B-17s OVER BERLIN

B-17s OVER BERLIN

Personal Stories from the 95th Bomb Group (H)

Edited by Ian L. Hawkins

Published with the cooperation of the
95th Bomb Group (H) Association

BRASSEY'S

Washington • London

Copyright © 1990 by the 95th Bomb Group (H) Association

Editorial Committee:
Leonard W. Herman, *Project Coordinator*
Ellis B. Scripture and David T. McKnight, *Coeditors*

First Brassey's trade paperback printing—1995
First Brassey's printing—1990
First published as Courage*Honor*Victory by Hunter Publishing Company,
Winston-Salem, NC—1987

Library of Congress Cataloging-in-Publication Data
Courage*honor*victory
    B-17s over Berlin: personal stories from the 95th Bomb Group (H)
    edited by Ian L. Hawkins.—1st trade paperback ed.
        p.   cm.
    "Published with the cooperation of the 95th Bomb Group (H)
Association."
    Originally published: Courage*honor*victory. Winston Salem, NC:
Hunter Pub. Co., 1987.
    Includes bibliographical references.
    ISBN 0-02-881129-1
    1. World War, 1939–1945—Aerial operations, American.   2. United
States. Army Air Forces Bomb Group (H), 95th—History. 3. World
War, 1939–1945—Personal narratives, American.   4. World War,
1939–1945—Personal narratives, British.   I. Hawkins, Ian.
    II. Title.
    [D790.C675 1995]
    940.54'4973—dc20   94-42451
                                                                                          CIP

Published in the United States of America
10   9   8   7   6   5   4   3   2

Prayer of an American Indian

When I'm dead cry for me a little
Think of me sometimes, but not too much
Think of me now and again as I was in life
At some moment that is pleasant to recall
But not for long
Leave me in peace and I shall leave you in peace
And while you live let your thoughts be with the living

EDITOR'S NOTE

By Ian Hawkins

Despite the ever increasing pressures and pace of present-day life in the 1980s, many kind people took the time and the trouble to relate and contribute their wartime experiences relevant to the 95th Bombardment Group (H) for this book.

This is the story of a collection of young American civilians who were suddenly thrown together amidst the maelstrom of a global war that took place nearly fifty years ago; how they rapidly adjusted to service life, how they lived, how they fought, and how they died.

Sadly, there are many, many episodes of extraordinary heroism and high endeavor that cannot be recorded because those valiant young men who were directly involved and the witnesses did not survive the war.

During these past four years Leonard Herman and Florence Rosenthal in Pennsylvania have patiently gathered, transcribed, and then relayed a constant stream of relevant data, including numerous tape recordings, which had been received from veterans and which revealed the dramatic, often humorous, sometimes gruesome, but always fascinating history of the 95th Bomb Group. Paul Andrews has prepared a most detailed and comprehensive Operational Record concerning the men, the aircraft, and their ultimate fate that possibly establishes a new standard in accuracy for the records of an Eighth Air Force combat group (see page 309). Norman Ottoway has completed a masterful collection of maps, illustrations, and formation charts for this book; John Rayson has re-created the dramatic scene of the 95th Bomb Group in action over Berlin during the first American daylight bombing raid to the capital city of Germany on 4 March 1944 (see page 310). William ("Ed") Charles is responsible for collecting, researching, and detailing all the original photographs in this book, while Ellis Scripture and Dave McKnight together have provided overall assistance and the necessary guidance as the project progressed to completion and publication. David Dorsey has kept the financial balance sheet in balance.

May I take this opportunity to extend my very grateful thanks and appreciation to all those who helped and contributed in any way to this illustrated history of the famous 95th, which, during WWII, had provided an outstanding and a significant contribution to a great victory. A victory and more significantly a lasting peace in Europe made possible primarily because of the strategic bombing campaign.

Who said so?

Certainly not the cynical postwar armchair historians and journalists, on both sides of the Atlantic, who find it so easy to criticize the Allied bombing campaign. Nor was it the devious British politicians who, with the war won, immediately condemned the bombing policy and the attacks on German cities and towns as if the German attacks on British, Dutch, Belgian, Polish, and Russian towns and cities had never happened.

The people who said so were those individuals who were in the ideal position to make an unbiased, sound, and proper judgment regarding the bombing offensive. They were the top German ministers and military commanders themselves who witnessed, often at first hand, the devastating and pulverizing effect of the Allied strategic bombing campaign.

Albert Speer, Hitler's minister for armaments and economics, said, "The strategic bombing of Germany was the greatest lost battle of the whole war for Germany." He then went on and gave the reasons and the evidence to substantiate that profound statement.

General Adolf Galland, commander of the Luftwaffe's fighter groups, said, "The bombers grounded our fighters by destroying our oil industry."

In June 1944 Field Marshal Erwin Rommel, one of the top German Army commanders, remarked to the German High Command: "If you cannot stop the bombing we cannot win. It's no good going on because all we get by going on is to lose another city every night. Either make peace or drop the atomic bomb . . . if you've got it."

The German High Command couldn't stop the bombing and they couldn't drop the atomic bomb because they didn't have one to drop, but in July 1944 some high-ranking German officers attempted to assassinate Hitler. They failed.

German Army General Sepp Dietrich, when ordered by Hitler to continue his advance during the bitterly fought Battle of the Bulge in December 1944, retorted: "Go on? Go on? How can we go on? We have no ammunition left and all our supply lines have been cut by air attack. . . . People don't understand that not even the best troops can stand this mass bombing. One experience of it and they lose all their fighting spirit. . . . "

Luftwaffe Field Marshal Hugo Sperrle confirmed emphatically: "Allied air power was the chief factor in Germany's defeat."

From the Allied side came the following assessments from two famous military commanders who undoubtedly knew what they were talking about because they were also in the ideal position to make an unbiased, sound, and proper judgment of the Allied strategic bombing campaign: Field Marshal Bernard Montgomery, British Army commander in North Africa and Europe, who co-signed the German surrender documents at the end of the war, stated, "The bombers did more than anyone toward winning the war."

General Dwight Eisenhower, Supreme Allied commander in Europe, added, "The Allied Air Force achieved the impossible."

This book is an attempt to tell the story of the 95th Bombardment Group from the viewpoint of those who are in an ideal position to relate the facts of what happened, when it happened, and how it happened.

CONTENTS

FOREWORD

I would not volunteer or dare to write a foreword concerning the activities of the mighty Eighth Air Force if I had not been closely associated with it at one period during the war.

At the peak of the United States Eighth Army Air Force's worst period of casualties, about the time of their second attack on the ball bearing factories at Schweinfurt in October 1943, our monarch King George VI and Prime Minister Churchill were most concerned about the enormous losses being suffered and accepted by the Americans. These were far and away above those that the Royal Air Force could endure. Subsequently, Air Marshal Arthur ("Bomber") Harris, commander of R.A.F. Bomber Command, was instructed to approach the U.S. commanding general to consider abandoning their daylight policy and joining the R.A.F. in the night bombing offensive.

I was one of the R.A.F. Bomber Command squadron leaders who had completed a tour of operations and, together with Leonard Cheshire and Guy Gibson, was seconded to the Eighth Air Force to wean the various American bomb groups and divisions away from their deadly daytime pursuits and to add their weight to the night offensive using our pathfinding technique associated with the British area bombing policy.

I was attached to General Jimmy Doolittle's staff and was made very welcome and given every facility to visit each American bomb group to lecture about the bomber command policy, particularly in connection with our mounting numbers and added weight. This was at the time of the relatively high casualties being suffered by the Eighth Air Force, and it was thought it would be welcomed by the Americans. However, it was rejected out of hand, and the daylight offensive pressed on despite these crippling losses.

I witnessed, at the sharp end of the American offensive, all the majesty, build-up, and the horror of broken bodies and the dead that were often the cargo returning aircraft brought back to their bases in England.

The 47,000 casualties added to Harris's 57,000 make somber reflection when we also consider the 'round-the-clock bombing policy fostered by Churchill and General Eaker. Although I deplore the decision to continue with the daylight offensive, I freely admit that once the long-range P-51 Mustang fighter with the Rolls Royce (Packard) Merlin engine could escort the Eighth Air Force anywhere in Germany, from then on the skies over Germany became untenable to the Luftwaffe, and Hitler's Third Reich was pounded into defeat by the Allied bomber offensive.

When we dwell on the total of 100,000-plus casualties, the price is hard to bear, but when we also learn from Albert Speer that after our joint attack on Hamburg, in July 1943, he said, "Six more Hamburgs and we are out of the war." But that effort had weakened both our bomber commands and we had to desist, more especially as we were being "milked" for the other theaters of the war.

Our partners and comrades in arms, the mighty Eighth, can take pride in their 'round-the-clock achievement, and we mourn their losses as we do our own.

The 95th, the only bombardment group in the Eighth Air Force to be awarded three Presidential Distinguished Unit citations, can take a special pride in its outstanding achievements and contributions to the Allied victory in Europe.

Group Captain Hamish Mahaddie,
D.S.O., D.F.C., A.F.C., R.A.F. (Ret.)

Group Captain Hamish Mahaddie (third from left, rear) with his crew and ground crew. Hamish was unable to fly one night and with a stand-in pilot their Stirling failed to return. All the crew perished.

THE 95TH BOMBARDMENT GROUP (H)

Station 119, Horham, England WWII

HISTORY

Activated 15 June 1942, Barksdale Field, La.

Formed October, 1942, Geiger Field, Wa. Trained at Ephrata, Wa.; Geiger Field, Wa.; Rapid City, S.D.

Departed for European theater of operations (ETO) 18 March 1943. Began operations 13 May 1943 from Alconbury, England. Later stationed Framlingham.

Permanent station 119, Horham.

Flew 321 combat missions, 13 May 1943 to 20 April 1945.

Flew 7 Chowhound missions to feed the starving Dutch people, May 1945; dropped 456.5 tons of food supplies.

Flew 4 Revival missions to return POWs and displaced persons.

Utilized a total of 359 B-17 Flying Fortresses. Dropped 19,769 tons of bombs. Completed 8,625 sorties.

Lost 156 B-17s in combat, 36 in other operations.

Battle damaged planes: 1,362.

61 planes force landed on the continent.

Claimed 425 enemy aircraft destroyed, 117 probables, 231 damaged.

Lost 569 men killed in action, 3 missing in action (assumed killed in action).

Lost 825 men as POWs, 61 internees, 61 evaders, 192 wounded in action; 63 killed in noncombat accidents (killed in service, or KIS).

Total casualties: 1,774.

SQUADRONS

334th, 335th, 336th, 412th.

MAJOR AWARDS

The only group in the Eighth Air Force to receive three (3) Presidential Distinguished Unit citations—Regensburg: 17 August 1943; Munster: 10 October 1943; Berlin: 4 March 1944. First U.S. Air Force Group to bomb Berlin, 4 March 1944.

The group was redeployed to the USA June–August 1945.
Inactivated 28 August 1945. Was reactivated during Korean conflict in B-36s, later with B-52s. Finally inactivated in 1967.

COMMANDING OFFICERS

Colonel Alfred A. Kessler, Colonel John K. Gerhart, Colonel Chester P. Gilger, Colonel Carl Truesdell, Jr., Colonel Jack E. Shuck, Lieutenant Colonel Robert H. Stuart.

RELATED ATTACHED UNITS AAF STATION 19 HORHAM, SUFFOLK, ENGLAND

1676th	Ordnance S&M Co. (AVN)
215th	Finance Office
49th	Service Group
64th	Service Squadron
1285th	Military Police Co.
271st	Medical Dispensary (AVN)
8th	Station Compliment
1210th	Quarter Master Co.
457th	Sub-Depot
433rd	Air Service Group
859th	Air Engineering Squadron
683rd	Air Material Squadron
433rd	Hqtrs. and Base Service Squadron
879th	Air Chemical Co. (AVN)
1029th	Ordnance Co.
18th	Weather Detachment
2022nd	Aviation Engineers Fire Fighting Platoon

BERLIN—"BIG B"

H. Griffin Mumford, Mission Commander

4 March 1944. 28,000 feet over Berlin. The first of many. God, it's cold. Look at that outside air temperature gauge—minus 65 degrees, and it isn't designed to indicate anything lower. Wonder what the temperature really is. Forget the temperature. Look at that flak. The bastards must have all 2,500 guns operational today. This has to be the longest bomb run yet. Krumph . . . boy, that was close and listen to the spent shrapnel hitting the airplane. Look at the gaping hole in the left wing of number three low element . . . an 88 must have gone right through without detonating. Damn, won't we ever drop those bombs? Bombs away . . . the sweetest words on any mission. OK, let's go home.

Wow, look at our little friends. Love those long-range droptanks! That old "escort you across the Channel" crap just wouldn't get the job done. Not to worry in the target area today about the Me 109s and the Fw 190s. Only wish our little friends could stay with us all the way home. What with the weather it would be nice to not have to contend with both the flak and the fighters on the way back.

What a great crew I have the good fortune to fly with today. Certainly makes a commander's job easier. Al Brown has fine-tuned his crew as well as any I have flown with: well-disciplined, possessing great esprit and courage, with each prepared to go to the limit and then a little something extra thrown in. Today certainly proves that point.

I wonder if they realize the significance of this mission, that it could be the turning point of the war. Stinking weather, fighter attacks, and flak over Berlin so heavy it could be walked upon is enough to make one anxious to get out of this wieners-and-krautland and back to Jolly Old. . . .

We made it. Wonder what old "Iron Ass" LeMay will think of the show his boys put on today.

Where did it start?

When will it end?

WAR! THE EARLY DAYS

Ellis B. Scripture

Everyone knew there would be war, but no one knew exactly how or when it would start. From early childhood we heard WWI veterans say that the political turmoil of Europe and the rest of the world had not been solved, that the great nations would fight again. Hitler became the focal point of all discussions on European affairs. The western world of the 1930s watched the aggressiveness of the Japanese with horror and amazement, but the primary interests of the United States at that time were obviously in Europe.

When Germany invaded Poland on 1 September 1939, the reality of U.S. participation became a matter of when rather than if. Nearly everyone in the United States watched events in the conflict as Hitler's armies swept across Western Europe with ruthless precision. The Battle of Britain brought the reality of combat closer. The dramatic words of Winston Churchill sounded a call to action as he said, "We will fight on the beaches . . . we will fight in the fields." When he told of the valiant victories of the R.A.F. in defending against great odds, saying, "Never have so many owed so much to so few," the urge to fly to the defense of freedom became the clarion call. Dreams of joining the air war were firmly implanted in the minds and hearts of tens of thousands of young Americans.

The attack on Pearl Harbor on 7 December 1941 shocked everyone into reality—War!—finally! Now the latent power of the United States could be brought into the struggle for freedom in full force. That quiet pleasant Sunday was shattered with the electrifying radio announcement all over America. It is interesting to note that everyone who was school age and above can remember precisely where they were at the moment of the initial announcement. The whole world seemed to stand silent the next day as President Franklin Delano Roosevelt told Congress with high drama that 7 December 1941 was "a day that will live in infamy." As expected, Congress voted war. War on the Axis powers—Germany, Japan, and Italy.

Now what? Join the armed forces! You've been waiting to prove that you're a grown-up man. Now go do it. But not the infantry, not the artillery! The United States Air Corps is the glamor service. These are the guys who fly the P-38s, the P-41s, and those big, beautiful, graceful B-17s. Yes, that'll be it—the Air Corps! Besides, there's more money in the Air Corps: flight pay. You'll get $30 a month as a private in the Army, but you'll get $50 as a cadet (later raised to $75), and then you'll be an officer—and they'll actually pay you to fly! The real trick is to volunteer before the draft catches up to your number.

This story could be told a thousand ways by a thousand men.

Well, you made it! After emotional goodbyes you've made the long train trip with 500 other cadets to Santa Ana, California, where construction crews are busily tearing up orange groves to build an Air Corps training center. It is February 1942. Only a few hundred cadets are here now—the parade ground is a sea of mud—but trains are arriving almost daily. Before the class 42-14 leaves here on 1 July there will be 50,000 young men marching, doing KP, getting shots, marching, saluting, doing twenty-mile hikes, taking psychological tests, marching, laughing, writing letters home, marching, marching.

It was exciting to meet new people and to learn about their lives, their loves, their jobs, their home towns. As we all remember, America was just emerging from the Great Depression at this time and very few people made much money. In one session, we were greeting a new group of cadets in our barracks. The first thing was to introduce yourself to all the barracks mates and to recite your home town and what you did before you became a cadet. One guy was asked what he did in civilian life. "I was a garbage man in Skokie, Illinois," was his answer. "Is that so?" he was asked. "How much money did you make hauling garbage?" "Twenty bucks a week and all I could eat!" And so it went, laughter, jokes, serious work, learning to be a soldier—marching, parades, inspections, discipline—a strange new way of life in a strange new world.

Then came assignment time. It finally dawned on the great number of guys that all of us cannot fit into a P-38! There are other things to do in the Air Corps. Important things like navigation, learning to drop bombs with the marvelously accurate Norden bomb sight, shoot guns, and operate a radio—all from that lovely big bird, the Flying Fortress.

As the story of the 95th Bomb Group (H) is told, it is indeed unfortunate that there will be so much left untold. Combat stories are the ones that attract the reader's attention and are the ones the flyers love to tell. (Some say the stories get better over the years!) But as one remembers events that happened over forty years ago, the many fine, interesting, dedicated people are an outstanding memory. People that one really never got to know as well as one would have liked. The team effort required was most important.

The success of the 95th is a story of team effort by many people in many and diverse disciplines, each an expert, putting forth that extra effort to achieve the ultimate goal: put combat-ready crews into combat-ready planes to fly the mission as planned. All of the men—those who flew and those who made flying possible—learned to love and respect one another in a relationship that will live as long as they do.

As in most war stories, the men who flew in combat get the most space, attention, and acclaim; but the people on the ground, the people who handled the million details and who made sure that men and planes would fly, deserve much more credit than they ever received. The longer we flew, the more we appreciated the people who made life bearable and high-altitude flying possible. The 95th became a proud group, proud of its excellence from top to bottom, every man proud of his own records as a contributor to victory.

As we began at Geiger Field in Spokane, Washington, and in Ephrata,

Washington, we were building an organization that would see *courage* beyond our wildest imagination, *honor* for all in a difficult job well done, and *victory* for freedom of our beloved country and throughout much of the world.

Fortunately for the greenhorn second lieutenants and flying sergeants who arrived at Geiger Field, there were more experienced people who seemed to know what they were doing. The average navigator and bombardier assigned to the 95th had about thirty-five total flying hours; the enlisted crewmen, even less. New first pilots had logged a total of about 150 hours through flight schools and multi-engine transition; co-pilots, even less. We soon learned to respect the men who really knew what flying is all about! This strange new world was exciting; we wanted to do the job, but we didn't know what the job was or how to do it. But we soon learned what to learn and how to learn to work together as a combat team.

The men who really put the 95th on the right track were the strong team of older, more experienced group and squadron leaders. Colonel Alfred A. Kessler, World War I veteran, West Point, 1922, put the group together. Tough, forgiving, demanding, understanding, we all came to know Colonel Kessler (affectionately called "Uncle Aaron" and "Old Ugly") as a fine leader who earned the respect of his men. There is no doubt in anyone's mind that John H. ("Jack") Gibson is the man who was the organizing genius behind the 95th. Lieutenant Colonel John H. Gibson was an Army pilot from the old school. Trained at Randolph Field and Kelly Field in 1934, Jack had flown the post–WWI planes; he was one of the Army pilots who flew the U.S. mail in the days when air mail was carried in small sacks behind the pilot's seat of a small, single-engine plane. Years of logging about 10,000 hours' flying time and organizational training at American Airlines had prepared Jack to be the air executive, the man who put the flying organization together. Much of what we were to become as a combat group was due to the background knowledge and patience of John H. Gibson. He was and is an inspiration to all who were fortunate enough to have him as their leader and a fine example of what a flyer should be, in the air and on the ground.

Other experienced pilots were chosen for key positions. Without exception, they were to prove to be leaders in every sense of the word: Ed Cole, Al Wilder, Dave McKnight, Cliff Cole, and Grif Mumford. Some had at least a few years of Army flying experience; some had trained with the Royal Canadian Air Force before the United States became involved in the war. All were respected leaders who were excellent examples to follow into combat. Other men who became flight leaders with more than average flying experience were Harry Stirwalt, brothers Richmond and Cliff Hamilton, Dexter Schnebly, Owen Cornett, Joel Bunch, Gale House, and Bill Lindley.

The expertise in fields other than flying also gave the younger crewmen and ground personnel much comfort and a feeling of security. These included Clarence D. ("Pappy") Fields as chief engineering officer. Pappy had been a master sergeant in the prewar Army Air Corps whose service had been in multi-engine bombers from their inception. Flight Surgeon Dr. Bill Harding headed a fine medical team. The "paperwork squad" of Lester ("Curly") Burt and Ed Russell, with their able assistants, kept the records straight. (As one would expect, Curly didn't have a hair on his head, but his head was filled with a well organized brain!) There were numerous others whose names will undoubtedly appear in the main text, each striving at peak capacity to bring the many required disciplines together in a coordinated training program to produce an outstanding, effective combat flying team.

The early flying days at Ephrata, Washington; Spokane (Geiger Field), Washington; and Rapid City, South Dakota, were frustrating for everyone. Starting in October 1942 and continuing through mid-March 1943, the weather everywhere we were stationed was atrocious. The bases in Washington were plagued with rain, fog, and snow to the point where the group was falling far behind in scheduled training flights. So, on to Rapid City, South Dakota, which should have been the training center for the Arctic sled forces. It was so cold that the thermometer fluid formed icicles! The cold weather had some advantages. It gave the married men additional time to spend with their wives in the hospitable town of Rapid City, where we learned that buffalo steaks weren't on the ration coupon list, and the Alex Johnson Hotel had the best bar in town. However, the miracles performed by the ground crews allowed enough flying to earn the Inspector General's report, "Ready for Combat Duty." An all-too-short leave at home for everyone, and the navigators got the chance to fly individually to Kearney, Nebraska, for overseas assignment—but where? At Kearney, the group was outfitted for war, and the orders were finally revealed: to the ETO—the European theater of operations! At least it will be a civilized war, or will it? Only time will tell. *Mr. Hitler, here comes the 95th Bombardment Group (H)!*

The trip to England involved stops along the way, the first of which was Gulfport, Mississippi. This relatively short trip from Kearney was planned as a navigation exercise over water, over the Gulf of Mexico with triangular legs to Gulfport, where equipment would be stowed for the long overseas trip. However, for one crew, it became an adventure that would teach us that Murphy's Law—"whatever can go wrong will go wrong"—works. The Charles Rubin crew soon learned that every part of the plane has to be fitted correctly or the bird won't fly right. This was the first time that B-17s had landed at this new base. Of course, the excitement ran heavy with the local people who were working there at that time.

As our airplane was taxiing to our assigned hardstand, one of the local boys who was driving a large dump-truck came under the left wing of our plane and slightly scraped the bottom of the wing. Charlie Rubin, our pilot, immediately shut down the engines, and everyone scrambled out of the aircraft. There was a very small tear in the underside of the wing. As the truck driver looked up at it he said, "That's not very badly damaged at all. If you guys report this I'll lose my job. Why don't you go ahead and you fellows have it repaired and I'll pay for it. That way it will be forgotten."

Unfortunately the tear, about eight inches long, was located right at the very point where one of the bulkheads formed a junction between two sections of the wing. Charlie Rubin studied the tear thoughtfully. Then he said, "Yes, I think we can probably handle it that way." The driver said, as he reached for his wallet, "How much do you estimate it's going to cost to fix it, mister?" Charlie replied, "Oh, I would guess somewhere in the neighborhood of $20,000." The driver almost fainted with shock.

But as it turned out the mechanics, working around the clock, had to first remove the two engines, then the entire wing, and replace it with a completely new unit and finally fit the two engines onto the new wing. So one can imagine $20,000 was a very conservative estimate of the total cost involved.

However, it didn't end there. After waiting about ten days for the necessary parts to arrive and our airplane to be repaired, we took it up for a test flight after the pilot, co-pilot, and flight engineer had given the plane a thorough inspection on the ground. The whole crew participated in this test flight, because we were now behind in our training and we needed as much experience as possible in the time available.

When we took off, however, and reach about 150 feet, the pilot banked the plane slightly to the left. Lo and behold! The left aileron stuck in position in about a 30° bank. We learned later that the people who had replaced the wing had put one of the aileron clamps on backward. The plane was in this shallow bank to the left, and the two pilots, wrestling with the controls, couldn't get the aircraft out of that dangerous predicament and under proper control.

We flew around at this low altitude for quite some time barely above the tall pine treetops. The B-17 was not under complete control, but the pilots managed to keep it in the air because we had full power from all four engines; but we didn't have any directional control. We stayed airborne for about three hours, flying round and round, coming over the base from time to time and in constant radio contact with the control tower. All this time the pilots and the air executive in the tower were trying to decide whether we should go up to higher altitude and bail out or risk crash-landing the airplane.

As it happened, some of our wives were sunbathing on the roof of their hotel near the airfield and everytime we flew low over their hotel they thought we were buzzing them. They were waving at us and shouting cheery hellos from the roof of the hotel, not realizing, of course, that we were in very serious trouble.

To cut a long story short, it was eventually decided that we should bring the plane back down. Charlie Rubin did a great job in lining the plane up for final approach but, unfortunately, as he brought it in, the low left wing clipped the ground at the same time that the left landing wheel made contact with the runway at a speed of about 95 miles per hour. We instantly went into a series of great and uncontrollable gyrations that wrecked the airplane completely. We had all assumed the proper crash-landing positions, and somewhat miraculously, all of our crew walked away without a single scratch. This was quite a harrowing experience for us all.

As a result we had to stay at Gulfport to wait for a new airplane, which took another twelve days to arrive. In the meantime, the rest of the 95th Group flew off to their final staging post at Morrison Field, Florida, prior to crossing the South Atlantic Ocean. We followed them alone, later, for our overseas assignment in the European theater of operations. Mechanical problems with the early models of combat aircraft were not publicized for obvious reasons. Later, records of the 95th Bomb Group (H) were to reveal that thirteen of the original thirty-nine B-17s outfitted for duty had to be replaced because of mechanical failure. The postwar records of the 95th Group would reveal that 77 percent of the combat crewmen who made up the original group would not complete a full tour of twenty-five missions. Among those killed in action were nine of the ten men who were with Charlie Rubin on the wild flight that cracked up at Gulfport.

THE FLIGHT TO EUROPE

David T. McKnight and Bill Lindley

The 95th Bombardment Group's move to Europe via the southern route is described by David McKnight, a squadron commander and later the group air executive officer.

From Gulfport, Mississippi, we flew to Morrison Field, West Palm Beach, Florida, in late March 1943. We used the southern route primarily because the weather over the North Atlantic was still acting up. Our plane flew out of Morrison Field on 30 March, leading nine airplanes of the 95th Group's total of thirty-nine B-17s, en route to Borinquen Field, Puerto Rico, a flight of six hours. Some of the group's airplanes were delayed in their departure for a variety of reasons. A number of engine problems developed. For example, we had a very bad series of components that would wear out quickly, like piston rings, due to sand being ingested into the engines. On 31 March we flew from Borinquen Field to Atkinson Field, British Guiana, a 7½-hour flight. On 1 April we proceeded to Belem, Brazil, which took almost six hours, and on 2 April we flew along the Brazilian coastline to Natal, Brazil, our last staging post before the long haul across the South Atlantic to West Africa.

One of the interesting aspects concerning the South American portion of the trip was the weather we encountered. The weather people at our stops on our way had warned us of the extremely heavy rain storms we would encounter occasionally. I recall approaching Belem when we hit the grandaddy of them all! About fifteen miles from the field we had to go under one of these things.

It was a solid sheet of rain with a very large black cloud on top, and it was so dark as we went through it that we had to switch on the cockpit lights to see our instrumentation. But, as they had predicted, we emerged after about five minutes and the base came into sight.

We landed without incident to a fine lunch with Brazilian butter, which was a sort of axle-grease substitute for butter. I guess someone got an award for inventing something that didn't melt in the tropics, or anywhere else for that matter. Personally, I think the person concerned should have been cashiered.

At midnight on 4 April we took off with full fuel tanks from Natal for Dakar, West Africa. Taking off into the middle of the South Atlantic on a pitch-black night is the ultimate into nothingness. We were briefed to climb at full rpm and full throttle, at 150 mph, leaving full throttle but slowly backing off on rpm while maintaining 150 mph indicated air speed; this is considerably more at that altitude in true flying speed. As time went by the load lightened as the fuel was gradually consumed, resulting in a slow increase to our true airspeed.

A couple of interesting things happened on the way over. About halfway across the "pond," my radio operator reported that somebody was on our frequency asking us for our position. We were briefed to maintain radio silence (and that is, of course, a two-way proposition). So I swallowed all my Brooklyn-boy desire to give whomever it was a snotty answer, and we maintained strict radio silence. A little later, while along the top of an undercast, a very bright light appeared through this undercast and tracked us. It wasn't on us but it was uncomfortably close. I never did know what it was about but the intelligence people at Dakar told us that it probably was a German submarine with a high-intensity light and an unpleasant piece of machinery on board with which to shoot at us.

We landed at Dakar, thanks entirely to our terrific navigator who was on loan to us from Air Transport Command. Without him I'm sure we wouldn't have been able to locate *Africa*! As we were taxiing, the control tower called and said we had to go out again and search for one of our planes. That shook us a bit but it turned out to be good news/bad news. One of our airplanes was down, ditched in the sea, due to engine trouble as described earlier. Its pilot, Raymond Abbott, our "all American boy," must have done a beautiful job because everyone got out and into the life rafts. Rumor has it that somebody, probably Ray (in fact, that's the story) went back into the sinking B-17 via the radio hatch, swam up front to the cockpit, retrieved a couple of quarts of Old Overholt "shaving lotion," got out, and swam back to the life raft. They were picked up safely the next day.

From Dakar we flew north to Marrakech in what used to be French Morocco, northwest Africa. While we were flying through a dust storm, the ground kept rising underneath us. I recalled the briefing about the Atlas Mountains being on our route, so I asked my navigator as we broke out and could see forward again, "Where were those mountains?" He said, "Look over your shoulder." And there were the mountains with the peaks rising above us, on either side. He had brought us safely through the middle of the lowest area of the forbidding Atlas Mountains.

After a one-day layover in Marrakech, we departed for England on the evening of 7 April, a 10½-hour night mission well out into the Bay of Biscay in order to evade the German fighters who were patrolling the bay with their night fighters, then north to the coast of Ireland and then back to the east to St. Eval in southwestern England. We landed safely at St. Eval despite the language barrier of the wonderful W.A.A.F. (or whatever they were called) in the control tower giving me landing instructions. As a result of my poor understanding of the language, or rather the strange sounding English accent (to a boy from Brooklyn), when I finally touched down I really wasn't sure where the hell we were. I knew it was in England somewhere and it turned out to be the right place, St. Eval.

It was here that we dropped off our hitchhiker, a young Royal Navy officer. He'd been on leave at Puerto Rico, our first stop, and had asked me where we were going. Of course, those being weird times, I wasn't able to tell him; but I asked him where *he* was going and he replied that he wanted to hitch a ride to England. I said that we could take him in that general direction for the first leg at least. We checked with the Intelligence people at each stop, and they cleared him each time. I guess that until then, it was one of the longest, if not *the* longest hitchhikes on record. It was definitely the cheapest way home, and we were glad to help him.

The next day we proceeded to Bovingdon, a base that received crews as they arrived and farmed them out to their assigned stations. Bovingdon apparently did not expect us as part of a completely new bombardment group, and we were told to unload our airplanes and get all our baggage off. It sounded as if something was wrong with the deal because I knew we shouldn't be giving up our airplanes at that point. I told them that I was working for a pretty tough boss and that if I gave the airplanes up and lost the crews, he'd have my you-know-what. Although they weren't too impressed, they called the Eighth Air Force headquarters and told them. As I watched and listened, their expression changed. As a result we were instructed to fly to Alconbury, near Huntingdon that same afternoon. At Alconbury we joined the 92nd Bomb Group, which was at that time "a training group for combat," and some of their personnel flew with us on several of our first combat missions.

It was at Alconbury that the rest of the 95th Group crews caught up with us, including our commanding officer, Colonel Alfred A. Kessler, who was nick-named "Aaron" when he was at West Point. We all referred to him as Uncle Aaron. He was a strict disciplinarian, but he also had a great deal of compassion. I saw him really take care of a couple of our bad boys and handle each situation beautifully. It was a great experience for us younger officers to watch him demonstrate this kind of leadership.

The following, however, is a "funny" on him. When we were training in the United States he used to tell the four squadron commanders that he was rather disgusted with all the boys wearing cowboy boots stomping around and speaking "western" talk when half of them were from the Bronx. Also he thought their stomping around the barracks at two o'clock in the morning singing "The Yellow Rose of Texas" was a little off balance because very few of them were from Texas. He also didn't think too much of the boys wearing cowboy boots.

Now, when we came through Brazil, there was quite a sale going on in gaucho cowboy boots. The boys were buying them, and when my crew asked me what I thought I replied, "I'm not going to tell you not to but I know for sure what Uncle Aaron is going to say."

But when Colonel Kessler showed up at Alconbury, guess who was wearing the finest pair of gaucho boots that you ever saw?

So much for my command judgment.

The story continues: One of several 95th Group Fortresses that were late arrivals at Alconbury was commanded by Lieutenant William Lindley, who describes the circumstances.

We took off from Morrison Field, Florida, one sunny morning for Trinidad, British West Indies. This should have been as easy as duck soup. It was anything but. My navigator, who was known to drink and stay up until the wee small hours, dozed off for about three hours during the flight. After his nap we weren't lost, just momentarily confused. A heated discussion concerning his ancestors took place during which time a loaded ".45" was waved underneath his nose. The big decision was to turn due south and make landfall on South America and go from there. The decision proved one point: South America is big and has lots of sandy beaches and jungles.

With red warning lights lit on the gas tank gauges, we finally spotted a small town with a very short gravel runway. Any old port in the storm. . . . I put her down on one end and almost immediately ran off the other end. The right wing clipped two thatched huts and scattered several irate natives. Having so much fun I turned the B-17 around, and hit another thatched hut with the same wing, and bent the number 4 propeller. The plane eventually finished up back on the airfield. All of us expected hell to break loose about then.

Some military-looking men approached in a very ancient car as did several curious natives on cows and on foot. It turned out that we had landed near Caracas, Venezuela. We asked the location of the nearest bar and were transported into town to a reasonable looking hotel. No one had raised any kind of protest. With hospitality like that the only thing to do was have a drink and talk the situation over. All we needed to get to England was a new propeller for number 4 and sufficient fuel.

A telephone call to Trinidad got us a new propeller that was flown in via a C-47 transport. Technical Sergeant Barnett and crew changed the prop; the local government supplied the gasoline and a bulldozer to extend the ends of the runway. All the crew except Barnett and me went back to Trinidad in the C-47. The next day with a most favorable headwind we got the B-17 airborne and headed back to Trinidad to collect the crew. To this day I have no idea who paid for the hotel rooms, the bar bill, the phone call, or the gasoline.

The short stay in Trinidad was uneventful, as was the visit to Belem and the flight to Natal. After a few days' rest, we took off for Dakar, West Africa. The flight time involved was about the maximum endurance for the B-17, and we were briefed to make a decision before reaching the point-of-no-return whether to continue to Dakar or return to Natal. Needless to say we didn't make it the first try. On the second attempt we made the mistake of eating a box of cookies about an hour out from Natal that made both my co-pilot and I violently sick. Back to Natal.

The next morning I'm in the local commander's office when he asked whether I had any objections regarding my going to the war in Europe. I almost hit him in the mouth. The next day we took off for the Ascension Islands, which made it a roundabout way of reaching Dakar. A refueling stop was also necessary at Accra, which was the first and last time that loincloth natives pumped gas from rusty fifty-gallon drums into the airplane.

With all the bad luck that we had been experiencing, it seemed that a lucky mascot was in order. While we were at Dakar the crew picked out a big green parrot with a mean and spiteful disposition. He didn't last too long. On the next flight he crapped all over the steering wheel, so I threw him out of the window.

Dakar was nothing to write home about and neither was Marrakech. When we eventually arrived there, we were billeted in what was probably the largest open bay barracks in the world. It was as long as a football field with a very high ceiling. Bunks were packed into every available space, two deep. Every row of bunks had poker, dice, and blackjack games in progress with people standing around waiting to get in. That was the only action available since we were warned not to go into Marrakech, particularly at night.

To heck with the warning. Steele, Barnett, several others, and I loaded up the second night and found a smelly Arab with a dilapidated buggy to take us to a night club. I was to protect us from marauders with the .45 if necessary. We were looking for and anticipating something like the night club featured in Humphrey Bogart's *Casablanca*.

Eventually our guide wound up in front of an unlit building and escorted us down into the cellar. I've been in better and cleaner chicken houses. The guide, I assume, assured the clientele that we were "good old boys from the U.S. of A." We went up to the bar and drank what is commonly known as paint remover but it had a slightly more pleasant smell. There were women around but rather on the greasy side. Not one of the locals in the joint had said a word after we arrived. Every one of them looked mean enough to take my .45 away and feed it to me in pieces. I wanted to stay, but the crew voted to depart in a hurry. They won and I beat them to the door. To hell with Bogart.

We were a good week to ten days behind the other 95th Group crews. The flight from Marrakech to England was uneventful. Landfall and the wandering around in the fog over England under British air-traffic control gave us a taste of the weather we could expect to encounter and operate in throughout the year.

The approach to the runway at Alconbury was located with B-17s of the 95th returning from their second mission. The crew and I took all the kidding that was expected and then some. John Storie made it all bearable when he said, "Bill, I'm glad you're here. We need you."

My crew proved to be among the most professional in the business. I was particularly proud of the enlisted members, and they stayed with me through the first tour of missions in England. Barnett, Steele, Macki, Cupp, Cowan, and Hockett were the best and absolutely dependable in any circumstances.

The 95th Bombardment Group's Route to England, 1942–1943. Permanent station: Horham, Suffolk.

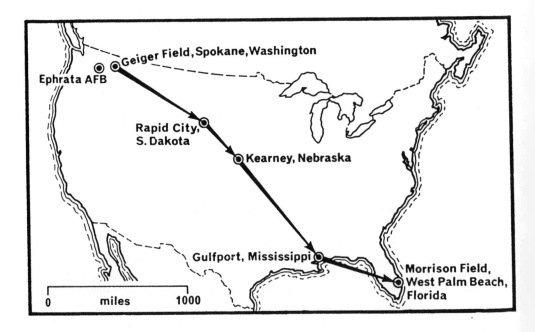

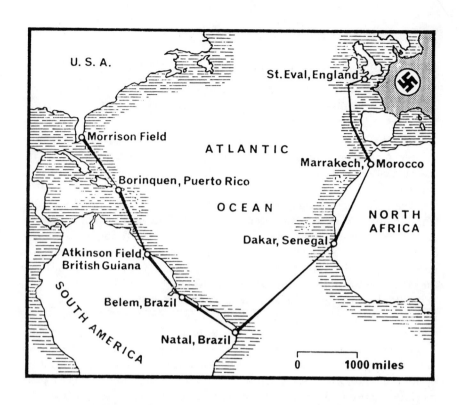

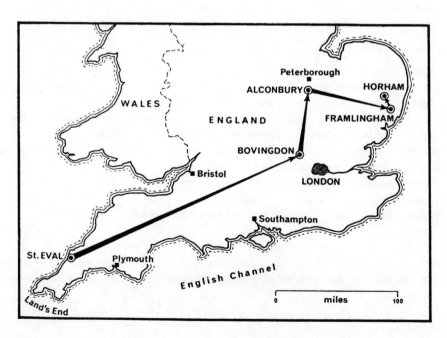

DISASTER AT ALCONBURY

Clifford Cole, also from *Contrails* (1947)

A brutal shock jolted the 95th as an overture to its earliest days in the combat theater. A tragic ground accident bit deeply into the heart of the group with the realization that we were in a lethal game where the very worst could happen.

The ground crews had arrived by troop ship two weeks previously; the 95th Group's planes were at Alconbury, flying their first missions with the 92nd Group. On 27 May 1943, the ground crews were loading the planes, checking radios and ordnance, going over the B-17s engines prior to tomorrow's mission. They buzzed around the aircraft, enthusiastic in their debut, the thing they had worked on in a hundred practice ways.

Without warning the bomb load on ship no. 229685 exploded with a horrifying blast. The plane, as such, literally disappeared, taking its ground crew with it. The sky rained debris from the blast. The shock waves traveled hundreds of feet in every direction. Nineteen men were killed, twenty seriously injured, and the grim caprice of the concussion took an erratic toll. GIs picked up an ordnance officer some distance away. He was dead, unmarked by so much as a piece of flying metal. An engineer, standing among other men at another point on the field, dropped to the ground, apparently in a faint. Men ran to aid him. He was gone. Others, feet from him, were untouched.

One combat crew was lounging in the afternoon sun near their plane. Nine of the crew members were lying flat on the ground. The navigator, Lieutenant Frank Metzger, was sitting upright. The nine men were not physically hurt by the blast; Lieutenant Metzger was killed by concussion. Their plane was broken in the center with the two sections completely separated.

Four other B-17s nearby were crumpled like old paper. Eleven others were written off with damage so severe they wouldn't fly again for months. The engines of the exploded plane were never found. The others, badly damaged, were blasted several feet into the ground.

Here, in one second, went the lives, the efforts, and the careful schooling of some of the Air Corps' most vital assets, the men on the line. They could get more planes, but dedicated, trained maintenance personnel were irreplaceable.

The cause of the accident was never determined and is still a matter of speculation. The 95th would fly 321 combat missions without a comparable ground catastrophe, but they were to take their share of good and bad fortune in the air.

REMEMBER KIEL . . .

The story begins with Ellis B. Scripture (navigator, 335th Squadron). Our first combat mission as a group was to St. Omer, France, 13 May 1943. The 95th Group was then based at Alconbury, Huntingdonshire. A little later, in late May 1943, we were transferred to Framlingham, Suffolk, and on 15 June 1943, we flew the short distance to what was to be the home of the 95th for the duration of the war, Horham, set deep in the beautiful countryside and amidst the gently undulating farmlands of Suffolk.

Our B-17 returned to England from that first mission to St. Omer and crash-landed. It was literally riddled with holes of varying sizes from flak and fighters, which we encountered over Nazi-occupied Europe. It was an absolute miracle that not one of our crew members was killed or even injured from that sort of withering firepower. Little did we realize that this was only the beginning.

Up to "Kiel Day" the 95th had flown to targets in France and Belgium, relatively close to the English Channel coast. We had also gone to Emden, Germany, which was the deepest penetration to date, and we had also bombed a refinery in Wilhelmshaven, Germany. We had put a relatively large number of airplanes into combat, and until 13 June 1943, the 95th Group had lost only four aircraft. During these first eight missions we had claimed thirty-six enemy fighters planes shot down. This would indicate, of course, that we had been under relatively heavy attack during each of these first few missions.

Then came Kiel . . . The Kiel mission, which we flew from Framlingham on 13 June 1943 I think will have to go down in history as the day the 95th Group became combat ready, and it is probably the one day that many of the original crew members will remember most of all of the days of WWII.

The day began just like any other mission day. Early that Sunday morning I was sitting in the briefing room with the rest of our crew, which was commanded by Charlie Rubin, our pilot. Lieutenant Colonel Jack Gibson, our group executive officer, came to our table and told me that I was going to fly the Kiel mission with another crew, commanded by Lieutenant William ("Bill") Lindley, as lead plane in the composite group. We were to fly above and to the right of the main force of the 95th.

I immediately protested, saying that I would much prefer to fly with my own crew since by that time with seven missions completed we had developed into a good fighting team. We had full confidence in each other. Jack Gibson paused and then said, "Lieutenant, this is an order. Get yourself over there with Lieutenant Lindley."

In early June we had been joined at Framlingham by Brigadier General Nathan Bedford Forrest III, a career officer straight from Washington who had been sent to Europe to take command of a B-17 Combat Bomb Wing. Nathan Bedford Forrest was the grandson of a very famous Confederate cavalry general who distinguished himself during the American Civil War. This man was known for his dash, verve, and for his outstanding bravery. The original General Forrest had earned a great reputation as a combat leader, and the United States Army tradition was carried on in his family. He had gone down in history of the Civil War as the general who said, "To win—git there fustest with the mostest." His son and his grandson both graduated from West Point and, of course, General Forrest III had become an Army Air Force pilot who was highly respected by his peers.

Before the Kiel mission, lengthy strategy sessions had been held, and it was eventually decided that a new type of formation would be flown. Colonel Curtis LeMay, while commander of the 305th Bomb Group of the First Air Division during 1942 and early 1943, had been the creator of the "box formation," in which the three squadrons of a bomb group—lead, high, and low— were staggered at slightly different altitudes within the group to present a boxlike defense configuration to the enemy fighters. Six airplanes to a squadron in flights of three and twelve 50-caliber heavy machine guns placed in various gun positions in each B-17 was the standard procedure adopted by the Eighth Air Force during each combat mission at that time. Experience had shown the First Air Division that the tighter and more compact a group formation was, the greater the concentration of firepower that could be brought to bear on the attacking German fighters. The vital necessity for close formation flying was constantly emphasized to our pilots. A B-17 lagging behind or to one side of the group formation, more often than not, became a sitting duck for the experienced German fighter pilots that we found ourselves up against at that time.

General Forrest, however, was convinced that we would gain better firepower if we flattened the formation and flew wing-tip to wing-tip so that we would be able to concentrate our firepower ahead, below, above, and to the rear. After a great deal of discussion, it was finally decided that we would fly that new type of flat formation on 13 June.

Lieutenant Robert Cozens, deputy group leader on the mission to Kiel that fateful day recalls that General Forrest had us practicing "his" formation for approximately two weeks prior to the mission. I don't recall how many crews were involved in the practice but I do remember that most of us failed to see any advantages the "new" formation offered over the "box" formation that had been flown on prior missions. However, as good military men, we did as directed by higher authority. It was apparent that General Forrest had strong convictions that his modification would serve us better. I am not sure how many other groups on the mission utilized the "Forrest" formation.

Ellis B. Scripture continues: General Forrest was in the co-pilot's seat of the lead airplane, which was piloted by Captain Harry Stirwalt. The group navigator flying with them was Lieutenant Willard Brown, who was a highly skilled and competent navigator. He was unquestionably the best choice as group navigator when the 95th was first formed.

The primary target was the shipyards at Kiel, beyond Bremen on the northwestern German coast, which of course, was the deepest penetration flown by the 95th up to that time. Twenty-six aircraft took off from Framlingham, and we had normal assembly with the 95th and 96th Bomb Groups over "Splasher 6," a radio homing beacon located near Diss in South Norfolk.

Our route, from Splasher 6 took us over the Wash, a large bay on the north Norfolk coast, across the North Sea, north of the Friesian Islands, and with a penetration toward the initial point (IP), which, as I recall, would take us about fifty miles inland for the turn on to our bombing run toward our target, the Kiel shipyards.

We were attacked by German fighters before we crossed the enemy coast. The concentrated attacks persisted during our entire penetration over German soil. It was an extremely vicious air battle, and it was unquestionably the longest period of intense combat we had seen to date.

Lieutenant William Lindley, pilot of B-17F 229967 leading the 95th's composite wing, remembers:

This was to be my first group lead, and Captain Grif Mumford was the command pilot. The flak was highly concentrated and the fighters were thicker than fleas. The Focke Wulfe [Fw] 190s and Messerschmitt [Me] 109s from several of the German Air Force airfields had started painting the noses of their aircraft with bright colors—red, yellow, and black-and-white checkerboard being the most predominant. They were known as Goering's Flying Circus. Just the thought of them still gives me the twitches.

General Nathan Bedford Forrest was the task force commander, and he flew ahead of us in the 95th's lead Fortress. What brought him to my attention was his order to use a new type of oil on the 50-caliber machine guns. The Fort's gunners had experienced some ejection problems at altitude, and this oil would solve them.

Landfall was made on the Kiel peninsula and within seconds the Luftwaffe fighters appeared. There were many more black dots on the horizon, thicker than gnats around the rear end of a camel. As they got closer, you couldn't miss the painted noses. About the time I made the turn from the IP toward the target, heavy and accurate flak began bursting among our formation; the fighters pulled in front of us. I told Grif, "Boy, we are in a heap of big trouble."

Then all hell broke loose. The flak looked awesome but the Fw 190s and the Me 109s would put the fear of God into anyone. To see them attack head-on from the twelve o'clock position with their wings flaring and smoking from their machine-gun fire is frightful to say the least. The 109s also firing their cannon located in the nose hub. . . . Awesome, particularly when one realized they are firing directly at us.

For the next fifteen minutes I was in a state of absolute and incredulous shock. Between the exploding flak shells, the burning aircraft going down, excited voices yelling over the radio, and those concentrated and continuous fighter attacks, I spent half the time with my head in my steel helmet ducked down behind the instrument panel. I glanced at Grif and he was as far below the panel as I was. Neither of us said a single word during the entire attack. The airplane was on automatic flight control equipment (autopilot) and was being steered by the bombardier in the nose of the ship. He managed to get the bombs away over the target area.

During these constant fighter attacks, I had noticed that the upper turret guns were not firing at all but I'd no idea what the problem was. Midway through the battle Sergeant Steel, my top-turret gunner, came down into the cockpit with his fingernails torn and his hands bleeding. I thought that he'd been hit, but we learned that both his guns had frozen. The charging handles had broken off, and he had tried to charge them with his bare fingers. He never fired a single shot.

In all, four of our ten guns froze, which was about average for all our aircraft. To make matters worse, General Forrest was killed when the lead ship was hit by fighters and went down over the target. The new oil wasn't used again.

Robert Cozens continues: General Forrest led us into battle that day flying in the lead aircraft. Flying as deputy lead, I was instructed to keep the nose of my B-17 "tucked up under the tail" of the lead aircraft. The Forrest formation was subjected to the "true test" when, just as we completed the bomb run, the formation received a massive diving frontal attack from German Fw 190s and Me 109s. In our position in the formation, as well as that of our wingmen, we were unable to clear any of our guns on the attacking aircraft because of the line of sight through our lead echelon aircraft. Consequently the lead aircraft was raked with enemy fire from one end to the other and immediately fell out of formation. As predirected, I immediately moved my aircraft into the lead position that had been vacated by the B-17 in which General Forrest had been flying.

Captain John Miller, pilot of B-17F 73090 "T'Ain't A Bird," gives a vivid eye-witness account of General Forrest's Fortress as it went down: We were badly outnumbered by the German fighters and the flak was highly accurate. I could see the orange bursts, then the black smoke, hear the MAARUMPH, and then feel the concussion. Frightening indeed. . . .

The enemy fighters were really boring in and putting it to us. I stayed on Harry Stirwalt's right wing and I could see right into his cockpit. Very shortly after the bomb run, there was obvious confusion in there as they were hit. I didn't realize they were going down, and I stayed right close on their right wing. Then I saw Bob Cozen's B-17 out of the corner of my eye, and we very nearly collided. I veered away to the right just in time and then we were hit again. As a result of this latest attack, I lost my regular flow of oxygen and things became very hazy and indistinct. I turned it on to emergency supply and prevented a blackout. Everything had happened so fast but we eventually managed to regroup around Bob Cozens, a rather ragged and beaten formation, but we never faltered.

My roommate, Don Scavato, was in the tail gunner's position of Harry Stirwalt's lead B-17, directing and observing our formation. I was devastated as I watched them spiral down.

Lieutenant Willard Brown, group navigator, B-17F 230164 (group lead, Kiel, 13 June 1943): Our plane took numerous hits from both flak and fighters before going down just beyond the target area. On board was a crew of thirteen, including Brigadier General Nathan Bedford Forrest. He and I were the last to leave the aircraft as it plunged to earth.

After bailing out I free-fell for about 20,000 feet before opening my parachute. I landed in the sea, very fortunately close to a fishing vessel and was immediately taken prisoner of war. After the war I learned that I was the only survivor from the lead aircraft. A strong offshore wind had carried the other twelve crewmen to their deaths in the bitterly cold Baltic Sea.

Sergeant Earl Underwood, tail gunner B-17 F 23091, 334th Squadron, recalls: As we approached the target, we came under attack by what seemed to be the entire German fighter force. We were flying in the second element of the lead squadron, just behind General Forrest's plane, and judging by the reports coming over the intercom at that time I could hear how hard the lead element was being hit. Of course, we were taking a pounding too, but the German fighter seemed to be intent on shooting down the lead Fortress.

As we were fighting our way through this hell I glanced down and saw a B-17 breaking in half, having taken a direct flak hit. The front half—radio room, wings, engines, cockpit, and nose—went straight down intact, but I didn't see any chutes because my attention was riveted on the incredible sight of the B-17's tail section. It was gliding steadily down as if in normal flight. Behind the tail section was a German fighter and in the tail, the gunner was *still firing* at the enemy plane, apparently unaware that the complete front half of his B-17 was gone.

Then our plane came under intense fighter attack and during that action I heard that General Forrest's plane had dropped its bombs and had gone down almost immediately afterward.

Waist gunner Sergeant Arlie Arneson, on board "T'Ain't A Bird," recalls: There were B-17s out of control doing unbelievable aerobatics, exploding, on fire, going straight down in near vertical dives, shedding parachutes; one was hit so hard that the complete ball turret fell free. Other B-17s that were badly damaged headed toward the target. I looked at the lead airplane just before we reached the target and could not believe that anyone could possibly be alive in there. When it eventually went down there was a near mid-air collision in our lead squadron because of an apparent misunderstanding. Thank God the collision was narrowly avoided.

I can't remember much after the bomb run except continual fighter attacks and the further loss of some of our aircraft. While returning over the North Sea our ball-turret gunner, Sergeant Floyd ("Chief") Thompson, reported that both his feet were frozen. Lieutenant Prochaska, our bombardier, came back to help me get Floyd out while Sergeant Cameron, our other waist gunner, went forward into the nose compartment. We got Floyd into the radio room and had his boots and shoes off when we were again attacked by fighters. Lieutenant Prochaska and I went to the waist guns, and Chief Thompson crawled back into the ball turret, frozen feet and all.

While firing from the right waist, I heard a loud crashing noise behind me. I turned, thinking a 20mm cannon shell had hit us. Lieutenant Prochaska, while firing at a 109, had somehow brought the gun muzzle inside the upper rear waist window and had blasted a big hole that, of course, considerably enlarged the waist-window opening. When the fighters again broke off their attacks, Lieutenant Prochaska and I helped Chief out of the ball turret and made him as comfortable as possible. He was only a young man but he was one hell of a gunner and a very fine buddy.

Lieutenant John Korman, navigator of B-17F 229737, recalls: Just before reaching the target, a flak shell exploded immediately beneath us jolting us upward. Shortly after bombing the target and turning for home, the warning lights on our oxygen supply outlets lit up simultaneously. Within a few short minutes the oxygen supply ceased flowing. The flak shrapnel had apparently hit and punctured the large oxygen bottles or broken the supply lines.

Fortunately there were twelve portable bail-out oxygen bottles located within easy reach of our ten crew members. By the time we approached the enemy coast on our way home, however, the oxygen in our bail-out bottles was almost exhausted. Prior to that, efforts to communicate with the lead ship requesting that we all go down to a lower altitude had either failed or couldn't be acknowledged in the confusion.

Very soon everyone except our co-pilot, Lieutenant Ralph Ziegler, was suffering varying degrees of anoxia (loss of oxygen), some losing consciousness. Lieutenant Ziegler kept the airplane in the safety of the formation as long as possible, but when he realized that he was no longer able to react or maintain formation, he immediately put the nose down and began an extremely rapid descent, exceeding the air-speed indicator redline by a considerable margin.

By the time most crew members regained consciousness the plane was very close to the surface of the North Sea and we were under severe fighter attacks, flying straight and level. The German fighters had hit our left wing, number 2 engine was burning, and number 1 was smoking badly. With the crew substantially incapacitated, and with the engine burning, the decision was made to ditch. The landing gear was lowered as a signal to the fighters of our intentions, and they thankfully stopped their attacks.

Just as the final preparations were being made for ditching, a sandbar appeared ahead, just above the surface of the water. Lieutenant Laurier Morissette, our pilot, again lowered the landing gear and he landed on the sand, making what was certainly one of the shortest landing rolls in the history of the B-17 due to the braking power of the soft, damp sand.

While we were helping and carrying our wounded crew members from the plane, the fighters circled low overhead, their pilots waving to us. By then the fire had spread over the entire left wing and was spreading rapidly to the fuselage. We retreated as far as possible to avoid the machine gun bullets that were exploding as the heat of the flames reached them. Someone had the presence of mind to grab two or three first-aid kits when leaving the plane so we were able to patch up the wounded people to a limited degree.

Shortly after we had finished the first aid process, a small, three-seater plane appeared and landed nearby. From it emerged a German soldier with a submachine gun, the pilot, and a civilian carrying a doctor's bag. The doctor approached us and, speaking English, offered to treat our wounded. We accepted gratefully. He told us that the pilot of the light plane was one of the fighter pilots who had shot us down. He also told us that a boat was coming from the mainland to pick us up and would arrive within two hours.

The sand bar was actually an extension at the southern end of the Friesian Islands and possibly was under water at high tide. After the light plane had taken off a German civilian appeared on a wagon pulled by a team of horses. He stopped nearby and took some photographs of our B-17, which by that time had stopped burning. Captain Vincent J. Gannon, the base communications officer who had tagged along on the mission, went over to the man and talked with him.

The boat eventually arrived, a fishing trawler manned by German naval personnel. We waded out, were loaded aboard, and taken back to the coastal town of Husum. The mayor offered us a drink of whiskey and soda or beer. The civilians were not hostile. Soon a Luftwaffe truck arrived and we were taken to a nearby military base to begin our prisoner-of-war status.

Captain Harry Conley, piloting B-17F 23202 "Blondie," remembers: The German boys were marvelous pilots and really were courageous. Of course, some were better than others. The best ones would dive on our formations and attempt to break them up by flying right between our planes. It took great nerve and skill with all our guns firing at them. The Kiel mission turned out to be the roughest raid we had experienced to date. I was leading the second flight of the composite formation, and our number 1 engine was shot out before we reached the target but we kept going. We fought an overwhelming force of enemy fighters for over an hour to and from the target. One after another I saw 95th Group B-17s going down.

Finally I got back out over the North Sea and stayed at very low altitude heading west. I couldn't catch up with the remnants of our formation with only three engines and, in addition, my bomb-bay doors were still open as the closing motor had been shot away during the bomb run to the target.

Lieutenant Ellis B. Scripture, navigator of B-17F 229967 leading the composite formation, recalls: Due to the intensity of attacks from enemy fighters, the bombing run was not particularly good. We couldn't really concentrate our efforts but we got through and released our bombs. The history books record the bombing results as poor to good.

We turned from the target and attempted to rally the remainder of our group over the North Sea. We had sustained severe damage and there was a question as to whether we should abandon our ship. Bill Lindley and Grif Mumford, being the great pilots that they were, said "No, we think we can keep it together," and so we decided to head for home. The fighters kept pecking away at us for quite some time, but gradually the battle died down to our relief and we made our way back to England at low altitude.

Along the way we were following another bomb group that was heading dangerously close to the Friesian Islands. I warned Bill Lindley, "We're getting too close to the Friesians, if we get too close we're sure to be hit again." Grif Mumford tried to warn our group and the group ahead of the new danger, but he couldn't establish radio contact.

When we were opposite the Friesian Islands at about 800-foot altitude, we were again hit by German fighters and again it was a very vicious attack. During these actions fought over the North Sea, our group lost four B-17s and the group ahead of us suffered similar losses. A German fighter collided with one of our B-17s, which in turn collided with another of our bombers on the way down. All three aircraft crashed in the sea.

I gave our pilots an alternate course home that took us away from that area, and one by one the fighters gave up the chase. Eventually we made landfall north of Great Yarmouth. Our airplane was badly shot up, and after we landed back at Framlingham it was found that we had two unexploded 20mm cannon shells in our self-sealing gasoline wing tanks. Numerous bullet holes were also evident throughout our ship.

Lieutenant Robert Cozens, deputy group leader, recalls: By that time we had lost a number of other aircraft and, to put it mildly, we were an extremely loose-knit formation as we straggled homeward over the North Sea. To make matters worse for us, in the heat of the battle the plexiglass over the pilot's compartment had disintegrated, and it was extremely cold for those of us in that area. When I thought that we were pretty much out of danger from further enemy attack, I went down into the navigator/bombardier compartment to try to warm up a little. Shortly thereafter we were once again under attack. The fact that we had not reformed into a tight defensive formation left us that much more vulnerable; consequently we lost additional aircraft.

Captain Harry Conley's Fortress had its number 4 engine shot out during this second attack, and he crash-landed "Blondie" in a barley field near Rack-heath, Norfolk, on two engines. He remembers: After the local civilians had ascertained that none of us were injured, they very kindly provided us with tea, sandwiches, cigarettes, and beer. They were a most hospitable and friendly group of people. I eventually got to a telephone, called the base, and they sent a truck to take us back. We were treated like royalty on our return to Framlingham. Apparently our ship had been reported shot down in the sea during the return flight.

Sergeant Arlie Arneson, waist gunner on the severely damaged "T'Ain't A Bird," recalls: We had taken a beating, a heavy beating. Before the debriefing we received a drink or two of Scotch whiskey instead of coffee and a spam sandwich. This was a first. All I wanted to do was to go off somewhere quiet to cry or get drunk. I did both.

Lieutenant William Isaacs, a 336th squadron navigator, describes his feelings and his fears on returning to Framlingham: As far as I was concerned that raid was the roughest of them all. Our squadron had lost five airplanes, and I recall how quiet and very lonely it was in our barracks that night with twenty of our close friends missing and whose fate was totally unknown to us at that time.

I sincerely felt that I couldn't possibly survive my tour of twenty-five missions. The odds were simply too overwhelming.

Lieutenant William Lindley made a solemn promise to himself on his return to Framlingham: On the way home we went down to very low altitude. One incident that remains vivid is the Fw 190 that made a head-on pass at two B-17s and tried to go underneath them. He miscalculated the clearance. He hung one wing in the water and instantly cartwheeled into the sea.

Several aircraft had feathered engines and one was smoking badly from number four. The largest remaining formation consisted of six planes; most were flying in twos and threes. When the German fighters bounced us again. There weren't many of them, but they had several B-17s as sitting ducks. On their first pass they shot down one aircraft, which crashed in the North Sea from an altitude of about 500 feet . . . straight in.

The debriefing was wild. Since Grif Mumford was the headknocker, he went to the briefing table while my crew and I sat in the corner on the floor. Very little was said as they passed the medicinal Scotch whisky around to each other, one drink per man, but since three of my crew were non-drinkers I drank theirs and bummed several others.

It was then that I swore never to let the German fighters scare me again. They never did.

Captain John Miller, pilot of the severely damaged Fortress "T'Ain't A Bird" and 412th squadron operations officer, vividly recalls the stunning impact the loss of 102 flight crew members had upon his group commander: Following a thoroughly depressing and sad debriefing during which he listened to the accounts of the surviving crews in silence Colonel Kessler, his eyes brimming with tears and very obviously extremely distressed, could only murmur, to no one in particular, "What's happened to my boys? What's happened to my boys?"

Robert Cozens continues: Those of us who returned safely were fortunate indeed. The 95th Bomb Group had just taken the worst beating that it would ever experience during its complete tour of combat duty. Needless to say, the "Forrest" formation was never again flown by the 95th or any other group. General Forrest had demonstrated his conviction that his leadership would be beneficial to the Allied air war by personally involving himself in this ill-fated mission—a mission that cost him his life and, unfortunately, the lives of many, many of the 95th Bomb Group's stalwart air crew members.

Ellis Scripture summarizes the Kiel mission, a day on which the other two

24   B-17S OVER BERLIN

groups in the Fourth Combat Wing at that time, the 94th based at Bury St. Edmunds, Suffolk, and the 96th at Snetterton Heath, Norfolk, had sustained losses of nine and three Fortresses, respectively: It had been an extremely harrowing day. The thing that made it the most dramatic and distressing day for me was that my own crew had been shot down during the mission. (Later confirmed as all KIA.) I became a survivor.

In the confusion of the debriefing, I was asked to make out a navigator's report for the mission. After the critique at Elveden Hall I became group navigator of the 95th Group. That's the hard way to do it, be one that survives.

We had lost ten aircraft. That was the greatest single-mission loss that the 95th Group suffered during the entire war. About half of our planes made it back to Framlingham, with several others managing to crash-land at alternate bases on the East Anglian coast. Colonel Kessler was completely stunned that evening. One hundred two of our crewmen were missing, all of whom he'd known very well, as we all did, since their assignment to the 95th Group.

That night, after the Kiel mission, Colonel Curtis LeMay (later promoted to general), the commander of the Third Air Division at Elveden Hall, Suffolk, telephoned to ask how many serviceable airplanes the 95th Group could put into the air the next day. He was told, "We have one plane and one crew. That's all."

He replied, "Fine. You're on an Alert to fly, and I will be at Framlingham early tomorrow morning to fly with them."

And he was there, ready to show us that he would not send crews where he was not willing to go himself and ready to lead personally. Needless to say everyone respected and admired General LeMay for this type of leadership. As it happened we didn't fly on that Monday, 14 June 1943. But we were ready and so was he.

With that type of outstanding leadership victory was certain. It was just a matter of time. It can be repeated that 13 June 1943 was the day that the 95th became a truly dedicated combat organization. From that point forward we knew we had to be good to survive. We began to rebuild the group with replacement crews immediately following that disaster. From that point on there was no better fighting organization in the entire Eighth Air Force.

The words "Remember Kiel" became our rallying cry for the remaining two long and often bitter years of the air war in Europe.

Local farmer Percy Kindred on whose land at Parham, near Framlingham, the 500-acre airfield had been built during late 1942 and early 1943, remembers: The first Fortress group to arrive at Framlingham, temporarily, was the 95th. On Sunday 13 June 1943, the whole group took off on another mission to Germany. About half of their B-17s returned, one crash-landed, and the remainder were literally shot to pieces.

This was one of my first sights, virtually outside my front door, of what those men were going through. I was stunned and shocked. What I saw that day I won't forget, ever. Then, in July 1943, came the 390th Group for the remainder of the war.

Most of the American airmen I met were nice fellows and extremely generous. In fact they were the most generous people I've ever met. If you were ever short of anything and they had it, you could be sure that they'd share it with you. They behaved like gentlemen and if ever they set a foot wrong I would only have to whisper, and they never did it again.

They were young men in a strange land fighting and dying for England, and it goes without saying that I held them in the very highest regard.

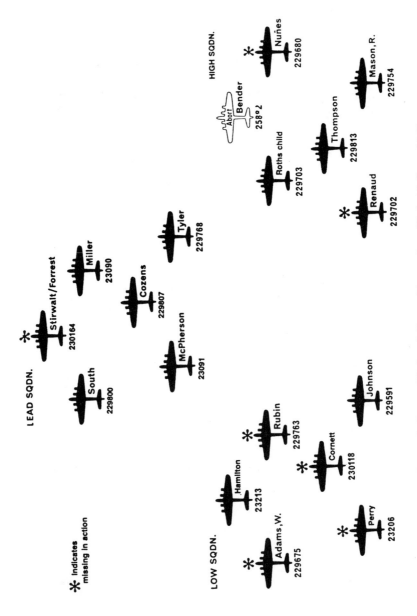

HIGH SQDN.

Nuñes 229680

Mason, R. 229754

Bender 258°2
Abort

Roths child 229703

Thompson 229813

Renaud 229702

LEAD SQDN.

Stirwalt/Forrest 230164

Miller 23090

Tyler 229768

Cozens 229807

McPherson 23091

South 229800

Rubin 229763

Johnson 229591

Cornett 230118

Hamilton 23213

Perry 23206

Indicates missing in action

Adams, W. 229675

LOW SQDN.

95th Bomb Group (H) Lead Group Formation, Kiel, 13 June 1943.

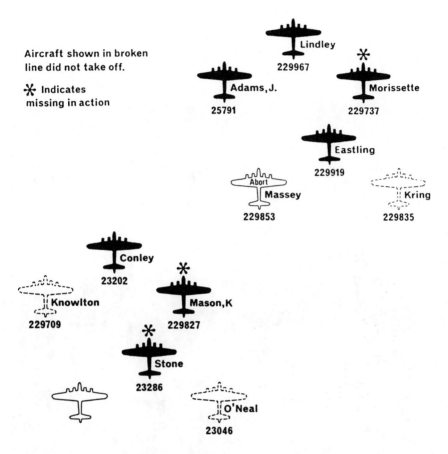

Aircraft shown in broken line did not take off.

✳ Indicates missing in action

Lindley
229967

Adams, J.
25791

Morissette
229737

Eastling
229919

Massey
229853

Kring
229835

Conley
23202

Knowlton
229709

Mason, K
229827

Stone
23286

O'Neal
23046

95th Bomb Group (H) Composite Group Formation, Kiel, 13 June 1943.

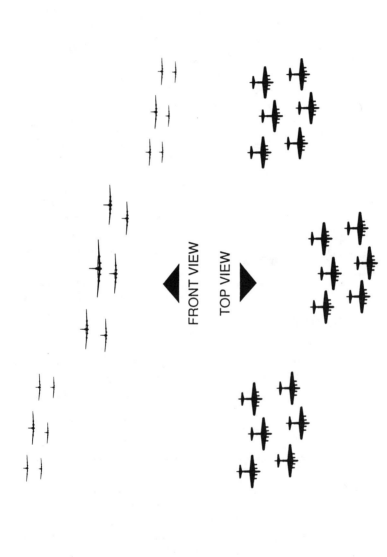

FRONT VIEW

TOP VIEW

Flat Combat Formation proposed by Brigadier General Nathan Bedford Forrest III and flown by the 95th Bomb Group (H) on the disastrous Kiel Mission 13 June 1943. (Reconstructed by Robert Cozens, deputy mission leader.) (Courtesy of Design Centre, Inc.)

OVER THERE

Joseph Florian, S-2 Intelligence Section

This is primarily the viewpoint of a civilian who was fortunate enough to gain a commission in the Army Air Forces due to my thirteen years' design and engineering experience. I was suddenly thrust into an entirely new and be-wildering life that was completely different to anything I'd known previously.

The harsh realities of the air war were brought savagely home to us all following the Kiel mission. Sunday, 13 June 1943, was a date never to be forgotten. We'd worked all through that Saturday night until 0700 hours the following morning, preparing the maps for the navigators, photographs of the target for the bombardiers, and route sheets for pilots. After snatching a few hours' sleep the tense wait for our combat crews to return began. Finally, we could see some of them in the distance, but as they circled the field we could only count half the number of planes that had taken off earlier that day.

After the surviving crews had been debriefed, we waited in vain for another three hours until all possible hope of any others returning disappeared. These missing men were close friends with whom we'd trained, swapped jokes, laughed, and traveled. It left a void that was impossible to write or think about.

Perhaps it sounds callous, but from that day on I made a silent resolve never to get to know aircrew members as well again, because the heartaches that accompany the sudden loss of such warm friendships were too great to bear.

Where and when did it all begin? After high-pressure courses in the varied aspects and techniques of intelligence at Miami Beach and the Army Intelli-gence School, I was assigned to the 95th Bomb Group at Rapid City in early 1943. After another period of intensive training and familiarization the great moment arrived. We were going overseas.

Troop trains took the 95th Group's ground personnel from Rapid City to Camp Kilmer and from there to Hoboken pier, New York. We boarded the *Queen Elizabeth*, a British 83,000-ton luxury liner in the Hudson River on 2 May 1943, for the five-day, zig-zag crossing of the U-boat–infested Atlantic ocean. We bade farewell to the magnificent skyline of New York City to the blasting of horns of every ship in the harbor. Little did the 16,000 troops, who were packed like sardines in a ship designed for 3,000 passengers and crew, realize that it would be exactly two years, almost to the day, when they would see the same sight and from the same ship, on their return journey.

We eventually arrived at Greenock, Scotland. The great liner made its way slowly and carefully past a maze of inlets and coves flanked by the greenest of rolling and wooded hills and the red-tiled roofs of gray stone cottages. A lasting memory of the sea voyage was seeing officers and men kneeling on the floor of the recreation rooms, gambling with dice and squinting at playing cards. I recall Lieutenant Stewart counting his $4,000 winnings at the end of the trip in ten-dollar bills. His uniform trousers also had two very shiny patches at the knees.

Although we docked during the morning we had to wait our turn to disembark, eventually going down the gangplank at 10:00 P.M. I looked at my watch several times and couldn't believe it was still daylight in those northern latitudes at that late hour.

The 400-mile train journey from Glasgow to Wickham Market, Suffolk, took twenty hours, and from there a convoy of trucks took 200 officers and 1,000 enlisted men to our new home at the U.S. Army Air base at Parham, near Framlingham. We arrived on 12 May and a week later 800 more men joined us. Rows and rows of what looked like large, black, corrugated-iron sewer pipes became our new living quarters.

Never before was it brought out so poignantly and forcibly how much comforts of home meant. Here we were faced with the biweekly chore of scrubbing our own laundry, early-morning shaving in a limited amount of cold water, and endless miles of walking from one building to the other across the 500-acre airfield. However, life took on a more cheerful aspect as the weeks went by. An English lady at nearby Wickham Market was persuaded and induced into doing my weekly laundry for three shillings and a bar of soap. British bicycles were issued, which helped greatly to alleviate foot weariness. Gradually too, over the next two years our mess hall food improved but never fully replaced the original staples—Spam, brussels sprouts, and powdered eggs!

Framlingham was to be our home for a short time only so we hastily saw and learned what we could of the geography and the history that surrounded us. Framlingham is located about twelve miles from the North Sea coast, which didn't allow much time for an air-raid warning against low-flying German bombers and fighter-bombers that occasionally came swooping over. However, Framlingham was a peaceful and picturesque country town in which was situated an ancient castle with crumbling sixteen-foot thick walls dating back a thousand years. It also had a local cinema, hotel, several pubs, a fish and chip shop, and a cycle shop. As the small automobiles were in storage for the duration, no gasoline was issued to the civilian population unless unusual circumstances arose. The accepted method of conveyance was the cycle.

The village pub was an important part of the community and center of activity during opening hours. The civilians, mostly farm workers, flocked to get their pint of bitter, light ale, or perhaps an 'arf an' arf." In such an atmosphere of timelessness, it was no wonder that the young American serviceman stood out like a sore thumb because he was always a busy and energetic person, prying in behind those solid English doors and, as a rule, being very well treated. It wasn't until a year or so later that the British began to resent the American invasion of their island kingdom and whispers began that we were "over-paid, over-sexed, overbearing, and over here."

I recall a dance that I attended at Parham, just to the south of our camp. It was held at a hostel where the Land Army girls were billeted. They did a lot of the agricultural work in East Anglia and they came from all parts of England. The dance ended early, about 10:30 P.M., because the girls had to start work in the fields again by 6:00 A.M. This schedule was maintained for six days a week and every three months they were allowed to visit their homes for a fortnight.

East Anglia is a totally unspoiled area of England, gently undulating farmlands, quaint old world villages, founded on the wealth of trade with Europe dating back to the Middle Ages, with half-timbered houses and ancient churches. It has immensely wide skies and a network of rivers and tributaries that meander quietly past tree-lined fields and marshlands to wind their way into the North Sea.

On 15 June 1943 the 95th Bomb Group moved by air and truck to our permanent base in England, Horham, an even smaller village set deep in the Suffolk countryside. It provided me with an opportunity to view the earth's pattern from the air, a green patchwork quilt of fields and dense, wooded areas. Red poppies appeared vividly from several fields and roadside verges during the short flight to our new airfield.

It wasn't long before we were able to launch missions from our new base. All S-2 intelligence officers and enlisted men were each given specific assignments, one primary job and one or perhaps two secondary ones. My primary assignment was to the war room, which contained the various war-front maps and a large-scale map of Europe on which all our mission routes were plotted. Of my two secondary assignments, one made me the map officer, which involved maintaining, filing, and issuing from a stockpile of 70,000 maps of various sizes, and also compiling a weekly commentary of the war news from the various fronts. My other secondary assignment was security officer for the airfield—briefing the boys on what they could or couldn't say in their letters home, and warning them of the very serious consequences that loose talk, both on and off the base, would bring them.

There was a great shortage of labor in England at this time because the majority of able-bodied men were away on active service. Consequently, it became necessary to import labor from southern Ireland, a neutral country. There were about 400 civilians working on our airfield, and about 150 came from Eire. These laborers worked for three months and then went home to Ireland for a short holiday. It was a well-known fact that some of them went directly to the German consul in Dublin to sell any information they'd been able to collect while working on Allied airfields.

However, we found that the majority of civilians who worked on our base, both British and Irish, were very sincere, friendly, and very helpful.

The 95th Bomb Group flew its last mission over Europe 7 May 1945. Much would happen before that final operation was completed.

SHOT DOWN

Joel Bunch, Group Operations Officer

On 22 June 1943 the primary target was a synthetic rubber producing plant at the West German town of Huls, located in the industrialized Ruhr Valley. "Happy Valley" was reputed to be defended by the most powerful antiaircraft batteries in the world.

As we passed over the initial point and began our bomb run the flak grew in intensity. Very shortly after "bombs away" we took a hit and things began to happen. Our aircraft (no. 230221) was seriously disabled; Lieutenant Harold King, our navigator, was mortally wounded; we were forced to leave the group's formation; and the order was given to abandon the plane.

Lieutenant Ernest Vielo (co-pilot) bailed out via the nose-exit hatch, and Lieutenant John Pearson (bombardier) managed to push Lieutenant King out of the nose hatch, pulling his ripcord in the hope that King would be found by the Germans in time to receive medical attention.

Lieutenant Pearson then bailed out but struck the still open bomb-bay doors as he fell, injuring one of his legs so severely that it had to be amputated by German doctors. He was eventually repatriated after several months. The remainder of the crew all survived, but I have no detailed knowledge of their experiences.

My back injury resulted from my parachute being caught in a lofty tree and I was slammed to the ground. Being temporarily unable to get to my feet, I crawled away from my chute to avoid detection and lay quietly in the nearby woods.

After an hour or so I set off in a westerly direction through dense forest. I came to a wide river that I couldn't swim because of my back injury. I made my way slowly along the river bank, keeping to the shelter of the trees, until I came to a bridge that didn't appear to be guarded. While attempting to cross the bridge German sentries suddenly appeared. I was immediately arrested and when they discovered my service pistol I was stripped of my clothing and beaten up. I spent that night in the city jail at Wesel, from there by railroad to Frankfurt for solitary confinement and questioning for the next four days, then to the permanent accommodation at Stalag Luft III in Sagan (now in Poland) for the next eighteen months as a prisoner of war.

Sagan was evacuated in early 1945 as a result of the Russian forces advancing from the east. On 28 January several thousand Allied POWs were force-marched westwards in sub-zero temperatures from Sagan to Spremburg, arriving there on 4 February. Then we were loaded onto trains, over fifty men to one rail car, for Mooseburg, Bavaria, another POW camp. Due to lengthy delays we didn't arrive there until 7 February. The camp was liberated on 29

April 1945, when the 14th Armoured Division (General Patton's Third Army) arrived.

Interestingly, I was in Rheims, France, where the peace was signed on 8 May, although I was unaware of it until the next day.

I feel that there is nothing heroic, or even creditable, about being shot down, other than the fact that the bombs were delivered accurately and effectively and that all but one of the crew survived.

THE ROBERT BENDER STORY

Don Merten, Co-pilot, 336th Squadron

"Spook" Bender . . . what a nick-name and it fitted him to a T. I first met Bob at Rapid City, South Dakota, on New Year's Day 1943. We were assigned to the 336th Squadron and within a week the full crew was formed. Bob was pilot, I was co-pilot, Willie Isaacs the bombardier, Jim Bader the navigator; the enlisted men were Don Bryant, flight engineer and top-turret gunner; Harold Van Arsdale, radio operator; Earl Bennett, ball turret; Hillabrant, tail gunner; and Lloyd Glick was one of the waist gunners but I can't recall the name of the other waist gunner.

The name "Spook" came about naturally. All his girlfriends were very attractive and with curves in the right places. Everyone else had spooks. Bob's favorite expression was, "Where did you manage to find that spook?"

In March 1943 we flew to Kearney, Nebraska, for overseas processing. Each crew member received his war gear; excess personal property was sent home. Spook had a small, black cocker spaniel and Isaacs had a small Pekingese that they used as contacts to meet the girls in each town. Both dogs proved to be highly effective in this regard.

We left Kearney and flew to West Palm Beach, Florida, and on 29 March we headed for Borinquin Field, Puerto Rico, where it was discovered that our pilot had acquired a rather unpleasant infection somewhere along the line that precluded his flying. While he was being treated with the necessary medication, we took the opportunity to enjoy the tropical climate and get lazy.

After two weeks Bender was pronounced ready for duty and we continued on our way to Trinidad, Belem, and then to Natal, Brazil. Between Belem and Natal we ran into some very rough weather. I've never seen it rain so hard. How all four engines could continue to run is quite beyond me. Also, the continuous Saint Elmo's Fire was running all over the place. It was particularly interesting to watch it leap across the rivets on the wide wings. From Natal we flew the long haul across the South Atlantic to Dakar, Senegal, via the Ascension Islands. From Dakar we flew in two stages to St. Eval in southwest England via Marrakech, Morocco. From there we were reunited with the 95th Group at Alconbury.

Our journey overseas had taken about a month since starting from Florida. During that time we had seen several very interesting sights; the lush, green rain forests of South America; the dense jungles and full running rivers of West Africa; the seemingly endless desert sands of the African desert and the tiny oases very occasionally where the natives could regroup and re-water during their long and lonely treks across this forbidding desert landscape; then the majestic and beautiful Atlas Mountains.

Easter 1943 was spent at Lammonia Hotel, Marrakech. This hotel was run by the French and was where Winston Churchill spent his winter holidays. The food was delicious, especially the fresh, large, juicy oranges. We loaded several sackfuls in our B-17, which, by this time, was pretty well loaded with cases of cigarettes and cases of rum, both of which had been acquired at little cost along the way, and all our gear. I will never forget how green and hazy the English countryside appeared through the early morning mists.

It had been quite an enlightening experience for this Kansas farm boy as it was to the remainder of our crew. Especially interesting was meeting the various people, all of differing lifestyles and of different cultures. They were very friendly and they were very helpful along the way.

While at Alconbury we did quite a bit of close-formation flying in preparation for the task ahead. Our first combat mission was uneventful. That state of affairs rapidly changed as the flak and enemy fighters became more than a reality. We began to get the feeling that Custer must have had when he said during his last stand: "Where the hell did all those Indians come from?"

To illustrate this point our crew lost four B-17s all named "Spook" during our first few combat missions. We lost "Spook I" on the Lorient raid during which we had two engines shot out by flak, and we crash-landed at a small fighter base near Exeter, southwest England. We skidded off the end of the short runway, down over a deep ditch, and knocked the sides off a bridge that carried the main highway between Exeter and London.

I remember leaving the end of the runway, sliding rapidly over the ditch, then seeing about eight British workmen digging a large hole near the bridge— eight startled faces staring up at us—and then they all scrambled for safety. Luckily we missed them all and none of our crew was injured. After things had settled down, I found one of the British chaps digging under our ball turret. I asked him what he was digging for and he replied, "Me jacket is under this lot."

Due to the fact that our wrecked B-17 had completely blocked the main highway, traffic began to build up on either side. As fate would have it, a British Army brigadier general and his driver who had been on their way to London in their staff car, were now stranded on the Exeter side of our shot-up airplane. The general was extremely irate and said so, which was a mistake because Spook Bender strode very purposefully across to the general's car, and in highly explicit and concise terms, he told the general and his driver that he and his crew were definitely not too worried or concerned with their predicament, nor of having caused them to miss their "regular night-out in London," at that particular moment in time. The brigadier general quickly wound his side window up.

That night the authorities arranged to put us up for the night with a British family near Exeter. During the night we had a German air raid and had to spend some of the time in an air raid shelter. The next day an aircraft returned us to our home base. The next two "Spooks," II and III, were so badly shot up that they were salvaged. I've forgotten the total extent of the damage each B-17 sustained, but they were about equal in flak and fighter shells. Here again it was an absolute miracle that not one of our crew was injured. It just scared the hell out of us—that was all.

It was during our eighth mission that we lost "Spook IV." The target was St. Nazaire, the U-boat submarine pens. We had an engine shot out over the target and had to apply excessive power on the other three in an attempt to get home. To make matters worse the refueling crew at Horham had somehow failed to fill our long-range "Tokyo" wing tanks with sufficient gasoline for us to make the mission. We learned later that two other 95th Group ships also had insufficient fuel, and they didn't make it back either.

We did everything possible to get back to England, throwing all excess equipment overboard in an effort to lighten the load but that wasn't enough. We finally ran out of gas and had to ditch our airplane about sixty miles short of the English coast and forty miles off the French coast in the English channel.

Everything went smoothly; each crew member knew his ditching procedure and Spook Bender performed an admirable demonstration of how to land 26 tons of B-17 on the surface of a fairly choppy sea at a speed of about 90 miles an hour. Our two life rafts inflated and we clambered aboard. We counted noses and everyone was in their proper place except a major from wing headquarters who had tagged along on the mission as an observer. We looked around and saw him standing on the wing of our slowly sinking B-17. He shouted across to us that he couldn't swim, so Willie Isaacs and I took off our clothes and went to his rescue. We got him back into one of the life rafts, but as he was clambering aboard the raft the knife he was wearing went through its sheath and punctured the raft's rubber skin. Spook Bender hollered that he could hear hissing.

Eventually we got the leak plugged with the repair kit about three hours later, during which Spook gave our "super-cargo" a non-stop verbal barrage while the major held his thumb on the leak.

We had ditched about 3 P.M. on 28 June within sight of the French coast. The weather was quite warm and the water not too cold. We spent the night trying to keep both life rafts, which were connected with a rope, heading into the wind to lessen the ungodly pitching and rolling of the ocean. All of us were sick, and I really mean sick, at one time or another. We had cans of fresh water to drink and big bars of unsweetened chocolate, which tasted better with the passage of time. We got our hand-operated and hand-generated radio transmitter working. The box kite with the thin wire antenna worked extremely well. Van Arsdale, our radio operator, tapped out distress signals throughout the night and well into the following morning.

It was about midday when two British motor torpedo boats (MTBs) of the Air-Sea Rescue Service came racing in to pick us up. We certainly were relieved and very glad to see that they were British and not German (we were in German-controlled waters at the time) and thought that they were going to run us down for a moment, they approached us so fast. Apparently Van's S.O.S. had been picked up by the British A.S.R. people over 400 miles away, and this was the reason that they had been able to locate and rescue us.

They supplied us with rum and tea, mostly rum, aboard the MTBs, which took very little time to get us back to the southern coast of England. It sure felt like home to us. We were flown back to Horham the following day. They gave us five days' rest and recuperation (R & R) over the 4th of July weekend, which we spent at a Red Cross rest home at Basingstoke near the south coast of England. Here the food was good; the soft beds, big bath towels, hot bath water, and clean, dry sheets were greatly appreciated by us all. In addition, we really appreciated the convivial atmosphere and the beer at the local pubs during the evening hours.

As it turned out St. Nazaire was Spook Bender's last mission. He'd lost a lot of weight and was usually shaking like a leaf. Who could blame him? All he could talk about was "all them Focke Wulfs" and "all that flak." It was about this time that Bill Lindley and Spook went to see a movie in the nearest big town, Ipswich. They sat in the first row of the balcony but the projectionist made a big mistake when he showed the latest newsreel before the movie, with nothing but German fighters attacking B-17s of the Eighth Air Force. Spook went slightly berserk. He crouched down behind the rail of the balcony and kept screaming for his gunners to "Shoot! Shoot! Shoot!" Bill managed to calm him, got him outside, and then they took a taxi back to Horham.

Bill Isaacs recalls Bob Bender's last flight with the 95th Group: We were given a brand new airplane which we named "Spook V." On our first test flight with it, after attaining take-off speed of 115 mph, Spook suddenly "froze on the stick" and couldn't pull it into the air. Don Merten overpowered him and jerked it off the runway just in time. When we landed, Bob Bender was taken to the base hospital, and this is the last I ever saw him. They said he'd suffered a breakdown.

Naturally I was very fond of him; he brought us safely through some rough, tough missions. Of course I'm slightly prejudiced; and I still think Spook Bender was one of the finest pilots of the Eighth Air Force.

Don Merten concludes, Bob stayed in the hospital for a rest and they finally sent him home to the United States. He suffered a massive heart attack a few years later and died. He was only 25 years old.

I got Spook V after I checked out as aircraft commander. Some crew members mentioned previously finished their missions with me, and we "lucked out" on 23 November 1943. Jim Bader finished soon thereafter with another crew, and Willie Isaacs finished his tour with the 100th Bomb Group at Thorpe Abbotts. Earl Bennett, our ball turret gunner who'd ditched with us in late June, went on another mission with Lieutenant Rothschild's crew. They ditched and floated for twenty-three hours before being rescued. Earl was a tough little cookie and a great crew member. He also had five German fighters, officially confirmed as shot down, to his credit.

A DAY TO REMEMBER

Joseph E. Mutz, Armorer/Waist Gunner, 336th Squadron

Our crew was commanded by Lieutenant O.V. Robichaud, and we were one of the original crews assigned to the 336th Squadron.

Our eighth mission was to Hanover, Germany, on 26 July 1943. Before reaching our target, our formation was attacked by swarms of Fw 190s and Me 109s. With two engines gone and on fire, our B-17 was forced to leave the 95th's formation; and as the fire grew in intensity, the situation became hopeless. Lieutenant Robichaud had no alternative but to give the order to abandon the aircraft before the fuel tanks in the wings exploded.

I was wearing a seat-pack type parachute that I always flew with during missions. The chest strap of the harness however wasn't properly adjusted. It was too tight, so I always left it unbuckled thinking that if I ever had to jump I'd hunch my shoulders forward and buckle the two clips before bailing out. Due to all the intense activity, both inside and outside our ship at this time, I completely forgot to buckle my chest straps when I jumped. Consequently, when I pulled the ripcord directly after bailing out, I was immediately flipped upside down and out of the harness with the exception of one leg strap.

That was the situation I found myself in when I regained consciousness at a lower altitude. My right arm was broken above the elbow, the sleeves of my flight jacket had been torn out at the shoulder and peeled down to my wrists. There I was, hanging upside down, swaying from side to side in the breeze, a broken arm dangling uselessly, hanging from only one leg strap and dreading what was about to happen when I hit the ground in this precarious position.

The closer to the ground I got, the faster it appeared to rush up to me. I landed very awkwardly and painfully on my broken arm, head and shoulder. I lost consciousness briefly, and when I came to, I was flat on my injured back and unable to move. Despite the pain, a feeling of intense relief swept over me. I'd escaped with my life.

However, it was to be the first of two narrow escapes that fateful day, because a few minutes later an armed German civilian approached me and stood about five yards in front of me. As I lay there unable to move, except to kick my legs and shake my head, he raised his rifle and shot me twice.

The first shot entered my lower thigh behind my knee and exited from my upper thigh. The reason for strange path of the bullet is that I was kicking my legs, shaking my head and screaming, "No! No!" His second shot grazed my right forehead, just above the eye. He obviously thought that second shot had finished me because he then left, and I fainted mercifully into unconsciousness.

I regained consciousness some time later when some German soldiers were loading me onto a horse-drawn wagon. The next nineteen months were spent in various prison camp hospitals in Germany, and I was finally repatriated in a prisoner-of-war exchange during March 1945.

I arrived home in the United States on board the Swedish exchange ship *Gripsholm.*

ESCAPE AND EVASION

Clifford Cole, Group Operations Officer

On 12 August 1943, the 95th Bomb Group was assigned to attack the marshaling yards near Bonn, Germany. I was the assigned mission commander and was flying co-pilot with the crew commanded by Lieutenant Cliff Hamilton, whose brother Dick was also a lead B-17 pilot with the 95th Bomb Group. Bonn was a relatively short mission in distance and was considered to be a "milk run." However, as we approached the target area the flak grew in intensity. We took a hit and lost number 4 engine with a runaway propellor that refused to feather. It acted as a brake and slowed us considerably, but we continued leading the group at reduced airspeed. Just short of the initial point, our number 1 engine was hit and put out of action. We had no alternative but to hand over our position to the deputy lead airplane and turn back for England.

Our crippled B-17 soon attracted a queue of German fighters, and the running battle lasted until our ammunition was exhausted. A 20mm cannon shell exploded just behind the cockpit, rupturing a highly volatile oxygen tank; our left wing was also on fire and we had taken numerous other hits. We had no alternative but to bail out.

Our altitude was 22,000 feet when Lieutenant Hamilton hit the bail-out bell that ordered the other crewmen to jump. I left my seat in the cockpit, grabbed my parachute, and headed down to the nose escape hatch, which was already open. As I knelt down, trying to snap on the second hook of my chest-type chute, a large boot shoved me out into space with only one hook properly fastened, and as I was free-falling I tried desperately to fasten the other metal hook but didn't succeed. As I was rapidly losing consciousness due to lack of oxygen, I pulled the ripcord. Mercifully my chute snapped open. I saw our ship explode in mid-air not far away and begin its slow spiraling on one wing on its way down.

I woke up on the ground, and my back gave me intense pain as I crawled around gathering my chute. I'd landed in a small clearing surrounded by pine trees. I hid my chute under a bush and examined the contents of my escape kit. Everything was quiet and peaceful so I decided to hide until darkness in a pile of brushwood, where some trees had been felled. The time was 1100 hours.

I had barely concealed myself when I heard voices calling in the surrounding woods. I caught glimpses of two men, less than fifty yards from my hiding place, as they continued calling and searching. To my great relief they didn't have dogs, and after a seemingly interminable length of time they left, going away from me and still calling.

I stayed under the brush pile until dusk and decided to head westward toward the Channel coast using my button compass. I eventually got clear of the forest after having to grope my way along in the darkness. A faint night vision came to me as my eyes adjusted to the dark, and I soon came to open fields and long, thick hedgerows. For the next three nights I continued my trek westward, hiding and sleeping in the hedgerows by day.

On the fourth day I was asleep in a hedgerow when I was awakened by the sound of hammering. It was a man repairing a wooden and wire fence about a hundred yards away and he had a dog with him. I remained hidden, hardly daring to breathe, but the dog came straight to my hiding place and began barking loudly. After one or two minutes of continual barking the fence repairer, a teenage boy, came across to see what his dog was excited about. He was startled when I stood up and said hello to him. To my great relief he appeared to be friendly and helpful, and using my slight knowledge of the French language we were able to communicate with each other with difficulty. I told him I was an American airman trying to get back to England and that I was thirsty and hungry. While attempting to explain to him how I got there, he suddenly motioned me to get down and out of sight. He then silenced his dog, and two or three minutes later an older man came walking along beside the hedgerow.

The two men greeted each other, talked briefly, then the older man continued on his way. After he'd disappeared from view, the boy indicated "all clear." He then told me that the man was a "Black Belgian," a term of contempt for those who collaborated with the German occupation forces in Belgium at that time. I learned that I was approximately twenty kilometers southwest of Brussels, the Belgian capital city. Between my poor French and the boy's equally poor English, I finally understood that he wanted to help me.

So began a series of extremely tense journeys during which I met many heroic Resistance workers and aircrew helpers in Belgium and France, all of whom risked their very lives to help Allied airmen evade capture and escape from Nazi-occupied Europe.

The boy took me to a seemingly impenetrable brier patch on a meadow, and he indicated a concealed opening. I crawled through the open "tunnel" and discovered a clear space, the size of a small room, which had obviously been used as a hiding place before. The boy told me to wait until night fall when someone would come to help me further. Then he crawled out and set off toward a cluster of houses on the distant horizon that I could see through the brier thicket.

As I waited I thought of the other members of Cliff Hamilton's crew and how they were managing. But thoughts of my home in Illinois predominated as they had done since my bail-out. My wife was due to give birth to our second child, and I was glad that I'd prearranged through a friend to have flowers sent to her daily while she was in the hospital. Thoughts of her and of getting back to England to reassure her that I was O.K. were foremost. I watched warily as a person approached my hiding place. It was a lady, and she constantly looked around to see if anyone else was in the vicinity. Apparently satisfied she called softly and I answered, "Ici." She entered the tunnel and took from her gathered apron a bottle of warm coffee, half a loaf of black bread, and two apples. She acknowledged my grateful thanks with a smile and then left, indicating that I was to stay where I was. Three more ladies appeared at intervals throughout the day, each bringing food and drink. The last one spoke reasonably good English, saying that a man would come for me at dusk with a bicycle.

Sure enough, a man arrived at dusk riding a bicycle made for two! He'd brought me a complete set of civilian clothes and a pair of large wooden shoes (clogs). As I was changing he kept assuring me that we would have no trouble riding the bike the few kilometers to his home. I climbed somewhat gingerly onto the back seat, my back was still painful, and sure enough we arrived at his house just after dark, having met several people along the way who paid not the slightest attention to us.

I was hidden in the hosts' attic that night, the first comfortable shelter I'd experienced since leaving Horham. The following morning, after a good breakfast, a member of the Belgian Underground took me by train into Brussels. The commuter train journey took about forty-five minutes or so, and my helper informed me that he would be in sight of me on the train but I was not to indicate in any way that I knew him. The train was very crowded as he'd predicted. No one paid any attention to me as I boarded although I couldn't help feeling extremely conspicuous. However I found it amazing that at the interim stops, as people crowded past me, some of them gently and quietly touched and squeezed my hand to indicate that they knew I was an evadee and that they were friends. When our stop eventually came, I saw my guide nod his head and I followed.

During my lengthy stay in Brussels, I was made very much aware of the calm and very efficient way in which the Belgian Resistance functioned virtually under the noses of the German occupation forces. After a thorough interrogation to establish that I was an American pilot, I was provided with forged identification papers, passport, photograph, and complete set of civilian clothing and shoes.

The home where I first stayed, near the Avenue Louise, was adjacent to offices occupied by a German military headquarters. My hosts, a Belgian lady who was a cleaner of those offices and her husband, a linesman technician for the Brussels telephone company, were both active members of the organization and both would be out of the house most of the time except for meals and sleeping.

The husband could speak English, German, and French fluently. He confided in me that with his equipment he could intercept nearly any telephone conversation he wanted to while he was "repairing" the lines. By this method the organization was kept thoroughly informed of all German movements in Brussels and, in some cases, other parts of Belgium and the low countries before they had actually taken place. It was priceless information.

The original plan for my escape was for a light aircraft from England to land on an open field near Brussels at night, pick me up and take me back to England, but after a few weeks this plan was dropped. During this time I was moved to different addresses in Brussels. At one of them I met a Resistance member who was himself on the run from the Nazis. He'd been a banker in Germany before the war, and because he was Jewish, he'd had to flee for his life. He had adequate funds and he took me for meals at "safe" restaurants and Sunday afternoon soccer matches during which we sat and watched the games from the stand surrounded by German soldiers. Apparently it was the safest place to be.

Eventually I left Brussels for the next stage of my escape. Two train journeys later I arrived in Paris, France, having been guided by a nurse in a white uniform on the first train who pointed out four other evadees by touching her cap as she passed each one. The uniformed German who inspected my forged papers said nothing, to my great relief, and he continued through the train.

In Paris I was taken by a different guide to an apartment. On the way there my guide asked me, "Who is George?" After reflecting a moment I told him George was the autopilot on an airplane. Reassured that I was not a German infiltrator, he continued to the apartment. Here I was greeted by a couple who were both involved in the escape line. The husband worked at a vehicle factory that supplied trucks to the German armed forces. He told me that he and his fellow workers were sabotaging as many of the trucks as possible by filing deep scratches in the cylinders, pouring sugar in the gas tanks, and many other ingenious tricks.

The following day another agent came to the apartment and told me I was leaving Paris early that evening for the bus journey south with several other evadees. There were no other passengers on the bus as we drove through the blacked-out countryside of occupied France, eventually arriving after a tension-filled journey, at a small village near the foothills of the Pyrenees Mountains. We stopped at a farmhouse, where we were treated to an excellent meal with wine.

After dinner we met our guide who would lead us over the Pyrenees into neutral Spain. He was a Basque, a man whom I judged was in his sixties and in excellent physical condition. We were given heavy socks, rope-soled shoes for mountain climbing, and warm clothing, all of which we needed during our subsequent and exhausting ascent and descent of that forbidding, snow-covered mountain range, the natural barrier between France and Spain. I vividly recall the feeling of profound relief mixed with joyous elation as I pulled myself to a crest and saw the lights of a Spanish town, San Sebastian, twinkling in the distance. I thought, too, of the tremendous risks my guides and helpers in Belgium and France had taken on my behalf. We descended in silence and in single file behind our guide. We continued heading toward the lights, and soon we stopped at a complex of buildings, which we discovered was a winery. After we were given a memorable breakfast, we slept until late afternoon on hay in a nearby barn.

That night a car from the British embassy collected us and took us to Madrid. There the American embassy would have nothing to do with us, so the British embassy took us in, provided new clothing, identity papers, and shelter in the embassy buildings. After a week in Madrid, a British embassy guide accompanied us by train to Gibraltar from where the Royal Air Force flew us to London on 7 December 1943.

Major Donohue came up from the 95th at Horham and positively identified me, and I was released. I learned the remainder of the crew were POWs except the tail gunner, who, sad to say, went down with the plane. After a period of debriefing at Horham, then a short course at a British intelligence school, I was instructed to tour several bomb groups and tell my experiences to combat crews. I flew home to the United States, arriving just before Christmas 1943, to Louise, my wife, and two daughters, the second of which had been born the day after I'd been shot down in August. Louise had been informed by a War Office telegram that I was MIA (missing in action) soon afterward but she didn't know any more details until she'd received the message I sent from London on 7 December to say I was safe. It was quite a homecoming.

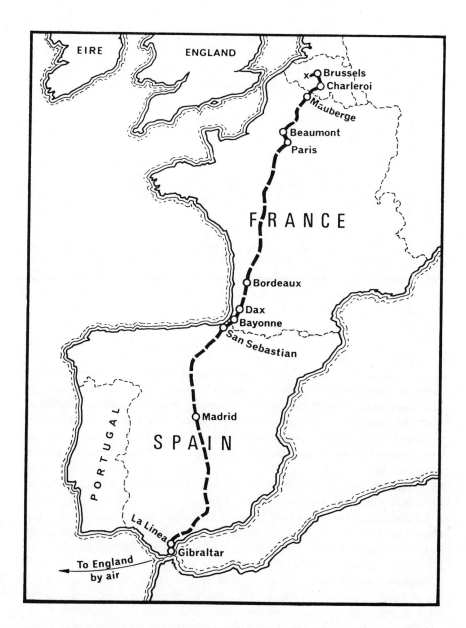

Escape route followed by hundreds of downed Allied airmen. The brave
people of the Underground risked their lives daily to keep the route open.

BETRAYED

Leroy ("Rocky") Lawson, Navigator, 335th Squadron

Ours was an original 95th crew and consisted of Captain Cliff Hamilton, pilot; myself; Lieutenant Virgil Jones, bombardier; Sergeant Anderson, top-turret/ engineer; Sergeant Ocheltree, radio operator; Sergeant Deverger, ball turret; Sergeant Dell, waist gunner. The other three crewmen who flew with us the day we were shot down while returning from the Bonn mission, 12 August 1943, were: Major Cole from group operations, co-pilot; Lieutenant Colonel Scott from 13th Wing H.Q., tail gunner, and Colonel Daniel Jenkins, waist gunner, from training command in the United States who was in England on a fact-finding tour concerning aerial gunnery. They replaced our regular co-pilot, Glen Ransom, and gunners Cleo Gardner and Frank Crooker.

"Jonesy" and I in the nose section never saw the enemy fighters because they attacked us from the rear. We heard a lot of talking on the interphone and the constant noisy sound of our defensive gunfire, but a deafening explosion in the nose compartment made us realize we were in deep trouble. The plane went out of control, so I clipped my parachute on and bailed out of the nose exit hatch.

I waited awhile, as instructed, before opening my chute and suddenly discovered I was bleeding profusely from my face, but it was only from plexiglass fragments, nothing serious. Then a German fighter circled me as I drifted down; presumably the pilot was organizing a reception committee for my arrival on the ground. As I descended the blood stopped flowing from my facial wounds and I landed in a farmyard very close to a pond. I gathered up my chute and buried it under a pile of loose earth in the farmyard. There was nobody around so I raced for the only cover available, a nearby field of yellowing grain and hid in the waist-high corn.

I stayed there for about half an hour and, hearing nothing, raised my head above the corn and saw a young boy at the edge of the field staring straight at me. He crawled toward me and with my limited knowledge of German and his knowledge of Dutch I managed to convey to him that I was an American airman and asked him for help. He told me the Germans were looking all round the area for me and that I'd better stay where I was for the time being while he went for assistance.

The help soon appeared in the form of a Dutch policeman who, after assuring me he would assist me, took me on his bicycle to a large wooded area. Once there, the policeman's scouts kept him constantly advised as to the whereabouts of the German search parties.

Eventually, just before dusk, the policeman, whose name was Maurice Cloostermans, hid me in some dense bushes at the edge of the woods, assuring me he'd return. Several people from the nearby village brought me food and drink. It certainly wasn't a secret that I was around. The local priest, who spoke excellent English, advised me that the policeman had connections with the local Underground movement. He impressed upon me not to remember any of my helpers' names in case I was captured because it would mean instant arrest and almost certain torture and death for the resistance members.

The policeman returned after dark and brought a set of civilian clothes that I changed into. He then took me across a field to a doctor's house. The doctor examined the wounds on my face, bathed them, and treated them with antiseptic while his wife prepared a hot meal of fried sausages and eggs.

Although the doctor spoke a little English, I had difficulty understanding him so I began using some German words from my high school days. He then left and a short time later returned with another Dutchman who spoke excellent English. The new arrival sat opposite me across the dining room table, asking me questions about myself. I saw no reason not to tell him. Finally he asked me where I'd learned German while claiming that I was American. I replied that I'd studied the language while in high school back in the United States. He then relaxed and placed a Luger automatic pistol on the table with which he'd been covering me during our talk from beneath the tabletop.

The policeman then returned and told me the safest place for me was in the local jail. If the Germans came he would have to tell them he'd arrested me, but I was free to leave any time I wanted. I decided to go along with the plan, went to jail and was soon asleep.

Very early the next morning the local village people, who appeared to be delighted to see me, brought me more food and hot drink. Apparently, I'd come down somewhere near Valkenswaard in southern Holland, quite close to the Belgian border. During that morning Maurice Cloostermans brought another Dutchman, who told me he was going to take me over the border into Belgium that afternoon.

We left the jail on our bicycles for Belgium, my guide riding about a hundred yards in front; along the way we collected another evadee. It was Virgil Jones, our bombardier.

Eventually we arrived in the small town of Overpelt, went to a farmhouse on the outskirts, and stayed for four days. Then our guide took us on to another small north Belgian town—Bree, I believe it was. There we stayed in hiding at a bakery for the next three days until our guide told us we would be leaving for Brussels the following day when a man known simply as "the chief" would collect us. During our stay at the bakery, Sergeant Anderson, our flight engineer, joined us.

The next morning the chief arrived and he was really gung-ho. He spoke excellent English and said he had spent several years in America before the war. He told us we would be going to Brussels by car and that we weren't to worry about anything, even though we would be driving right past a German military camp because, he said, they wouldn't bother him.

With us three evadees packed into the rear seat of that little car, a Renault, as I recall, the chief drove us without incident to a very large and impressive house in Brussels. Here we were greeted by over a dozen other Allied evadees, among them were Britons, Canadians, Australians, Americans, and two Polish flyers who had been funnelled there by the Underground.

The chief told us we would stay there until arrangements were made to take us on to the next stage of the escape line which extended south to Spain or, alternatively, by ship or submarine from the Belgian or French coast back to England. During my stay in Brussels I was taken into a clothing and a department store, outfitted with a new set of clothes, had my photograph taken for my false passport, and issued forged paper and documents complete with a false name. Each day one or two evadees left the house and continued on their way, hopefully to freedom.

After seven or eight days in Brussels, I was told to follow my assigned guide onto a train at Brussels railroad station for Paris, which stopped at the Belgian/French border for a customs and passenger check. The Underground members, however, had everything organized, and there were no problems.

On my arrival in Paris I changed guides, as prearranged, and followed a man with a briefcase. We walked to a small hotel, the Hotel Brussels, which was about three blocks from the railroad station. My guide collected a key from the reception desk, and I followed him up the stairs and into a small room. He then said, "Wait here, I'll be back in a few minutes," and left.

I sat down on the bed and after a few minutes the door suddenly burst open. In rushed three men in civilian clothes brandishing Lugers. "For you the war is over," one of them yelled. I was searched thoroughly and my papers taken. My passport said I was Flemish and a traveling salesman for a plumbing company. One of the Gestapo men said, "A very good likeness, Mr. Lawson," as he looked at the photograph in my passport. So they knew my real name. I was stunned.

It was impossible to believe I'd been on the loose for nearly three weeks and had gotten this far. Quite obviously the Gestapo had been tipped off, but by whom? And where? They bundled me downstairs and into a bus with a big swastika on its side and I was driven to a huge prison called Les Fresnes and put in solitary confinement in a very cramped cell.

After four days I was taken to the main part of the prison and put in a larger cell with two other captives, both of whom were American sergeants, and had been there for three weeks. They told me they'd come through that same house in Brussels. We immediately realized we'd been betrayed by the man known as the chief.

It was a well-known fact throughout occupied Europe at that time the penalty for helping escaping Allied airmen was death and that for any information leading to the arrest of evadees large financial rewards were offered by the Germans.

The two sergeants told me they'd been informed that unless they could prove they were shot-down airmen they would be treated and considered as

COL. A.A. KESSLER, JR.

COL. JOHN K. GERHART

COL. CHESTER P. GILGER

LT. COL. ROBERT H. STUART

COL. CARL TRUESDELL, JR.

COL. JACK E. SHUCK

95th Bomb Group (H)
Headquarters Staff Officers
Rapid City, S.D.—Jan. 1943

First Row — Left to Right
Maj. "Jiggs" Donohue — S-2
Lt. Col. L.E. Burt — Exec.
Col. A.A. Kessler, Jr. — Commander
Maj. J.H. Gibson — S-3
Maj. E.P. Russell — S-1

Second Row — Left to Right
2nd Lt. Joe Florian — Asst. S-2
1st Lt. R.F. Knox — Gp. Communications
Capt. Cliff Cole — Asst. S-3
1st Lt. "Sandy" Baldwin — Asst. S-4

Third Row — Left to Right
2nd Lt. Charles J. Brickley — Phy. Ed.
Capt. Bob Petraitis — Dentist
1st Lt. Geo. Myers — Chaplain
2nd Lt. David Olsson — Statistical

Fourth Row — Left to Right
1st Lt. Leon. "Joe" Dawson — Bombing Off.
Capt. Bill Harding — Surgeon
1st Lt. W.W. Brown — Navigator
Capt. C.D. Fields — S-4.

Officers, 334th Squadron
Rapid City, S.D. — Jan. 1943

1.	2nd Lt. Warner	Navigator
2.	1st Lt. Lochrie	Photo Interpreter
3.	1st Lt. McNutt	Bombardier
4.	1st Lt. Thimm	Navigator
5.	Capt. Cramer	Sq. Surgeon
6.	Major Wilder	Sq. Commander
7.	Capt. Strader	Sq. S-3
8.	2nd Lt. Moreland	Navigator
9.	2nd Lt. Prees	Co-Pilot
10.	2nd Lt. Rice	Bombardier
11.	2nd Lt. Baille	Co-Pilot
12.	2nd Lt. Orme	Bombardier
13.	2nd Lt. Staley	Navigator
14.	2nd Lt. Miller	Co-Pilot
15.	F/O Noyes	Co-Pilot
16.	1st Lt. McPherson	Pilot
17.	1st Lt. Ford	Sq. Communications
18.	2nd Lt. Hargrove	Asst. Sq. S-3
19.	2nd Lt. DeWolf	Bombardier
20.	2nd Lt. Winnegar	Navigator
21.	1st Lt. Sanders	Sq. Ordnance
22.	2nd Lt. Manriquez	Bombardier
23.	F/O Greed	Co-Pilot
24.	2nd Lt. Lasher	Co-Pilot
25.	2nd Lt. Titus	Navigator
26.	1st Lt. Tyler	Pilot
27.	2nd Lt. Haynes	Navigator
28.	2nd Lt. Prochaska	Bombardier
29.	1st Lt. Watson	Pilot
30.	1st Lt. South	Pilot
31.	1st Lt. Thomas	Pilot
32.	2nd Lt. Stapleton	Co-Pilot
33.	2nd Lt. Neeley	Bombardier
34.	1st Lt. Wallrich	Sq. S-4
35.	1st Lt. Scavotto	Pilot
36.	1st Lt. Cozens	Flight Commander
37.	2nd Lt. Baxter	Asst. Sq. Engineer
38.	1st Lt. Holt	Asst. S-2
39.	2nd Lt. Fitzgerald	Bombardier
40.	1st Lt. Conley	Flight Commander
41.	1st Lt. Brown	Navigator
42.	Major McKnight	335th Sq. Commander
43.	2nd Lt. Alweiss	Sq. Statistical
44.	1st Lt. Wolf	Sq. S-1
45.	Capt. Eickemeyer	Sq. S-2
46.	2nd Lt. Hamby	Sq. BSM Officer
47.	1st Lt. Dowlin	Sq. Engineer
48.	1st Lt. Welborn	Sq. Mess.

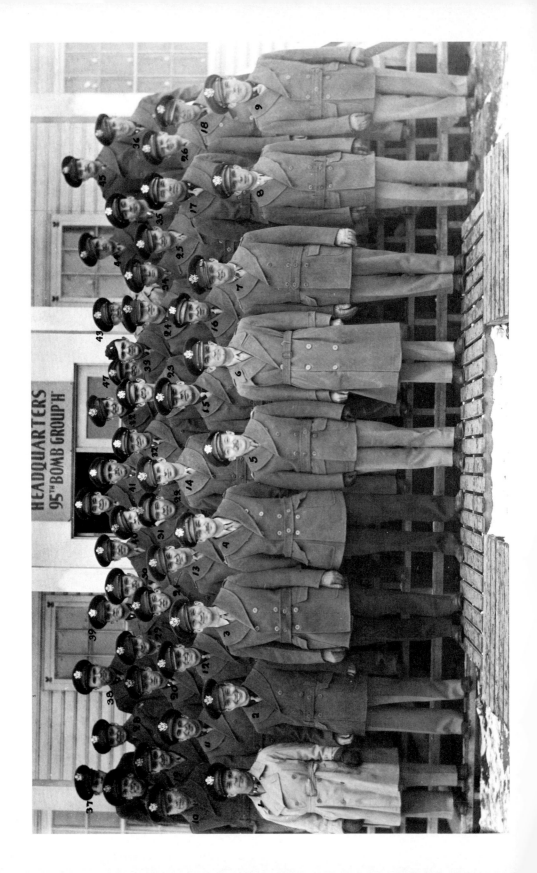

Officers, 335th Squadron
Rapid City, S.D. — Jan. 1943

1. 1st Lt. Moore — Photo Interpreter
2. 1st Lt. Murray — Sq. Bombardier
3. 1st Lt. Kelley — Sq. Adjutant
4. Captain Imes — Sq. Flight Surgeon
5. Major McKnight — Sq. Commander
6. Captain Bunch — Sq. Operations Officer
7. Captain King — Sq. S-2
8. 2nd Lt. White — Co-Pilot
9. 2nd Lt. Wagner — Co-Pilot
10. 2nd Lt. Lawton — Bombardier
11. 2nd Lt. Herman — Bombardier
12. 2nd Lt. Lees — Navigator
13. 1st Lt. Swift — Pilot
14. 1st Lt. Mason — Pilot
15. 2nd Lt. Wizaski — Bombardier
16. F/O Veck — Co-Pilot
17. 2nd Lt. Herried — Bombardier
18. Capt. Hamilton, R.L. — Flight Commander
19. 2nd Lt. Copeland — Navigator
20. 2nd Lt. McKinney — Sq. Mess & Adm. Officer
21. 1st Lt. Adams — Pilot
22. 1st Lt. Mulkin — Sq. Engineering Officer
23. 2nd Lt. Pepry — Co-Pilot
24. F/O Carson — Pilot
25. 1st Lt. Foutz — Pilot
26. 2nd Lt. Sparks — Sq. Operations Officer
27. 2nd Lt. Laskey — Bombardier
28. 1st Lt. Rubin — Pilot
29. 2nd Lt. Payne — Bombardier
30. 2nd Lt. Smith — Navigator
31. 2nd Lt. Fedderson — Navigator
32. 2nd Lt. Johnson — Bombardier
33. 2nd Lt. McKinney — Sq. Mess Officer
34. 2nd Lt. Jenkins — Co-Pilot
35. 2nd Lt. Scripture — Navigator
36. Capt. Hamilton, C.B. — Flight Commander
37. 2nd Lt. Hughes — Navigator
38. Capt. Cornett — Flight Commander
39. 1st Lt. Dodson — Navigator
40. 2nd Lt. Jones — Bombardier
41. 1st Lt. McKinley — Pilot
42. 2nd Lt. Ransom — Co-Pilot
43. 1st Lt. Moody — Supply & Trans. Officer
44. 2nd Lt. Hapner — Navigator
45. 1st Lt. Schnebly — Pilot
46. 2nd Lt. McDonald — Bombardier
47. Major Wilder — 334th Sq. Commander

Officers, 336th Squadron
Rapid City, S.D. — Jan. 1943

1.	1st Lt. Campbell	Asst. Operations Officer
2.	F/O Vacek	Pilot
3.	2nd Lt. Johnson	Bombardier
4.	2nd Lt. Merten	Pilot
5.	2nd Lt. Storck	Pilot
6.	2nd Lt. Nix	Navigator
7.	Major Cole	Squadron Commander
8.	2nd Lt. Johnson, D.W.	Bombardier
9.	2nd Lt. Isaacs	Bombardier
10.	2nd Lt. Messersmith	Navigator
11.	2nd Lt. Robichaud	Pilot
12.	2nd Lt. Katz	Bombardier
13.	1st Lt. Parker	Asst. Operations Officer
14.	2nd Lt. Nichols	Bombardier
15.	1st Lt. Rothschild	Pilot
16.	2nd Lt. Belson	Pilot
17.	2nd Lt. Walter	Pilot
18.	2nd Lt. Heathcote	Navigator
19.	2nd Lt. Sharpe	Pilot
20.	F/O Berntzen	Bombardier
21.	1st Lt. Francis	Pilot
22.	1st Lt. Nunes	Operations Officer
23.	1st Lt. Abbott	Squadron S-2
24.	Captain Probst	Squadron Adjutant
25.	1st Lt. Roberts	
26.	2nd Lt. Finch Jr.	Navigator
27.	Captain McKittrick	Squadron Surgeon
28.	2nd Lt. Kurz Jr.	Bombardier
29.	F/O Perceful	Pilot
30.	Captain Landrum	Navigator
31.	2nd Lt. Lambert	Navigator
32.	2nd Lt. Sipple	Navigator
33.	1st Lt. Fisher	Bombardier
34.	1st Lt. Mason	Pilot
35.	1st Lt. Renaud	Pilot
36.	1st Lt. West	Engineering Officer
37.	2nd Lt. Bader	Navigator
38.	1st Lt. Stone	Pilot
39.	1st Lt. Peek	Asst. Engineering Officer
40.	W/O Caouette	Armament Officer
41.	2nd Lt. Huthmacker	Bombsight Maint. Officer
42.	2nd Lt. Petry	Asst. Intell. Officer
43.	1st Lt. Mohr	Supply-Trans. Officer
44.	1st Lt. Wilderson	Ordnance Officer
45.	1st Lt. Nastasiak	Communications Officer
46.	1st Lt. Clark	Pilot
47.	2nd Lt. Henderson	Asst. Intell. Officer
48.	1st Lt. Bender Jr.	Pilot
49.	2nd Lt. Mytinger	Navigator
50.	2nd Lt. Reinecke	Bombardier

Officers, 412th Squadron
Rapid City, S.D. — Jan. 1943

1.	1st Lt. Eastling	Pilot
2.	Captain House	Flight Commander
3.	1st Lt. Zajicek	Co-Pilot
4.	1st Lt. Morissette	Pilot
5.	1st Lt. Lindley	Flight Commander
6.	Captain Mumford	Squadron Commander
7.	1st Lt. Metzger	Squadron Navigator
8.	1st Lt. Storie	Flight Commander
9.	1st Lt. Smook	Squadron S-2
10.	1st Lt. Krause	Squadron Photo Interp.
11.	1st Lt. Stewart	Squadron Mess
12.	2nd Lt. Roy	Navigator
13.	1st Lt. MacKinnon	Pilot
14.	2nd Lt. Jenkins	Bombardier
15.	1st Lt. Imand	Bombardier
16.	2nd Lt. Tigerman	Co-Pilot
17.	2nd Lt. Powell	Navigator
18.	1st Lt. Bingham	Squadron S-2
19.	1st Lt. Meek	Ordnance Officer
20.	1st Lt. Nelson	Bombardier
21.	2nd Lt. Cone	Armament Officer
22.	1st Lt. Stone	Squadron Adjutant
23.	2nd Lt. Ruh	Navigator
24.	1st Lt. Adams	Pilot
25.	2nd Lt. Matarazzo	Bombardier
26.	Captain Miller	Squadron Operations
27.	1st Lt. Ogden	Asst. Operations
28.	1st Lt. Messeck	Pilot
29.	1st Lt. Herron	Squadron Supply & Trans.
30.	2nd Lt. Munn	Bombardier
31.	2nd Lt. McCrory	Bombsight Maintenance
32.	F/O Woods	Co-Pilot
33.	Captain Noble	Squadron Flight Surgeon
34.	2nd Lt. Bonham	Armament Squadron
35.	2nd Lt. Korman	Navigator
36.	2nd Lt. MacIntosh	Navigator
37.	2nd Lt. Hoag	Bombardier
38.	2nd Lt. Beall	Asst. Engineering Officer
39.	2nd Lt. Melroy	Navigator
40.	2nd Lt. Ziegler	Co-Pilot
41.	2nd Lt. Krava	Bombardier
42.	2nd Lt. Miller	Co-Pilot
43.	2nd Lt. Sharp	Co-Pilot
44.	1st Lt. Davis	Engineering
45.	1st Lt. Gannon	Communications Officer
46.	2nd Lt. Hines	Co-Pilot

Colonel John H. ("Jack") Gibson
95th Bomb Group, Air Executive
1942–43

Cold weather and snow plagued training during the winter of 1942–43 in Washington and South Dakota.

Waldo Cleveland atop a snow pile, Rapid City Air Base, early April 1943.

High-altitude flying suits still not warm enough. Lieutenants Walker and Mattice, Sergeants Green and Schwartz. Photos at Rapid City, S.D., 1943.

The crater where a fully loaded B-17 exploded while being made ready for a mission. Alconbury, 27 May 1943.

Planes destroyed in the explosion at Alconbury, 27 May 1943. Nineteen men were killed, twenty injured.

The dream of the American airman,
1943–1945: To fly, to fight courageously
in great air battles, to seek honor, to win
victory, to keep the world free from
tyranny and oppression, to help all people
seek an honorable destiny in peace.

Horham Airfield (under construction)

Dave McKnight in his favorite seat. Clarence ("Pappy") Fields rides as co-pilot.

Jay J.G. Schatz awarded first Purple Heart in 95th Bomb Group 14 May 1943. (Note leg brace.) Pictured in early 1945 on War Bond sales tour.

Pilot Laurier Morrissette and crew crash-landed on a sandbar in the Friesian Islands after being shot down on the Kiel Mission. The 95th Group lost 10 planes and 103 men on this day, 13 June 1943.

Captured crew lined up by German captors. "Ihr Krieg ist
Fertig."

German smokescreen attempts to cover a vital target area Gdynia, 9
October 1943.

Rare photo of Belgian Underground people with downed American flyers. Overpelt, northern Belgium. *L to R:* Leroy Lawson, Mrs. P. Specters, Alda Spoiren, Virgil Jones. 15 August 1943.

All Underground people in Holland, Belgium, and France risked their lives daily to help Allied flyers escape. *Shown L to R, Back Row:* J. Spelters, M. Vandlers Feesten, M. Spelters. *Seated:* M. Royers, Sgt. T. Anderson, Mrs. Spelters, Sr., 17 August 1943.

Colonel Jack Gibson, Major "Jiggs" Donohue, Colonel John Gerhart check out flak positions on war room map.

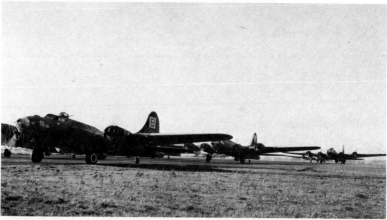

Dramatic series of photos 3 November 1943.
Target Wilhelmshaven. Assembly, takeoff,
formations return peel for landing. All 27 planes
returned safely.

Contrails.

Captain Eddie Rickenbacker addresses the 95th 27 July
1943.

Colonel Kessler poses with an early group of medal awardees.

Colonel LeMay, Colonel Gerhart, and Colonel Kessler with crewmen being decorated, 8 October 1943.

Sergeant Don Crossley receives one of his medals from Colonel LeMay. Don was credited with twelve enemy planes shot down—the most for any U.S. Eighth Air Force gunner.

"Roger the Lodger" returning from Marienburg, 9 October 1943. A
few moments later the plane exploded. There were no survivors.

Ellis B. Scripture, 95th Group
navigator and lead navigator of
the mission to Munster 10
October 1943; later, staff
navigator at Third Air Division,
Eighth Air Force.

Munster—target as seen by
the bombardier.

Bombs hit
target.

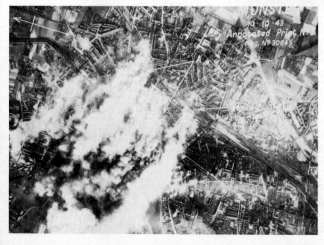

Munster—all of city
destroyed around the
cathedral.

Bombardier briefing
for mission, summer
1943.

Crews are
interrogated following
the mission.

Bill Lindley's crew and the "Zoot Suiter." Composite group lead crew, Kiel Mission, 13 June 1943. Gordon McIntosh (*second from left, rear*) flew Munster mission with the Charles Rubin crew and was KIA.

Removing wounded flyer. Note care of medics and concern on the faces of fellow flyers and ground crewmen.

Me 109 plant at Regensburg is destroyed in first shuttle mission to
Africa, 17 August 1943.

Regensburg shuttle to Africa, 17 August 1943, loading bombs with crude equipment and gasoline from 50-gallon drums in Africa for the trip back to Horham.

Some of the guys brought this small donkey and cart from Africa. *Shown are:* Sergeant Fitzsimmons, Ed Russell, Jack Gibson, and "Jiggs" Donohue. When the creature died, he was dropped over Germany in full uniform with dog tags.

Typical all-night planning session in the War Room. Sleepy Colonel Gerhart checks his watch. Jack Gibson and "Jiggs" Donohue recheck the field order.

Rodney ("Frosty") Snow.

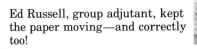

Ed Russell, group adjutant, kept the paper moving—and correctly too!

Skill, determination, and teamwork combined to bring damage planes like this back from rough missions.

Sometimes it was a miracle that the plane got back to base.

Ground crews and specialists put hundreds of planes back into service after severe battle damage.

Intelligence information dictated regular attacks on sub pens. This is the result of one mission to St. Lorient.

The lead plane in the group (or squadron) always dropped a smoke bomb to synchronize the bomb drop in the formation.

spies and executed. I really didn't know what to think, but they pointed out that they'd been at the prison for over three weeks and nothing had happened.

During my imprisonment at Fresnes I almost got eaten alive by fleas. My legs, arms, and body were badly swollen by flea bites. When I asked the prison guard for help from the prison medical staff, he merely laughed and said, "Little eagles, little eagles."

After about a week I was taken for interrogation by a Luftwaffe officer who told me I would be treated as a spy and shot unless I could prove I was an American airman. I just gave him my name, rank, and serial number and was immediately returned to my cell. Two days later the Luftwaffe officer again interviewed me and repeated his warning.

I figured he probably knew much more about me than he was prepared to say, so I said, "I can tell you all about the chief. He's the one who's working for you, but I don't know anything about the others. I can't recall them telling me their names. I didn't even know where I was after I was shot down."

He replied, "Very well . . . but we need a list of the crew you were shot down with." This I refused to tell him and reminded him of the terms of the Geneva Convention that stated that every prisoner of war need only divulge his name, rank, and serial number. I was returned to my cell.

The two sergeants and I then decided to make up three fictional crew lists. We couldn't see any harm in it, and they would have to have really good intelligence to see that we were deceiving them. Little did we know.

The Luftwaffe officer, however, seemed satisfied with my fictional crew list, and five weeks later, about mid-October 1943, the three of us were transported by rail from Paris to the interrogation center, Dulag Luft, in Frankfurt, Germany.

Shortly after my arrival I was again questioned by a Luftwaffe officer who, to my complete amazement, produced a comprehensive 95th Bomb Group file with a full listing of names of my original crew. The one query that seem to mystify him, however, was the name of Colonel Daniel Jenkins. He had been captured while flying with our crew, but he wasn't a member of the 95th Bomb Group. Needless to say, after my recent experience in Paris I was in no mood to satisfy the Luftwaffe's curiosity. I spent the following nineteen months as a prisoner of war.

GENTLEMEN SONGSTERS OFF ON A SPREE . . .

Trammel ("Ace") Hollis, Waist Gunner, B-17F, "Fritz Blitz," 335th Squadron

On the afternoon of 15 August 1943, four of us crewmen of "Fritz Blitz" decided to go to London. It was raining very heavily and we all felt that there was absolutely no chance that we would be flying the next day. So we proceeded to write out our passes (which was slightly against regulations), went to Diss railway station, and boarded the train for London.

We registered at the Hamilton House Hotel, near Hyde Park where we always stayed, and the party was on. The next morning the sun was shining from a clear blue sky, and we felt then that we might be in just a little bit of trouble.

Our suspicions were confirmed on our arrival at the "Rainbow" Red Cross Club. There on the bulletin board was a notice that meant Uncle Sam had caught up with us and that the party was well and truly over: "LT. BROMAN'S CREW REPORT TO BASE IMMEDIATELY."

We knew for sure that we'd goofed up because Major David McKnight, 335th squadron commander at that time, had warned us that he didn't care what we got up to, within reason, just as long as we were on base at mission time, and that if we ever missed a raid through absenteeism he promised he would "burn us off a really hot new one."

By the time we arrived back at Horham it was in the very early morning hours of 17 August. As we were walking back to our barracks we ran into our crew, with four replacement gunners, heading for the trucks to take them to the hardstand where "Fritz Blitz" was parked.

I said to Lieutenant Willie Fowler, our navigator, "What's up?" and he replied "You ought to be glad that you're missing this one. We're to hit Regensburg and then fly on to North Africa. It's the first shuttle mission."

They made it all right and hit Bordeaux on the way home several days later. Meanwhile, the four of us were court-martialed, immediately grounded, and reduced to the rank of private. Then we were given the most menial jobs such as garbage and "honey-bucket" detail, keeping the base neat and tidy, and clearing and building concrete walkways through the woods.

Our original crew went on subsequent raids with the four replacements filling in for us. They were on their twenty-third mission when "Fritz Blitz" was shot down over Munster in October 1943. All the crew managed to bail out except for one of the replacements Technical Sergeant Roy Rightmire, who was killed during a fighter attack.

Eventually we were assigned to another replacement crew, and we all completed our tour of combat missions safely.

THE REGENSBURG SHUTTLE MISSION

17 August 1943
William ("Bill") Lindley, Harry Conley, and John Storie

Bill Lindley: The Regensburg shuttle mission to North Africa was my kind of action. You never knew what would happen, but you looked forward to a change of scenery. Since Dave McKnight had taken an outstanding set of fighter attack photographs with a hand-held camera, I thought we could do better. Lieutenant Orville Tigerman, my co-pilot, was issued a camera with a short barrel and the sights set at least eight inches above the lens. We had plenty of film.

The formation took off with full gas tanks and headed into Germany with General LeMay (at that time Colonel), the task force commander. Fighter escort stayed with us most of the way to the target. Enemy fighters pecked away at our formation for two hours, never very many, but with continuous replacements.

Tigerman worked that camera like a professional, and it was confidently anticipated that our pictures would at least be as good, if not better, than McKnight's. Tigerman was just about out of film when I suddenly noticed that every time he took a photograph of an attacking fighter the sights on the camera were above the instrument panel but the lens was below. Not one picture came out! In Tigerman's defense he was rather short in stature (he had to sit on three cushions to reach the pedals) but I still thought about dropping him out when we crossed the Alps. He was immediately fired as cameraman—but was a damn good pilot.

The bomb strikes were right on target—the Messerschmitt fighter plane factories. It was one of the most successful bombings of the war. Minutes later we were over the Alps. Visibility was forever and never have I seen anything, either before or since, that could rival that magnificent picture of majestic splendor.

The Italian fighters decided not to get into the act over the Italian mainland and the formation landed at Bone, North Africa, without incident. The

95th had come through with the loss of four B-17s during a raid that had cost the Eighth Air Force sixty aircraft. It cost the Germans much more.

Bone had a few tents and mud shacks where we could sleep on the ground. Almost everyone opted for underneath the wing of their aircraft. The tent bar was going full blast, with plenty of whiskey and a piano. There were a few foreigners around, Australians, and the Aussies sang songs that made the British look like nuns in a convent.

Colonel LeMay walked past our aircraft while we were cleaning the mess of shells and debris from the mission. I called the crew to attention, and we put on a snappy salute for "Ole Iron Ass." He returned our salute left-handed while smoking a long cigar clenched between his teeth. I do believe the 'ole boy smiled.

The shuttle back to England was over France and a piece of cake.

Harry Conley (from a letter to his mother dated 28 August, 1943):

Since I last wrote I've traveled some 4,000 miles. Yes, we had our "summer vacation"—at least we had a change of scenery. Of course, we combined business with pleasure and left a few "calling cards" both on the way down and on the way back—the results were most gratifying! In fact, the best we've ever had. It really hit Adolf where it hurts. We also pulled a fast one on him by keeping right on going to North Africa after we dropped our eggs.

It was a rough risk going in, as you can well imagine, flying over the depth of Germany then across the Alps and Italy in broad daylight. We met around 300 fighters, and for over two hours the battle raged. It was a terrible fight—even worse than Kiel in my opinion. However, except for a few holes in our ship, we came through O.K.

We had to sit in North Africa for several days due to weather conditions before we could return. The return journey across France was uneventful.

Had a wonderful time in Africa. Got to see lots of my old classmates who are flying down there. They certainly have a picnic. Just to show you the difference, our operational tour from England is twenty-five missions, down there they have to go sixty-five. In the Pacific theater, it's even more. The greatest treat of all was that we got all the fresh eggs, vegetables, and fruit that we could eat. Also white bread (French), which is unheard of up here. For a week we just laid around in the nice warm sun and swam and ate and went to town.

We had lots of fun trading soap and mattress covers to the Arabs for eggs, chickens, watermelons, and some of our boys even got a donkey for which they made an oxygen mask and brought him back to England with them. For one bar of Army soap, we got nine dozen eggs!! The Arabs love the mattress covers. They cut a couple of holes in them and wear them.

There are hundreds of Italian prisoners of war all over the place. It's most amazing. No one guards them. In fact, it would be impossible to drive them away. They say that every time they count them there are more than at the previous count because they apparently keep coming down out of the surrounding hills. They are a wonderfully happy lot; they work in the kitchens, wait on the tables, and do all sorts of general work around the bases. No one guards them, and they come and go into town as they please. In fact, they don't even wear a "P" on their backs. They can't do enough for you and are really interesting people.

Talked to a boy in London who had just returned after being shot down over the continent. He gave me word about nine of our boys who are missing. He said that he walked into a bar in a little French town and met all nine of our guys. According to him, they will all be back shortly.

John Storie: The Regensburg shuttle mission resulted in one bomber crew returning to Horham with a North African donkey in tow. It subsequently provided many local English children with cart rides, in an improvised wagon, around the base and into Horham village. Although the donkey survived the comparatively cold English climate for some time, it finally succumbed to pneumonia or distemper during the winter months of 1943–44.

The problem of disposing of the animal's carcass was solved in a typical bomber crew manner. Enough surplus GI clothing was assembled, including suitably inscribed dog-tags, and the deceased donkey was attired as only proper air crewman could be.

The next available raid gave the opportunity to drop the unfortunate animal (without a parachute) at the initial point (IP). Unfortunately no one can record the confusion and consternation of the German people assigned to grave registration.

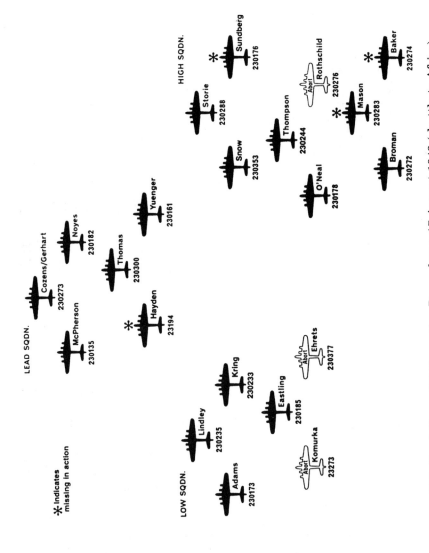

LEAD SQDN.

McPherson
230135

Cozens/Gerhart
230273

Noyes
230182

Thomas
230300

Yuenger
230161

* Hayden
23194

HIGH SQDN.

Storie
230288

Sundberg
230176

Snow
230353

Thompson
230244

Rothschild
Abort
230276

Mason
230283

Baker
230274

O'Neal
230178

Broman
230272

LOW SQDN.

Lindley
230235

Kring
230233

Adams
230173

Eastling
230185

Ehrets
Abort
230377

Komurka
Abort
23273

* Indicates
missing in action

95th Bomb Group (H) Formation Regensburg, 17 August 1943 (shuttle to Africa).

SHORT BURSTS

William ("Catfish" or "Wild Bill") Lindley

My first contact with the B-17 was at Sebring, Florida, in the late summer of 1942. While the checkout and other training was boring and tedious, I met an individual who was to become a future 95th Bomb Group standout and a good friend.

I checked into Sebring about two o'clock in the afternoon; the temperature was in the hundreds. I signed in and headed for the bar. Only one other person was in the bar and he introduced himself as Dave McKnight. He was a cocky little redhead then and hasn't changed since.

By four o'clock we were well under way and had exchanged enough personal information to make a preacher blush. Dave was married and he insisted on me coming with him to meet his wife. We fired up from the parking lot with Dave in the lead and got at least two blocks down the main boulevard when the military police pulled us over. Off to the stockade to be written up for speeding and a slight smell of alcohol.

All I can remember was the speeding ticket ended with the words "... closely followed by a blue coupe." I've been following Dave around ever since. The next day we were both hauled into the commander's office and severely chastized. Dave didn't even look sorry.

****

Things began to pick up in Spokane, Washington, where the initial cadre of the 95th Bomb Group was formed during the following October. While there I once got the opportunity to go hunting. I hiked off to the edge of the base to shoot ducks with a borrowed shotgun. It was zero degrees with a heavy fog. The lake was barren of ducks, and it began to snow heavily. In order to keep warm, I began walking around the edge of the lake, being able to see only twenty or thirty feet ahead. Lo and behold, I walked upon a green-headed Mallard duck sitting on a rock at the water's edge. I raised the shotgun and aimed right at his head, but he just sat there and looked straight at me as if asking, "What in the hell are we both doing out in this kind of weather?"

I lowered the gun and walked back to the base. For all I know he is still sitting there.

****

The 95th was activated with John Storie, Gale House, Harry Conley, Bob Cozens, Dave McKnight, Grif Mumford, Joel Bunch, and me on the original orders. One of the incredible and amazing things is that in this group of pilots were some of the few originals who made it through the war. Storie and House were severely wounded, and even old Harry shed a little blood during the tough mission to Munster in the fall of 1943.

The 95th commander was Colonel A.A. Kessler, an individual whom I will never forget. Well over six feet tall and probably one of the most homely individuals know to man, we nicknamed him "Uncle Ug," not in disrespect but because it was his expertise and command ability that undoubtedly got us off on the right foot. Then it was off to Rapid City where it was cold but it was there that we cemented friendships that will last forever.

An incident of note that happened at Rapid City involved the deputy base commander. I don't even recall his name. He called a meeting of all pilots to give us a pep talk before we headed off to war. He should have worn a black armband because within two minutes he had us all in a state of absolute shock. When he finally started crying and carrying on about the number of us that were certain to be killed, guess who came to our rescue? Dave McKnight. . . .

In no uncertain terms Dave cast strong doubts on the guy's leadership ability and took violent exception to his pathetic remarks. This broke up the meeting. Colonel Kessler threw the deputy off the base that same day.

****

An incident at Kearney, Nebraska, adjusted my crew slightly. My original bombardier, Lee Lockwood, John Storie, and I stayed too long at the bar and arrived back at the barracks about 2:00 A.M. We were the only ones there except the janitor sweeping the floor. Storie asked him to stop since dust was flying everywhere. The young janitor didn't even look up as he continued his work.

Storie is big but Lockwood is even bigger. They both asked him to quit, or else. No reply. Lockwood said to Storie that it appeared they would have to, very reluctantly, take drastic action. Lockwood said, "Storie, you hold him above you and I'll shoot him." Storie picked the janitor up by his armpits, Lockwood walked behind them, pulled his .45, and fired a shot through the barracks roof. The janitor turned white as a sheet and took off. Everyone hit the sack. Not for long.

In marched the military police and hauled us off to the stockade. I was totally innocent. Lockwood was kicked off my crew, and Storie and I were put "on the wagon" until further notice. This happened after a session with Colonel Kessler during which he pointed out, "it is not normal practice, and it's not nice, to go around shooting up the barracks and scaring the hell out of janitors."

****

Grif Mumford and I flew together on another mission very shortly after the disastrous Kiel raid in mid-June 1943, that we flew from Framlingham. This mission, one of the first we flew from Horham, our permanent base in England, wasn't too exciting but there was a little action in our aircraft. At the Thirteenth Wing assembly point, it was customary to fire off a "double-red" flare from the lead group for identification purposes.

Grif was flying the aircraft while I loaded the flare pistol. Somehow I accidentally fired the thing off in the cockpit. There we were at 20,000 feet, on oxygen, with a full load of fuel and high-explosive bombs with two red balls of fire bouncing around at a high number of knots between the central control pedestal, the instrument panel, and the floor of the cockpit. Grif immediately got to his feet and went from a nifty "heel and toe" dance to "the black-bottom stomp." And I didn't even know he could dance.

Grif didn't speak to me for two days.

****

About once a month a bus would haul in a load of English girls from Ipswich and Norwich to our base at Horham, situated about midway between two towns. These were fun times and gave everyone a chance to relax and enjoy themselves.

A party was in full swing at the officers' club during one of these occasions when, about midnight, Fitzgerald, one of our bombardiers, wandered out of the front door with a lass in close attendance. Immediately in front of the club was a tree-lined ditch that was always knee-deep in leaves and mud.

A short time later Fitz, all 6'4" of him, came running back in the club hollering for assistance. About ten of us responded to the call and followed Fitz out the door and into the night.

For the next fifteen minutes we were all down in the ditch scratching and searching around in the leaves and the mud, not looking for the gal, but for her false teeth. Matches and cigarette lighters were not much help, and the search was eventually abandoned.

The gal lost her teeth and Fitz had lost a dear friend.

****

By the end of July 1943, the 95th Group had lost thirty B-17s, either shot down or ditched on the way home. Such thoughts didn't lead to contemplating postwar plans.

It was about this time some of the funny stuff started popping up. One of the waist gunners on another crew had solved the problem of dirty laundry. He had two barracks bags, one full of clothes. As he dirtied one set of clothes it was placed in the empty bag. When the first bag was empty he started wearing the full bag.

It was a good thing that the mission limit was twenty-five at that time, because he was pretty ripe when he rotated. Fortunately, the fully ventilated B-17 kept his crew from being asphyxiated.

****

General Curtis LeMay, Third Air Division commander, personally critiqued each bomb group's lead pilot and crew after each mission at Elveden Hall, Third Air Division headquarters. In the early days especially, things didn't always go as planned, and I've seen him chew up and spit out those pilots who'd deviated from the mission plan without good cause. I've seen pilots, navigators, and bombardiers grow pale and start to shake as they stood in front of the briefing map. Luckily, he never really got his teeth into me.

Right near Horham was a large, wooded country estate loaded with pheasants that, we learned, was the king's private game preserve. It didn't take Rodney Snow, several other "dead-eyes," and me very long to realize that here was fresh meat for the taking. Many of these beautiful birds were subsequently brought to the mess and prepared for the tables with tender loving care. We were wise enough to realize that the roof would cave in sooner or later and that we would need an out. That's when we started sending General LeMay a brace of pheasants on a fairly regular basis.

Sure enough, the muck hit the fan, and complaints began flooding in from the local dignitary and officials about taking the king's game. However, we were not shot at sunrise, we were merely told to cease our safaris—forthwith.

****

Shortly after the series of Berlin raids, in March 1944, the 95th completed its 100th mission. The celebration was a beaut. A name band orchestra provided the music, and Ipswich and Norwich provided the gals. The walking wounded were still being cleaned up days later.

Even the base hospital commander came to the party, bringing with him his deputy and two head nurses. I adopted all four of them and made sure they had a good time. Why not? They were the people who patched up Jay Schatz, John Storie, Gale House, and countless other injured 95th men.

Around midnight the nurses decided they wanted to see the inside of a B-17 for a change. Fine with me. They loaded up in a jeep and off we went. Across runways, taxi-ways, empty hardstands, and what have you until we found the B-17 with the "Zoot Suiter" nose. Have you ever tried to lift a 150-pound female into the nose hatch of a B-17? Finally we were all aboard and one nurse fired up an engine while the other explored the upper turret. I do believe she would have fired both 50-caliber guns if she could have gotten them cocked. On the way back I was amazed that the only casualty was the deputy who'd cut his head.

The sobering thought about the 100th mission celebration was the cost: 97 aircraft and their ten-man crews.

****

Time rolls along and although targets like Schweinfurt, Emden, Bremen, and Frankfurt were hit, the missions were never routine. Not so with Brunswick where the 95th lost seven aircraft.

It was about this time that a U.S. Army Lieutenant Colonel, a paratrooper, talked the Eighth Air Force into letting him fly a combat mission, and they assigned him to the 95th. He picked the wrong time because the aircraft in which he flew was shot up so severely by 109s and 190s that it had to land at Woodbridge, the emergency landing field, just in from the Suffolk coast.

When he was asked if he wanted to fly back to Horham with the crew, he declined with the words, "I don't want to fly back to Horham. I may never set foot in an airplane again. I'll walk!"

****

From all the combat crews of the 95th that I knew, I've seen many scared and nervous troops. But only once during my forty-four missions did I come across a so-called case of combat fatigue. He was a pilot who, after completing his first two missions, couldn't crawl back into the cockpit of a B-17. He wasn't from my squadron, and I didn't know him personally.

Somehow I was selected to interview, counsel, and recommend the appropriate action. Here was a six-foot hulk of a man who cried like a baby and was ashamed that he couldn't be a credit to the organization. He was flat out through and adamant. No amount of talk and encouragement could get him back into the cockpit. All he was really worried about was what the people back home would think. To tell the truth I was baffled.

My recommendation was to send him home and take his pilot's wings away. The idea was that taking his wings away would be harder for him to accept than any combat mission, and he would think about himself and his responsibility to others for the rest of his life.

LIGHT RELIEF FROM "FROSTY"

David ("Dave") T. McKnight, Air Executive

I first met Rodney Snow when he joined the 95th Group as a replacement pilot in the late summer of 1943. He was the epitome of Hollywood's idea of the Air Corps pilot; handsome, happy-go-lucky, and an outstanding flyer, except he was *for real*. His nickname was "Frosty." He flew many tough missions and was a resourceful and fearless leader. He took on all of the trials and tribulations of those very difficult days and retained his moral fiber and sense of purpose. Not that these traits of character were that rare among the fine young men surrounding us at that time, but he stood a shade above most.

Rodney also had an invaluable talent for making those of us who associated with him cheerful despite the many problems confronting us during those difficult and dangerous times. He had a delightful, puckish, sense of humor that he would employ to cut through the sometimes overwhelming monotony of wartime regulations and routines.

I recall a specific incident that occurred as an illustration of the above. Our briefings for combat missions usually took place at the unearthly hour of 4:00 A.M. after a 2:00 A.M. awakening and a 3:00 A.M. breakfast. The latter was generally a powdered egg and greasy Spam specialty of the day, not enhanced by the sickly glare of the fluorescent lighting! The point here is not to downgrade the food—under those spartan and frugal conditions it was great—but to illustrate why the combat crews were not exactly in an enthusiastic state of mind at that time of day.

The briefing consisted of presentations by our intelligence section relevant to known flak concentrations, enemy fighter defenses, and escape and evasion routes. Other headquarters men briefed on air sea rescue, primary target information, communications, maintenance, and then the "biggy"—operations. The operations officer would conclude his presentation and the *great moment* would arrive . . . the synchronization, or setting, of every crewman's watch with the correct time.

This would be accomplished by having a junior operations officer come up on the briefing platform with the "master clock" and name a moment occurring a minute or so away by saying, "In so many seconds it will be . . .," whereupon all present would dutifully pull out the stems of their GI-issue watches and await the momentous word—"Hack!" Then they would solemnly push in the stems and feel that they had all been a part of history. It was really overdone, but it served the additional purpose of making everyone feel that something important had happened. After all, the master clock was set to the 1/100th of a second by the international time signal from Greenwich, London!

On this occasion Rodney was the designated on-stage junior operations officer and at the point where he was saying, "The time is now exactly ...," he looked hard at the master clock very doubtfully, shook it, and raised it to his ear, repeated the process—at which point every crewman present broke into laughter. The tension created by the impending tough mission was completely broken up, and it was a great lift and boost to morale for those individuals who could use one.

HIGH-ALTITUDE ATMOSPHERIC CONTAMINATION

Robert ("Bob") Carter, Pilot, 336th Squadron

It was to be another one of those days—a "maximum effort" mission. That means that anything with wings and a couple of engines must take to the air and go if at all possible. We were flying the lead airplane in the low squadron. For this particular effort, we were to have an extra aircraft to fly in the slot below and behind us. This dubious honor was given to a ship from the 412th Squadron, piloted by Dave G. To know Dave was to love him. We were buddies from way back in phase training in the United States; we went through the replacement procedures and arrived at Horham together. I was assigned to the 336th and Dave to the 412th squadron.

He was a boisterous and uproarious product of Brooklyn, New York, and flew an aircraft with the inelegant and ungraceful name of "Floozie Flossie." He always joked about his two sets of dog-tags. One set read Dave G. and the other read Dave O'Brien. As he put it, "I'm not going to be caught with a name like Dave G., if I'm shot down over Germany." Incidentally, Dave is Jewish, and he has the map of Israel all over his face.

After a normal take-off, we circled for an hour in the pre-dawn darkness to gain altitude and assemble into group formation. We leveled off at 23,000 feet and headed east toward "Fortress Europe."

If you've never seen a sunrise from five miles up, then you're missing something really special. The sky gradually changes from its inky, Stygian blackness to quite beautiful and spectacular shades of purple, to various and exquisite hues of blue and then to reflections of orange, pink, and red. Then, inexorably and inevitably, the rim of a huge ball of fire peeps inquisitively and cautiously over the eastern horizon. The rising sun is on its way to herald in a new day, lighting our way to the target and, unfortunately, also lighting the German fighters' way to find us. This day the contrails streaming from our engines in the sub-stratosphere pointed like an arrow straight to our Fortress formations. The Lord was showing no favorites that day.

As we were crossing the North Sea and approaching the Dutch coast, our co-pilot, Joe A., called me over the intercom to advise me of a condition that was causing him much inconvenience and extreme discomfort—the "GIs." He requested information as to how to solve his embarrassing and delicate predicament.

I reminded him of the large, canvas shell-casing bags on the two side nose 50-caliber machine guns, one of which would be more than adequate to solve the problem. Now, how to dispose of the canvas bag on completion of the exercise?

I advised Joe to go back to the radio operator's compartment, remove the overhead plexiglass hatch, and just throw the shell casing bag, with its contents, up through the open hatch. The force of the slip-stream across the opening would suck the bag up and out.

We completed the mission successfully and returned to Horham without further incident. As we were leaving the debriefing room, Dave G. and his crew came in.

"How did it go, Dave?" we inquired.

"Don't ask," replied Dave, "I must have hit a bird or something. You should see the state of my splattered windshield!"

Needless to say we didn't tell Dave about the bird that had hit his windshield.

IHR KRIEG IST FERTIG

Gus Mencow, Navigator, 13th Combat Wing

While it is difficult to recall the momentous events of forty-odd years ago, certain happenings do creep into our minds during our daily travels. The Second World War was one of the most important events in our lives, so it is only natural that this should occur. Was it all a dream? Did we really accomplish those many impossible missions over Nazi-occupied Europe? Is it all a miracle that we are still living, and the many thousands that were shot down are gone and remain only in our memories of the dim and distant past? How many crews never came back and are now forgotten? What happened to our many close friends who went down during their second or third mission? The following few paragraphs may possibly bring back the names, and the memories, of some who disappeared.

I first met Bill Savage on the train going to Santa Ana, California, on 6 March 1942 for cadet training. He had just transferred from the artillery to the Army Air Corps and I had transferred from the infantry. After discovering that we both came from the same city in Massachusetts we formed a close relationship. The weekends in Los Angeles, studying together, and the camaraderie that existed formed a bond between us during those few months. We were then separated, he to bombardier school at Carlsbad, New Mexico, and I to Mather Field, California, for navigation training.

By coincidence we were both assigned to the Thirteenth Combat Wing after completion of our training: Bill to the 334th Squadron, 95th Bomb Group at Horham with the crew of Lieutenant Max Crowder; I went to the 570th Squadron, 390th Bomb Group at Framlingham with the crew of Lieutenant Jim Geary. It was not until April 1944 that I became aware that Bill was with the 95th Group and had been shot down following the mission to Saarlauten, Germany, on 4 October 1943 and had ditched in the North Sea.

Douglas Gordon-Forbes and I came to Thirteenth Wing headquarters at Horham from Framlingham as wing bombardier and navigator, respectively, when Colonel Edgar Wittan, the 390th group commander, was promoted to command that organization in April 1944. We were located just below the 334th Squadron area commanded by Bill Lindley when I learned of the fate of Max Crowder's crew. They were all taken prisoner.

When the shooting stopped and the prisoners of war came home with the rest of us, Bill Savage was one of the first to contact me. We subsequently got together a few times with other Eighth Air Force veterans. However, marriage, children, and careers made us both go on our separate ways. I found Bill was very reluctant to discuss his POW days, although he would talk about those times when specifically asked. Each time he had that far away look in his eyes, and I knew he had experiences that couldn't be shared with anyone. On one occasion he related that part of their last mission when they'd ditched in the North Sea. A German patrol boat picked them up and the first words they heard were, "Ihr krieg ist fertig" (Your war is over). "How wrong they were. That was the beginning of my real war," Bill said.

Those nineteen months in the Stalag Luft took their toll on Bill and his crew. Years later the story emerged how the prisoners were forced to march for six weeks to the west, near Munich, to avoid the advancing Russian Army from the east. All during that forced march, Bill carried the vestments of the church so that a daily mass could be said. The inhuman conditions at the camp, the constant alerts, and surveillance stretched them to the limit of their endurance.

Bill died on 8 August 1963; he'd never really recovered from his ordeals. The memories weighed him down. They were such that he couldn't live with them and he couldn't live without them.

Those who knew him will always remember Bill Savage. As perfect a gentleman as God ever created, a true soldier, patriot, and friend—one of many for whom the war could never end.

KEEP 'EM FLYING

George Peterson, Crew Chief, 334th Squadron

One of the first B-17G models of the Fortress to be assigned to the 95th Bomb Group arrived at Horham in early October 1943. The new airplane, which differed from the F models, incorporated several improvements, including a two-gun chin turret. This was a replacement for B-17F 4230045, "She's My Gal," missing in action during the mission to Saarlauten, Germany, on 4 October 1943.

The replacement, B-17G 4231299, was assigned to the 334th Squadron and I was her crew chief. She was named "She's My Gal II," and an appropriate picture of a female was painted on the nose of the airplane underneath its name. The squadron call letters on the fuselage were BG-M with a yellow letter M on the vertical stabilizer just below the airplane's serial number.

Following the initial acceptance inspection, the plane was released for a test flight. A pilot, co-pilot, and flight engineer arrived on the flight line for the test flight but while they were taxiing round the perimeter track near the end of runway 31, the pilots momentarily lost control and the airplane ran off the perimeter track, crossed a grassed area, and ended up straddling a drainage ditch at the edge of Horham Airfield.

It wasn't a pretty sight for a brand new camouflaged aircraft, lying pathetically in the ditch near runway number 31. The left landing gear had been forced up and back under the wing, and a main-frame member inside number 2 engine nacelle had been broken completely into two pieces.

Fortunately the plane could be repaired, but it required the services of the mobile repair unit, which had the facilities to fabricate the necessary parts required. Keeping the aircraft intact while waiting for the mobile repair unit to arrive got quite hectic at times. Other crew chiefs from the 334th and the three other squadrons hovered like vultures around the stranded new arrival, just waiting for the chance to pounce and salvage spare parts urgently needed for the repair of their own ships.

The mobile repair unit finally arrived and we jacked the plane up by using inflatable air bags (borrowed from the Royal Air Force) under the left wing. The damaged landing gear was temporarily secured so that the airplane could be towed back to the hardstand. Once there, the necessary replacement parts and repairs were speedily completed. In order to gain access to replace the damaged parts, a large section of the outer metal skin on the outboard side of number 2 engine nacelle was removed. After the completion of repairs this skin was replaced but it didn't get painted with olive drab to match the rest of the airplane's camouflage. This turned out to be a means of quick and easy identification of my aircraft when it was returning from a mission and circling the base.

"She's My Gal II" flew two or three missions with spare crews before Lieutenant Garland Lloyd and his crew were assigned to the plane. When they weren't flying, Lieutenant Lloyd and his crew came out to their bomber to assist in its maintenance and to learn more about the mechanics and engineering of their plane itself. I flew with Lieutenant Lloyd several times during test flights, and I had complete confidence in his ability to fly that aircraft.

I'm reasonably certain that Lieutenant Lloyd and his crew flew over twenty-two missions before that fateful day, 6 March 1944, when they were shot down over Holland during the second mission to Berlin. Mercifully, all ten crewmen managed to bail out in time, and Lieutenant Lloyd was apparently on the loose in occupied Europe for two months before being captured by the Germans.

In 1986 I learned that Klass Niemeijer, a WWII aircraft researcher in Holland, had located the crash site of "She's My Gal II" in a farmer's field in northeastern Holland. She will supply many interesting souvenirs and museum pieces for the new generation of WWII aircraft researchers, as she provides fond memories for me as her crew chief.

A DAY AT THE OFFICE

Major General David Grant, Surgeon General, U.S.A.A.F.

One look into the pilot's cabin of a B-17 will convince you that its flight is actually an engineering operation demanding manual and mental skills that put the driving of an automobile into the kiddy-car class.

The compartment is lined—front, sides, ceiling, and part of the floor—with controls, switches, levers, dials, and gauges. I once counted around one hundred thirty. The coordinated operations of all these gadgets would be difficult in the swivel-chair comfort of your office. But reduce your office to a five-foot cube size, engulf it in the constant roar of four 1,200-horsepower engines, and increase your height to around five miles. Then get into a flying suit, gloves, and flying boots—all heated by electricity—put on a helmet with earphones, cover your eyes with goggles and the rest of your face with an oxygen mask containing a microphone, strap on your parachute, and it might be as well to add on about sixteen pounds of body armor contained in your flak jacket.

That will give you an idea of the normal conditions under which these men worked out the higher mathematical relationships of engine revolutions, manifold and fuel pressures, aerodynamics, barometric pressure, altitude, wind drift, airspeed, ground speed, position, and direction.

You may have to face an occasional pain from ears, bends or intestinal gas expansion, a touch of dizziness, numbness from cold, or the subtle comatosity of anoxia. There will be interruptions to man machine guns against enemy fighter attacks. Due allowance must also be made for a stream of machine-gun bullets and cannon shells, or the burst of flak and air-to-air rockets in your immediate vicinity.

As a final touch to this bizarre picture of intense concentration, add the thoughts of death, bail-out, escape, or Stalag Luft.

THE PREMONITION

James F. Goff, Navigator, 412th Squadron

I was assigned to Lieutenant Barraclough's crew flying the "Impatient Virgin" for the longest mission flown by the Eighth Air Force. The date was 9 October 1943 and the target was the Focke Wulf 190 assembly plant at Marienburg, beyond Berlin, in East Prussia. Everything seemed unusually serene as we droned eastward toward occupied Poland. We spotted only one German plane, apparently an observation aircraft, flying at our 21,000-foot altitude and far out to the left of our formation.

There was no flak at the target and the bombing of the fighter aircraft factories was extremely accurate; in fact the Marienburg raid was subsequently acclaimed as a perfect example of strategic aerial bombardment. As we swung away from the target and flew north before heading for home, I recall seeing hundreds of contrails over Gdynia and Danzig, large ports on the Baltic coast of occupied Poland. The contrails appeared to be heading straight for us. My heart skipped several beats and I thought, "My God! Here comes the whole German Air Force." Then I realized to my intense relief, that what I was seeing were the Eighth Air Force bomb groups of the First and Second Air divisions,

B-17s, and B-24 Liberators, turning off their targets at Gdynia and Danzig. As we passed over Danzig, we could clearly see a huge ship circling frantically in the harbor.

The long flight back to England across the Baltic Sea and Denmark was uneventful except for some flak on the Danish coast. When we were well over the North Sea, we relaxed and unwrapped the sandwiches that were provided for us to eat during the long flight. We never finished those sandwiches because suddenly the intercom came alive with warnings that German fighters were approaching our formation from the rear. They were Ju [Junker] 88s and Me 210s.

The fighters laid back about 1,000 yards, out of range of our 50-caliber machine guns, and began firing air-to-air rockets and 37mm cannon fire into our formation. We saw Lieutenant Ehert's B-17, "Roger The Lodger II," take a series of hits in its number 2 engine, which caught fire. Then a rocket hit number 3 engine and the aircraft immediately went down in flames. Seven parachutes emerged from the stricken ship but the last two chutes were on fire. We saw five parachutes splash down as Lieutenant Barraclough circled the area long enough for me to determine the coordinates and give them to our radio operator to relay the downed crewmen's position to the British Air-Sea Rescue Service. But we all knew that even if the Air-Sea Rescue launches could find them in that vast expanse of sea it was too far from England and too much time would elapse before the frigid and unforgiving North Sea would claim them.

I felt particularly saddened with the loss of Lieutenant Ehert's crew. His bombardier had occupied the bunk next to mine and in the short time I knew him we had become friends. His name was Robert Wing and his nickname was Catfish (not to be confused with Bill "Catfish" Lindley). The night before the Marienburg raid we'd sat on our bunks and talked and he told me he'd been assigned to Lieutenant Ehert's crew. He then said he didn't want to go because he knew he would never return. I scoffed at this remark, but he said he was serious and his feelings of impending death were very strong.

Was it premonition? I will never know.

In late November 1985 Jim Goff wrote: "In my mind's eye I can still see that ill-fated Fortress going down in flames and those pitiful parachutes drifting down to the cold North Sea. I suppose it was etched so deeply in my memory because it was only my second mission and because I was witnessing the death of my friend, Bob "Catfish" Wing . . . just as he had predicted."

"THE CHARGE OF THE LIGHT BRIGADE"

Munster: 10 October 1943

For the third time in three days, the flight crews of the 95th Bomb Group assembled in the briefing rooms at group operations. They were informed they were to lead the other fifteen selected bomb groups of the First and Third Air divisions on the mission to Munster. Three more bomb groups from the Second Air Division, equipped with B-24 Liberators, would form a third task force, and fly a diversion route toward northern Germany before withdrawing. Six P-47 Thunderbolt fighter groups would provide escort to the main force at different stages to and from the target.

Major F.J. ("Jiggs") Donohue, the group's intelligence officer, briefed: Munster is a vital rail junction between Germany's northern coastal ports and the heavy industries and the munition plants of the Ruhr Valley immediately to the south of your primary target. Through Munster's marshaling yards, each day and each night, roll hundreds of tons of armament and war material produced in the Ruhr Valley and destined for all points north, west, and east.

However, unlike all previous military and industrial targets attacked to date by the Eighth Air Force, today it will be different—very different— because today you will hit the center of that city, the homes of the working population of those marshaling yards. You will disrupt their lives so completely that their morale will be seriously affected, and their will to work and fight will be substantially reduced.

Should the primary target be obscured by cloud or industrial haze, the secondary target is Hamm, located in the Ruhr Valley itself, and as a last resort, any industrial town in Germany.

Captain Ellis B. Scripture, lead navigator, B-17F 230235, "The Zoot Suiters": I'd been raised in a strict Protestant home. My parents were God-oriented people and were quite active church members. I was shocked to learn that we were to bomb civilians as our primary target for the first time in the war and that our aiming point was to be the front steps of Munster Cathedral at noon on Sunday, just as mass was completed. (Later the field order was revised so that "bombs away" was scheduled for 1500 hours [3 P.M.]; this undoubtedly saved many lives!) I was very reluctant to fly this mission; in fact I had a hard time realizing that we would have such a target.

I approached Colonel John Gerhart in the war room as we were planning the mission and told him that I didn't think I could fly this particular raid and I explained my reasons. His reaction was exactly what one would expect (in retrospect) of a career officer and a very fine commander.

He said something like this: "Look, captain, this is war—spelled W-A-R.

We're in an all-out fight; the Germans have been killing innocent people all over Europe for years. We're here to beat the hell out of them, and we're going to do it.

"We have, to date, been very diligent and concentrated all our efforts in U-boat yards, aircraft plants, oil installations, and other industrial targets connected with the German war machine. We have astutely avoided the possibility of bombing civilians. This decision has only been reached after great consideration. It has become very apparent to the Allied leaders that we must now carry the war to the German people to make them realize that there is a war going on and that they are the victims of their own military leadership in Germany. People there are beginning to have real doubts about the Nazis' capability of winning this war. All of us are well aware of the countless atrocities committed by the Nazis in the name of the German people.

"Now, I'm leading this mission and you're my navigator. You're leading this mission also; this could be an important turning point in the war. You have no option! If you do not fly, I'll have to court martial you. Any questions?"

I said, "No, sir," and that ended the incident.

This was to be my eighteenth mission and my tenth time to lead the task force. I made up my mind then and there that war is not a gentleman's duel. I never again had doubts about the strategy of our leaders. They had tough decisions to make—and they made them.

Captain Rodney Snow, pilot, B-17F 230181, "Herky Jerky II": Reaction at the briefing really didn't register for awhile. What got to me was that it was a Sunday mission, and probably the only one I flew on the sabbath. Being of Scots-Irish descent and a regular Presbyterian did give me some deep reservations about the need for Sunday bombings.

Quite frankly, my first concern was my position in the formation. Leading the third element of three airplanes in the high squadron is the worst position in the group. You are on the whip-end, which means to say that when the group lead airplane makes a turn to the left or right you have to anticipate and react very quickly or you find yourself out of the formation and all alone.

Lieutenant Paul Perceful, co-pilot, B-17F 230218: In my case it was only a momentary question mark because by October 1943 our group's losses were almost 100 percent. We had also heard stories concerning the Luftwaffe's lack of chivalry, not to mention how the German Army was conducting itself. In the early days we might have had second thoughts, but not at that point.

Captain William Lindley, lead pilot, B-17F "The Zoot Suiters": About the only thing I can remember about the briefing was this was the first American mission where the target was the city itself and not an industrial complex. One of the purposes of the strike was to destroy a university in the city center. Apparently it was being used as a center for developing hard-line Nazis.

Some of the crews at Horham had misgivings about using the city center for an aiming point.

Not me, I thought it was great.

Technical Sergeant Warren Thomas, radio operator/gunner, B-17F 230272, "Fritz Blitz": This was to be my twenty-fifth mission and completion of my tour of bombing raids. Upon arrival at the "Fritz Blitz" I stowed my gear, triple-checked my parachute, and began the dreaded waiting period until take-off time. This countdown was always the worst part of every raid for me personally.

Mission doubts, the ever lengthening odds on returning, and other black thoughts clouded other matters. The longer the wait, the worse my condition of mind. The summons to board the bomber was always a very welcome call. The actions required to taxi, take off, and assemble into formation were the ideal antidote to clear the nagging doubts and fears.

Captain Rodney Snow, pilot, B-17F, "Herky Jerky II": The mission looked relatively short in duration, although we knew that we would be in for considerable trouble any time we penetrated Germany. This was my twenty-first mission, and I was to lead the third element in the high squadron. Shortly after take-off my two wingmen—Lieutenant Smith in "Slightly Dangerous" and Lieutenant Tucker in "Cuddle Cat"—developed engine and oxygen trouble, respectively, and were forced to abort. In addition, Lieutenant Glenn Infield piloting "Peggy Ann," one of the spare B-17s, had to turn back with his interphone out. That left me flying alone as an element in the high squadron, so I elected to fly the diamond behind Captain Lindley's lead squadron of six aircraft, that is I was flying low behind the second element of three ships.

Things proceeded normally when I suddenly noticed that my mixture control was too rich and I had burned up far too much fuel if the mission was to be anywhere near as long as indicated at take-off. Our gasoline tanks were filled with only about half-an-hour or so more capacity than the mission required; that is, if the mission was of six-hour duration we would have enough fuel for about seven hours at the most. I cut the mixture back and decided that maybe I could go ahead and complete the mission with the remaining fuel on board. We proceeded across the North Sea, where the gunners tested their machine guns to be sure they were functioning properly, and crossed the coast of Holland.

Being an unusually clear and beautiful autumn day for flying with not a cloud in the sky, we could see for about forty to fifty miles from our altitude of 24,000 feet.

As we approached the German border towns, which we could see quite clearly, the enemy fighters were concentrated in numbers such as we had not seen on any of my crew's twenty previous missions. I'll digress here for a moment to say that the Luftwaffe were never able to turn back an Eighth Air Force bomber effort. I think this particular mission was aimed at turning back the attack. The ensuing events are extremely difficult to describe because of the number of enemy fighters we encountered.

The German fighters elected first to take on the 100th Group which was flying low group in the wing. On the first pass I remember there were eight to ten Me109s, 410s, and Fw 190s coming in waves directly through our formation in a frontal attack from twelve o'clock level. Following their first pass, which took out three airplanes from the 100th's lead squadron, wave after wave kept attacking these low squadrons. I thought that the enemy had successfully shot down all of the 100th Group, certainly most of them were smoking or had exploded in mid-air due to direct hits. American and German parachutes from the planes considerably below were soon visible to my gunners in the rear of our ship.

We were sure these German pilots were the cream of the Luftwaffe as it was evident that the "Abbeville Kids" and "Goering's Flying Circus" were leading this enemy attack because of the gaily painted engine cowlings on their fighters and also the scarves and headgear of the pilots.

Captain Ellis Scripture: Never before had we seen the great concentration of enemy fighters—nor would we in the months ahead. They were everywhere, attacking from every direction, every level. It was similar to fighting off an aroused swarm of bees. I could look out the gun ports on both sides of the navigator's compartment and find new fighters attacking. This continued literally from the Dutch-German border to the initial point, on the target while Dewey was concentrating on the bomb run, to the target, and the withdrawal to the rendezvous with American fighter cover near the Dutch border. It was always the navigator's responsibility to record every aspect of the flight. That day it was impossible to record all attacks reported by the gunners. The navigator also had the responsibility to direct the pilot at critical flight path corrections (turns) and to follow the flight plan. One most important job was to assist the bombardier in finding the exact aiming point in the target area. Fortunately, on this day, Dewey Johnson could identify the target easily because of the clear visibility, so I could concentrate more on the guns while he flew the plane on the A.F.C.E. (automatic flight control equipment).

While Dewey Johnson, our bombardier, and I were busy getting to the target and getting in quite a few shots en route, we heard many reports over the intercom regarding 100th Group bombers being hit and going down in every stage of distress. We could also tune in on the command frequency and hear their chatter among themselves and to Colonel Gerhart as the battle continued.

Captain Rodney Snow: The field order specified that Bill Lindley make a long bomb run in order to give the bombardiers ample time—too much, I thought—for straight and level flight to ensure that the twelve 500-pound bombs that each Fortress carried would reach their primary objective, the target area.

I clearly remember that on this particular day our bomb run was nearly six minutes—two minutes longer than we liked to fly straight and level as enemy antiaircraft fire was quite heavy, as were the fighter attacks, and our evasive action was eliminated during this period. Also, we lowered our bomb-bay doors during the turn over the IP, thereby creating extra drag, which in turn reduced our airspeed.

After they had practically destroyed the 100th Bomb Group in the low position of our wing, the fighters' next concentrated effort was on the 390th Bomb Group, which was flying at about a thousand feet above and behind us. Here again, they took their toll with straight, head-on attacks through the 95th, against the three squadrons of the 390th. The sky seemed full of tracer bullets and burning airplanes, both theirs and ours. It was later estimated that we were being attacked by about 250 fighters all through the bomb-run.

Captain William Lindley, leading the other fifteen heavy bombardment groups of the Third and First Air Divisions to Munster in the 95th's Fortress "The Zoot Suiters," remembers: Well before we got to Munster the flak guns began putting up heavy barrages of antiaircraft fire over every city and town along our flight path. Every target zone we passed had a black layer of flak smoke thick enough to walk on, but barrage flak always looked worse than it actually was. The radar-tracking guns were by far the most accurate. However, we could still give the flak gunners fits of apoplexy. By looking over the side of the cockpit at the gun emplacements, we could see every time the battery fired in unison. A slight turn in either direction of a few degrees, and the 88mm shell bursts would appear off to the side of our formation, an exciting spectacle to behold. When the battery stopped firing, the gunners were adjusting to allow for our change in course. The next time they fired a salvo we would begin a slight turn in the opposite direction. Radar tracking, with manual feed to the guns, made this maneuver possible. We didn't use this maneuver during the bomb run from the IP to the primary target.

Enemy fighters picked us up long before we reached the target area, and it quickly became very obvious that we were about to get worked over again. There were just as many fighters as on the Kiel raid, but this time our task force was much larger. Our P-47 Thunderbolt escort fighters diverted many of the attacks, but shortly after we left the Dutch border they had to break off and return to the barn.

The enemy fighters then concentrated their efforts on the 100th Group, flying in the low position of our lead Thirteenth Combat Wing. Most of the 100th aircraft were lost in the first few minutes before we reached the IP area. The fighters then switched to the 390th Group, which were in the high position. Flak increased as we made our turn over the IP and two more B-17s went down. It was about then that the number 4 engine took a light hit and began to vibrate. Colonel Gerhart reached over to push the feathering button to number 4 but before he could press it I knocked his arm away. A feathered engine at that critical time would have played hell with the formation and the bomb run.

A few minutes later Dewey Johnson made the final adjustment with the bomb sight. The bombs didn't release automatically so Dewey hit the salvo switch. Much credit has to be given to the other pilots in our formation. In spite of all the fighter attacks and the heavy flak, they flew as tight a formation as you would ever see. The resultant bomb pattern was perfect—right on target. We all sang Dewey's praises! Number 4 engine still shook and puffed a little smoke, but it eventually got us back to Horham.

Captain Ellis Scripture, lead navigator: We had made all the navigational check points en route and we approached the city from the southwest. Dewey Johnson, our bombardier, had taken control of the airplane through the A.F.C.E. by this time. Between the IP and the target area, the wing had encountered intense fighter opposition; this was certainly the greatest concentration of German fighters we had seen to date. They seemed to lose the classical attack patterns and become a jumbled mass before, over, and beyond the target. Tracers filled the air, and it was like shooting at fish in a tank when the slow, heavy, twin-engined night fighters became entangled in the bomber formations.

At 1503 hours, three minutes later than scheduled, the bombs curved down, and we hit the target exactly as planned, in spite of intense fighter opposition. And as we turned away from the target, I shot down a twin-engined German fighter. It was an Me 410, flying ever so slowly, as if he was trying to turn away after his attack on our formation. At the time, I felt we had to clear him out of the way or run over him!

Quite frankly, I didn't experience a particular thrill over the situation, either at the time or later. As one who had grown up on stories of fair fights in Western novels and stories of First World War dog fights, I could take no particular pleasure in shooting down a guy who was trying to run away, even though he came in shooting and had undoubtedly been firing at other B-17s in our formation just previously.

Captain Lesley Kring, pilot, B-17F 230233, "Rhapsody in Flak": Following the bomb run Sergeant Cunningham, our tail gunner, called me on the interphone and yelled, "Move this damn airplane around a little! Jerry is behind us shooting rockets; I can't reach him!" I took instant evasive action even though I was leading the second element of three ships in our lead squadron.

Almost immediately after that, while glancing at numbers 1 and 2 engines, I saw an air-to-air rocket streak past about a foot above the wing. My heart skipped a beat. Cunningham called that one, and saved us all a lot of grief.

Lieutenant William Overstreet, co-pilot, B-17F 943, "Situation Normal": Munster was our crew's thirteenth mission, and it was by far the roughest. The Germans hit us with everything they had. The whole sky was a fantastic panorama of black flak bursts, burning and exploding B-17s, spinning and tumbling crazily ... German fighters blowing up and going down streaming flames and long plumes of grey and black smoke ... intense flak over the target.

During the battle Lieutenant Harry Meintz, our navigator, was seriously injured. His left arm was blown off and shredded by a 20mm cannon shell from a German fighter. One Fw 190, with a black-and-white checkered cowling, came within a few feet of colliding with our B-17. The enemy pilot was slumped over in his shattered cockpit, apparently dead.

Lieutenant Paul Perceful, co-pilot, B-17F 230218: I vividly recall seeing a B-17 that had been simply cut in two halves by the concentrated cannon fire from a German fighter. I think that the mental process does strange things to you at times like that because the whole incident, from start to finish, appeared to me to happen in slow motion. The Fortress was struck and slowly came apart at the radio room. The front half of the fuselage, wings, still functioning engines, and the cockpit, seemed to slowly rise upward, completely separate from the rear fuselage and tail unit. Then both halves twisted and tumbled down and away. The battle continued without respite.

The bombing run of the Third and First Air divisions targeted the city center of Munster, October 1943.

Lieutenant Theodore Bozarth, navigator, B-17F 25918, "Heavenly Daze": During and after the bomb run our tail gunner kept up a running commentary on the battle: ". . . two Forts from the low group going down . . . both on fire . . . six chutes from one; . . . B-17 from the high group leaving formation . . . one engine feathered . . . under control . . . no chutes yet; . . . There goes another one from our low squadron . . . two . . . three . . . four chutes. . . ."

It only seemed a matter of time before it became our turn to come under the hammer.

Lieutenant James Goff, navigator, "Rhapsody in Flak": To this day I am very grateful that I was assigned to Captain Kring's crew. He was an experienced, veteran pilot and his crew were likewise. I am convinced that the 95th Group suffered the fewest losses in the Thirteenth Combat Wing that day due to the skill and determination of the 95th Group pilots to fly a tight, defensive formation no matter how fierce the opposition.

I can remember few specific details of those terrifying twenty-five minutes over Munster when all hell broke loose. My mouth felt as though it was full of cotton, and in spite of the numbing subzero temperature, I was perspiring freely. I can recall slipping and sliding on the growing mound of shell casings as I moved hastily and clumsily from the left nose gun to the right nose gun and back again. I found later that I'd fired some 1,600 rounds. If I did any damage to the German fighters, I never knew, because they were coming in so fast and furiously.

It all seemed like a blurred nightmare . . . wave after wave of enemy fighters . . . pieces of aircraft littering the clear blue sky . . . ugly black smoke of flak bursts . . . men in drifting parachutes . . . burning bombers and fighters all around us . . . Twenty-five minutes that lasted an eternity.

Editor's note: The 355th Fighter Group, which had been scheduled to provide escort to the B-17s of the Third Air Division with its 48 P-47 Thunderbolts from the IP of Haltern to the target of Munster, had been unable to take off from its base at Steeple Morden because of dense ground fog. Three other fighter groups were, however, at that time over Holland on their way to provide withdrawal cover for the Fortresses. Meanwhile the Luftwaffe had amassed approximately 250 unopposed fighters in the battle area and concentrated their efforts against the Third Air Division and, in particular, the lead Thirteenth Combat Wing.

Following the bomb run of the Thirteenth Wing, Sergeant Mackie, radio operator in the task force commander's Fortress "The Zoot Suiters," tapped out on his morse key a code message to Third Air Division Headquarters at Elveden Hall relayed to him via interphone by Colonel Gerhart. He sent it slowly, with a distinct spacing between the dots and dashes for each letter, to ensure clarity of transmission above the static:

PRIMARY STRIKE SUCCESSFUL STOP DIVISION UNDER SEVERE REPEAT SEVERE ATTACK STOP PRESENT POSITION FIVE TWO ZERO SEVEN NORTH ZERO SEVEN FIVE TWO EAST STOP COURSE TWO SEVEN THREE STOP ALT TWO FOUR STOP IMPERATIVE GET ESCORT REPEAT IMPERATIVE END.

GERHART

****

B-17F 25986, "Brown's Mule," was the first of five 95th Group Fortresses to be shot down shortly after bombing Munster. Its pilot, Lieutenant John Riggs, was the last of eight surviving crewmen to bail out before his plane crashed and exploded in a forest clearing near Saarbeck, twenty kilometers north of Munster.

"Miss Flower III," leading the 95th Group's low squadron, staggered as it received a direct flak hit and slowly glided down with an engine on fire, its propellor feathered. Captain John Adams held the B-17 steady, thereby enabling all his crew to bail out safely before he also abandoned the aircraft over the rally point of Emsdetten.

Flying left wingman and deputy lead to Captain Adams was Lieutenant Eldon Broman piloting "Fritz Blitz."

****

Sergeant Warren Thomas, radio operator, "Fritz Blitz": The fighters were now hitting us with everything they had. Suddenly a B-17 that had been hit loomed over and in front of us. Our pilot, Lieutenant Broman, swung clear. We were then hit by flak or a rocket, setting our hydraulic and oxygen systems ablaze. The entire bomb-bay area was on fire as was the right wing.

I fought to open the door leading to the ball-turret area, which had been jammed by spent cartridge cases. Frantically I forced it open, kicking and hammering until the gunner exited and bailed out. The tail and waist gunners had already left but our top-turret gunner, Sergeant Rightmire, was killed in his position by 20mm fire from enemy fighters.

I reached the waist door and jumped. Almost immediately afterward our bomber exploded. I yanked the ripcord and was overjoyed to have the chute deploy in a normal manner. I then noticed during my descent that I had several nicks and burns.

I landed in a nice, soft ploughed field and a young lad armed with a rifle approached. He motioned me to a nearby farmhouse where his mother looked at my burns. She brought a handful of damp tea-leaves and pressed them to my face, which soothed the pain.

A policeman eventually arrived and escorted me and two other airmen who had also been picked up to the local jail. The two captured airmen carried me around wherever we went as my wounds had stiffened the joints and skin and I was unable to walk. A Luftwaffe doctor dressed my burns and lacerations. He informed me I'd be taken to a prison at Lingen, Germany, to recover from my wounds.

I thought myself lucky to be alive at all after twenty-five missions.

****

B-17F 23497, commanded by Lieutenant Lionel Correia, came under concentrated attack by fighters over Greven, northwest of Munster. Nine parachutes billowed from the blazing bomber before it eventually exploded in the air and crashed near Haaksbergen, Holland, near the Dutch/German border and within a few miles of the crash site of "Fritz Blitz." Sergeant Jerome Schneider, 23497's radio operator was killed in action.

"Patsy Ann III," piloted by Lieutenant William Buckley, curved slowly away from the 95th's formation with both its wing fuel tanks blazing and a fire in the radio room.

****

Lieutenant Robert Barto, navigator, "Patsy Ann III": Our interphone was not working during this emergency. A few seconds later we received a direct hit, either by flak or rocket, that broke off the entire tail assembly, and the plane went into a spinning dive. Our bombardier, Lieutenant Ed Jannly, and I bailed out through the nose exit hatch. I then saw our aircraft crash and explode in a corner of the same field where I landed.

****

Co-pilot Lieutenant Frederick Kennie, tail gunner Sergeant Edward Burlingham, and waist gunner Sergeant Donald Reinhart also managed to parachute to safety before their B-17 crashed near Lingen, thirty-five kilometers north-west of Munster.

****

Major Harry Conley, commander of the 334th squadron, leading the 95th's high squadron in a B-17 named "Holy Terror," recalls, Munster was the roughest raid we had experienced up to that time. We lost five ships, including three of my crews, but we claimed forty-two fighters shot down and many more damaged.

The Jerries attacked us in great force with their new air-to-air rockets, a very potent weapon that was fitted with a time fuse. They really raised hell with whatever they hit when they exploded. One of them burst just outside our cockpit, it took out three of the four windows, the cockpit roof and most of the instrument panel. A large chunk of very hot metal struck me at the base of my neck on the left side. It felt as if someone had hit me with a baseball bat but all the damage it did was to give me a stiff neck, a slight burn from the hot metal and a big black and blue bruise. It must have hit me with its flattest side as it ended up on my lap. I subsequently used it as a paper-weight in my office. That was the baby that had my name on it. From then on I sweated out those addressed to "whom it may concern."

Not one of our ships returned from Munster without at least a dozen holes in it. That really was an air battle on a gigantic scale and the Germans were out to stop us at any cost. They didn't succeed in stopping us, and it cost them very heavily.

Captain Ellis B. Scripture, lead navigator: One memory stands out in this and other difficult missions that I flew. That was the calm way young men reacted to extreme danger, and especially during the vicious air battles with German fighters. This stands out as a lasting tribute to the men of the Eighth Air Force.

On this mission, calm prevailed in the planes. When planes were going down, we heard their pilots say over the command radio such things as: "We're hit badly. . . . We're going down. . . . Carry on. . . .We'll be O.K. . . . We'll see you later." No panic, but rapid talk, men doing a difficult and hazardous job well.

On the way home, the remnants of the 390th and the single survivor from the 100th gathered around us. We heard one statement from the group leader of the 390th. Speaking to Colonel Gerhart, he said, "Thanks, it was a good show and a great lead."

Lieutenant William Isaacs, bombardier, B-17F, "Holy Terror": From our position in the high squadron, the last time I saw the only remaining 100th Bomb Group plane over Holland was trailing smoke and lagging further behind our formation. I didn't think that he could possibly make it back to base.

Lieutenant Marshall Thixton, bombardier, B-17F 230322, "Liberty Belle":
We'd had to shut down our number 3 engine after sustaining battle damage while in the target area and were forced to leave the formation near the Dutch coast. Our ship was badly shot up and we'd lost most of the plexiglass nose to cannon fire. We crossed the North Sea fully expecting to ditch at any time.

Captain Rodney Snow, pilot, "Herky Jerky II": During the flight home we were attacked only occasionally. However, I lost oil pressure on my number 2 engine and was unable to feather the propeller, so that it was aimlessly and harmlessly windmilling. There was nothing I could do about it except add extra power in an effort to stay up with the formation.

On crossing the Dutch coast, I advised our group leader that I was going to have to leave the formation because of the considerable drag the windmilling propeller was causing. Also, my gas supply was getting uncomfortably low. To lighten the plane we dumped all excess equipment into the sea. An English-woman, a British Air-Sea Rescue Service operator, picked up our Mayday signals and gave us directions.

As we approached the vicinity of our own base, the weather was deteriorating rapidly. The scud from the North Sea had moved in quite quickly so that visibility was extremely restricted. Our main concern was the cloud ceiling, which appeared to be 1,000 feet or less. We were in bad shape because of our shot-up condition, our near-empty fuel tanks, and the inevitable fatigue that had begun to set in.

After we had cranked the right-hand landing gear down manually because of an electrical malfunction, we prepared to land. We saw a runway, and I tried a big right-hand turn to line the plane up with it. Suddenly the waist gunner yelled, "Pull up, Cap! Pull her up! You're heading straight for a church steeple!" With a violent maneuver to the right we just missed hitting a church spire that had been obscured by the mist and fog. We then completed the turn, and saying a little prayer, let down at an unidentified base.

While we were taxiing back to hardstand, the tower told us we were at Thorpe Abbotts. The commanding officer of the 100th then inquired as to the whereabouts of his group as they should have at least been in radio contact with the tower by that time. The colonel refused to believe me when I told him, "I'm sorry to say this, sir, but I don't think that you will have anyone from your group home this day." But I could not convince him of what we had seen less then two hours earlier, so I advised him to contact Colonel Gerhart at Horham by phone.

Lieutenant William Owen, pilot, B-17F 230322: The "Liberty Belle" lost two engines and the turbo-supercharger was shot out on a third between the period of time when the fighter attacks first began and shortly after "bombs away."

With only one good engine at high altitude we left the formation, descending at so steep an angle I think the enemy fighters assumed we were finished. It wasn't until we'd dived down to 4,000 feet and leveled off that I realized we had two good engines because the turbo wasn't needed at lower altitudes.

We headed for England. By the time we saw the Dutch coast ahead our radio operator, Sergeant Cain, although badly wounded in the throat, had managed to contact British Air-Sea Rescue. The crew took up ditching positions, but they were convinced that we could make it back to Horham at low altitude, which we eventually did, despite rapidly worsening visibility.

I am convinced that the luck of losing the turbo, leaving only one engine at altitude and the resultant very steep descent, saved us. The following day the crew counted 242 holes in the ship.

Lieutenant James Goff, navigator, "Rhapsody in Flak": When we landed at Horham with one engine out and less than ten minutes of fuel in our tanks, I wondered how I could ever have been so eager to see combat. Back in January 1943, I'd graduated from Midland Bombardier School and I was among a group of graduates who were selected to train as navigators at Hondo, Texas. I can remember the keen disappointment we felt because our fellow bombardiers would be sent to combat and we were left behind to study navigation. It didn't seem fair.

The performance of all those splendid young men, both friend and foe, during those traumatic minutes over Munster that day taught me something about bravery. Brave men are not necessarily fearless, but rather they are men who can perform their duties in spite of great fear.

Lieutenant Perceful, co-pilot, B-17F 230218: After the debriefing, I met Captain Dewey Johnson, our lead bombardier, in the 336th Squadron operations room. I had already heard that Dewey had been knocked away from his bomb sight shortly after we had passed the IP. It was later discovered that a flattened bullet had struck him. He had climbed back to the bomb sight and placed the bombs right on the target.

I said to him, "How goes it, Dewey?" His quiet reply was, "Perceful, I've got the horrors. . . .I think I'll go up to the officers' club." I did not go with him.

****

Captain Dewey Johnson was awarded the British Distinguished Flying Cross (DFC) and was personally decorated by King George VI at Buckingham Palace, London, a few days later. For the accuracy of their bombing the 95th Bomb Group was awarded their second Presidential Distinguished Unit Citation. During the Munster raid, the Eighth Air Force lost thirty Fortresses, twenty-five of which were from the lead Thirteenth Bomb Wing, all in approximately twenty-five minutes.

****

Captain Frank Murphy, navigator aboard 230275—one of the twelve B-17s shot down from the 100th Bomb Group—summarized those twenty-five traumatic minutes: Historically, the correct perspective for judging the men of a military unit is not the final outcome of the battle but their dedication in carrying out their mission and, in the last instance, how they performed when called upon to fight to the end against impossible odds, as was the case at Munster.

In this proper historical sense the performance by the men of the 95th, the 100th, and the 390th Bombardment groups over Munster on 10 October 1943, as I saw them, could quite rightly and with full justification, be considered the United States Air Force equivalent of the charge of the Light Brigade in the Crimea or General George Pickett's charge at Gettysburg during the American Civil War.

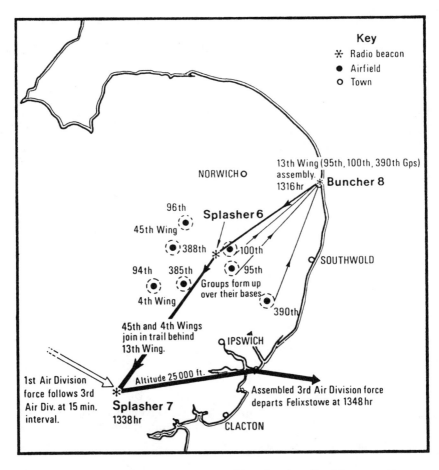

Assembly route for Thirteenth Combat Wing heading for Munster, 10 October 1943.

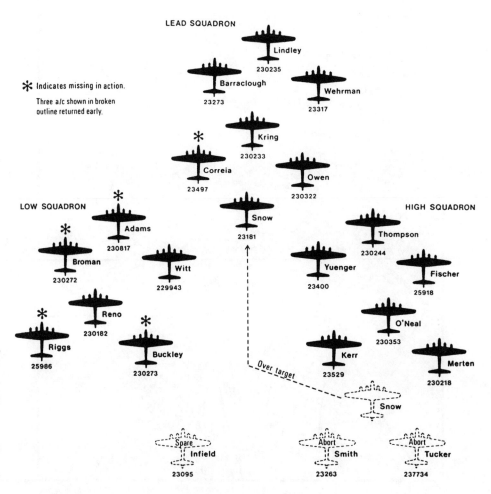

LEAD SQUADRON

Lindley
230235

Barraclough
23273

Wehrman
23317

Kring
230233

Correia
23497

Owen
230322

Snow
23181

* Indicates missing in action.

Three a/c shown in broken
outline returned early.

LOW SQUADRON

Adams
230817

Broman
230272

Witt
229943

Reno
230182

Riggs
25986

Buckley
230273

HIGH SQUADRON

Thompson
230244

Yuenger
23400

Fischer
25918

O'Neal
230353

Kerr
23529

Merten
230218

Over target

Snow

Spare
Infield
23095

Abort
Smith
23263

Abort
Tucker
237734

95th Bomb Group (H) Formation, Munster Mission, 10 October 1943.

79

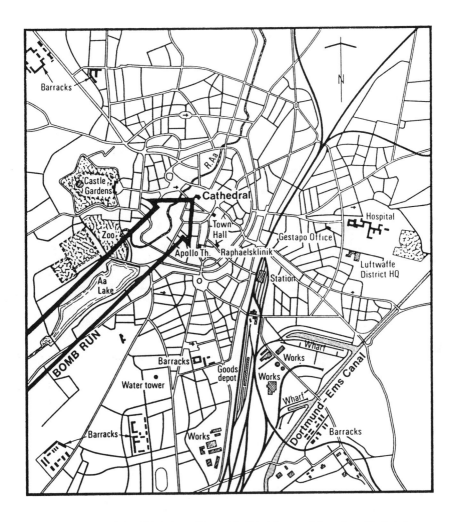

Bomb run, Third Air Division, First Air Division on Munster, 10 October 1943.

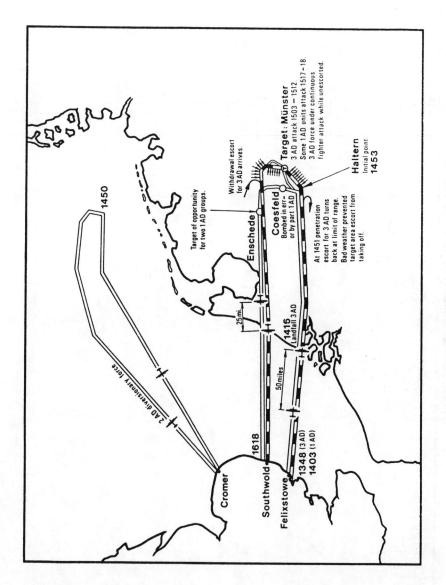

Mission summary, Munster, 10 October 1943.

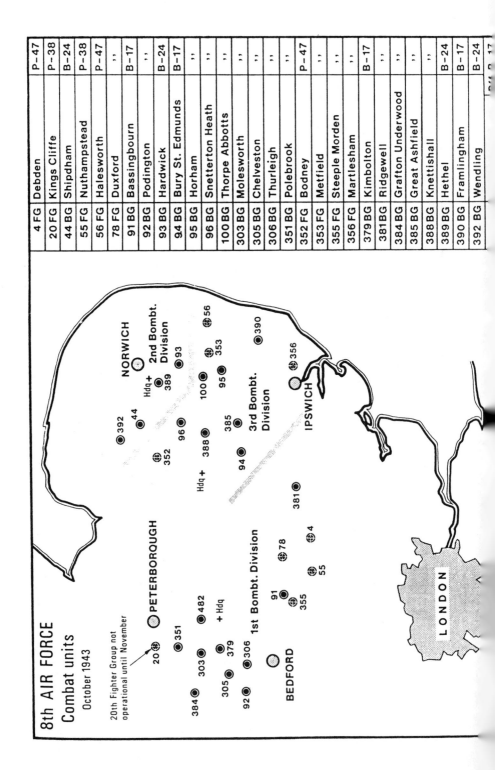

8th AIR FORCE
Combat units
October 1943

20th Fighter Group not operational until November

4 FG	Debden	P–47
20 FG	Kings Cliffe	P–38
44 BG	Shipdham	B–24
55 FG	Nuthampstead	P–38
56 FG	Halesworth	P–47
78 FG	Duxford	,,
91 BG	Bassingbourn	B–17
92 BG	Podington	,,
93 BG	Hardwick	B–24
94 BG	Bury St. Edmunds	B–17
95 BG	Horham	,,
96 BG	Snetterton Heath	,,
100 BG	Thorpe Abbotts	,,
303 BG	Molesworth	,,
305 BG	Chelveston	,,
306 BG	Thurleigh	,,
351 BG	Polebrook	,,
352 FG	Bodney	P–47
353 FG	Metfield	,,
355 FG	Steeple Morden	,,
356 FG	Martlesham	,,
379 BG	Kimbolton	B–17
381 BG	Ridgewell	,,
384 BG	Grafton Underwood	,,
385 BG	Great Ashfield	,,
388 BG	Knettishall	,,
389 BG	Hethel	B–24
390 BG	Framlingham	B–17
392 BG	Wendling	B–24

NORWICH

2nd Bombt. Division

IPSWICH

3rd Bombt. Division

PETERBOROUGH

1st Bombt. Division

BEDFORD

LONDON

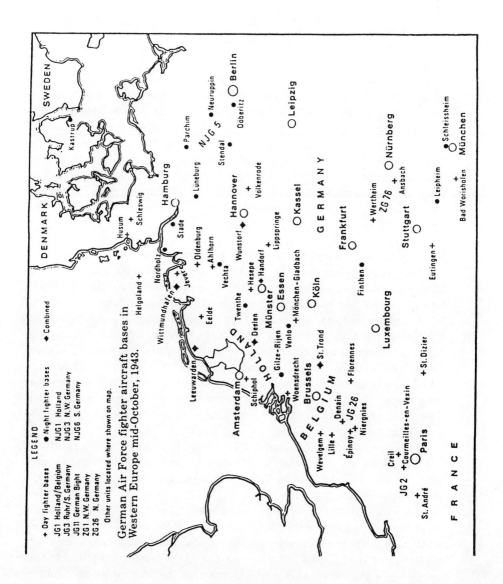

German Air Force fighter aircraft bases in Western Europe mid-October, 1943.

LEGEND

+ Day fighter bases
● Night fighter bases
◆ Combined

JG1 Holland/Belgium   NJG1 Holland
JG3 Ruhr/S. Germany   NJG3 N.W. Germany
JG11 German Bight   NJG6 S. Germany
ZG1 N.W. Germany
ZG26 N. Germany

Other units located where shown on map.

ONE-WAY TICKET TO MUNSTER

Eldon Broman, Pilot, B-17F 230272, "Fritz Blitz" 335th Squadron

Our mission assignment for the attack on Munster, 10 October 1943, was to fly deputy lead in the low squadron. We encountered extremely heavy fighter opposition as we approached the target, and the battle damage sustained during the bomb run resulted in a substantial loss of power to number 2 engine.

The low squadron leader was hit very hard and fell back from the main formation shortly after the bomb run. I decided to stay with him to provide defensive firepower until his crew began bailing out, then we headed back to rejoin the main 95th Group formation. During this time we were hit hard by cannon fire, or a rocket, which created a fire in the top turret and in the oxygen storage area directly behind the cockpit.

I still had the airplane under control, but the fire rapidly grew in intensity so we had no alternative but to abandon the aircraft. Both the alarm bell and the interphone system were inoperative during this time, so I tapped my co-pilot, Lieutenant Chaffin, on the shoulder and pointed down. He knew what that meant, left the cockpit, and bailed out via the nose hatch.

I trimmed the plane up as best I could and got out of my seat to retrieve my British chest-type parachute. This meant stepping into the worst part of the flames momentarily as it was stored under the top turret platform. Once I'd snapped it to my harness I lost no time in leaving via the front hatch.

After a delayed fall through space, I opened the chute and a few minutes later landed among the branches of a large tree in a densely wooded area. Fortunately I was close enough to the ground to release the chute from the harness and drop to the ground.

I heard a machine gun nearby fire a short burst, and with my parachute in the branches of the tree clearly indicating my present position to the search party, I decided to put as much distance between my chute and myself in the shortest possible time.

I ran through the woods until I was exhausted and then some more to get away from the telltale chute. I was still in the woods when I stumbled across what must have been an old foxhole. I rested there and buried my flight coveralls and flying boots. After taking a couple of benzedrine pills from my escape kit, I started off in a westerly direction, navigating by my "button" compass.

I crossed several fences, which apparently was the Dutch/German border, while still in the woods and continued heading westward until eventually I came to a large, busy highway. I deduced from the names marked in large lettering on the sides of the passing trucks that I'd arrived in Holland. I waited until the road was clear of traffic, scurried across, and continued west on a minor road that had a path for bicycles alongside.

By this time the sun was getting low on the western horizon and I decided to approach a farmhouse. In the adjacent yard a woman was busily milking a cow. The woman looked up; as I started to explain to her that I was an American airman in need of assistance, she suddenly started screaming hysterically. I discovered later that the flames in the plane had burned my forehead and upper parts of my face; consequently, my face was very puffy and swollen. I looked positively ghoulish, but I was quite unaware of my injuries probably because of the adrenalin flow due to the dramatic happenings of that day.

Hearing the screams, her husband came running out of the nearby barn. Eventually I managed to convince them who I was, and they invited me into their farmhouse where I was given a refreshing glass of milk and a mirror. I could hardly recognize myself. I knew that I couldn't travel looking like that so I requested their immediate help in contacting the Dutch Underground.

The man agreed to help me and then left to make contact. He returned a short while later saying that help was on its way. I then had a very anxious half-hour wait or so until, just as it began to get dark, a young man, riding one bicycle and guiding another bicycle alongside him, arrived. After thanking my hosts for their hospitality and apologizing to the Dutch lady for scaring her, I left with my helper for his small, camouflaged cabin/hideout located in another densely wooded area.

For the next three weeks, I stayed with my helper while my burns gradually healed and my eyebrows and eyelashes grew again. My newfound friend provided me with civilian clothes and false identity papers. My new name became Jean Seprinee.

My helper's name was Patrick Laming, an English-born, Cambridge-educated Dutchman. He spoke six languages and was actively engaged in sabotage and espionage with the Dutch resistance. He was particularly proud of the fact that the Gestapo had a 6,000 guilder reward for his capture, "dead or alive," and was disappointed that I didn't have my .45 service pistol to add to his armory.

Toward the end of October 1943, I left Patrick's hideout and he saw me onto a train. I then traveled south through Holland, sometimes on foot, all fours, bicycle, street-car, train, a Pontiac automobile, and a row boat. I eventually crossed the Dutch/Belgian border and made my way to the large town of Liege, Belgium.

Ross Repp, a 91st Bomb Group radio operator, who had also been shot down on 10 October 1943, and I were guided to the second floor of an apartment building in Liege, Belgium, one afternoon in late November. Two other Eighth Air Force evadees arrived at the apartment at about the same time. Introductions were made by a Belgian Resistance member, a rather short, wiry individual, who spoke to us in a mixture of half Flemish or French and broken English.

We chatted cordially between ourselves for a few minutes and explored our new hiding place. I noticed, with concern, that there was no rear exit from the apartment. The only apparent access, to and from, was via the stairs.

One of the airmen whom I'd just met then went downstairs to the toilet and our Belgian helper then announced he was going to the kitchen across the landing to prepare some food for us. We hadn't eaten anything since early morning breakfast, about ten hours previously.

As he was crossing the landing from the living room to the kitchen he suddenly yelled a warning to us. Several German S.S. troops were sneaking silently up the stairs. They'd apparently had the building under constant surveillance for some time.

The Resistance man pulled out a small, semi-automatic hand gun and fired about six shots in rapid succession at the troops. Several of them returned his fire as they retreated hurriedly back down the stairs amidst confused yelling and shouting. After emptying his gun, the Belgian hurled it down the stairs at the retreating Germans. He then raced into the kitchen and dived headlong through a closed window, landing on a small lean-to directly below the shattered window that I'd noticed earlier, picked himself up, and made a dash for his freedom.

After the initial and almost hysterical noise had subsided the S.S. troops could be heard creeping cautiously back up the stairs. I'd taken refuge behind the sofa when I saw the ominous barrel of a Luger pistol in the open doorway followed by the equally ominous and notorious skull and crossbones emblem on one of the S.S. troops' caps. As soon as they realized we were unarmed, they all rushed into the room.

The shouting began again, and the three of us were lined up against the wall with our hands up. It was at that moment when I feared the worst because we were all in civilian clothes and we could be executed as spies. Then one of the S.S. troops began yelling at the airman whose buddy was missing. Evidently they'd seen four of us brought to the building. The German then grabbed the airman with one hand and gestured as if to pistol-whip him with the other. I tried to explain, as best I could, that none of us could understand German. Each of us remained silent, but it was a futile gesture because after a thorough search of the premises he was found and brought back upstairs. One of the troops asked mockingly in English, "How do you like the trap we set for you?"

A short time later the very gallant Belgian Resistance man was brought back to the apartment. His face was almost unrecognizable, just a mass of ugly welts and bruises. Either he'd injured himself diving through the kitchen window, or far more likely, he'd been viciously pistol-whipped after capture. Naturally, we were all extremely concerned for him because we knew he was undoubtedly in for a very rough time—one that in all probability he was not likely to survive.

Perhaps, fortunately for us, none of the S.S. troops appeared to have been injured by the Belgian's gunfire, despite the close range of all the shooting.

Being the only officer among the four of us, I was separated from the others and driven to a nearby Luftwaffe air base where I was put into solitary confinement. The prison cell was spartan, but dry and clean with a narrow iron-frame bed with a mattress. Although we'd been searched for weapons at the time of capture they hadn't discovered the hacksaw blade from my escape kit hidden in my shoe.

I promptly went to work on the window bars of my ground-floor cell but four cuts through the three-quarter inch diameter steel would take a considerable time. However, I was only halfway through the first cut when I was transferred to St. Gilles prison in Brussels, Belgium, with Ross Repp and the other two airmen.

This was a grim, fortress-like prison dating back to the Middle Ages. On arrival I was again put in solitary confinement. In direct contrast to my former cell, this was dirty, dank, smelly, cramped, and with a thin, lumpy straw mattress directly on the stone floor. The toilet facilities consisted of a small steel bucket that was emptied only once a day. Breakfast was a small cup of luke-warm ersatz coffee (made from scorched barley, I believe), lunch was a bowl of cabbage soup, and dinner was a chunk of black bread with a spoonful of preserves of some kind.

The only redeeming feature was the fact that Ross and the two other evadees were in the adjacent cell. We found we were able to communicate by talking with our mouths close to a water pipe that extended continuously along the interior prison walls. The pipe was a good sound conductor. Our conversations were innocuous and governed by the assumption that both cells were bugged.

As time went by we heard many messages being tapped out in a code of some sort along the pipes. The tapping went on throughout most of the nights. Blood-curdling and spine-chilling screams of agony and other equally ominous and distressing sounds could also be heard quite distinctly at various times during the nights. Almost certainly, our Belgian friend was here undergoing interrogation, although we hadn't seen him since our capture. All in all, this wasn't a place to get a good night's sleep.

We were interrogated daily by members of the Gestapo, sometimes in civilian clothes and sometimes in black uniform, during our first few days at St. Gilles and several times weekly thereafter. After I'd identified myself by name, rank, and serial number the Gestapo agent told me I was considered a spy because I'd been arrested in German-occupied territory in civilian clothes. There were many threats of mistreatment. Of course, what he really wanted to know were the names of my helpers and where they'd helped me.

After about a month of solitary confinement and interrogation, I decided to demand an interview with the prison kommandant. During that month I'd determined from comments passed by the guards, who accompanied trustee prisoners when food was brought to the cells, that the German Army personnel who administered and operated the prison had about the same feeling and contempt as did the prisoners for the Gestapo types who were interrogating many of the inmates.

It was just before Christmas 1943, and I reasoned that the timing of my interview with the kommandant would never be better. One morning after coffee, I hammered on the cell door until the guard came. I demanded to see the kommandant. He nodded his head and left. In a few minutes he was back and I was escorted up to see the kommandant who, it transpired, was a colonel in the German Army.

Upon entering his office, I thanked the kommandant for permitting me to confer with him, which was duly translated by the German soldier standing by his chair. The kommandant appeared to be very Prussian and very much a professional soldier.

I began my statement by mentioning that it had always been my understanding that the Germans were a Christmas-loving people and that the close proximity of Christmas 1943 had some bearing on why I'd asked to confer with him. I went on to state that we four American airmen who'd been brought to St. Gilles near the end of November had not been engaged in espionage as accused by the Gestapo interrogators. The truth was that we were just airmen whose aircraft had been shot down during daylight operations over German-held territory; that all concerned really knew that to be the truth; that we, as evadees, had been doing only what any loyal German airman would do in similar circumstances; that is, we were simply trying to avoid capture and trying to get out of enemy territory. I continued by saying that we were all keenly aware that what the Gestapo really wanted from us were the names and locations of the people who'd helped us along the way. I added that even if we knew the correct names we couldn't live with ourselves if we turned informer and I would prefer to be executed under a false spy charge than to endure remaining in solitary confinement.

I concluded by stating that it was my firm belief that he had the necessary authority to transfer us from his prison so that we could be with other military airmen, Allied prisoners of war, for Christmas and thereafter as circumstances dictated.

There was no response from the kommandant as I completed my statement and was escorted from his office.

Later that same day I was taken out of solitary confinement and put in the same cell as Ross and the other two airmen. A day or two after that the four of us were released from St. Gilles and, still in civilian clothes, transported by train to the temporary POW camp at Frankfurt, Germany.

The night before our arrival, Frankfurt had been heavily bombed (20–21 December) by Royal Air Force Bomber Command and the Royal Canadian Air Force. Great damage had been done to the city, and a number of aircraft had been shot down.

As a result of the cells being needed to interrogate new prisoners at Dulag Luft, we were marched several miles to another POW camp in Frankfurt. As we marched, a number of angry and probably newly bombed-out civilians gathered along the way, cursing and hurling rubble at us. I was helping support a Royal Canadian Air Force airman with a very badly injured ankle and foot.

One of the German civilians pointed to the Canadian's injury and shouted angrily, "Das ist gute!" Fortunately and perhaps because of his obvious injury, none of the bricks were thrown at the two of us. The guards made no attempt at stopping the rubble throwing or the name calling, but no civilian was permitted to strike any prisoner of war.

We eventually reached the camp where, to our relief, hot showers, strong soap, clean uniforms, and ample food were all available, courtesy of the British and American Red Cross and under the supervision of the International Red Cross organization.

The four evadees who'd been arrested together in Liege a month previously spent Christmas Eve 1943 together, but we couldn't help thinking and wondering about our far less fortunate Belgian Resistance friend, presumably still imprisoned at St. Gilles.

Several days later I was included with a group of POW officers who began a rail journey to Stalag Luft I in Pomerania near Barth, northern Germany. Ross Repp and the other two airmen were sent to a different stalag. We were about to begin another phase of our prisoner of war experience.

This Allied prisoner of war camp was liberated by tough, hard-fighting Russian troops from Marshal Rokasovky's army in early May 1945. I returned to the 95th Bomb Group at Horham for a brief visit shortly afterward, just before returning to the United States via a hospital ship.

POSTSCRIPT FROM THE UNDERGROUND

Wim Willemsen, Peter Wijnen, Dr. J. Bussels

The following additional information was received during July and August 1986 from former members of the Dutch Resistance, Mr. Wim Willemsen and Mr. Peter Wijnen and from Dr. J. Bussels, a Belgian schoolmaster.

In 1981 Dr. Bussels wrote a book (which he published himself) called *De Doodstraf Als Risico* (The Death Sentence as a Risk), which includes many of the incidents as described in the accounts titled, "Betrayed" by Leroy Lawson and "One-Way Ticket To Munster" by Eldon Broman.

"The chief," or "the captain" as he was sometimes called, was a traitor who, together with his Spanish mistress, betrayed about five hundred Allied air crew members and an unknown number of Resistance members in Holland, Belgium, and France to the Gestapo in Nazi-occupied Europe.

Prosper de Zitter (the chief) and his mistress, Florentine Giralt, worked together with a British Army deserter, Harold Cole, who had fought with the British Expeditionary Force in France and Belgium during the summer of 1940. These three were infiltrated by the Gestapo into the escape line code-named "Luctor et Emergo" and worked for a highly specialized secret service group within the Gestapo code-named MI 9. They also cooperated with other traitors from the organization headed by the infamous Christian Lindemanns, otherwise known as "King Kong," a notorious Dutch traitor who was executed after the war.

Leroy Lawson was found by a boy who informed Maurice Cloostermans, a Belgian policeman, who then took him to Dr. Vrancken in Hechtel, northern Belgium, close to the Dutch border. Maurice Cloostermans then took Leroy Lawson to a farm at Overpelt owned by an elderly widow, Mrs. Spelters, a very brave lady, and her sons. From Overpelt Lawson was guided to Bree, also in northern Belgium. At Bree he was hidden at a café and bakery owned by Alfons ("Uncle Fons") Bergmans and his equally brave family.

It was at Bree where the American escapees met the chief, who took them to Brussels by car.

The chief was a Belgian who had emigrated to Canada and lived there for ten years before returning to England and being parachuted into occupied Belgium by the Allies in 1940 in order to help in the organization of escape lines for shot-down Allied airmen.

Prosper de Zitter and his mistress, Florentine Giralt, were tried, found guilty of treachery, and executed in Brussels on 17 September 1948. Sergeant Harold Cole was killed during the liberation of Paris in August 1944 when many members of the French Resistance movement in Paris took the law into their own hands.

Eldon Broman, who was shot down 10 October 1943, was hidden by the Loven family at Roermond, southeastern Holland, from 30 October 1943 until 5 November 1943 with William Whitlow and John Ashcraft, (385th Bomb Group) and Ross Repp (91st Bomb Group), who had also been shot down over Holland on 10 October 1943. They all left Roermond for Neeritter to be met by a famous Resistance man, Reinier van de Vin, who hid them until his friend, Theodor Florquin, came at midnight on 6 November and transported the escapers to his home at Geistingen, just inside the Belgian border.

From Geistingen a policeman, Peter Koolen, transported the airmen to Jan Hilven who took them on to Gertrude Hendrikx at Maaseik. Eldon Broman remained in hiding there until 23 November and on that day he was guided to Liege by Leopold and Anna Erkens.

TO WHOM IT MAY CONCERN

Leonard Herman, Bombardier, 335th Squadron

As soon as we learned that fresh eggs were on the menu for our pre-dawn breakfast that morning, 14 October 1943, we knew we were in for a real tough mission. Fresh eggs were always an accurate indicator. The better the chow, the rougher the mission.

Schweinfurt would be the twenty-fourth mission for the crew of "the Brass Rail." When you've flown that many missions, you learn to accept the combat routine and the basics. We were a "no chatter" crew, and we didn't get this far without being sharp. Our original pilot, John Johnson, had been killed during a mission to Kiel on 25 July; several of us had been wounded but the majority of our original crew was still together. We made it because we were good and worked together as a team.

Flak we can't do anything about. We fly our course, stay in formation, and pray we don't get hit. At least with the fighters we can shoot back. We are busy, . . . busy watching them as they line up to attack our tight formation, . . . busy following them as they swoop in, . . . crazy busy, . . .short bursts, . . . short bursting them to death.

We're on pure oxygen and can feel the adrenalin flowing. There's no fear at this time because we're too busy to think about anything but doing our job. We see planes hit, we count the chutes as our buddies bail out, and we wonder when the hell the fighters are going to stop coming.

We're on the bomb run, flying straight and level. Then it's "Bombs away! . . . Bomb-bay doors coming up! . . . Let's get the hell out of here!"

We peer down seeing the bombs hit, watching the explosions, the flames, and the smoke boiling up from the largest ball-bearing manufacturing complex in Europe. Now the purpose of our mission is complete. Good, bad, or indifferent. We know one thing—we're going home. We'd dropped our bomb load, and we're going home. Our planes will be faster on the way back. Sure, there's still going to be plenty of fighters and flak to fly through and there will be further losses, but somehow we got through and got back. That was Schweinfurt.

It was after that mission (Schweinfurt) that I was notified that I would be flying lead bombardier on a practice mission with a pilot for whom I had no special love or respect.

Just a few days previously I'd been to see group operations and asked if they would give me credit for two missions instead of one, because the Schweinfurt mission had been so rough. The Eighth Air Force had lost sixty B-17s that day, which speaks for itself. However, my request was turned down so the result was that I still had one more mission to fly to complete my tour of twenty-five combat missions.

After I had adamantly refused to fly the practice mission with the afore-mentioned pilot, I heard myself being paged over the loud-speaker system. I was being requested to report to group operations immediately.

Upon reporting I was asked by the operations officer to recount what had happened and to explain why I had refused to fly the practice mission that day. My reply was as follows: "During the Schweinfurt mission every German fighter plane and every German flak gun was shooting at me personally. It seemed the whole German Air Force was out to get me and keep me from completing my twenty-five missions. This they were not able to accomplish, so I don't see why I should jeopardize the last chance I have of completing a tour by flying with a very unstable and erratic pilot on a practice mission.

"Furthermore, I don't mind too much if I get hit by a piece of flak or a machine gun bullet that had got my name on it, even if I get caught by one or the other that is labeled 'to whom it may concern.' This I have little control over, but I'll be damned if I'll put my life in the hands of him."

I was told to return to my barracks and to stand by for further action.

After forty-two years I'm still waiting for a decision. However, shortly thereafter I flew my twenty-fifth mission to complete my tour and a few days later received orders returning me to the United States. The only conclusion I can reach is that the entire matter was dropped, but I often wonder why.

A VIEW FROM THE GROUND UP

(Part I)
Ted Lucey, Radio Technician, 336th Squadron
(Written as personal notes, not originally intended for publication)

18 October 1943: Went on leave yesterday. Left the base in time for the London-bound train from Diss. Arrived Liverpool Street station 1900 hours. Took the underground train to Marble Arch. As always, it was very sad to see hundreds of civilians camping in subway stations for the night. First arrivals got cots hinged to station walls; others, whatever platform space they can find. Many people have gone through this ordeal every night since the beginning of the blitz on London in 1940. Little children sleep somehow, oblivious to all the noise and bustle going on around them. Train services cease at 2300 hours, so there's relative peace and quiet for these poor souls until early morning.

Tajewski and I found our way through the pitch dark of the blackout to the Columbia Red Cross Club, where we were lucky enough to get a room with two single cots. There was an air raid that night in which two Jerry bombers were said to have been shot down, but we slept right through it.

19 October: Met a Yank from Camden, New Jersey, an American Merchant Mariner who has lived in Dover on England's southeast coast for the past six years. He said Dover had been hit hard, mainly by shell fire from German heavy artillery gun emplacements on the French coast, a mere twenty-two miles across the English Channel. Twenty thousand people live in Dover.

Strolled through Hyde Park. Today we stopped to listen to the soap box orators at Speaker's Corner, bellowing forth their widely varying views on politics and religion. One chap in particular, was extremely odd. A chubby, hatless, toothless fellow of about fifty. He was dressed in a dirty fuzzy sweater and once-white trousers. The only recognizable word that he roared intermittently was "somewhere." Every time the explosive word came out, the large circle of onlookers joined in a gleeful chorus of "somewhere!"

20 October: Left Liverpool Street at 1000 hours. Arrived back at base 1545 hours due to derailment of another train. Went straight to work on flight line, pre-flighting ships radios and interphone connections.

A buddy and I teamed up to pre-flight a plane. While I was checking the flight engineer's interphone, he was examining the fuses on the bulkhead in front of the bomb bay. This should never be done while the power is switched on. He unintentionally caused a short circuit resulting in a vivid flash of flame.

I stood staring and waiting, not so much scared as angered, because the accident had been so unnecessary. Fright came later on thinking about the incident. There were twelve 500-pound demolition bombs on board. And all around us were full oxygen tanks. Even the slightest leak from one of these— not at all unusual—could have triggered a massive explosion.

Bitterman, DeBrown, Raymond, and Shilton were working in and around a ship when the combat crew came aboard. The flight engineer was tinkering with his guns in the upper turret and accidentally touched off a short burst of gunfire. Luckily no one was injured.

21 October: Spent last night on the line until early morning. Just after the group's last plane was in the air and they were circling the field, word came over the radio: "Boston." Mission scrubbed.

22 October: 1840 hours. Sounds like thunder overhead, R.A.F. bomber command planes are streaming out in force. Some place in Germany will catch hell tonight.

Red signal at 1945 hours. Searchlights probing the night sky all around. A German bomber dropped flares. Cloudy sky. We can hear him wandering about overhead. Antiaircraft fire to the south of Horham, probably Ipswich.

23 October: BBC announced London was bombed last night for the seventh night in succession. VHF radio set brought into radio shop for repairs. It had apparently been shot up by guns of a nearby ship.

Party on tonight, first anniversary of activation of the 95th Bomb Group. Beer hall, recently opened, seems to be going great guns. Haven't been there yet. The boys say the beer is quite potent, and there are signs that this may be so. As for me, I don't care much for warm 'arf and 'arf.

24 October: Tried again for combat crew status, radio operator-gunner. Asked for waivers on age and color-blindness but was definitely turned down. I'm on the ground for the duration, and far luckier than I have any right to be.

Purple warning 1940 hours; red alert at 1947 hours. Bombing and ack-ack (antiaircraft fire) in direction of Norwich and Great Yarmouth. Tannoy order repeated red signal, directed all lights to be switched off despite the blackout curtains. This was unusual, but there were no further developments although we could hear the Jerry bombers wandering around overhead.

25 October: First Christmas mail arrived today, causing much joy in squadron. I received four letters and six packages!

27 October: Awakened by much noise. Someone tried to light the reluctant stove by using a bottle of high-octane aviation gasoline!! Naturally it blazed right up, burning the holder's hand. He threw the bottle away from him; it hit the floor next to Dixon's bunk, across the aisle from mine. Flames licked the floor. Someone tossed a blanket over them. It also began to burn merrily. More blankets were thrown and eventually smothered the fire, but not before Dixon's bed was badly charred and his shoes set on fire.

Only yesterday Dixon was involved in another and potentially much more dangerous fire on the flight line. He was about to work on a ship's radar. A large puddle of gasoline had been spilled on the concrete hardstand directly under the B-17s nose. Apparently someone had cleaned the portable generator with gasoline, and when the "putt-putt" was started up, a spark caused a fire. Luckily, the ground crew was able to get fire extinguishers from the ship before the blazing generator touched off the gas on the hardstand.

3 November: Today was swing-shift, 0900 to 1900 hours. Arrived on the line to find the ships scheduled for today's mission already pre-flighted and so I had little actual work until the group's planes returned from Wilhelmshaven about 1600 hours. Worked on miscellaneous tasks until about 1900 hours. Heard the constant drone of R.A.F. bombers going out again in the gathering dusk.

5 November: As Jack Shilton and I left the radio shack for the day and started back to the barracks, a red alert flashed. Directly afterward came the sound of ack-ack fire. The sky was streaked with dozens of searchlight beams although they seemed weak in the moonlight. The *hrumm-hrumm* of Jerry bombers could be heard as the Germans dropped chandelier flares on three sides of our airfield and others drifted down not far away. Very soon it was almost as bright as day on the ground. Then the Jerries unloaded; luckily their bombs exploded some distance off. Very soon came the hum of night-fighters going after the Germans. A red flare zoomed up from the control tower, a belated signal to put out all lights and stop work on the airfield. By this time Jerry's chandelier flares were flaming all around. A base defense machine-gunner, mistaking the tower flare for a chandelier, let go a stream of tracer bullets at it.

Now the night-fighters were busy ... tracer bullets cut dizzy patterns through the night sky. Bursting ack-ack shells were also very plentiful. Some fellows claimed at least six Jerry bombers were shot down. I don't know. We eventually reached our barracks with the show still going on. All the lights were out because someone with brains had thrown the master switch. A little later the all-clear siren sounded.

Usually there's a period of five or ten minutes between the white alarm and Jerry's arrival. Just lately he's arrived almost with the white warning. Presumably he flies low over the North Sea to avoid radar detection, then climbs at the coast to go to work. But he's been consistently considerate in one respect. He comes early, and often only once in a single night, so we can all go to sleep undisturbed.

9 November: Explosion about 0500 hours. I didn't even hear it. Said to result from bombers of another group colliding during assembly and burning as they fell. The bombs exploding as they hit the ground. Pitifully few survivors from the two crews involved.

21 November: Forty-eight-hour passes issued in time to catch truck at 1520 hours for Diss then to London by train. Spent the night at the Columbia Club. Al Higgins and I shared a room with a couple of American airborne paratroopers. They'd been forty-two days crossing the Atlantic! Their small steamer started out in a westbound convoy, developed engine trouble, turned back in mid-Atlantic, returning to Halifax, Nova Scotia, for repairs and to await another convoy. Their only freedom was an hour's daily walk along the dockside. And we thought our five days' trans-Atlantic voyage on the converted passenger liner *Queen Elizabeth* was tough!

Airborne paratroopers' work is really rough; they are infantry, carried in gliders. It's a young man's job, but one of these fellows is thirty-four years old.

I went for a long walk in the St. Paul's Cathedral area. Neither the cathedral nor the buildings facing it had been badly damaged. On the other three sides, however, virtually nothing was left standing. Just a huge desert of broken bricks, caved-in walls, steel girders twisted by the heat, and very little wood; that had been consumed in the firestorms. Here and there odd things came into view; high up on a jagged wall a toilet bowl was held in place by its pipework ... no floor ... no ceiling. What a horrible experience for these unfortunate Londoners. And we are here to do the same thing to the Germans.

28 November: On a recent mission (19 November) one of our Forts banked too sharply at low altitude just after take-off and crashed about a half mile from the hangers. It instantly burst into flames. Most of the bomb load went off in ragged explosions. Fifty-caliber bullets shot all over the immediate area. The entire crew was killed, of course.

I'm assigned temporarily to SBA (blind landing approach) receiver work. It is to be installed in a number of our planes. Five months ago I went to R.A.F. Cranwell, Lincolnshire, to study the subject.

1 December: Tonight purple warning was followed almost immediately by red alert. Bombs falling somewhere nearby as occasional concussions can be felt.

2 December: Spent all day on the line, modifying jackboxes. Got soaking wet, thoroughly dirty and cold. Red Cross Club mobile, with its steaming hot coffee and creamy doughnuts, was a very welcome sight, and enjoyable break from the bitterly cold east wind that blows straight across the airfield from the North Sea. Returned to the radio shack hours later and found orders to suspend all SBA work!

Rumors say a P-47 Thunderbolt crashed about five miles away today. Didn't see it, although it is probable. We often see P-47s and P-38 Lightnings practice-raiding the field and buzzing the control tower. Those planes can f-l-y!

4 December: R.A.F. Bomber Command Lancaster made an emergency landing on our field this morning while returning from a night raid. It was badly shot up. When our ground crews lifted the tail gunner out from his shattered rear turret, they found he'd been shot eleven times, once squarely between the eyes. The Germans may be getting a beating, but they still fight back.

THE DAY TIME STOOD STILL

Ruby Gooderham

Friday, 19 November 1943, dawned clear, cold, and frosty. At that time my husband Victor, two-year-old daughter Ann, and I lived in Green Farm Cottage, Redlingfield. It was a tidy farm cottage with a thatched roof, and my husband worked on the neighboring farm. I was expecting our second baby the following month.

Redlingfield, about three miles from Horham as the crow flies, was on a direct line with the main runway at Horham airfield. We used to watch the big four-engined bombers as they took off in the early morning, and we saw them return from their bombing raids in the twilight of the evenings. If the wind was in a certain direction the Fortresses used to fly directly over Redlingfield, one after the other at low altitude, as they came into land or when they were taking off.

We often saw the American airmen in the village during their off-duty hours either in their jeeps, trucks, or on their bicycles. Many local people did their laundry for them, and it was often amusing to hear the villagers discussing the different prices charged for different items of washing.

That Friday morning my husband had gone to work in a nearby field with the farm horses. The planes were taking off on another raid when about 8:30 A.M. one of the huge bombers failed to gain enough height for some unknown reason, and, with a full load of fuel and high-explosive bombs, crashed to earth and immediately exploded very close to our cottage. It completely demolished a nearby house, which, very fortunately, was unoccupied at the time.

The first indication I had that something terrible was about to happen was a terrific high-pitched screeching sound of a falling plane. I was standing by the open kitchen window at the time, having just let our cat in. As the screeching grew louder and louder, I just stood there, frozen with fear. Then I was hurled bodily backward against the kitchen table by the blast from the exploding bomber. Falling plaster from the walls and ceiling filled the room with clouds of choking dust, doors were blown from their hinges, the thatched roof of our cottage was set on fire, large trees outside our home were flattened in an instant by the tremendous blast, chunks of white hot metal from the exploding bombs were flying and falling everywhere, and parts of the burning plane were blown into our house and garden by the force of the explosion. It was an absolute miracle that Ann and I were mercifully unharmed. She appeared to be stunned as I picked her up from the rubble and rushed her outside to safety in her pram.

My husband had watched, horror-stricken, as he saw the Fortress plunge to the ground and explode almost in our back garden. He immediately ran across the fields to our burning home, fearing the worst. At the scene of the crash he saw the dreadful sight of the pitiful remains of the bomber's crew. A few heads, arms, and legs, all blown to pieces and scattered haphazardly among and near the burning wreckage was all that remained of what had been ten human beings a few minutes earlier. It was a shocking sight, but he was immensely relieved when he saw us and that we had survived virtually unscratched.

The American Air Force and British fire engines, ambulances, and crash tenders were very quickly on the scene, but there was little they could do except put out the fires from the blazing fuel, collect the human remains for burial, and gather up the shattered remnants of the bomber that had been scattered over a wide area. An American ambulance from the base took Ann and me, suffering from shock, to my parents' home in Redlingfield.

Our home was partially destroyed and we'd lost most of our possessions, including all our wedding presents in the fire, but we eventually received compensation to cover our losses. The village folk were very kind. They organized a collection for us to buy clothes and presents for our new baby, a boy, who was born on 18 December 1943. We eventually moved into another tidy cottage at Redlingfield, and later on we had another daughter.

Our three children have now grown, married, and have children of their own. Even today (1986) I still jump with fear when I hear a sudden and unexpected bang or similar noise nearby. We thank God for sparing our lives on that fateful November day when ten young American airmen tragically died, so cruelly.

From the official police report submitted by police constable Henry J. Kimber: On Friday, 19 November 1943, at 8:30 A.M., an American Fortress, aircraft no. 231123, crashed at Green Farm, Redlingfield.

On the above date this aircraft was taking off from the Horham Aerodrome on a mission, when it failed to gain sufficient flying speed, and was banking to turn when it stalled, crashing about forty yards from the rear of the farm house.

A list of personnel of the 334th squadron crew was later obtained from the officer in charge of the Horham airfield as follows: Second Lieutenant K.B. Rongstad, pilot; Second Lieutenant W.M. Straw, co-pilot; Second Lieutenant R.E. Diete, navigator; Second Lieutenant J.E. Spicer, bombardier; Technical Sergeant G.E. Richmond, top-turret, gunner/flight engineer; Technical Sergeant G.U. Soreason, radio operator; Staff Sergeant C.E. Phinney, Ball turret gunner; Staff Sergeant L.M. Mirabel, left waist gunner; Staff Sergeant J.W. Tarck, right waist gunner; and Staff Sergeant K. Cosby, tail gunner.

REACTION TO DISASTER

Elvin D. ("Doc") Imes, M.D.

On Friday, 19 November 1943, I was a captain in the medical corps, serving as flight surgeon for the 335th squadron, 95th Bomb Group.

I attended a briefing that morning, one of about 300 that I attended during the war. The target for the day was Gelsenkierken. After the briefing I went to the line along with the ambulance and driver to watch the planes take off. That morning I was in the tower along with Lieutenant Colonel David McKnight, the air executive, and others.

Everything was more or less routine; it was unusually clear, no fog, chilly—not the normal English weather. The planes took off in orderly fashion until suddenly a plane failed to gain altitude and nosed into the ground about three-quarters of a mile from the end and to the left of the runway.

I was on the balcony of the tower, and I immediately jumped down and into my ambulance, which was a square English type with the steering wheel on the right. Dave McKnight had a jeep that he was driving himself. My driver, a boy from Tennessee, knew all the roads around Horham and Redlingfield, and we took off at top speed for the wrecked airplane, with McKnight right behind us in the jeep. We arrived at the scene of the crash within three or four minutes.

The road, I think, ran north and south. The plane crashed about seventy-five feet southeast of a house on the east side of the road. We stopped the vehicles about twenty-five feet south of the house. We could see the plane burning, and all that time there had been only the one explosion that had occurred on impact.

As I got out of the ambulance there was another explosion, a bomb I suppose, and a large piece of engine cowling landed about six feet from me in the road. I ran up the road north, and my driver stayed with the ambulance.

There was a kidney-shaped pond or almost a medieval moat (as I remember forty-three years later) and a bridge to cross to get to the house. Dave McKnight and I ran across this bridge. We went into the house, and I looked around the north side of the house at the burning airplane. There was a crewman lying on the ground at the corner. I don't remember his rank. I could see no marks on him, and I didn't know whether he was alive or dead. I took hold of his feet to pull him around the corner of the house. At that point there was another explosion, the blast of which knocked me back. When I got up and looked around the corner of the house again the crewman was partially decapitated. I then went back to the front of the house, the thatched roof of which was then burning, and went inside.

Inside the house I found Lieutenant Colonel McKnight comforting a very pregnant woman and a small child, both of whom were very frightened and hysterical. By this time the floor of the house was covered with glass, plaster, and other debris. We took them out of the house and into the ambulance.

There were still sporadic explosions as bombs were going off, and it was a complete nightmare. After a short time, the explosions stopped, and other base personnel began to arrive, running across the fields.

I left with the pregnant woman and the child and took them by the base hospital, because the woman was complaining of abdominal pains. After some time the woman's discomfort had subsided, and I determined that she was not in labor. We then took her to her mother's home in Redlingfield, and I advised her to see her own physician or obstetrician.

THE GOOD SAMARITANS

Earl Underwood, Tail Gunner, B-17F 230135, "Trouble Shooter," 334th Squadron

On 24 July 1943, the briefed target was the heavy water plant at Rjukan, Norway. This installation was believed to be connected with Nazi Germany's experimental work (relevant to the atomic bomb, as we learned later).

During our climb to altitude, we had our customary 10,000 feet check for all personnel and equipment. All went well until I discovered I wasn't wearing my "Mae West" life jacket. Frantically, I checked all around the tail-turret area and inquired, via interphone, if the other crewmen had a spare. No luck, but I knew from that moment on who would be the first in line in the queue of ten to get into the first of two life rafts if we had to ditch in the sea.

After a long six-hour flight, we bombed our primary target with good results and turned for home. We then came under attack by German fighters and were forced out of formation. Lieutenant McPherson, our pilot, then told us to hang on as he pointed the plane's nose down and dived toward the sea at a tremendous speed. A fighter tried to follow us, but our firepower and the speed of our dive obviously changed his mind, and he finally gave up the chase.

Shortly after we'd leveled out and got on course for the long haul back to England, we spotted a 390th Bomb Group B-17 down in the sea. The familiar "Square J" on the plane's vertical stabilizer was clearly visible as we flew over, seeing the crew clambering into their life rafts. We then saw a small fishing boat not too far away, but out of sight from the ditched Fortress. As we flew at low level toward the boat, the fishermen must have thought we were about to attack them because one of the crewmen hastily climbed the boat's mast and waved a Norwegian flag above his head.

We circled the boat, then flew toward the downed plane, then back to the boat. We did this two or three times until they got the message and followed us. As we left the scene, the last we saw was the boat picking the B-17's crew up from their life rafts.

It was a very satisfying feeling to know we had helped in the rescue, but we now faced the worry of getting home ourselves because we had used up a considerable amount of our dwindling and precious fuel, even during that short time.

However, after twelve hours' total flying time, during which we covered 1,800 miles, dear old "Trouble Shooter" brought us safely home to Horham. I never thought a B-17 could fly so far on gasoline fumes.

THE GREAT DOUGHNUT FEAST

Emerson Kuder, Group Gunnery (N.C.O.)

During the latter half of 1943 I recall several air and ground crew members of the 412th Squadron were enjoying the regular card game in our Nissen hut, shooting the bull about anything and everything, when somebody happened to mention, very wistfully, how much he missed the delicious taste of some real, homemade doughnuts.

It so happened that one of my civilian-life occupations before the war was as assistant to a baker in a large restaurant, and I'd help make many large batches of fancy doughnuts. The next day I went to the aircrew mess and persuaded the head cook to lend me a recipe for doughnuts, which I subsequently converted down to a four-dozen batch.

That evening I told everyone in the barracks if they could "acquire" the necessary ingredients and cooking utensils required, I would make the doughnuts for them the next night. Then followed a lot of furtive scurrying to and fro between the two buildings with each man somehow making a raid on the aircrew mess. All the required staples and supplies that I needed appeared, including one of the mess tables.

The following afternoon I began mixing the dough in the pans, then rolled out the dough on the table. Things were going great. We weren't able to get a proper doughnut cutter, but a biscuit cutter and the brass cartridge case from an empty 50-caliber shell (which had been boiled until clean) made the ideal substitute doughnut-cutter. The pot-bellied stove in our barracks was soon glowing red, a large pan filled with lard was put on top of the stove, and we were in business.

I made the four dozen doughnuts and handed them out. I was getting ready to tidy up when it seemed every enlisted man and officer in the 412th squadron suddenly appeared, all wanting one of our doughnuts. We only had the exact ingredients for the one batch, and I tried to explain I couldn't make any more. As if by magic everything I needed to make more doughnuts appeared and more men literally elbowed their way in with yet more supplies. I was making doughnuts until lights out.

The next day I received a reprimand from Captain Stone, squadron adjutant, for cooking in the barracks, the untidy mess and shambles in the barracks, and a severe reprimand for not inviting him to share in the feast.

But the reprimands, or "chewing-out," were well worth it just to see the expressions of delight and obvious pleasure on all those men's faces as they enjoyed the great doughnut feast.

LETTERS TO MOTHER

Harry Conley, 334th Squadron (The following are extracts from letters written by Harry Conley)

14 November 1943: As for our tour of duty, it is still twenty-five raids regardless of rank. It will take me quite a while to complete my tour as we have five command pilots in the group, which includes Bob Cozens and myself. We take our turn to fly as lead pilot. However, it will progress more quickly now as this week we are doubling the size of our group. Instead of having nine crews in our squadron, we now have eighteen, and from now on we will put two groups, 95A and 95B, in the air on all raids. That means each of us will fly twice as often, hot dog! What will happen after I've flown twenty-five missions will depend largely on the circumstances at that time. To be very frank with you, I'm not very anxious to go home. Quite a few of us want to stay over here and see this thing through. All hell is going to break loose over here one of these fine days, and we want to be here to see it.

20 November 1943: We all have our new crews and airplanes now, and we are in the middle of a prodigious training program. That means eighteen crews and airplanes to all four 95th Group squadrons.

These new replacement crews are filled with trepidation as to what the future holds for them. Evidently the stories that they heard in the states about fighting in the European theatre are pretty gruesome. They all seem to expect the worst. We, of course, just laugh at them and try to make them see that it isn't as bad as it's cracked up to be. I certainly hope they get a few easy missions to bolster their morale.

The base is very crowded now. We had to erect new buildings to accommodate them all. It is strange to see so many new faces. It makes the few remaining aircrew members of the original 95th Group, there are only twelve of us, feel like strangers. It's as though we're on a strange base.

You once mentioned German air raids and hoped that we all take cover in the shelters. While these raids are probably well publicized in the papers at home, they really don't amount to much. We are situated between two heavily bomb-damaged towns in eastern England, Norwich and Ipswich. The Jerries come over almost every night that they can, but these days it's only individual aircraft and they don't do much damage.

The British newspapers call them "scared cat" raids. All they usually amount to are solitary enemy fighter planes, with one or two bombs, tearing across the English coast at high speed, dumping their bombs and tearing for home before the British night fighters can get at them. They are certainly not bombing raids in the same volume or intensity of the ones we are carrying out.

For the past month, things have been a lot easier for several reasons.

Primarily because we've been doing a lot of blind bombing through the clouds. The clouds over continental Europe are anywhere from five to twenty thousand feet thick and are usually full of turbulence and ice. That makes it practically impossible for the enemy fighter pilots to get up to attack us in any great numbers, because fighter pilots, as a rule, are not good instrument pilots and fighter planes are difficult to handle under instrument conditions. Secondly, our fighter force over here has increased tremendously, and we get fighter cover during most of our raids. Fighter cover, however, isn't foolproof, but it does help to break up organized enemy fighter attacks. They still knock down a few B-17s, but not as many as in the early days when we went out unescorted in clear weather.

It's as cold as the devil up there now. We were out the day before yesterday, and at 27,000 feet, it is fifty-five degrees below zero. It is so cold that the metal on the interior of the B-17 sweats and the moisture forms a coating of ice on the inside surfaces of the ship. You probably wonder how we overcome the weather if the enemy can't. Well, due to some meteorological phenomenon, the overcast is rarely more than 10,000 feet thick over eastern England and usually has breaks that our fighters can climb through. No breaks, then we get no fighter support. Our bomber pilots, however, as you may recall my experiences back in the states, are well trained in instrument flight. We can assemble the Eighth Bomber Command on top of any overcast that has yet confronted us. Today, for example, the boys were out. It was raining when they took off, the ceiling was 300 feet, and they didn't break out until they'd reached 11,000 feet, yet all our B-17s made their rendezvous and carried out a very successful mission. It is absolutely amazing what these youngsters are doing over here. We fly as a matter of course in weather that back home would ground every aircraft in the country. That is the side of the picture that gets the least publicity, yet calls for the most skillful and precise flying technique on the part of our pilots.

9 December 1943: The training of our new crews is now complete. Tomorrow we take them across to introduce them to Hermann Goering's boys. I hope, for their sakes, they have learned their lessons well. This is one school where "A" is the only passing grade.

11 December 1943: Back in my quarters again after a long, long day.

Got up at 2:30 A.M. Had breakfast, attended the briefing, and then sat down for a couple of hours to study the plan and the maps of all the country adjacent to our route, made my necessary operational notes, and finally got out to the airplane five minutes before take-off time.

The boys had a real initiation. The weather was so bad here at the base that we had to assemble the group on top of the overcast. We took off in a snowstorm and finally broke out at 12,000 feet into the most beautiful sunlit scene imaginable. The top of the overcast was just like a model of the mountainous Sierra Nevada country. There were peaks and valleys and plains and rolling hills of clouds exquisitely tinted with the delicate colors of early morning sunrise. Everywhere, as far as the eye could see, straining B-17s and B-24s were emerging from the billowing mass, climbing to their assigned assembly altitude and joining their respective groups. A tremendously awe-inspiring sight. It is always a source of the greatest amazement and pride to me to witness such a performance and achievement. Those young pilots had taken off under the most adverse conditions, climbed for 12,000 feet, circling the base, through clouds so dense that they couldn't see their own wing tips; then they all came out on top in close enough order to form into group formation with a minimum of trouble. It is a tremendous tribute to the young crews and to the Training Command back home.

We formed our groups and then our combat wing with the 100th and 390th groups and slotted into our position as scheduled. As our navigator told us we were leaving the English coast and starting across the North Sea, it was undercast as far as we could see in every direction. We climbed on course and reached our bombing altitude about twenty minutes before we reached the German coast. As we reached our assigned altitude, we could see the undercast break away, and the Friesian Islands and the German coast were visible through the haze. We flew parallel to the coast for a time and then turned inland to our primary target, Emden.

Friendly fighters were supposed to meet us at the coast. We were met at the coast by fighters, but they were Hermann's boys and not friendly. We later learned that our P-47s had been jumped over the Zuider Zee by the Jerries, and consequently they were late in picking us up. The Jerries put on quite a show for a few minutes. There were only about a hundred of them, so our fight wasn't too bad, but our new boys were greatly impressed. The flak didn't amount to much, either.

The German fighters tried some brand-new tactics I'd never seen before. They attacked us head-on, in line abreast, with four to six twin-engine fighters in each wave, firing rockets and cannon. They flew right through our group, and it was effective as hell. Their single-engine boys stayed above us as top cover for them and pecked away at our stragglers. We lost only two planes, but we were luckier than some of the other groups. The attacks continued from the time we crossed the coast until we bombed, about half an hour in all.

Soon after leaving the target, our friendly fighters arrived, and as far as we were concerned the battle was over. We flew along and watched the opposing fighters dog-fight around us. Soon we were out over the sea, and the clouds once again formed below us. We started our let-down, and by the time we'd reached the English coast, we were at cloud level. Fortunately we found a gap and immediately spiraled down. The ceiling was 2,000 feet, so we continued home with no trouble.

Just another day's work. Oh yes. We hit the target.

29 December 1943: Friday, Christmas Eve, the boys went hunting over France. It wasn't my turn to go, so I took a shotgun and went hunting in the sugar-beet fields and woods surrounding our base. Shooting was good, and I came home with two pheasants, three grouse, and a cottontail rabbit. That evening Colonel Gerhart returned from the hospital where he'd been confined for the past few days with a throat ailment. About a dozen of us had a special dinner with him in the Mess and a party full of good liquid Christmas cheer in his quarters afterward.

Christmas Day I staggered out of bed at noon just in time to eat an excellent meal at the Mess. Christmas afternoon, believe it or not, was spent behind the desk catching up on odds and ends. Then about 4:30 P.M., Grif Mumford, the group operations officer, and I went down to Ipswich to a really marvelous Christmas dinner at the home of a British couple who were being kind to us. We respect the British most highly, and they return the favor. They haven't much food to share, but they do it graciously.

We're out again tomorrow and it's my turn to lead the wing, so I think I'll get a little sleep. It just might help a bit. It will be a long one because we have a full gas load. That means around ten to thirteen hours.

INCIDENT AT KREMS

WHAT A WAY TO EARN A PURPLE HEART!

William Binnebose, Waist Gunner, 335th Squadron

Our plane was shot down on 17 August 1943 during the shuttle mission to North Africa. I was taken prisoner by the Germans on that date and held until released by American troops on 3 May 1945.

After being taken prisoner I was moved from one camp to another until mid-November 1943 when I was assigned to barracks number 35-B, Stalag 17-B at Krems, Austria.

On the night of 3 December 1943, I was in my bunk, still awake, when at about 2200 hours I heard several rifle shots fired somewhere near the barracks, close to the rear barbed-wire fence. Someone then said that two American airmen were attempting an escape.

The shooting continued. Then I heard screams and yells of "Don't shoot! Kamerad!" Screams of pain were heard as someone was hit by the shots.

I'd counted about thirty shots when I said to my buddy, Albert Bergeron, the tail gunner on our crew, "Let's lie on the floor, some of those shots sounded mighty close." I'd just pulled myself up into a sitting position when I was hit in the right buttock by one of the stray rifle shots. I rolled from my bunk to the wooden floor, yelling to Albert I'd been hit.

The firing continued as I lay on the floor with my hand on the wound. My hand was covered in blood as I held it up to show my buddies to prove I wasn't fooling. I tore my underwear open and felt around for more blood or pain to determine where the bullet had come out. There was only one wound; the bullet was lodged somewhere inside me.

Several of my buddies then rolled me onto a blanket, and escorted by one of the German guards, they carried me to the camp dispensary. The people at the dispensary then advised the camp hospital, about half a mile from the actual POW camp, to prepare the operating room.

I was transferred to a stretcher and carried to the main gate of the camp. There I had to wait for about forty-five minutes on that stretcher, in the snow, with just a thin blanket over me, for the two boys who'd made the escape attempt. When the other two stretchers eventually arrived, the gate was opened, and we were carried to the hospital.

On arrival it was found that one of the escapees had died from his wounds, and the other, named Ralph La Voie, had been shot through both legs. He was operated on first. In the meantime I was taken to the x-ray room. I was then operated on by a French surgeon who was also a prisoner of war.

Apparently, the bullet had lodged in my stomach between the intestines, and I was on the operating table for almost three hours. After three months' recuperation at the hospital, I was returned to the camp and barracks 35-B at the end of February 1944.

THE LONG ROUTE BACK

Richard M. Smith, Pilot, 336th Squadron, and Jerry Eshuis, Ball-turret Gunner

On 30 December 1943, our crew was briefed for its thirteenth mission. The target was Ludwigshaven, Germany, about forty miles from the German border with northeastern France, a relatively short mission.

It was a beautiful, late December day, clear skies, no enemy fighters in sight, the flak was comparatively light, and as we hit the target and turned for home, we were in a good frame of mind. Our B-17, 230674, "Destiny's Tot," was functioning smoothly when suddenly number 4 propellor "ran away" as the engine took a flak hit. We tried in vain to feather the prop, but there was insufficient oil pressure to do so. As the 95th Group was the last to bomb the target that day, we soon found ourselves all alone at 28,000 feet straggling far behind the formation. The frustrating thing was that although we could

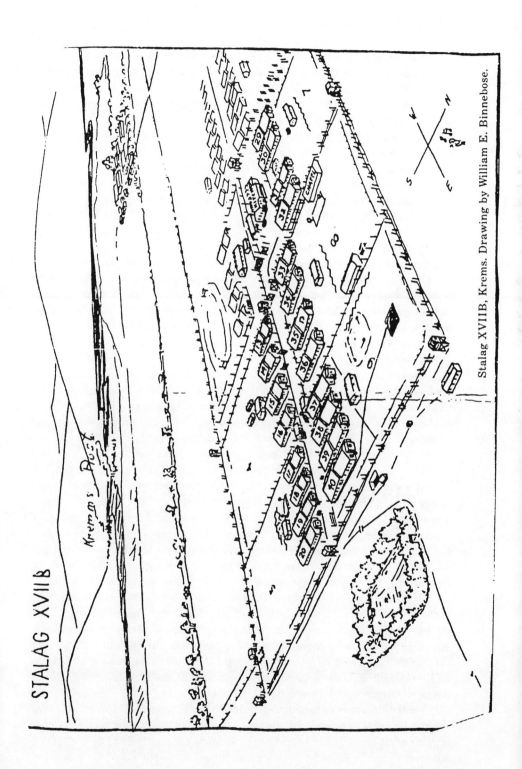

STALAG XVIIB

Krems Düst

Stalag XVIIB, Krems. Drawing by William E. Binnebose.

see our escorting fighters clearly, covering the withdrawal of the main bomber force in the distance, we couldn't raise any of them on the radio to come back to give us a little personal attention.

We decided to get down to the deck as quickly as possible to try and hedge-hop our way home. We had reached about 15,000 feet when we were intercepted by an Me 109 and six Fw 190s. A furious air battle instantly developed, but it was all over in about eight or ten minutes. "Destiny's Tot" was quickly reduced to a flying wreck by the well-coordinated fighter attacks. The radio room was on fire, my instrument panel was completely gone, there were large holes in both wings, and the intercom was shot out. There was no alternative but to hit the alarm bell as I maintained level flight as best I could to enable everyone time to buckle up and get out.

To this day I recall every move I made in bailing out of the nose hatch, pulling the ripcord after a free fall and really whacking into the legstraps of my parachute harness as the canopy blossomed out above me. The sudden, profound silence after the deafening din of the battle made the war seem a million miles away. As I drifted in space an Me 109 approached and circled me. I was terrified that he was going to open fire on me, but the pilot merely dipped one wing and waved so I waved back at him. Then the ground appeared to rise swiftly to meet me.

I landed in a field that was being plowed by a very elderly French farmer. He had a yoke of oxen pulling a single blade plow with which he buried my chute and flying boots. He then indicated one direction, saying "Alleman" and in the opposite direction he said "Kamerad." At that time I didn't know what "Alleman" meant but I sure understood "Kamerad," and after thanking the farmer profusely I took off in that direction toward a small forest.

After walking cautiously through the heavily wooded area, I concealed myself in an overgrown hedgerow, well hidden from all four directions. It was really quite a beautiful winter afternoon and I decided not to travel further across open countryside in broad daylight. Presently I heard the sound of distant shouting, motorcycles and trucks as the German search parties combed the area for my crew members and me. In the distance I also heard the distinct whistling and rumbling of a train and immediately thought the railroad would be a source of transport if I wasn't discovered by the German military first.

Darkness fell eventually and I'd decided to make a move in the direction of the railroad when I heard muffled voices approaching. Three men in civilian clothes stopped right outside my hiding place and indicated that I come out. All three carried a handgun. One had a sack over his shoulder containing civilian clothes, which he proceeded to empty. I couldn't believe my good fortune as I swiftly changed into them. It transpired that the men had watched my parachute descent and observed my subsequent hiding place.

We then walked for about two miles in the direction of the railroad and eventually came to a small village that I discovered much later was Wavenieu in the region of Oise, northern France. I was taken to the local police station where the three men and the policeman talked incessantly, but they couldn't speak English and I couldn't speak French, so the conversation was quite one-sided.

All during my subsequent evasion, I was never told where I was nor the full names of my numerous helpers. Everybody was Jacques, Pierre, Alphonse, Paulette, or similar names. This, of course, was absolutely essential for the security of the French Resistance movement. If we were caught by the Gestapo, and subsequently tortured, what we didn't know we could not possibly tell.

Eventually the conversation ended. Evidently they were convinced that I was an Allied airman and needed their help. I was taken outside and crammed into the trunk of the smallest car I'd ever seen, and after an extremely uncomfortable one-hour journey over rough country roads, we arrived at a large farmhouse where I was overjoyed to be reunited with my co-pilot Bill Booher and Al Mele, our radio operator, who was of Italian descent and could speak a little French. For the first time we could communicate to some extent instead of using sign language.

However, we were told that the farmhouse was occupied by two separate families: one older couple was very pro-German and the younger French farmer and his wife were pro-Allies. We were close enough to the German border that this situation prevailed with many families and had done so over the centuries. Subsequently, there were many people of German extraction throughout the border area.

It was an eerie feeling to realize that one half of the household was harboring three fugitives and that the other half would be more than happy to turn us over to the German authorities. However, after two days in hiding, we were transported to a fairly large city, St. Just (unknown to us at that time), and accommodated in an unoccupied, but fully furnished house. We were told that the owners had gone south to visit relatives. We were under strict orders not to go outside in daylight nor to stand by windows where we might be seen. Our food was brought to us twice daily by Paulette, a young, blonde French girl who was married to the local Resistance leader, Captain Jacques.

While we were there, we were joined by Jerry Eshuis, our ball-turret gunner. He'd been wounded in the legs and back during the air battle, but his French rescuers had taken him to a local village doctor who had operated and stitched him up. Although the doctor had done a very admirable job for Jerry, his wounds were serious enough that they restricted his mobility considerably.

Jerry Eshuis recalls: We managed to down two of the seven German fighters during our rapid descent, but they proved too much for us. I bailed out at 12,000 feet and landed in a beet field near the edge of some woods, grabbed my chute, and hid in the woods that night. I'd been wounded in the leg, eye, and back, and was bleeding rather badly. By morning, weakened by loss of blood, I decided to take the risk of seeking help, and luckily quite by chance, it wasn't long in coming. I saw a boy, about my age, in the beet field apparently searching. I fervently hoped he was an aircrew helper, and fortunately, this was soon confirmed.

His name was Gervais Gorge, and he took me to his parents' home, cleaned my wounds with hot water, hid me in the barn under some hay, and brought me food and drink.

Gervais contacted the French Resistance, and the next day I was moved by them to a French castle owned by Count and Countess Baynast. A doctor tended my wounds and removed a large fragment of shrapnel from my leg. I stayed at the castle for about a week until I recuperated sufficiently to be moved on.

Richard Smith continues: We also discovered that our two waist gunners Robert Southard and Tony Onesi and tailgunner Tom O'Hearn had been so seriously injured during the air battle that they'd had to be turned over to the German authorities for hospitalization and eventually to prisoner of war camps in Germany.

An incident that caused us great concern happened when Captain Jacques visited the house and relieved us of our dog tags. Although we argued and pleaded with him, he was adamant. It was a case of give them up or we would have to continue on by ourselves. Very reluctantly we handed them over.

After our move to a new address, the home of Paul and Yvonne Beques, in St. Just (due to our previous neighbors asking too many awkward questions among themselves regarding the sudden increase in activity at the house, smoking chimney, strangers coming and going, etc.), it was decided we would go to Paris for the next stage of our escape. At this stage we had no papers, no dog tags, no identification of any kind, and quite scruffy and threadbare civilian clothes.

It was around mid-January when we walked to the center of St. Just to await our early morning transportation to Paris. What happened next could have been taken from a movie script, but it actually happened. A beautiful old limousine, from the late 1920s or early 1930s era, appeared and glided noiselessly to a stop. Its driver, a large unsmiling man, was the roughest, toughest, and meanest looking individual I've ever laid eyes on, before or since. As we got into the car he gave each of us a loaded .45 pistol and told us if we got stopped by German authorities along the way we were to start shooting and run. And he meant it because, as we no longer had our dog tags to identify us as Allied evadees, we would be lined up against a wall and shot as spies.

The first of several heart-stoppers happened at a railroad crossing at Beauvais when we were forced to stop to allow a very long and very slow freight train through. As fate would have it a large black German staff car pulled up right beside us complete with four or five uniformed German officers. They appeared to be in good spirits, laughing and talking among themselves. Had they looked sideways at us I'm certain our guilt would have been very apparent. It was an extremely tense seven or eight minutes while we secretly prayed for the freight train to pass because I'm absolutely certain that our driver was not a man who would answer any questions or take any prisoners.

We eventually arrived in Paris, and after he'd made a brief telephone call, our chauffeur delivered us safely to the tiny flat of a very delightful little old

English lady. Truly a super person. Obviously she couldn't look after all four of us, and after the traditional tea and crumpets, our hostess made a phone call. It was decided that Al Mele and I would be transferred to another address.

We made contact as instructed with another guide who took us to 34 rue Madelaine, an office building that had apartments on the upper floors. Al and I were billeted on the fifth floor, and we were to discover that the entire third floor had been taken over by a large contingent of German staff officers. Inevitably this led to more heart-stopping incidents during the next few days, but Alphonse and his wife, our hosts, protected us admirably.

During this period, we had several visits from the leaders of the French Resistance in Paris. They were extremely concerned at our lack of positive identity. They all lived in constant fear that the Germans would infiltrate one of their escape routes with a highly skilled English-speaking impersonator who would then betray everyone connected with the French Underground.

During our stay in Paris, we ate very well: fresh meat, eggs, cheese, butter, fresh white bread, lots of good wine along with fresh fruit and vegetables. This Underground section was well financed, enabling Alphonse's wife to go out into the countryside and buy black-market food. We spent lots of time reading, and on several occasions Alphonse took us to a nearby bar and to a local movie house.

Very early one morning I was told by a very pretty young French girl, about eighteen years old, that I was to be moved. I bade my friends Alphonse, his wife, and Al Mele a warm farewell and was taken by the young girl on the subway train to the Gare West, or west depot. On our arrival, two Resistance men gave me a complete set of ID papers. These included discharge documents from the French Army, papers to report for work in Germany in sixty days' time. I was given identity papers that identified me as a French geologist! We also received ration cards. In fact we got everything that all French people had to carry with them at all times.

After a long and tortuous train journey from Gare West, during which I changed trains and guides twice, I finally arrived at my destination, St. Brieuc, on the Brest peninsula. The city square was teeming with all kinds of German military personnel, Army, Navy, and Air Force, because the area was one of the prime candidates for the Allied invasion. The construction work to fortify the coastline and its approaches was very much in evidence. Following a comparatively short train ride, four other evadees and I were escorted by another young French girl to a very modest home near the village of Plouha where Germaine lived with her elderly mother. This was where we were to stay until the British Royal Navy came to pick us up from the nearby beaches. A Royal Navy gunboat, powered by electric motors for silence, could only come three nights in every month when there was no moon.

It was claustrophobic with all five of us crammed into one small bedroom. The window shades had to be permanently drawn because the road and the railroad to the coastal defense area both passed directly in front of the house.

They were both very busy with German military people going to and from work. We could also observe work trains with two flak cars just behind the engine and just in front of the caboose, with many cars full of laborers and construction material in between. Without my knowledge Al Mele, Bill Booher, and Jerry Eshius had also made the train trip and were then in the St. Brieuc area.

The BBC in London broadcast coded messages to the Nazi-occupied countries at 1000 hours and 1730 hours so that the local Resistance leaders were kept informed of developments. The first two nights we heard that the mission was scrubbed as high seas were running. Needless to say everyone was depressed, evadees and resistance workers alike. On the third night, jubilation! The Royal Navy was on its way.

The various resistance cells collected their small groups of evadees, a total of twenty-five evadees per trip, one trip by the Royal Navy every month. During our walk down to the beach, our guide led us through farmyards and pigsties to help fool the tracker dogs that the Germans used to patrol the beaches every night. We walked in single file in absolute silence through the darkness, and soon we could hear the surf. We all made it safely down a steep cliff and were directed to a cave about fifty yards from the shoreline to wait. If the Royal Navy didn't show up we were to be taken overland to the south of France for a long walk over the Pyrenees Mountains into Spain.

When the blinker lights showed up, we were elated! The first of the long-boats came ashore loaded with clothes, medicines, arms and ammunition, and other supplies for the Resistance . . . but no money! The boat returned to the mother ship offshore, empty of evadees to collect the money. Some way to fight a war!—with no faith even between Allies. Apparently the British and American governments were paying $15,000 for each repatriated national. We had one "wanted" French Resistance fighter and a very young and tough Russian tank commander in our group. We never learned how he got into the mainstream of the French Resistance.

It was a nerve-wracking situation sitting in that cold, dank cave waiting to be called to the beach. On the third trip, about 0200 hours, it was my turn with several others, and I recall I helped to row out to the anchored gunboat. Once we were all aboard and the longboats secured, we started for England. The date was 31 January 1944.

Once clear of the land shelter, the open sea became very rough and miserable. At times the ship's propeller rose up clear of the water, and we could hear and feel the tremendous slam as a large wave crashed against the bow. Only Bill Booher and I of the twenty-five didn't get violently seasick as the ship plowed its turbulent way toward Plymouth, A Royal Navy port on the southwest coast of England.

From Plymouth we went to London by train, and after a thorough debriefing and positive identification we traveled back to Horham, Suffolk. Full circle.

Postscript: Our navigator Louis Feingold and bombardier Warren Tarkington arrived safely back in England one month later via the same escape route. After the war I established contact with our top-turret gunner, Ken Morrison. He'd been hidden in a Frenchman's cellar only a few blocks from us in St. Just. Unfortunately his host, a good and brave man, was not in contact with the local Resistance movement, and Ken spent the next eighteen months in hiding at his host's home.

In June 1975 Jerry Eshuis and his wife went back to France to retrace his escape route and contacted several of his wartime French helpers. In 1981 Gervais Gorge, his first helper, visited Jerry at his home in Washington state to renew friendships and share memories.

I keep in frequent touch with the Beques at St. Just, and I've made trips back to see my helpers. The young lady who helped me in Paris was eventually caught by the Gestapo. They made a vegetable of her, and while she still lives physically she is unaware mentally. Alphonse and his wife, the couple I stayed with in Paris, have both died. In June 1985 the Escape and Evasion Society went back to Europe to be with our helpers to celebrate their liberation. It was a memorable occasion.

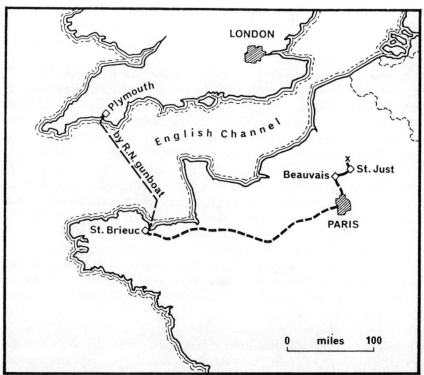

Escape route of Lieutenant Richard Smith and many downed flyers from France to England.

INCIDENT OVER HELIGOLAND

James F. Goff, Navigator, 412th Squadron

On 4 January 1944 we were briefed for a mission to Kiel, the 95th to be led by a pathfinder. Eddie Sharp, our regular co-pilot, had just returned from a 48-hour pass, was nursing a terrible hangover, and begged to be excused from the mission because he was really sick. Instead of excusing him, Colonel Mumford, our squadron commander, assigned Eddie to fly tail-gunner in the pathfinder ship to keep an eye on the 95th's formation.

As it happened we were flying left wing on the lead plane, and we could observe Eddie very clearly at close range. He looked as green as the North Sea and was obviously quite ill. On our return, as we passed over the small island of Heligoland, a few bursts of flak appeared, but we regarded them as insignificant. Suddenly the pathfinder ship heeled over and went into a steep dive; it had taken a direct hit. The pilot had been killed; the command pilot, Major Gale House, was severely wounded; and the flight engineer had also been seriously wounded.

Somehow Eddie managed to struggle his way frantically from the tail-gunner's position up to the cockpit and was able to pull the plane's nose up before it hit the water. He then flew the damaged aircraft back to Horham single-handedly and modestly accepted the gratitude of the wounded men and the rest of the crew. Later, Eddie was written up in *Stars and Stripes* and was subsequently awarded the Distinguished Flying Cross for his heroism.

Another story concerning Eddie Sharp: As navigator, I always rode in the nose, even on take-off and landing. It was a superb view from that position, and it was fascinating for me to watch the ground gradually recede from us on take-off and slowly rise up to meet us on our return to earth as we landed.

Tom Batcha was an excellent pilot and I had complete confidence in him at all times, so I had no qualms about landing and taking off in the nose. But on returning from one bombing mission Tom, without my knowing it, decided to let Eddie land our 26-ton B-17. Now I'm not criticizing Eddie's ability as a pilot—he was as good or better than most—but a pilot can get rusty without frequent practice in landing.

When Tom Batcha landed it was, more often than not, difficult to realize that we were actually on the runway, such was his expertise. Well, that day we hit that runway so hard that everything went flying except the airplane. The left nose-gun, weighing about 65 pounds, came off the hook and came crashing down, just brushing my forehead. If I'd been leaning forward a mere inch further, they would have undoubtedly had to ship me home in a box.

That was absolutely the last time I ever landed in the "greenhouse" regardless of who was at the controls.

ALL IN A DAY'S WORK

Lieutenant Deryk Wakem, Royal Navy (Ret'd.)

Tuesday, 4 January 1944, saw me serving aboard the destroyer H.M.S. *Verdun* as a sort of supercargo. I was a Royal Navy writer, which meant that there wasn't much to do apart from the times when we were called to "action stations," except act as the captain's secretary, (to complete and compile convoy reports from the ship's and captain's log, plus my own gleanings).

During January 1944 H.M.S. *Verdun* was assigned east coast convoy escort duty, north and southbound, through "E-boat alley" from the Thames estuary up to Britain's northeast ports. Among the many problems facing us at that time—besides the bitterly cold winter weather with sleet and snow driven almost horizontally by icy east winds, together with the endless pitching and rolling in the cramped and claustrophobic living conditions of a wartime destroyer—was the ever present menace of high-speed German E-boats.

When we were in action against them, I operated the A.R.L. plotting machine, which was very crude by today's refined technology. Basically it worked from the speed and direction of the E-boat's movements, and I drew in bearing and distances of targets that I received from two radar sets. This enabled me to calculate the enemy's course and speed and also to work out their angle of attack relative to our course.

Apart from our radar we often received reports from the R.A.F. and the American Air Force that the E-boats were leaving their pens at Ijmuiden, Holland, usually just before dusk, prior to a night operation against our convoys. Seated beside me were two radio listeners who both spoke fluent German. They listened on the E-boats' radio frequencies and reported the German squadron commanders' orders to their boats. The "confidential book" on all this had a remarkably comprehensive listing of the German Codes of Orders to the E-boats, e.g., "make smoke," "retreat to the north," "re-group," etc. The names of the E-boat commanders were also well known, and we knew exactly who and what we were up against. We even knew how the German commanders spent their time ashore in Holland, which was reported to us via the Dutch Resistance movement. I suspect that German intelligence had exactly the same sort of information on our chaps.

Some of our destroyers had quick-firing Bofors guns mounted on their bows. During one particularly vicious night action, I vividly recall seeing one destroyer's Bofors gun firing *downward*, at point-blank range, on an E-boat. A trawler used to lie astern of the convoy in order to pick up survivors of sunken ships. Men couldn't be expected to live for any length of time in those freezing waters of the North sea, especially during the winter months. Speed was absolutely essential in locating the small dots that were sighted bobbing about amongst the floating wreckage. It was very much a case of looking for a needle in a haystack. This is where the high-speed launches and motor torpedo boats of the R.A.F. air-sea rescue did such sterling work throughout the length of the war. MTBs quite often went in right under the noses of the German defenses to within a few miles of the enemy coast to rescue ditched Allied aircrews.

On 4 January 1944, we were part of a northbound convoy of twenty merchant ships. The escorts were the destroyers *Charleston, Verdun,* and H.M. Tug *Attentif.* The weather was fine with good visibility although extremely cold. The wind was force 6, northerly and increasing. At 1510 hours a Mayday call was received from a B-17 that was about to ditch in the vicinity of number 41 buoy, which was about five miles off Felixstowe. Speed was immediately increased as *Verdun* left the convoy and moved eastward. A signal was sent to commander in chief of the Nore and the flag officer at Harwich: "AIRCRAFT CRASHED IN SEA AT BUOY 41. INVESTIGATING."

A Walrus flying boat appeared and passed low overhead, heading for the scene. Within a very few minutes, the tall tail fin of the ditch Fortress, in a vertical altitude, was sighted. Drifting down to the south and away from the wallowing B-17 were two bright yellow circular inflatable life rafts containing all ten crew members.

The freshening wind was blowing foam from the near-freezing wave crests as *Verdun* maneuvered to pick up the rafts. This took some minutes as they were drifting quite rapidly. Meanwhile the Walrus had returned and dropped a smoke-marker into a huge patch of green florescent-dyed water.

From *Verdun's* bridge a Coston gun-line was fired from a .303 rifle, but the first two lines fired were carried away by the wind. On the third attempt, which also blew way, one of the B-17's crewmen jumped overboard and swam to retrieve it. He then struggled back with the line to the rafts, which were lashed together.

At 1535 hours both rafts were hauled alongside, and a scramble net lowered over the port side and, one by one, the ten American airmen were pulled up on deck. Both rafts were awash with the green dye, and some of the airmen were also colored with it. The were all taken down to the wardroom, given hot rum, and survivor's kit clothing. I then collected their names, rank, and number for entry into the log and convoy report.

My report reads: "Rescue of American airmen from Fortress No. 26098, 'Superstitious Aloysius,' 95th Bomb Group, Horham, Suffolk, was effected in twenty-nine minutes from the time they hit the sea until they were aboard the 'Verdun.' The B-17 sank after about thirty minutes in position; Lat.52 01.3 N. Long.01 37.4E. The crew were Lt. P.V. Milward (Pilot), Lt. A. Farris (Co-pilot), Lt. W.J. Milton (Navigator), Lt. A.R. Scroggins (Bombardier), T/Sgt. R.L. Spears (Top Turret), T/Sgt. E.S. Winstead (Radio Operator), Staff Sgt. C.R. McComber (Ball-turret Gunner), Staff Sgt. W.L. Weeks (R. Waist Gun), Staff Sgt. F.P. Miles (L. Waist Gun), and Staff Sgt. J.L. Kolarik (Tail Gunner). One of the crew members was still dry beneath his flying clothes."

The two life rafts were also hauled aboard and stowed between the two funnels. They were eventually landed at Rosyth dockyard, Scotland, for salvage. Souvenir hunters among the ship's crew came up with a pistol, lots of Horlicks type tablets, morphia syrettes, paddles, and some interesting cans of drinking water, canned in the midwest of the United States.

By 1650 hours we'd rejoined the convoy and an R.A.F. high-speed launch arrived on the scene. Astride the gun turret an airman signalled with semaphore flags, which seemed odd, even in those comparatively primitive times.

The ten airmen were brought up and transferred to the HSL, no mean task with the launch bouncing up and down some ten or twelve feet. They were taken back to Felixstowe and taken by truck back to Horham that same night.

Most of the flying kit was left behind with us, and it very rapidly appeared on the *Verdun's* crew. The leather helmets and sheepskin flying jackets were especially welcome during the winter, as we were about to experience some of the roughest and worst weather imaginable. In fact, sadly, we lost a man overboard from the after gundeck during one very stormy night.

There are two postscripts to this story. During the summer of 1944 some of the *Verdun* crew met, by pure chance, two of the B-17's crew in Southend, of all places. Secondly, the *Verdun* received a huge cardboard box of American cigarettes, enough for 120 men, from the crew of "Superstitious Aloysius."

My own history since that day was to be sent out to the Far East with the Royal Navy, return home, go up to Cambridge University to read geography, and became a schoolmaster at a public school. I stayed at the same school for over thirty years, became a housemaster, commanded the cadets, running the geography department, films, looked after cricket, soccer, and hockey, etc. Rather dull it looks in type like this, but a very full life at any time. I became a "Scandinavia-phile" about fifteen years ago and have camped all over Norway and Finland.

I'm in contact with the 95th Bomb Group Association in the United States. What I would like to do is follow up each of the B-17's crew from that day on the North Sea in 1944 until the present. Ambitious at this time but not impossible as I have already established contact with the B-17's former pilot and bombardier.

LONG TIME NO SEE

Lieutenant Deryk Wakem, Royal Navy (Ret'd.)

I wrote an earlier article about the rescue of the crew of B-17 "Superstitious Aloysius" by H.M.S. *Verdun* after their Fortress had ditched in the North Sea off the Suffolk coast. Following several letters to the United States, I managed to contact six out of the ten crew members of that B-17.

So, on Sunday, 14 September 1986, I had arranged to meet Peter Milward, the pilot of "Superstitious Aloysius." The rendezvous was to be the control tower at Duxford Airfield at 1300 hours.

I had not seen Peter since that afternoon of 4 January 1944, when we had all given the crew a hand up the scrambling nets of the *Verdun* and I had subsequently collected their valuables for safekeeping.

We now move forward a matter of forty-two years and find that 14 September 1986 was the big anniversary flying day and that twenty to thirty thousand people were also milling around the control tower.

Peter's idea that we should both display placards giving our names turned out to be a brilliant move. We shuffled through the crowds, holding up our cards and being watched curiously by the surrounding people. After a few minutes I made another foray and bumped into Peter, and we shook hands for the first time in nearly half a century.

Peter is, without a doubt, one of the most anglicized Americans that I have encountered. But then, what would you expect from the son of a father who worked for Rolls Royce, both in Derby and later in their brief American operation? Peter therefore has many relatives living in England, and it was to visit them that he made his three-week pilgrimage to England this summer, his first in fourteen years.

We walked and talked, to the roar of the modern jets on display and then stood back to admire the smoothness of the Spitfire, the Hurricane, the Lancaster, the B-17, and the Mustang. We then paid a visit to the B-17 "Sally 'B" in her hangar, and I videofilmed Peter, describing the good habits of the Fortress.

Peter then said goodbye to his cousins with whom he had been staying in Suffolk, and my wife and I took him to our home in Lincolnshire.

We continued talking until it was time to take Peter to the station for his return to London, from which he intended to take off for Elgin on another family-tracing expedition before finally returning to California.

The actual meeting made my day, of course, but it also answered several questions that had been in my mind, on and off, for those forty years.

The weather in the North Sea on 4 January 1944 was very poor; the tail end of a gale was still blowing, the seas were still quite high, and there was more than a hint of the snow to come. The tops of the waves were being blown away into long columns of spume down to leeward. When the Coston gun-line was fired across to the two life rafts, the first three lines were blown away. In the end, one of the American flyers jumped overboard and swam to pick up the floating line and towed it back to the inflatables.

The gallant swimmer turned out to have been Peter.

Only one of the ten men was totally dry beneath his flying clothes, I recorded at the time that I made out the report. Which one and how come?

It was Staff Sergeant McComber, the giant of the crew, and the unlikely ball-turret gunner. How these two events came about I heard from Peter Wilward for the first time at Duxford this year.

The first life raft had inflated with no problems and eight of the crew took off in her. McComber volunteered to stay with Peter and attempt to inflate the second life raft. As they stood atop the fuselage, rolling in the sea, they struggled with the equipment, especially the lines that had become tightened by immersion. It was still possible, however, to walk along the top of the Fortress from one end to the other.

At last the second dinghy was inflated and just before climbing aboard, Peter decided that it was time to "take a leak" from the stable platform afforded by the Fortress' fuselage. This he duly did with some sage advice from McComber as to which direction was downwind. Then they both dropped into the circular dinghy, cast off, and drifted down to join the others.

Almost thirty minutes later an R.A.F. Walrus arrived and dropped two large smoke floats. Peter said that it was a little unsettling to see them tumble out of the flying boat and land in the water nearby. Immediately afterwards the *Verdun* arrived and began the difficult task of catching the dinghies that were moving rapidly down wind to the southeast.

This was the moment when Peter got wet, and how McComber managed to stay dry in the lightly loaded dinghy. The other life raft with eight men aboard was full of water by this time, much of the gear having been washed away initially, while the rest was rolling about in the water-filled raft.

This had been their first and last flight in "Superstitious Aloysius," which had lost three engines on the way back from Kiel. As they dropped steadily back from the 95th's formation until they were alone, they were approached by two Spitfires. This alone produced its own doubts and problems. The Spitfires were obviously reluctant to approach too closely, unaware that the Fortress had ditched her guns and ammunition to keep themselves airborne for as long as possible. The Fortress crew, on their side were suspicious of the two fighter planes that were standing off at some distance. However, the Spits rolled to display their friendly markings and then, having been identified, approached more closely and remained with them for a time, until fuel levels forced them to leave.

As we drove away from Duxford, on that autumn afternoon, Concorde was flying across our path and the Red Arrows were tightening up their formation preparatory to giving their last flying display of the afternoon. Meeting Peter once again after our earlier, brief meeting on that winter's afternoon so many years ago was one of the high spots of my researches, and we have found a new friend, Peter Milward, a gentleman in all senses of the word. Stop Press: I have just received a letter from Eddie Winstead, the radio operator of "Superstitious Aloysius."

OBSERVATIONS

James F. Goff, Navigator
412th Squadron

I was assigned to Lieutenant Alden Witt's crew for the long trip to Schweinfurt on 14 October 1943. As we left the target area, we saw one of our planes in trouble and falling behind. I believe it was Lieutenant McPherson on his twenty-fifth mission. Lieutenant Witt immediately advised his crew that he was throttling back to stay with the crippled ship and offer what protection we could. But we knew that stragglers attracted hostile fighters like flies to honey and our action was futile. The heavily outnumbered bomber was shot down, and we watched it fall like a great wounded bird.

By that time we were attracting plenty of fighters, and our gunners were firing almost without pause trying to ward them off. However, Lieutenant Witt was able to rejoin the comparative safety of the 95th's formation eventually. Our crew claimed twelve fighters but I don't know how many they were eventually credited with, and I doubt very much if anyone can accurately determine which gunner shot down which enemy aircraft, especially when all our twelve guns were firing.

Following the Schweinfurt raid, through the remainder of October and November, I flew ten missions with my own crew (commanded by Lieutenant Tom Batcha) during which time the 95th Bomb Group suffered relatively light losses. On 13 November 1943, however, I found myself assigned to Lieutenant Robinson's crew for the Bremen mission. Before this raid we were briefed by the meteorology section to expect winds at our altitude to reach 120 mph.

We encountered a solid overcast, and it transpired that the weather boys were right about the exceptionally strong winds but wrong about the direction.

When we reached what we assumed to be the vicinity of Bremen, a brief break in the clouds revealed an unrecognizable coastline. It wasn't on any of our maps, and we then encountered heavy flak from a cloud-covered city that was later identified as Kiel. But not knowing where we were, we didn't release our bombs and later dumped them in the North Sea on our way home.

During that mission we were attacked by about forty enemy fighters, and although the 95th didn't lose a ship, Captain Miller's waist gunner and tail gunner were killed by cannon fire while defending their B-17. I watched three B-24 Liberators go down in flames.

We'd been blown some 120 miles north of our intended course and had to fly against an extremely strong headwind on the return trip. We finally made landfall on the northern tip of Scotland and eventually arrived at Horham an hour and a quarter late. There were a number of ditchings in the North Sea due to fuel exhaustion, and I vividly recall all four engines on our airplane stopped, one after the other, as we rolled toward the end of Horham's main runway after landing.

One unfortunate incident occurred 19 November 1943 on a mission, led by Pathfinders, to Gelsenkirchen, Germany. Lined up at the end of the main runway, we watched Lieutenant K.B. Rongstad's Fortress, just ahead of us, lift off, and then we were rolling, one bomber every thirty seconds. Halfway down the runway I watched Lieutenant Rongstad's B-17 make a gradual left turn, then it suddenly fell and exploded in a ball of fire and black smoke behind some trees in the nearby village of Redlingfield.

We passed directly over the crashed bomber at 100-foot altitude, and as I looked down I could see the entire Fortress engulfed in flames. There couldn't possibly be any survivors from that fiery hell.

Takeoffs for the rest of the group continued without pause—one bomber every thirty seconds. We were shocked and shaken at the sight of that flaming wreckage but well aware that once committed, the "show must go on." The sudden and tragic loss of our ten comrades couldn't deter the mission of several hundred other men.

Ironically, the losses for the entire Eighth Air Force that day totalled just one—Lieutenant Rongstad's crew.

On 11 December 1943, a mission was scheduled, but our crew was about to go on a forty-eight–hour pass. When the orderlies came to the huts early that morning to awaken a crew for briefing, I decided to go with them to breakfast and enjoy some fresh eggs. Since I had no immediate plans, I decided to attend the briefing, just to see where the 95th would be going.

On my arrival Major Lindley collared me immediately and informed me that a navigator was urgently required for Captain Miller's crew and asked would I like to go?

"No, thanks; I'm on a forty-eight–hour pass," I said.

Major Lindley could have ordered me to go, but instead he told me that if I'd take the mission he would see that I got a forty-eight–hour pass anytime I wanted one. I remember thinking of my friend Bob ("Catfish") Wing who'd gone down on the Marienburg raid, but I said, "O.K., Major, I'll go, but if I'm killed during this mission, just remember that I'm coming back to haunt you."

The mission to Emden was considered somewhat of a milk-run so I wasn't really worried. After takeoff we climbed through the 10,000-foot overcast for group assembly above the clouds, always a hazardous and tension-filled procedure because of the everpresent threat and distinct possibility of a mid-air collision.

It was a really beautiful sight when we eventually broke through the comparative gloom of the claustrophobic overcast into an entirely different world of bright and brilliant sunshine. We watched bomber after bomber emerging in rapid succession through the clouds below us as we searched the skies for the familiar "Square B" identification of the 95th Bomb Group. We looked far and wide for our group but couldn't find them.

Eventually, when the great formation began streaming out across the coast we flew alone over the North Sea in pursuit of the lead wing. We were nearing the Dutch coast before we were finally able to join the 390th Bomb Group's low squadron and slide into the "tail-end Charlie" position—not the healthiest place to be.

We crossed the Friesian Islands and the German coast on our bomb run at the point where we were due to rendezvous with our fighter escort. At that moment fighters appeared in the distance ahead of us and a voice on the intercom announced, "Here come our little friends." We relaxed, but in the next instant we were shocked to see Ju 88s coming straight at us, four abreast. At about a hundred yards' range, they fired rockets and were immediately followed by Me 109s attacking from front and rear.

In their first pass, the took out every ship in the 390th lead squadron and two in the low squadron. I heard Captain Miller's voice on the intercom yell out, "Oh, my God!" and our ship immediately nosed over in steep dive. Thinking we'd been hit and were going down, Lieutenant Bowen, our bombardier, and I snapped on our chest chutes and headed for the nose exit hatch. As I reached for the emergency release handle and waited for the bail-out bell, I recall thinking, Damn! Fifteen missions and the odds have finally caught up with me. Now I'll be spending the rest of the war in a prison camp. Then our ship leveled off.

Bowen and I had been concentrating on the attacking fighters and hadn't seen the B-17s from the 390th's lead squadron suddenly plunge down directly in our path, but Captain Miller had seen them and his instantaneous reactions had saved us from an almost certain fatal mid-air collision.

Now we were all alone and taking a pounding from the German fighters as Captain Miller sought cover in some contrails; then he headed for the clouds below us. I never relished flying through clouds but what a blessed relief it was that day to see that white fluffy stuff close in around us and envelop our airplane like the protective arms of a loving mother.

The action had lasted for about ten minutes, and our crew was credited with three enemy fighters. In the safety of the clouds, Captain Miller called for a crew check. There was no response from Sergeant Petzack, our tail gunner, and the pilot sent one of the waist gunners, Sergeant Loren Fetter, back to investigate. The report came back that Petzack was dead and appeared to have been hit in the face by a 20mm cannon shell.

During the flight back to Horham, none of the usual chatter on the intercom was heard; the crew was quiet. We weren't indifferent to death, but after many missions we'd learned to expect it and to accept it.

Tragedy struck again, although to a lesser extent, during a mission to the well-defended port of Bremen on 20 December 1943.

In the heat of another vicious air battle with German fighter planes, our newly assigned ball-turret gunner wet his pants and shorted out his electrically heated suit. The temperature at our altitude was fifty-five degrees below zero, and we were unable to get him out of his turret until we landed back at Horham.

On the truck going back to Operations for debriefing he sat across from me, shivering uncontrollably. I remember that he looked directly at me and smiled, almost as if he was apologizing. The poor kid had frozen his feet so severely that both had to be amputated above the ankle. When we visited him at the base hospital later, he could still manage a courageous smile.

I'm still haunted by that brave lad's smile. And when I think of him and all the others like him, I am both sad and angry . . . innocent young boys doing a man's job. If wars have to be fought, they should be fought by old men like me, not by mere youngsters whose whole lives lie ahead of them.

There were other missions, some rough—Bremen, Solingen, Kiel, Ludwigshaven, Frankfurt—and some easy, Bordeaux, Pas de Calais, Paris. But one mission I sweated more than any since that notorious "black week" in October was my twenty-fifth and last mission to Wilhelmshaven on 3 February 1944.

It was a Pathfinder operation with bombing to be carried out at 23,000 feet but high, thick clouds forced us up to 28,000 feet and scattered the formation. The Thirteenth Combat Wing was leading the raid, and I was certain that the Luftwaffe would be all over us. However, our "little friends" provided excellent support, and an opening in the clouds at Wilhelmshaven gave us the opportunity for visual bombing.

As we turned off the target, our replacement ball-turret gunner began babbling incoherently over the intercom, then suddenly was silent, and unresponsive to our calls. We realized he'd lost his oxygen supply, and at that altitude couldn't survive for long. In order to save his life, Lieutenant Batcha left the formation and began a rapid descent through 25,000 feet of solid clouds during which we encountered snow, rain, sleet, and icing.

Forty minutes later we broke through the undercast at 1,000 feet somewhere over the North Sea. No other aircraft, friend or foe, could be seen. Lieutenant Batcha called me for a heading to England, and I really didn't have the foggiest idea of our position except that we were over the North Sea. Perhaps it was an educated guess or pure luck, but I told him to take a heading of 242°—a number I've never forgotten. We flew that heading all the way back and came in right over Horham Airfield. My combat tour was over; I had beaten the odds.

I thought back to those many crewmen who hadn't been so fortunate. It was always a very sad and moving sight to watch a four-engined bomber sustain fatal damage—from either flak or fighters, and go down, and I certainly witnessed my share. But it occurred to me that there was a marked difference in watching the demise of a B-24 Liberator as compared to a B-17 Fortress. The end of a Liberator appeared to come suddenly, ugly and rather clumsily. In marked contrast the death of a Fortress seemed to happen slowly, gracefully, and with great dignity. It was like watching a large, beautiful eagle, mortally wounded but still proud and gallant to the end.

I departed Horham on 12 February 1944, but not with the elation I'd anticipated. Two days earlier, 10 February, the 95th had lost seven bombers over Brunswick including the crews of Tuberose, Kelly, Cole, Huddleston, Bowman, and Pierce, all good friends of mine.

THE BRUNSWICK STORY

Charles A. Wayman, Bombardier, 336th Squadron

The weatherman's predictions held good and 11 January 1944 dawned as a bright, clear winter day. As usual the bombers circled almost endlessly, straining for altitude over eastern England to get into formation and alignment in the specified formations, heading east across the cold and forbidding North Sea. The strike force was a big one, some 550 B-17s and B-24s strung out in a bomber stream some seventy-five miles in length, hanging like motionless insects in the cloudless eastern sky.

While crossing the North Sea, we performed the usual preparatory chores such as arming the twelve 500-pound high explosive bombs and clearing our 50-caliber machine guns. Then a bad omen appeared. Our nose gun jammed as we attempted to clear it. Even the efforts of our expert waist gunners couldn't correct the malfunction.

Apart from that, things went smoothly as we crossed the coast of Holland and approached the German border. Our pilot, Lieutenant Jim Foley, was at his best in holding formation, with one wingtip almost tucked into the adjacent B-17's waist gunner's window. Our co-pilot, Lieutenant Paul Keith, made the rounds on the intercom to ensure that all positions were ready. Down in the nose position with me, navigator Lieutenant Chuck Shaughnessy checked the flight path to confirm that we were on course as planned. The sun was in our eyes and Brunswick was ahead.

Thirty minutes short of the target disaster struck. The Navigator and I noticed our instrument needles flopping around wildly. We checked our electrical connections, including the intercom, and found that nothing worked. We quickly scrambled up the crawlway to tell the pilot. The failed electrical system meant that we couldn't operate the gun turrets, couldn't communicate, and would have to crank open the bomb bay doors manually.

Possibly due to the electrical system being out, Lieutenant Foley believed that one engine was "running away." He promptly feathered that one and dropped us out of the formation. That was the cardinal sin. We had been told to stay in formation at all costs. We became sitting ducks for the Luftwaffe fighters. Lieutenant Foley turned for England, dumped our bombs, and let down to "hit the deck" in order to avoid detection. Around 10,000 feet two Me 109s picked us up. We began to hear the dreaded sound of bullets and cannon shells striking along the length of our fuselage. Our own guns on top in the rear and the two waist gunners were also extremely busy at this time, banging away at both fighters at every opportunity. We could clearly see the fighter's gun ports glittering and flashing as they concentrated their fire on our B-17's midsection.

It was all over very quickly. Without electrical power to our gun turrets, we were no match for the German fighters and probably wouldn't have been even if it had been working. I saw a fire starting on one wing, close to the fuselage, grabbed a tiny fire extinguisher and entered the empty bomb bay. One side of the compartment, next to the wing, was burning furiously. The fire extinguisher had no effect whatsoever. The fire blocked access to the rear of the ship, so I returned to the cockpit and gave Lieutenant Foley the bad news. He promptly gave the order to bail out. Even though the crewmen in the rear of ship couldn't hear the order, they sensed the desperate situation. They all got out successfully apart from Sergeant W.S. Cadle who, we believe, was trapped in the ball turret. Two of the gunners had been wounded but recovered later.

Due to the fire, the nose hatch became the only escape for those remaining in the front section of the ship. The Engineer Sergeant Irv Rothman, radio operator Sergeant E.O. Carter, Keith, and Shaughnessy jumped. That left Lieutenant Foley and me. I wasn't in any hurry, because I'd heard stories of B-17s coming back to England with only one or two men aboard.

I knelt in front of the open hatch for an eternity, it seemed. Feeling Lieutenant Foley's boot on my back, I rolled out with my head down and my GI shoes tied to my parachute harness, as instructed.

Once clear of the nose hatch, the approved first move was a free fall to ensure clearing the propellors. People have always asked me if we practiced parachuting. The answer is, "No, but we listened very closely." I rolled over several times, waited until I was face up, and pulled the ripcord. The chute, with lines behind it, went up like a shot, and opened far above me. It was the most beautiful sight imaginable. But the chute looked so small way up there above me. I was swinging back and forth and I had no sensation of falling although I had heard that a parachutist descends at the rate of 1,000 feet a minute.

When I was on my back the force of the opening chute had split the front of one pant leg, the one with the pocket containing my escape map, compass, and emergency rations. I saw those extremely precious items floating downward.

Suddenly an Me 109 fighter started to circle me. He was close enough for me to see the Luftwaffe cross very clearly. The German pilot slid back his cockpit canopy to wave to me. I waved back, thinking of the stories I'd heard of airmen shot at while parachuting. I guess that his purpose was to alert the people on the ground by radio to come and capture the enemy *Terrorflieger*.

The greatest surprise was the sudden quiet. Now I could hear birds chirping and cows mooing on the ground. I landed in a grove of low brush and scrubs, cushioning my landing in a featherbed fashion. I was down all in one piece, with hardly a scratch, my shoes still tied to the chute harness. I unbuckled my chute straps, put on my shoes, and hurriedly rolled up my chute in order to hide it. I was in a small wooded ravine completely surrounded by plowed fields with nowhere to hide.

I looked out of my sparse hiding place and saw several people assembling and forming a line to march across the field in my direction. No guns were in evidence, but some of them had pitchforks in hand as they advanced toward me.

They were startled as they stumbled across my hiding place and saw me. They chattered excitedly as I raised my arms in surrender. It was then that I was thankful for the orders we received in the 95th Bomb Group: "Don't carry a sidearm on a raid into Germany. It will give them an excuse to shoot first and ask questions later." My raised arms came down as soon as the German discovered I had a pack of American cigarettes in my torn leg pocket. I passed them around, to the obvious relish of my captors, who weren't accustomed to such quality.

Instead of threatening me, the Germans exhibited more curiosity and self-congratulations than anything else. These rural people, I learned, were members of the *Volksturm* (Home Guard), whose duties included picking up downed enemy airmen. I learned later that my fate would have been far different had I landed in a city recently devastated by Allied bombing raids.

My captors marched me down a nearby road. The people were talking all at once, and the crowd increased as we moved along. I wasn't tied up or restrained in any way. At one point we passed an elderly German man. I was wearing my leather flying jacket with officer's silver bars on each shoulder. The old man saluted me, and I recall thinking he was probably a First World War veteran. I was too surprised to return the old veteran's salute. Further along the road, a German girl pedaled her bicycle beside me and proceeded to try out her high school English on me. "You're American?" "Yes." "Where are you from in the United States?" My answer, "Ohio," seemed to puzzle her. "Are you married?" I hesitated for a moment wondering if this girl could succumb to my charm and get me out of this. But I looked at the crowd around me and answered, "Yes."

Within half an hour or so, we arrived at a village with medieval archi-
tecture, just like a picture postcard. My captors marched me into the village
tavern and sat me down. Within a few minutes the proprietor set before me
a bowl of good potato soup and a glass of apple wine. I was the only customer,
and for the first time I could relax. Meanwhile, people were shouting on the
telephone in the next room.

Thus far I had seen neither a military uniform nor a swastika. But that
soon changed. The door opened and a sharp featured, angry-looking man wearing civilian clothes and a swastika armband strode into the tavern. He motioned for me to stand, started shouting questions, and waved his fist under
my nose. Each time I pleaded ignorance of the German language, he grew
more excited and angry. I figured he was the local Nazi party leader and had
to make an impression on the locals. I was relieved that he didn't bring an
interpreter to force me to answer.

A small, beetle-shaped Volkswagen chugged up to the tavern soon after
the Nazi had left. A youthful man in a grey German uniform limped in and
told me, in English, to come with him. I got in the back seat and off we drove,
making a couple of stops within a few miles to pick up other captured American
flyers. Finally, there were three of us as passengers in the car. We didn't know
each other and we didn't talk much because we had been warned that the
Germans sometimes planted spies among prisoners of war.

It was getting late in the afternoon as our driver dashed around the countryside, stopping at several well-camouflaged military bases, apparently to
find someone to take us in. One of the first towns we passed through was
Hamlin (fifty-two miles west-southwest of Brunswick), of Pied Piper fame. At
one stop, the driver pulled out his wallet and showed us photographs of American girls and other scenery that he said were taken at the 1932 Los Angeles
Olympics. Apparently he had been a member of the German Olympic team.
He said he liked the United States and its girls, a statement we resented. He
also told us that he had been in the Luftwaffe, was wounded during the Battle
of Britain in 1940, and had been invalided back to his home district for part-
time duty such as this.

We were finally dropped off for the night at a place where a number of
American prisoners were assembled. We received some food and a welcome
bed. That ended the exhausting day of 11 January 1944.

We moved on the next day by car and truck. Each stop brought forth a
growing number of prisoners, caught by the very efficient German dragnet.
By nightfall we filled a church basement, where we spent the night. In the
crowd were two or three members of my crew. All of us were unhurt, and we
were happy to be reunited. By that time we had German military guards who
took the opportunity to search us. That was the last I saw of my wristwatch
and leather flight jacket, now, no doubt, regarded by some guard as the spoils
of war.

We were then taken to Frankfurt by train. There, as the bustling city
went about its ordinary business, we rode through the city center in the back

of an antiquated streetcar. We were separated by the guards from the curious civilians staring at us from the front section of the car.

Dulag Luft, our destination on the outskirts of Frankfurt, was a large brick building surrounded by wooden barracks. There we heard conflicting opinions of what would happen to us inside—from "nothing to it" to "solitary confinement for God knows how long."

I was led to a bare cell containing a light bulb that was never switched off, a narrow bed, and a small barred window set up high on one wall. There was nothing whatsoever to do but sit on the cot or pace the bare floor and look at the square patch of sky through the window. We were fed porridge and bread through a hinged opening in the cell door.

The wait was mercifully brief. On the second day of solitary confinement, I was taken down the hallway to a large office and behind a large desk was a German officer, impeccably uniformed and speaking flawless English. He wasted no time.

"For you, Lieutenant Wayman, the war is over," he said emphatically. "You will be well-advised to cooperate with us so that you can be immediately shipped out to join your comrades in a permanent and comfortable prison camp."

I met a pained expression when I told the officer that, as he knew, we were allowed to give only name, rank, and serial number. He was brusque with me. "All right. You will change your mind after a few weeks in solitary here." I was escorted back to the cell.

Fortunately for me Dulag Luft had too many prisoners from the big raid to process. On the very next day, I was called back before the same officer. His mood was different, conciliatory. He offered me a seat and a cigarette. The questions came as though we were having a friendly chat. "What missions have you flown? What kind of bomb load were you carrying to Brunswick? How many Pathfinders (radar-equipped B-17s) were leading your group?" We sparred back and forth. My interrogator became more exasperated with each repetition of name, rank, and serial number. I thought to myself, how little I could tell him, even if I'd wanted to. At Horham all they'd told us was when and where to go.

Finally, the officer lost his patience. Perhaps he had to hurry on to his next captive, maybe someone more important than a deputy squadron bombardier. "All right," he said, "if you won't tell me, I'll tell you." He pulled a file from a desk drawer and began reading from it. He told me where I had been trained in the states, what my mother's maiden name was, when I had arrived in England, and when I'd joined the 95th Group. He also told me of some trouble with some Negro troops at a town near Horham, the name of our group commander, and the names of some of the targets of our raids. He was in error a few times, but I wondered to myself how the Germans could devote all of this effort to getting information on each of us, even though some of it probably came from U.S. newspaper clippings.

Within hours of this finale, I was out of Dulag Luft and, with dozens of others, riding the cattle cars of a train that was to take us on the several days' journey to our permanent prisoner of war camp, Stalag Luft I at Barth, Pomerania, far to the north on the Baltic Sea. It was the start of sixteen months in captivity.

THE WAY IT WAS

Louis Feingold, Navigator, B-17, "Destiny's Tot," 336th Squadron

After successfully bombing the primary target at Ludwigshaven, Germany, on 30 December 1943, we were attacked by several German fighters after being forced to leave the 95th Bomb Group's formation because of battle damage sustained over the target. Further crippling damage was sustained, and our crew had no alternative but to bail out.

Shortly after my landing in occupied France, I was joined by Warren Tarkington, our bombardier. We were extremely fortunate in making almost immediate contact with friendly and helpful French peasants, one of whom guided us to a heavily wooded area, telling us to wait while he went to get us some civilian clothing. When our helper returned, we lost no time in changing our clothes. Now disguised, we followed the man through the woods and out onto a main road. Another man on a bicycle then approached us and, in perfect English, said, "Follow the main road until you come to the overhead wires. I'll meet you there in two hours' time. There will be plenty to eat and drink."

This all sounded too easy and we didn't trust him. After he'd gone we asked our peasant guide what he knew about the man on the bicycle and learned that he owned a very large house. Remembering all the S-2 (Intelligence Section) advice against big houses, we decided to pay no attention, but after we'd continued down the road a short way, our guide stopped and asked a farmer, who was ploughing his field next to the road, about the man on the bicycle. The farmer was enthusiastic. We then decided he must be a safe bet, in spite of his house and apparent glibness. The peasant then left us, and we continued on up the road to our appointed rendezvous. It was bitterly cold waiting for him in our thin and somewhat threadbare secondhand civilian clothes. The mournful sound of the wind from the overhead electricity lines seemed to convey a warning of impending danger as we ate some candy from our escape boxes . . . and waited.

At the appointed time the man on the bicycle returned. He led us to a shack where we were given rum, tea and sandwiches. We waited for another hour or so, and then the remainder of our journey from occupied Europe back to England was arranged.

****

The following is a word-by-word copy of the Escape and Evasion Report dated 3 March 1944, London, England.

HEADQUARTERS
EUROPEAN THEATER OF OPERATIONS
P/W and X Detachment
Military Intelligence Service

SECRET—AMERICAN
MOST SECRET—BRITISH

E & E Report No. *419-420* APPENDIX "C"

The following information has been obtained from American personnel who have been repatriated. *If further circulation of this information is made it is important that the source should not be divulged.*

Evador's name, etc.: Louis Feingold. 2nd Lt.
0-747085 (419)
Warren C. Tarkington, 2nd Lt.,
0-673752 (420)
336 Bomb Sq., 95 Bomb Group
Date of interviews 27 February 1944

The man on the bicycle turned out to be the *Chief of the ST. JUST en CHAUSSEE* Organization. His name is *JEAN CROUET* and he is a chemical engineer for Ford. We spent the night of 30 December 1943 in his chateau.

On 31 December he took us to his factory. He makes camouflage paint for the Germans. This paint has been sabotaged so that it gives no protection from aerial photography. He is the regional sabotage chief and blew up fifteen locomotives on the night of 5 January. He had planned to blow twenty-five but he was stopped by a premature explosion. This information was given to us by *BERNADETTE*. He hid us in a tunnel under the factory until noon when we were fed in his office while the workers were at lunch. We spent the night and all of New Year's Day in his office. During this time truckloads of Germans searched the town for us. A month previously an entire Fortress crew had been spirited away by the townspeople, and the Germans had announced that they would shoot anyone found waiting in the field to help airmen.

That night we were taken to *M. HARRY, a baker*, in a house on the main street. We were here until 3 January when we returned to *JEAN's* for a day. On the night of 4 January we went to *M. and Mme. ROUSSEAU* near *HARRY's*.

On the afternoon of 6 January we left the town by following JEAN until a truck picked us up. Before he left us M. JEAN gave TARKINGTON his own shoes, slacks, and overcoat. He gave FEINGOLD another overcoat. From the truck we were transferred to cars which took us to CLERMONT. Here we were whisked into the home of *Mme. ODETTE and her son EDMUND SAUVAGE*. She owns a dairy. Her husband is a collaborater who went to Germany in '35. She lives with *GASTON LEGRAND* an ex-P/W who is a black market butcher. He spends his time shooting collaboraters, and our stay delayed a shooting as he did not want to add to our danger. Mme. is in such good standing with the German commandant that he lets her use his car. EDMUND had been watering the milk sold to the Germans for two years so that he could pass on real milk to French children. When the commandant found out he kicked him downstairs. He took advantage of his mother's good standing to steal cigarettes for evaders from the German HQ. When we arrived here on 6 January we met Lt. Edward DONALDSON (Escape & Evasion Report Number 460).

During our stay we visited *Mlle. BERNADETTE* every other evening. She is an organization member who speaks English and brought us books. She had been to Cambridge and was a governess in Scotland. She had been a dressmaker in CLERMONT for seven years. She twice took letters for our families. We also met *LUCIEN and MAURICE LECLERC*, sons of one of the CLERMONT's biggest businessmen (owns saw mill, etc.) and therefore exempt from the German labor draft. They brought us food and cigarettes. Their mother sent us each a good new sweater and shirt.

On 8 January we were joined by Lt. DONALDSON'S pilot, Lt. GLENN CAMP; the navigator, Lt. JARVIS COOPER, and a gunner Sgt. PARKER (E & E Number 461). On 20 January Mlle. BERNADETTE told us that four of us would leave the next day and the remaining two the following Tuesday. We decided that the three of us who had been there longest would go plus one of the remaining three who was lucky in a card cut. Sgt PARKER won the cut.

The guides came for us that very day. (Lt. DONALDSON was the fourth member of the party). We walked to the station while LUCIEN LECLERC patrolled in his car. We expected to go to *BEAUVAIS* but got off at *CREIL*. Here we were separated due to a mix-up. TARKINGTON went with PARKER and FEINGOLD went with DONALDSON. TARKINGTON spent the night in an unidentified woman's house. FEINGOLD was picked up in a Woolworth's and taken to a man's house. His wife thought they were leaving by submarine.

On 22 January we four rejoined each other at the railroad station. ED-MUND SAUVAGE and a guide of the previous day took us to *NOAILLES* by train. Here a car was waiting. The guides left, and the chauffeur drove us ten miles to the farmhouse of M. and Mme. *ROBERT ECKERT*. On 24 January a small truck took us to *ANNEUIL*, where we were taken to the home of our guide *M. GILBERT*, a justice of the peace. He had been an officer in the army and had escaped from Germany. He is the local organization chief. A doctor came to see TARKINGTON who had asked in vain to see a doctor at ECKERT's.

GILBERT took our pictures and made us identity cards. On 26 January, Sgt. REEVES, who had been shot down on 21 January, joined us. A *barber* gave us all haircuts. He later appeared as our PARIS guide.

On 27 January we drove twenty-five miles to the station and left for PARIS with GILBERT and the barber. We took the metro to the home of *Mme. SCHMITT*. Here we met *OLOF* and an English Typhoon pilot. We spent the day here (27 January). TARKINGTON soon told GILBERT that he thought OLOF was an imposter. GILBERT told TARKINGTON to interrogate him without letting him realize what was happening.

OLOF told me that he was a private in the U.S. Army making recordings for the BBC. He was shot down on a U.S. raid on KASSEL on 13 October. The crew was Canadian; they were flying a Fortress. I knew this story could not be true. I asked him where he took off, and he said IPSWICH. He could not remember his group, or the letter in his A/C. He said he did not live on the base, but in town with friends. The Army gave him no allowance for this, and he did not know the name of his friends. The BBC paid him $4 a day, and the army, $50 a month. He wrote articles in Dutch, French, and German and could speak the three languages.

The Typhoon pilot took TARKINGTON aside and told him that OLOF was no good. TARKINGTON told him he had reported this to GILBERT. The Typhoon pilot then told him that OLOF used to pose as a Norwegian, but as the Englishman spoke Norwegian he soon found out that OLOF could not. OLOF then claimed that his parents were Dutch, and that his father was in charge of a radio station in Norway.

CLAUDETTE came at dinner time. She told us that she had handled Lt. SMITH (E & E Number 349) and Lt. BOOHER (E & E Number 350) of our crew. After dinner she took TARKINGTON to one of the bedrooms to discuss OLOF.

She told me that the organization suspected him, but thought him a Dutchman trying to get to England through the organization. He was thought too stupid to be a spy. He had been sent to CLAUDETTE by an organization in North France. He claimed to have escaped from Germany.

CLAUDETTE was a domineering Wellesley graduate, thirty-three to thirty-five years old. She said the rest of our crew had left PARIS on 26 January and that she had looked all over North France for us. She had arranged a rendezvous to pick us up but we had not appeared. That afternoon at 1700 hours she took PARKER and DONALDSON to another house. She returned for us at 1900 hours and was to take REEVES at 2100 hours. We had been told we were leaving France by boat, but that OLOF was not to know this. He asked us our route, and we said Spain; he said that was the only way.

We got off the metro at Pasteur Station and went to *10 rue d'Ernest Renan* to the flat of *Mme. KOCERA MASSENETT*. Her husband owned a Czechoslovakian sugar factory and she had last seen him four years ago in Sofia. MASSENETT was her maiden name. CLAUDETTE was to return on 28 January with cigarettes. She came back twice with toothbrushes, razor blades, and cigarettes. We saw her for the last time on 3 February. She said she was going to the north of France and would not be back until 8 February. She had taken us to be photographed on this day. We stayed with Mme. KOCERA for four more weeks. *JEAN KOCERA*, her son, is in the organization. He is married to a Norwegian girl, and they have two children. *RAYMOND MAURET, 11 rue de Vieux Point, COURBEVOIE*, is always with JEAN. He is also a member of the organization. He drove a tank at Dunkirk and was evacuated to England. His father is a wealthy industrialist. Neither man seemed to have any information on *CLAUDETTE*.

MARCELL, a French Canadian, came on 16 February. He interrogated us for identification and told us that he was the new contact man. He was taking CLAUDETTE's place, as she had been caught by the Gestapo when OLOF got away from Mme. SCHMITT. He knew nothing of PARKER, DONALDSON, REEVES, or the Typhoon pilot. He said they had sent women to the houses in which CLAUDETTE had been known to place fliers. On arrival, however, these women had been arrested by the Gestapo. Mme. SCHMITT had also been arrested. MARCEL said the organization had carried on because CLAUDETTE was the only actual organization member caught. He returned on 21 February to take our pictures and said we would leave for the coast Wednesday or Thursday. This was the last time we saw him.

On 14 February JEAN and RAYMOND brought S/Sgt. FRUTH (E & E Number 462) and T/Sgt. VINES (E & E Number 457) into PARIS. We saw them for half an hour, before they went on to another flat in the same block. Later Mme. took us to visit them; they were staying with *ANITA LE MONNIER*. On 23 February RAYMOND and JEAN told us that we would be leaving the next evening. We did.

JEAN took us to the station on foot where we met RAYMOND who had Sgt. OLYNIK (E & E Number 431) and Sgt. QUINN (E & E Number 433). We had a compartment reserved for the six of us and reached QUINCAMP at 0915 hours on 25 February. We carried folded newspapers as a signal. We were turned over to *LOUISETTE and a man*. She took OLYNIK and QUINN, while the man took us to a house across the street.

We waited an hour and the couple returned. They took us to another house where we rejoined OLYNIK and QUINN. We remained here until 2000 hours. During the afternoon we were interrogated by *THE CAPTAIN*, a shrewd man who spoke excellent English. That night we were picked up in a truck. We kept stopping for people until we were a party of seventeen. As we passed along the road there were flashlight signals at regular intervals. At one stop, nine got out of the truck. We went on to an unoccupied farm, where Lt. Smith and the rest of the crew had stayed. It was prepared to receive airmen with mattresses and blankets.

At 2145 hours on 26 February two men came for us. We walked three kilometers to rejoin the nine who had left us. One, a Belgian, had been bound.

Here we met *THE CHIEF*, a short black-haired Canadian. He collected our money. We went down to the coast in a hand-holding chain. The tide was too high so we climbed back up the cliff and down another. Here the gunboat picked us up.

Lt. TARKINGTON was told that the Germans now check ration books as well as identity cards.

Compiled by DOROTHY A. SMITH, Captain, WAC

HEADQUARTERS
EUROPEAN THEATER OF OPERATIONS
P/W and X Detachment

Military Intelligence Service
SECRET—AMERICAN
MOST SECRET—BRITISH

10 March 1944

APPENDIX "B" TO E&E REPORT, NOS. 419 & 420

1. The following information has been obtained after an interview with two officers who evaded capture in enemy-occupied territory.
2. Further circulation of this information may be made, *but when doing so no information as to the source may be divulged.*

Statement of information covering period from 30 December 1943 to 24 February 1944.

a. Hearsay on 29 January that there is a radar installation near ST. JUST en CHAUSSEE. It is situated in an angle in the road between the town and BEAUVAIS. Also hearsay that there is a large gasoline and oil storage dump in a wooded area on both sides of the railroad between ST. JUST en CHAUSSEE and BULLES. A new spur has been built from the railway into the woods.

b. Hearsay on 17 January that there are tank traps in the wooded areas near all the small towns that circle AMIENS.

c. Hearsay on 5 January that the Germans were looking for billets in JUST en CHAUSSEE for marines who were being transferred there from DUN-KIRK.

d. Hearsay that troops from the Russian front passed through PARIS around 15 January while on their way to the west coast.

e. On 14 January a troop train carrying 600 Germans was observed on a siding between CLERMONT and CREIL. Everyone was engaged in washing and it appeared as though the train had been put on the siding at mealtime.

f. On 5 February a first class railroad carriage full of high-ranking German officers was observed at GUINCAMP. The train was moving west toward the coast.

g. Hearsay that advanced flying cadets are being sent up as fighter pilots during heavy raids.

MEMORIES OF HORHAM AIRFIELD, 1943–1945

David Warne, Farm Foreman and Home Guard Corporal

During the war my wife and I lived at Grove Cottage near Horham Airfield. Late one night, during the late summer months of 1943, I was suddenly awakened from my sleep by the sound of someone shouting loudly followed by the bangs of two gunshots. Startled, I went to the open bedroom window. About two hundred yards away on the meadow beyond the sentry post, there were several MPs talking loudly. Presently a jeep drove up, and by its lights I saw something, or somebody, lying on the ground. After about another ten minutes of loud discussion, the MPs lifted whomever or whatever it was into the jeep and departed.

About three weeks later, all the local Home Guard detachments received an official letter stating that a person had been discovered on a local airfield carrying a very powerful radio transmitter in a large attaché case. A detailed description of the attaché case was in the letter, and it also requested us to report immediately anyone we saw carry a similar attaché case. However, what I saw that night was shrouded in mystery, and despite my making discreet inquiries I never discovered anything further.

After a crew had completed their tour of combat missions, they used to fly very low over the control tower firing off flares in celebration and then circle the airfield two or three times at low level, still firing flares.

I recall one amusing occasion when one of these flares landed in George Roper's stackyard and set fire to one of his stacks of corn. Along came the fire engine to put the fire out, but the damn thing wouldn't work, much to the consternation of George, a neighboring farmer. However, he eventually got compensated for his loss.

I'll also never forget the day I was topping sugar beet one misty day in the autumn of 1944 when about five American bombers collided and came down in surrounding villages. One Fortress was cut in two; the four engines seemed to suddenly scream so loudly that it was nearly deafening and the completely separate tail section started zig-zagging down. Suddenly, the parachute of the tail gunner appeared and came down safely, but I didn't see any more parachutes.

About a week later I was in the Red Feather Club on the base when, lo and behold, I was introduced to the young tail gunner whom I'd seen come down. I was told that the collision had affected his nerves and he was undergoing rehabilitation. He actually fainted in the club that night, but they eventually got him right. It must have been a truly dreadful experience.

Another graphic illustration of what those boys endured was the story of the chap who got shot down over France. Incidentally, he was a regular guest at our home, and my wife Violet used to do his laundry for him.

After he was shot down he evaded capture and escaped back to England after many months with the help of the French Resistance. He managed to bring a piece of his parachute back with him that my wife made into a silk headscarf for his mother in America, and as a Christmas gift for our children he brought the biggest box of chocolates that I've ever seen in my life.

However, the strain of his experiences during his escape had turned his previously dark hair completely white.

In my opinion, and I'm not alone, if we hadn't had all those American bombers going out on bombing missions during the day and our own Royal Air Force during the night, we would have certainly lost the war.

Sadly, my wife passed away in 1978. Among several souvenirs I've kept of those wartime years is a press clipping from a Pennsylvania, U.S.A., newspaper dated 24 January 1944. It concerns Sergeant John Brown, who I believe was a mechanic with the 95th Bomb Group. He and several other sergeants were frequent visitors to our home. The clipping reads as follows:

A FINE LETTER FROM ENGLAND—Mrs. Jarvis W. Frazer has received the following letter from England: Grove Cottage, Denham, 8 Nr. Diss; 2 January 1944.

"Dear Mrs. Frazer: Please accept our most humble thanks for the lovely things you sent to our children for Christmas. Your brother John, made them up into four lovely parcels, complete with all the trimmings and greetings. We have two little girls: Betty, age 9 years, and Molly, age 6.

"I only wish that you people in America can understand how grateful we in England are for all that you have done for us. Our children had a lovely party given to them by the American boys at their camp with everything they could wish to eat and drink. Each child also received a present from one of your lads dressed up as Father Christmas. The children wouldn't have received much for Christmas if it hadn't been for you over in America, as here in England it is very hard to get toys as so many people are at war work and what few we could get are very expensive.

"It seems strange to think there has to be wars to join our two countries together in bonds of friendship, as we in England have seen the results of air warfare. Living as we do about midway between Norwich and Ipswich near the east coast of England we saw many German planes come over, and we could do little to stop them. Now, thanks to our own glorious R.A.F. and the magnificent U.S.A.A.F., the tables are turned and the air vibrates with sound.

"We also get a great amount of your canned foods over here to help us with our rations. We are very well treated with food when one remembers that this is our fifth year of war. I say from the bottom of my heart, God bless the U.S.A.

"Again, thanking you very much indeed for everything. I'm sure the clothes will come in most useful to them in the summer. They are wearing the little coats now; it's just what they needed. We have great difficulty due to the clothing coupons. John has shown us your little girls' photograph. We all send our kindest regards.

"I remain,

"Yours sincerely,
"Mrs. D. Warne."

A FORT CALLED "SITUATION NORMAL"

William Overstreet, Co-pilot, 334th Squadron

Our original crew was assigned B-17F, serial number 423456, and we departed Kearney, Nebraska, in July 1943 as part of a provisional group commanded by Colonel George Mason. From Kearney we flew in stages to Prestwick, Scotland, via Bangor, Maine; Goose Bay, Labrador; and Keflavík, Iceland.

On arrival at Prestwick, the aircraft was taken over by the authorities for combat modifications, and our crew traveled to London by train for combat crew school training. On completion of this course on 15 August 1943 we were assigned to the 334th Squadron, 95th Bomb Group, at Horham, Suffolk.

A replacement Fortress was assigned to us, and the crew made a unanimous selection and named B-17F 229943 "Situation Normal."

The original crew of "Situation Normal" was: Lieutenant Alden Witt, pilot; Lieutenant William Overstreet, co-pilot; Lieutenant Harry Meintz, navigator; Lieutenant Richard Holmes, bombardier; Technical Sergeant Kingsley Spitzer, top turret/engineer; Technical Sergeant Roy Baughman, radio operator/gunner; Staff Sergeant Wendall Verbulecz, ball-turret gunner; Staff Sergeant Charles Schrack, waist gunner; Staff Sergeant Everett Lewis, waist gunner; and Staff Sergeant William Jackson, tail gunner.

Staff Sergeant Jackson was replaced on the crew shortly after we started flying combat missions by Staff Sergeant Sandy Sanchez.

The following is a complete record of my tour of combat operations.

3 September 1943—Target, Renault Works (Paris); Flight Time, 05.35. Remarks: Encountered fighters and flak. Confirmed: One fighter destroyed, one fighter damaged.

6 September 1943—Target, Stuttgart; 08.45; target overcast. Bombed airfield in France. Confirmed: One fighter destroyed.

7 September 1943—Target, Watten (V weapon site); 03.25; could see English coast throughout the mission. Accurate flak over the target.

9 September 1943—Target, Paris; 05.00 (flight time); our first P-47 escort and they mixed it up in some dogfights. Mission recalled over Belgium.

16 September 1943—Target, La Pallice (port area); 11.30; solid hits on target. Encountered weather and darkness on return to England. Landed at R.A.F. field after ducking barrage balloons.

23 September 1943—Vannes Airfield (France); 09.45; flew with Lieutenant Adams in low squadron lead. Poor formation this day but excellent P-47 cover saved us.

27 September 1943—Emden (industrial area); 06.00; cold. Minus 42 degrees centigrade. Bombed target through overcast.

2 October 1943—Emden (industrial area); 05.40; bombed through total overcast. Confirmed: One fighter damaged.

4 October 1943—Hanau (industrial area); 08.30; countered 100 mph winds 180 degrees from forecast with complete undercast en route. Bombed somewhere near Saarbrucken. Returned over Paris instead of Brussels. Left formation over Paris because of oxygen depletion. Descended into undercast.

8 October 1943—Bremen (shipyards); 06.30; destroyed the target but had plenty of activity. Confirmed: Five fighters destroyed, two fighters damaged.

9 October 1943—Marienburg, East Prussia (aircraft factory); 11.00; led flight of 95th aircraft to augment the 100th Bomb Group. Losses had been so heavy they did not have the aircraft available for a complete group. Almost perfect bombing. Long mission.

10 October 1943—Munster (built-up area); 06.50; the 95th Bomb Group led the Eighth Air Force on this one. The Germans hit us with everything they had. The sky was a panorama of dogfights. B-17s spinning in, exploding, etc., and intense flak over the target. Harry Meintz, navigator, was wounded. His arm was shot off by a German fighter. Confirmed: Eight fighters destroyed, two probable, and two fighters damaged. One Fw 190, with a black-and-white checkered cowling, came within a few feet of colliding with our B-17. The German pilot was slumped over the cockpit, apparently dead. Note: Harry Meintz was replaced on the crew by Lieutenant Pratt.

14 October 1943—Schweinfurt (ball-bearing factories); 08.30; the target we'd been anticipating. Eighth Air Force lost sixty bombers. Not as rough on us as Munster but more so on the leading division. Confirmed: Two fighters destroyed.

20 October 1943—Duren (industrial area); 06.10; bombed from 29,000 feet on Pathfinder aircraft through total overcast. Good P-47 and Spitfire coverage. We lost number 2 engine. It wouldn't feather, and windmilling caused us to leave the formation. The crew was thankful for the P-47 that stayed with us all the way to the French coast. We landed at an emergency field on the coast of England.

3 November 1943—Wilhelmshaven (port area); 05.15; the sky was clear and looked as if it was full of B-17s, B-24s, P-47s, and P-38s. We didn't lose a ship. Bombed through overcast in target area on Pathfinder aircraft.

16 November 1943—Rjukan, Norway; 10.30; bombed heavy water facility. Couldn't transfer fuel from the Tokyo tanks on outbound flight. Left formation at Norwegian coast for most direct route to the English coast to minimize probability of ditching in the North Sea. Landed at the 91st Bomb Group's base at Bassingbourn. Note: "Situation Normal" was replaced by a new aircraft after this, our sixteenth mission.

30 November 1943—Solingen (industrial area); 07.00; flew with Captain Thompson. Another extremely cold mission.

11 December 1943—Emden (industrial area); 06.30; the 95th put two groups in the air. Influx of new personnel. Formation reflected it. Some fighter opposition. Confirmed: One fighter destroyed.

13 December 1943—Kiel (port area); bombed through overcast on Pathfinder aircraft. Very heavy flak. Note: Lieutenant Witt and Sergeants Spitzer, Baughman, and Verbulecz were all killed in a B-17 crash.

30 January 1944—Brunswick (city); 6.30; my first mission as pilot. Bombed on Pathfinder aircraft. Crew: Overstreet, pilot; Giles, co-pilot; Geirtsen, navigator; Fisher, bombardier; Hickey, top-turret/engineer; Hoopes, radio operator; Kinnebrew, ball turret; Schrack, waist gunner; Lewis, waist gunner; Sanchez, tail gunner. Note: Schrack completed his twenty-five missions on 10 February and was replaced by Bohl for my twenty-fifth mission. Holmes, the original bombardier, was assigned to another crew and completed his twenty-five missions with them.

3 February 1944—Wilhelmshaven (port area); 06.00; Thirteenth Combat Wing led the Third Division. Bombed on Pathfinder aircraft. Sighted no enemy fighters. Excellent P-51, P-47, and P-38 escort. Logged some instrument time during our descent over the North Sea.

4 February 1944—Frankfurt (marshaling yards); 07.30; bombed on Pathfinder. Encountered a few enemy fighters and intense flak.

6 February 1944—Villa Coublay, France (airfield); 06.00; primary target overcast. Bombed target of opportunity, which turned out to be a high-priority target. Some Fw 190s sighted. Group led by Lieutenant Colonel McKnight.

10 February 1944—Brunswick (industrial area); 08.25; aggressive enemy fighter opposition; 95th lost seven aircraft. Confirmed: One fighter destroyed.

20 February 1944—Rostock (target of opportunity); 10.15; primary target was in Poland. It was overcast and bombed secondary target. (Completion of my twenty-five missions.)

****

The enemy aircraft listed as destroyed and damaged were confirmed through intelligence information to specific gunners on the crew. They received confirmation for a total of nineteen enemy fighters destroyed, two probably destroyed, and six damaged. Mission remarks are from notes I made in 1943–44 after each mission was flown.

It is very much regretted that the names of the ground crew of "Situation Normal" are not remembered, because they were as much a part of the crew as we were.

Staff Sergeant Sanchez volunteered for additional combat missions after completing his required twenty-five and flew a total of forty-four missions as tail gunner. He was awarded the Silver Star, his fourth medal, and the first Flying Fortress in the Eighth Air Force to be named after an airmen was "Smiling Sandy Sanchez."

Finally, what happened to our Fort "Situation Normal"? Like a very large number of her gallant breed, she died nobly, and sadly so did half the crewmembers who were flying her on that fateful day, 6 March 1944, when the Eighth Air Force sustained its heaviest loss of the war—sixty-nine bombers on the second mission to Berlin.

THE MAN WHO CAME FOR BREAKFAST

William ("Ed") Charles, Navigator, 336th Squadron

Late one night in mid-February 1944 after we had gone to bed and were halfway into a needed night's sleep, the door of our barracks suddenly opened. The C.Q. (charge of quarters) entered, the bright beam of his flashlight probing the darkness.

"Is there an empty bunk in there? We have a new arrival and he needs a place to sleep." I said the bunk next to mine was vacant. I offered to get up and help the new arrival to unpack, but he said, "No thanks, I'll do it tomorrow. . . . I feel very tired, and I think I'll hit the sack." I didn't even get a good look at his face as we shook hands. He took the bunk next to mine, saying that he was a replacement navigator and that his name was Spencer. We all went back to bed and were soon asleep.

About two o'clock the following morning we were again awakened by the C.Q. with his flashlight. He said, "Lieutenant Spencer, you're to come with me. We need a navigator for today's mission, and you're on the list to fly." Lieutenant Spencer dressed and left for breakfast and the early morning briefing.

When we eventually got up, I noticed Lieutenant Spencer's brand-new leather A-2 flying jacket lying on his bunk with his initials and the last four numbers of his serial number stamped on the inside.

Later on that day we, as most crewmen who were not assigned to that day's mission, went up to the flight line to watch our returning B-17s peel off and land. It became obvious that the 95th had experienced a rough mission; about five of our ships were missing, several others landed with either one or two propellors feathered. We later learned that Lieutenant Spencer's B-17 237971 was one of those that had been shot down. He had only spent one short night as a member of the 95th Bomb Group at Horham and from that day forward he was known as "the man who came for breakfast."

I subsequently took his A-2 flight jacket before they collected his belongings, and it is now on display in the Memorial Air Museum at Framlingham, the 95th Group's first airfield in Suffolk, England.

"BIG B": 4 March 1944

Lieutenant Glenn Infield, pilot, B-17 231329, 334th Squadron: Every American combat crew in the Eighth Air Force had been waiting, expecting, and dreading the day they would be sent out to accomplish the raid that the commander in chief of the Luftwaffe, the bemedaled Hermann Goering, said couldn't be flown: a daylight attack by the American heavy bombers on Berlin, the capital city of Hitler's 1,000-year reich.

Field order no. 477 came to the 95th Bomb Group from Eighth Air Force headquarters late on the bitterly cold, blustery night of 3 March 1944. It was blunt, matter-of-fact, and very ominous: MAXIMUM FORCES WILL BE DISPATCHED AGAINST OBJECTIVES IN THE BERLIN AREA ON 4 MARCH 1944. CLOUD COVER OF 6 TO 8/10 FROM 12,000 TO 18,000 FEET PREDICTED FOR THE TARGET AREA. OVER THE NORTH SEA, NORTH OF 53 DEGREES LATITUDE, CLOUD TOPS ARE EXPECTED AT OPERATIONAL LEVELS, RESTRICTING OVER-WATER ROUTES BETWEEN ENGLAND AND THE CONTINENT TO AREAS NORTH OF THAT PARALLEL.

In those unemotional impersonal words clicking over the teletype machine at our group headquarters building, the fate of the mission was sealed.

Lieutenant Marshall Thixton, bombardier, B-17 731 (pathfinder), 482nd Bomb Group: In November 1943 selected crews from each bomb group were sent to Alconbury to undergo specialized training in the new Pathfinder (radar-equipped) aircraft. Our crew, commanded by Lieutenant William Owen, was chosen from the 95th.

On completing our training, we remained at Alconbury and flew to the bases of the lead groups in the Thirteenth Wing prior to each mission. Later, in the summer of 1944, each bomb group in the Eighth Air Force had their own Pathfinder aircraft, based permanently at their own airfield, after selected crews had been trained by us at Alconbury.

During the night of 3 March 1944, we flew to Horham from Alconbury to attend a briefing for the raid on Berlin the next day.

Sergeant James Johnson, S-2 (Intelligence Section): We didn't get any sleep during the night of 3–4 March 1944. The various sections of the group's administrative and planning staff were busily engaged in finalizing every aspect of the Berlin mission down to the last detail. This procedure was routine, of course, for every raid flown by the 95th, but Berlin was something very special.

The crews scheduled for the mission were awakened by the squadron C.Q.s about 0300 hours, had breakfast, and assembled for the briefing. When the curtain was pulled aside revealing the route and the target, indicated by colored strings stretching from East Anglia to the German capital, there was considerably more reaction and exclamations, whistles, groans, etc., from the crews than usual. It was the second time in twenty-four hours that their assigned target was Berlin; yesterday's mission had been recalled because of the atrocious weather conditions. There had been no appreciable improvement in the weather conditions in the meantime.

I operated the projection machine for showing pictures of the targets in Berlin to be hit. Captain Frank Eickemeyer briefed the crews on that particular aspect of the operation, and Major Donohue completed the main briefing. Some of the boys were convinced that this was their last briefing and that they wouldn't be coming back. They left their personal belongings in safe hands.

At about 0700 hours the boys went out to their planes hoping, some of them, that the mission would be scrubbed. I went to bed but I couldn't sleep; I was really concerned about this mission. I heard the planes taking off, one after the other, on the long flight to Berlin.

Many of us at group headquarters had vivid recollections of the 13 June 1943 Kiel mission disaster when ten of our planes and crews were lost. We feared the worst.

Lieutenant Vincent Fox, navigator, B-17 231600, "Spirit of New Mexico," 335th Squadron: If Berlin could be attacked in daylight, then all of Germany would become accessible to the full weight of American bombs. For us, the bomber crews who were assigned the mission, Berlin was a giant mental hazard, the toughest of all missions, for which we had little genuine enthusiasm. However, the briefing officer, Major Jiggs Donohue, the silver-tongued lawyer from Washington, D.C., had the ability to make it sound like a gallant adventure into the wild blue yonder to be cherished.

But the procedure wasn't new to us, we were on our twenty-fourth mission. We'd been briefed for Berlin on five previous occasions, but each time the adverse European winter weather had forced us to abandon the mission short of "Big B." The previous day we'd climbed to 30,000 feet over the Danish peninsula only to be confronted by a solid bank of swirling, turbulent clouds.

Emergency dinghy practice was more fun than the real thing. Even
the audience wanted to see someone get wet.

The Yanks always enjoy
playing or watching baseball!

The 95th Red
Feather
Orchestra—
always well
received.

One of the longest overwater missions to Rjukan destroyed the "heavy water" plant. This ended Germany's hopes of producing an atom bomb.

This plane was hit in Norway and the engine fire smoldered all the way back to Scotland.

Snow storm slows action, December 1943.

Cold weather gear. Sergeants Bright
and Zimmerman, 335th squadron,
winter 1943–44.

R.A.F. Lancaster makes
emergency landing in
snow storm, December
1943.

Strong men brave the
weather to keep 'em flying.

A vital German ball bearing plant is hit hard. Pinpoint bombing of
strategic materials sources crippled the Nazi war machine.

John Miller, lead pilot, served with the 95th and the 100th.

Sergeant Lawrence "McDuff" Robbins, 334th Squadron, uses cold weather outfit in action.

Congressman Baldwin of NY visits Horham and visits his brother "Sandy" Baldwin.

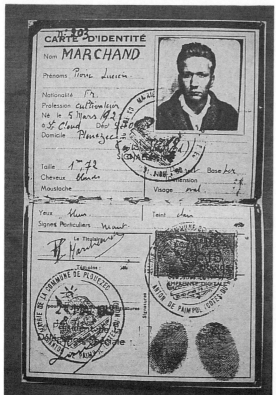

Forged papers prepared by members of the Underground for Jerry Eshuis.

Colonel Chester Gilger presides at an awards ceremony, 4 February 1944.

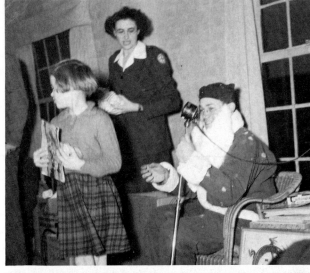

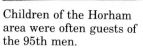

Children of the Horham
area were often guests of
the 95th men.

Christmas 1943. The Red Cross girls play Christmas carols for a sing-along.

Three on one—bicycle, that is.

88mm gun and crew at Munster (date unknown).

The 412th Ordnance personnel pose with their famous plane "Zoot Suiter."

A Queen dies hard—a direct hit—and she goes down in flames. Mission and date unknown.

Red Feather Club, Horham.

Everybody remembers Mother!

P-51 Mustang added a new depth to fighter protection for American daylight bombers.

P-47 Thunderbolt always gave comfort to bomber crews with superior firepower and excellent pilots.

Thunderbolt "little friends" give close support.

Four famous American Aces from the 56th Fighter Group: Colonel Hubert ("Hub") Zemke, Colonel Dave Schilling, Colonel "Gabby" Gabreski, Captain F.J. Christensen.

Lieutenant "Chuck" Yeager got his first confirmed Air Victory on 4 March 1944 over Berlin during the first American daylight bombing mission to the German capital.

Chuck Yeager's famous P-51 "Glamorous Glen III," 357th Fighter Group.

General Curtis LeMay briefs the Mission Commanders for D-Day, 5 June 1944. Colonel Gerhart is front, center.

E.D. "Doc" Imes and Sergeant Quickie. Reaction to disaster was always a way of life.

Contrails—a familiar sight over Germany on clear, cold days. American P-51s and P-47s streak ahead searching out enemy fighters.

P-47s line up for takeoff to escort bombers on a deep penetration mission. Note drop tanks.

H.M.S. *Verdun* picked up Lieutenant Milward's crew after ditching.

Crew of "Superstitious Aloysius" in R.A.F. uniforms after rescue by *Verdun*.
L to R: L.R. Spears, P.V. Milward, A.R. Scroggins, F.P. Miles,
E.S. Winstead, C.R. McCoomber, W.L. Weeks, J.C. Kolarik, W.J. Milton,
A. Farris.

Al Brown's lead crew pose with "I'll Be Around" for news photographers after first daylight mission to Berlin, 4 March 1944.

Bill Owen's crew flew the Pathfinder B-17 and dropped the first American bombs on the German capital city, 4 March 1944.

Standing L to R: Donald White, Eng.; Harlin Sours, WG; Edmund Aken, R.O.; Leo Moffatt, Ball; John O'Neil, Tail; E.A. Beans, W.G.; *Kneeling:* William Owen, P.; Marshall Thixton, Bomb; Albert Englehardt, Nav; Frank McAllister, CP.

CO Colonel Chester Gilger congratulates the members of the crew of "I'll Be Around"—lead plane, Berlin, 4 March 1944.

Marshall Thixton, Pathfinder bombardier, dropped the first American bombs on Berlin, 4 March 1944.

Lieutenant Colonel H. Griffin ("Grif") Mumford is awarded the Silver Star as mission commander of the first American daylight bombing of Berlin, 4 March 1944. Presenting the award is Major General Curtis E. LeMay, commander, Third Air division.

Flying in heavy cloud cover became an accepted fact of combat in the E.T.O. Pathfinders and radar bombing made successful bombing missions possible. 1944–45.

Other crews who flew the "Berlin First" mission pose with the lead crew for newsreel photos.

"First to Berlin," 4 March 1944. The whole group gets into the act. For this mission the 95th Group was awarded its third Presidential Unit Citation, the only combat group in the Eighth Air Force to be so honored.

One of the better days
for visiting the continent.

Climbing high
into the sun.

Thousands of maps for all
possible routes and
targets.

Smilin' Sandy Sanchez smiles from "his" plane. He was the only crewman known to have a B-17 named in his honor, after completing forty-four combat missions.

Sandy Sanchez plays host to Red Cross girls atop his namesake plane.

Ground crew personnel enjoy a great American pastime (with British money) during a stand down.

95th B-17 was forced to crash-land in Switzerland after mission to Augsburg, 16 March 1944. Lieutenant James Redd, pilot.

Lieutenant Robichaud's crew shot down 26 July 1943. Joe Mutz (3rd from left, kneeling) was wounded, then shot by an armed German civilian.

General Matthew Ridgway was flown over the battlefield at Arnhem in a 95th Group B-17.

Awards ceremony, headquarters building, Horham.

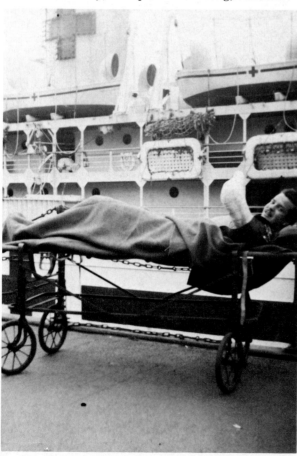

R.E. ("Lefty") Nairn boards a Red Cross ship in Liverpool for the trip home.

"Tokyo Raider" greets "Berlin
Raider." Grif Mumford with General
Doolittle.

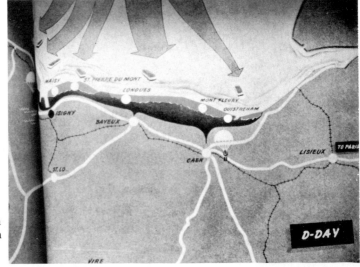

D-Day invasion route.
The 95th and the
other groups of the
Eighth Air Force each
flew three missions on
6 June 1944 in
support of the
Invasion.

Now we can relax and smile. Coffee time at crew interrogation, summer 1944.

OK men, stand at attention and act like real soldiers—just this once!

Official group picture tells the world that 200 missions have been successfully completed.

Three news reporters join the 200th mission party. The party lasted far into the night for two days.

The meteorology officer glibly promised better weather for today's mission, but our faith in his predictions had suffered numerous setbacks before.

After the general briefing, I went to the navigators' special briefing, and it seemed like I'd collected enough maps, charts, and photos to navigate halfway round the world. Then it was off to the equipment hut to collect chutes, oxygen masks, Mae West lifejackets, electrically heated "blue bunny" suits, throat mikes, flak suits, escape kits, and candy bars. A 6 x 6 truck took us to the hardstand where our aircraft, bombed up and with a full gas load for a maximum effort, waited, menacing and eager to go.

We warmed ourselves as we mingled with our ground crew in their tent at the revetment. There was a bond of deep friendship between our ground and flight crews. After all, our lives were in their hands, and they always did their utmost to assure our safety. We couldn't have come through all our previous missions safely otherwise.

While we mounted our machine guns, bombardier Herbie Levine scratched a personal message to Hitler on one of the 500-pound demolition bombs as he checked the fusing. Powers, McLeod, and Knipper circled the big bomber, doing their pre-flight rituals, then climbed aboard through the nose hatch to run through the cockpit checklist.

It was only 0700 hours, but it seemed like we'd already been working for half the day. It was still dark with occasional snow showers blustering across the airfield.

All around the perimeter track, engines were coughing and then roaring to life. Soon a ponderous procession of drab-looking war machines lumbered toward the end of the main runway, finding their places in line.

Lieutenant Alvin Brown, pilot, B-17 231320, "I'll Be Around," 412th Squadron: For the maximum effort that day the 95th put thirty-eight planes up, including two Pathfinder aircraft. Our group was divided into two flights of nineteen ships, A and B. The 100th and 390th Bomb groups made up the wing. My crew, with Lieutenant Colonel "Grif" Mumford as command pilot, was to lead the wing and flight B. Lieutenant Hal Powers was to lead flight A.

Lieutenant Vincent Fox, B-17 231600: A green flare from the control tower signaled the start of the mission. Hal Powers lined up for takeoff, locked the tail-wheel, pushed the throttle column fully forward, released the brakes, and we felt the sudden surge as our four 1,200-horsepower Wright Cyclone engines, roaring at maximum revolutions, pulled us rapidly down the runway toward air speed. Powers used all the available runway before easing the twenty-six ton bomber into the air and into a gentle left turn.

At our takeoff time of 0730 hours, scattered snow squalls limited visibility down to a scant 300 yards as we peered apprehensively into the eerie pre-dawn light while we spiraled up to group assembly altitude. During the tension-filled climb, the English countryside was visible only momentarily through multilayered clouds.

We were the lead ship in our squadron, and as the other planes formed up behind us, our tail gunner reported who was in position. The rendezvous was accomplished as planned with the cold early morning air frequently being illuminated by multicolored identification flares as each bomb group in the Third Air Division assembled over Suffolk. This spectacular display was being repeated high over the various other counties of eastern England as the bombers of the First and Second Air divisions assembled their respective groups.

We formed up in group formation behind the 95th's *B* flight led by Lieutenant Brown and Lieutenant Colonel Mumford, left the English coast behind, and continued to climb on course over the North Sea. It was time to test fire the guns; each gunner checked in by interphone as he squeezed off a short burst. During this time, several of our group's B-17s had to abort the mission (forced to return to base) because of engine problems or oxygen failures.

We leveled off at an altitude of 27,000 feet over eastern Belgium. There was a solid floor of clouds between us and the continental landscape. Ahead of us loomed an imposing barrier of dark gray cirro-stratus cloud, towering up to 29,000 feet, as if presenting a forbidding and impenetrable defense to the interior of the reich.

It was necessary to climb again, and we finally leveled off at 29,000 feet, just above the cloud bank. The thermometer read minus sixty-five degrees fahrenheit.

Lieutenant William ("Ed") Charles, navigator, B-17 231939, 336th Squadron: One bomb group aborted before we left England due to an inability to attain a combat formation. Another group was scattered all over the sky crossing the North Sea and abandoned the mission when they reached the enemy coast. As we climbed on course and finally got above the clouds, the contrails from the planes in front became so dense that they formed complete cloud decks themselves which added to our problems.

Shortly after crossing into Germany, for the second time in two days, Eighth Air Force headquarters sent out over VHF a recall signal. All the other formations immediately began 180° turns to return to base and attack targets of opportunity on the way home. It quickly became apparent however that Colonel Mumford, leading the 95th Group, wasn't turning around with the other groups. Our pilot Bob Kroeger and co-pilot Hearty Fitchko checked with our radio operator, George Green, and all were positive there had been a recall. Bob said, "What's going on anyway? What's the guy doing?" Another pilot in the group broke the absolute silence radio code by calling on the command frequency, "Colonel Mumford, there's been a recall."

I'm sure there was as much aircraft intercom chatter in the other planes as there was in ours, but every plane in our formation continued on to the assigned primary target.

Lieutenant ("Doc") Thayer, co-pilot, B-17 231410, 336th Squadron: When we'd almost reached the Rhine, I saw group after group turning back and passing by on our left. I'd heard the recall several times earlier, and remember two or three radio comments from returning planes saying, "You'll be sorry. . . ."

Lieutenant Glenn Infield, pilot, B-17 231329: My radio operator, Sergeant Ellis Steere, called me on the interphone: "Division has instructed all combat wing leaders to use their own discretion on continuing the mission. They can bomb targets of opportunity or return to base."

Formations all around us began making 180° turns. Within minutes they were all gone, disappeared to the west, but our formation kept on course for Berlin. Our twenty-nine Forts, mere dots in the sky over the continent, droned deeper into Germany.

The minutes passed and I fully realized that our planes had been registering on the German radar screens on the Dutch coast, and further inland, ever since our group assembly over East Anglia that morning. The Luftwaffe fighter controllers had, without any doubt at all, alerted their *staffels* of Focke-Wulfs and Messerschmitts. I began to get very edgy.

Then the tense radio silence decreed by the field order was broken by a nervous pilot in the low squadron; "The other formations have turned back, Colonel."

There was a momentary pause, then the crisp voice of the mission commander crackled in my earphones: "We will continue to the assigned target."

I was momentarily stunned. Twenty-nine B-17s against the entire Lutfwaffe? Less than one complete combat wing of American bombers opposing the entire might of the Nazi air armada dedicated to keeping daylight heavy bombers from their capital city. It was suicide! I swore softly. Had the colonel gone mad?

Unknown to us at the time, Colonel Mumford and Al Brown, his lead pilot, had made an on-the-spot decision that was as courageous and wise as any made during the aerial war over Europe. Knowing that the wing was already deep in enemy territory, too deep to slip back unnoticed, Mumford decided to take advantage of the extremely bad weather. Rather than backtrack over the same course we had used for penetration and running the gauntlet of Nazi fighters that would be waiting, he stuck to the original flight plan. By taking this desperate gamble, he hoped to accomplish two things: get the formation out of enemy territory without overwhelming losses and bomb Berlin. He was well aware of the morale and propaganda value of an American heavy bomber raid on Berlin. We continued on toward Berlin and the Robert Bosch AG factory in the Klein Machnow suburb of the city, our assigned objective.

Technical Sergeant Frank Atterbury, radio operator, B-17 231320, "I'll Be Around": For the sake of brevity, I'll skip all the details of the horrendous weather conditions that day and how the 95th lead corraled a small force of B-17s and took them to Berlin and back. These events, I believe, are well known. What apparently isn't well known is the true story of the Berlin recall. Hopefully, this will clarify the conjecture.

The message came in bomber code that consisted of groups of four letters without any particular sequence but corresponded to a particular word. An example might be, PQAM, which might have been the code word for "obscured."

The collective code word for that day was, RZNC̄—the dash above the letter *C* meant that in our particular use of the International Morse Code the letter *C* would have an extra dash in it and to come across as "dash dot dash dot dash." The collective call sign <u>RZNC</u> was the call sign that our base station would use to call everyone on the mission. It was the greeting or salutation of the message.

The actual decoding message came across as follows: ABANDON OPS. RETURN TO BASE, 1200 HOURS. RZNC̄. The message came from a nearby source. That was obvious from the clarity, sound, and tone of the signal. The collective call was used as a signature to the message—which was an error—and there was no greeting call-sign used at all. The messages came across several times, but with a significant interval. There was no possibility that I could have mistaken the signature for a greeting.

I reported the message as received to the cockpit and told the pilots that the message as sent did not constitute a recall per standard operating procedure.

Upon returning to Horham, it was confirmed to me by Colonel Chester Gilger, 95th Group commander at that time, that there had not been a recall sent from England. Where then, did the message come from? I am sure that it came from an enemy radio transmitter in an almost successful attempt to turn back an historic event.

The courageous decision to continue toward our assigned target, Berlin, came from the cockpit, naturally. If I may paraphrase a familiar newscaster: ". . . and that's the way it was for March 4, 1944."

Lieutenant Al Brown, pilot, B-17, "I'll Be Around": Sergeant Atterbury's report was relayed to Colonel Mumford, and we decided to continue on, being able to abort at any time if the weather got too bad.

Lieutenant Malcolm Durr, lead navigator, B-17, "I'll Be Around": It was the coldest day that I'd ever flown. We eventually reached 29,600 feet to get above the clouds. I checked our position constantly by Gee fixes (navigational aid that used radio beams transmitted from ground stations in England) as far as the Belgian coast and calculated the westerly wind at fifteen knots rather than the forty-two or forty-five knots that had been forecast at briefing. We were unable to obtain any Gee fixes beyond Ostend on the Belgian coast, because that device didn't have the necessary range thereafter.

We didn't see the ground from takeoff until we reached Magdeburg, Germany, one of our checkpoints, having flown a dead reckoning course all the way. Flak came up to meet us and we lost a plane from our lead squadron flown by Lieutenant "Tex" Worthy whose crew shared a Nissen hut at Horham. They were good friends of ours, and their navigator, Frank Gaynor, and I had been through navigation school together. We saw their airplane go down; four or five crewmen bailed out before the ship disappeared into the clouds below. We later learned that all ten crewmen managed to bail out and became POWs.

The next checkpoint that I was able to positively identify through breaks in the cloud was Oranienburg, about twenty-five miles north of Berlin. We changed course accordingly and headed toward our IP (initial point).

Despite the adverse weather conditions, extreme wind differentials, distance flown to the target, and abnormal altitude, the route to Berlin was flown as briefed by dead reckoning. If I had made the wrong decision while crossing the Belgian coast, with about three more hours of flying to the target area ahead of us, instead of being at the target we would have probably been eighty or ninety miles east of Berlin.

Lieutenant Vincent Fox, navigator, B-17 231600, "Spirit of New Mexico": We soon had the chilling realization that we were alone in our undertaking. Our ball-turret gunner could identify squadrons with 95th "Square B" tail markings and elements with the "Square D" of the 100th Group still maintaining the integrity of the formation. It seemed incredible that our token force was still bearing east toward the German capital.

We got a brief glimpse of the ground near the city of Brunswick and were greeted by a barrage of enemy flak bursts, as though we needed to be reminded of the stark reality of our situation. The clouds continued to thin, and as we approached to the northwest of our assigned target, only 50 percent cloud coverage obscured our vision of the ground.

A new menace to our mission soon presented itself in the form of about twenty Me 109 fighter planes. They began their attacks from the direction of the sun in defense of their capital city. Our right wingman was shot down before eight P-51 Mustang escort fighters put in a miraculous appearance from nowhere and broke up the attack. Those P-51s were really beautiful as they challenged the German fighter pilots. How our little friends ever managed to find us through the maze of clouds that day is one of the incredible mysteries of air combat.

Lieutenant Joe Blagg, navigator, B-17 231410, 336th Squadron: The flak was intensifying as we approached Berlin. I recall looking at a damaged B-17 on our left; it had a huge hole in its fuselage directly behind the right wing and several crewmen were bailing out.

We had no fighter support at that time and assumed that our fighters had been recalled along with the bombers. There were many Luftwaffe fighter bases and radar-controlled antiaircraft guns between us and the English Channel, and it was an absolute certainty that our small force of bombers was being tracked all the way on German radar. The chances of any of us returning to England looked extremely remote, and I remember thinking, We'll sure be lucky to get out of this one . . . only hope we have a chance to bail out.

Then some P-51s showed up . . . just like in the movies. I doubt if any of us would have got back to base if the P-51s hadn't been there.

Lieutenant "Doc" Thayer, co-pilot, B-17 231410: We flew through a vertical cloud bank and emerged into good forward visibility. There was new snow on the ground, which made it easy to see roads, railroads, and cities ahead.

When the flak started firing, I could see the vivid red flashes of flame from the gun barrels, and then, for the first time ever, I saw the 88mm flak shells themselves, distinct against the white snowy background, coming all the way up as if in slow motion, then rapidly accelerating the closer they got.

Fortunately, the flak barrage burst above us. Then another flak shell came up through the bomb-bay doors, knocked the fuse off one of our bombs, and kept on going completely through the top of the fuselage.

Our bomb ended up on the catwalk between the two bomb bays, making a noise like a volcano-type sparkler, and spewing out what looked like small shiny pieces of aluminum. How we got the bomb-bay doors open and that smoldering bomb out of our aircraft in less then ten seconds I will never really understand. Apparently, there was another B-17 almost directly below us that the falling bomb missed by a matter of inches.

A minute or so later flak knocked a hole in our left wing and the left side gas tanks, which shut down numbers 1 and 2 fans for the rest of the day. By the time things had settled down, we could see Berlin in the distance through gaps in the clouds, and it soon became obvious that our P-51s were in charge of the Luftwaffe.

Without a shadow of doubt, the Mustangs saved our lives that day.

Sergeant Philip Kanarkowski, top-turret gunner, B-17 239884, 336th Squadron: We had reached the outskirts of Berlin when a flak shell bored a six-inch hole through the bottom of the fuselage of our Fortress and blew a hole three feet across in the top as it burst. The explosion knocked our right-waist gunner, James Kollmeyer, against the ball-turret gears six feet away without a shell splinter hitting him, but it blasted the left-waist gunner, John Hurley, full in the face and chest and out of the plane.

Despite the huge hole in our plane, our pilot, Lieutenant William Reis, continued on to the target, holding formation with the group.

Captain Raymond Abbott, pilot, B-17 232019, 336th Squadron: I saw Lieutenant Reis's airplane take a direct flak hit; so much stuff came up through the hole that I thought it had exploded. Quite frankly, I expected his plane to break in half.

Sergeant Lawrence Pifer, ball-turret gunner, B-17 231785, 335th Squadron: This was our eighteenth mission, and it turned out to be our last. We had crossed the IP and were on the bomb run, flying straight and level, when a flak shell hit our number 1 engine, which exploded into flames. I recall seeing the propeller blades bent back against the remaining cowling and engine cylinders by the force of the blast; the blades were not feathered, causing us to leave the formation in a rapid descent.

As we began going down, flight engineer Marvin Anderson had to crank the bomb-bay doors open because they wouldn't open from the bombardier's remote control in the nose section. By the time we'd dropped the bombs, the German fighters were upon us and kept up relentless attacks from all directions. Our pilot, Lieutenant Melvin Dunham, tried to stay in the sanctuary of the clouds, but the lower we were forced to descend, the more scattered the clouds became.

Due to our rapid descent, the ball turret frosted up completely and as I couldn't see out of it at all I decided to get out and help the other gunners.

Just as I clambered out of the turret, both waist gunners were hit by 20mm cannon fire. Both collapsed to the floor, not moving.

I had no communication with the cockpit due to the interphone lines being severed during the fighter attacks; consequently, I didn't hear the order to bail out so I kept alternating from one waist gun to the other until flames and smoke came streaming past the waist window. I looked out to see the extent of the damage to the engines and saw some tree tops not too far away. It was then that I knew we weren't going back to England and I had to get out— fast. After grabbing my chest chute, frantically clipping it on, I bailed out via the bomb bay. I pulled the ripcord as I went past the ball turret, and after what seemed an eternity, the chute snapped open. The first thought that came to mind was that I didn't lose my boots. They'd told us that the sudden jolt of the chute opening would cause my sheepskin flying boots and shoes to come off. Then I hit the ground unexpectedly; landing awkwardly I broke my left ankle and fractured my ribs. Needless to say, the pain was intense. I saw two large columns of smoke and flame erupt as our bomber crashed in open country about a quarter of a mile away. At the time I had no idea as to the fate of my crew apart from the two waist gunners, Clarence Barstow and Vince Aiello, who went down with the plane.

Eventually however, the other seven crewmen were all rounded up and taken prisoner. We were taken by truck to a nearby Luftwaffe base and from there we were transported by rail, via Berlin, to various prison camps in Germany. We had the dubious distinction of being the first Americans in Berlin—but under less than ideal conditions.

Lieutenant Glenn Infield, pilot, B-17 231329: Through breaks in the overcast I caught occasional glimpses of the city as we began our bomb run, but I knew visual bombing was impossible. We would have to drop our five-hundred pounders on a signal from the Pathfinder plane.

Lieutenant Hal Powers, pilot, B-17 231600: We had just started our bomb run when several Me 109s appeared out of the sky ahead of us and came right through our formation. If you want to know the crude word for describing the thoughts of bomber crewmen while under head-on fighter attack it was "pucker-time."

Apparently there were only about twelve P-51s up there protecting us, but they very soon cleared the air of enemy fighters. I thank God for the 51s that day, because they did a wonderful job.

Lieutenant Al Brown, pilot, B-17 231320: At the IP, Lieutenant Forrest Flagler, our lead bombardier, advised that he believed he could see the target, and we would make a visual bomb run. Then he advised that the bomb-bay doors were frozen shut, and we were unable to crank them down. The heating system in our plane had malfunctioned and was partly responsible. The temperature was minus 65 degrees fahrenheit. We were at an altitude of 25,500 feet and although the ground was mostly obscured by clouds, visibility over Berlin was reasonably good at our altitude. Me

109 fighters had come through our formation earlier, but they were closely followed by P-51s.

During the bomb run, Colonel Mumford and I had continuing dialogue with Bill Owen, pilot of the Pathfinder. Bill positioned his plane alongside our lead plane; the other planes in the formation closed as much as possible to get a good, tight, bomb pattern. Forrest Flagler, our bombardier, continued to report that he had reasonable visual contact with the target through his Norden bombsight. However, because our bomb-bay doors were frozen closed, we all realized that the following planes in the formation would have to drop their bombs on our flare signal in addition to the sight of the bombs from the Pathfinder. It was agreed that both the visual run and the back-up radar sighting on the target would be utilized in case Forrest's visual sighting was obscured at the last moment. The coordination was a credit to both crews, who had never practiced this type of maneuver. We fired the signal flare at the exact instant the Pathfinder navigator, Albert J. Englehardt, signaled Marshall Thixton to hit the bomb release. The bomb drop was achieved against all odds! Enemy fighters attacking, flak everywhere, lousy weather; in spite of all the negative factors, Berlin had received the first bombs dropped by American planes in daylight! It was a momentous moment—and a great group achievement. As a team, and as individual airmen, we had proved that Germany's most prized and protected target—Berlin—was no longer safe from Eighth Air Force daylight attacks. All of us were extremely proud and relieved. Even though we could not measure the precise bombing results at that moment because of the cloud cover, we had shown that diligent training, personal air discipline by dedicated crew members, and teamwork beyond the ordinary had brought the Allied war effort to the pinnacle of achievement. As we turned for home, we knew in our hearts that the end of the war in Europe was possible.

Lieutenant Marshall Thixton, bombardier of the Pathfinder B-17 from the 482nd Bomb Group: During the bomb run, the intercom came alive with shouted warnings: "Fighters at twelve o'clock high! Fighters at three o'clock low!" Guns swung into action as numerous enemy fighters came swarming in with little flashing lights glittering from their wings. Every gun on our ship was in constant action, and the intercom was full of chatter as the attacking fighters were passed from one gun position to the next. I recall, most vividly, our top-turret gunner hollering a warning as our P-51s followed the Me-109s right through our bomber formation: "Watch your fire . . . P-51s . . . little friends . . . watch your fire!"

Reports came over the interphone from our tail gunner: "B-17 just blew up; . . . two more ships hit . . . smoking . . . leaving formation . . . going down under control; . . . five . . . six chutes . . . 109 burning . . . going down . . . pilot bailing out. . . ."

During that action, some of Berlin's 2,500 heavy flak guns were firing at our formation, but the 109s flew straight through their own flak regardless. Everyone was so busy with the fighters and the bomb run, that the flak was almost unnoticed.

I touched the button, and the first American bombs were on their way down to the enemy's capital city from a very few of the planned 850 bombers scheduled for the mission.

"Bombs away!..." And we were on our way home. Homeward bound, struggling airmen homeward bound! Two or three bombers had one or two of their propellers feathered and engines smoking, but they managed to keep up with the formation as we gradually descended after leaving the target.

Lieutenant Ed Charles, navigator, B-17 231939: While we were on the bomb run, one German fighter passed so close that I could actually see the pilot's face.

At the release of the Pathfinder's bombs, all the other ships dropped their loads in unison. The time was 1335 hours. We'd beaten all the odds but were a long, long way from home, and we fully expected big trouble on the return flight.

Lieutenant Al Brown, pilot, B-17 231320: After leaving the target area, it became apparent that our oxygen supplies were dwindling, forcing the group to descend as soon as possible. About an hour and a half later, our bomb-bay doors were opened, and we dropped our bombs on a target of opportunity, which happened to be a bridge, from an altitude of 12,000 feet. The intermittent cloud banks at this lower altitude through which we flew made holding formation difficult.

In all, twenty-one 95th and eight 100th Bomb Group Forts had made it through to Berlin, but our group lost four airplanes and the 100th had one shot down. However, the main purpose of the mission was to prove that Berlin, despite its formidable defenses, could be hit by a daylight raid. This had been accomplished.

Lieutenant Vincent Fox, navigator, B-17 231600: There was very little chatter during the long return flight. The numbing cold affected us all, and due to low pressure, our oxygen system wasn't functioning properly. We were fully expecting the Luftwaffe to show up at any time, but we were intent on making a fight of it, if and when they attacked. For a couple of hours I made very few entries in my log as the drama of the flight was being played out. My fingers were almost too numb with cold to write anyway. During the flight to Berlin, we'd been working for General Jimmy Doolittle, but now we were working for ourselves—to survive and return to England.

As we gradually descended through the cloud layers, it was necessary to break formation; each time we entered a cloud bank, our formation became more scattered. When at last we reached the Belgian coast, only a single plane was flying on our wing; the remainder were either strung out somewhere in front or behind us. As we approached the coastline, two ugly black bursts of flak exploded in front of our left wing and two more burst behind us. That was the last we heard from Jerry.

It was time for a little ritual, always a moment to be eagerly anticipated: our first food for twelve hours on that occasion, a bit of a frozen Mars bar.

Our friendly coastline finally came into view. England had never looked so good to us at that moment! After all the horrendous weather we'd flown through, conditions over the East Anglian countryside were practically cloudless.

While over Berlin, our radio operator, Felix Knipper, had been wounded in the leg. The other gunners gathered around Felix in his radio room and made him as comfortable as possible for the landing. The blood from his leg wound had frozen, but he managed a wry little smile.

We landed at 1716 hours, and an ambulance was beside our plane within seconds at the end of our landing roll. The medics gently lifted our radio operator onto a stretcher and took him to the base hospital.

We were the first crew in the 335th Squadron to return from Berlin. The myth that Berlin was inaccessible to daylight bombers had been broken, and it was done by the Thirteenth Combat Wing. At that moment I didn't consider myself anyone special, just grateful to be one of the survivors.

Lieutenant Ed Charles, navigator, B-17 231939: When we were taken to the debriefing room, we found the area loaded with Eighth Air Force top brass, various other VIPs, reporters from the leading newspapers and magazines, newsreel cameramen from Movie-Tone News, and overall confusion. The group "scuttle butt" was that the top brass had come to Horham to discipline Lieutenant Colonel Mumford for the direct disobedience of an order in combat. Whether this was actually true or not I never discovered, but when they had confirmation that we'd actually become the first American bomb group to hit Berlin, the propaganda boost was immense and it was utilized to the fullest. General LeMay awarded the Silver Star to Lieutenant Colonel Mumford in the debriefing room and the Distinguished Flying Cross to Al Brown.

The next morning photographers from *LIFE* magazine assembled all the surviving crews that had returned from the mission and took pictures of us all standing in front of and on top of one of our B-17s, "Berlin First," Lieutenant Barksdale's ship, which had flown to Berlin and back. *LIFE* magazine featured the story and photographs in its issue of 20 March 1944.

Lieutenant Glenn Infield, pilot, B-17 231329: We were desperately short of fuel, two of our engines had already run out of gas, and we only just managed to make the English coast at Manston, Kent, a British fighter-bomber airfield, also used as an emergency landing strip because of its lengthened runway.

The 4 March 1944 mission was significant, not because of the 69.3 tons of bombs dropped by our combat wing, but because it was proof that Berlin was not invincible to day bombers. The London *Evening Standard*, in a leading editorial, "Allies over Berlin," saw in this first daylight raid a sign of unshakable comradeship between the British and American peoples, dispelling German rumors of dissension.

The sight of American heavy bombers with their fighter escorts also made a deep impression on the Berliners, because this was something that Goering had said was impossible. The Berlin *Boersen-Zeitung* tried hard to explain: "If the inhabitants of the capital were surprised that isolated enemy formations reached the city, it must be remembered that this need not be interpreted as a sign of enemy strength."

This raid, however, was the beginning of the end for Berlin and the 95th Bomb Group was subsequently awarded its third Presidential Unit citation for leading the offensive against the German capital.

Editor's note: Although the bulk of the escorting fighters had been recalled with the bombers, some elements of the Fourth Fighter Group from Debden, Essex, and the 357th Fighter Group based at Leiston, Suffolk, kept their rendezvous with the B-17s as scheduled. The Fourth Fighter Group was led to Berlin by its outstanding Commander, Lieutenant Colonel Donald Blakeslee, a veteran of the R.A.F. Eagle squadrons. Lieutenant Charles ("Chuck") Yeager, 357th Fighter Group, shot down his first enemy fighter over Berlin, one of a total of eleven lost by the Luftwaffe on 4 March 1944. A total of twenty-four fighters was lost by the Eighth Air Force that day. Most were due to the adverse weather conditions. Sixteen of these were from the Fourth and 357th Fighter Groups.

HEADQUARTERS
FOUR HUNDRED EIGHTY SECOND BOMBARDMENT GROUP
(P) AAF (D-D-2)
APO 639

7 March 1944

SUBJECT: Outstanding Performance of DR Navigator.

TO: Commanding Officer, 95th Bombardment Group, APO 634, U.S. Army.

1. On the mission to Berlin on 4 March 1944, one of our airplanes flew as deputy lead in the combat wing led by your group. Weather conditions forced the seven other combat wings to seek targets of opportunity or abort, this one formation alone reaching its objective.

2. According to the pilot and special equipment navigator in our plane, an outstanding job of dead reckoning was accomplished by the navigator in the lead aircraft, 1st Lt. MALCOLM D. DURR of your group. The route is said to have been flown almost exactly as briefed in spite of almost impossible difficulties encountered. The combat men here give high praise to Lt. DURR'S ability.

HOWARD MOORE,
Colonel, AC,
Commanding

HEADQUARTERS
FOUR HUNDRED EIGHTY SECOND BOMBARDMENT GROUP
(P) AAF APO 639

14 March 1944

SUBJECT: Recommendations for Awards.

TO: Commanding General, Eighth Air Force Composite Command, APO 639, U.S. Army.

1. Teletype number F221D, dated 9 March 1944, from the 95th Bombardment Group refers to aircraft 731, flown by Lt. Owen and Lt. Engelhardt on the mission of 4 March 1944, as follows:

Thru frequent calls on VHF, the personnel of NC number 731 gave invaluable assistance to the group leader in holding the formation on course and avoiding dangerous flak areas, both to and from the target. At the IP the lead A/C could not open their bomb doors and A/C 731 was called to "take over" on the bomb run from their number 2 position. The personnel of A/C 731 then sighted and bombed thru the undercast and the other A/C of their group and following groups dropped on their markers. A visual run was first tried but a cloud covered the target before the bombardier could synchronize. The change to instrument technique was made very efficiently.

For the Commanding Officer:

RICHARD M. COILGROVE,
1st Lt., Air Corps,
Adjutant

(*Editor's note:* The first Berlin mission on 4 March 1944 was the ninety-first bombing raid completed by the 95th Bomb Group [H]. From that date until the end of strategic bombing on 20 April 1945, the 95th flew 230 more missions, fifteen of which were to Berlin—in which 375 95th B-17s participated.)

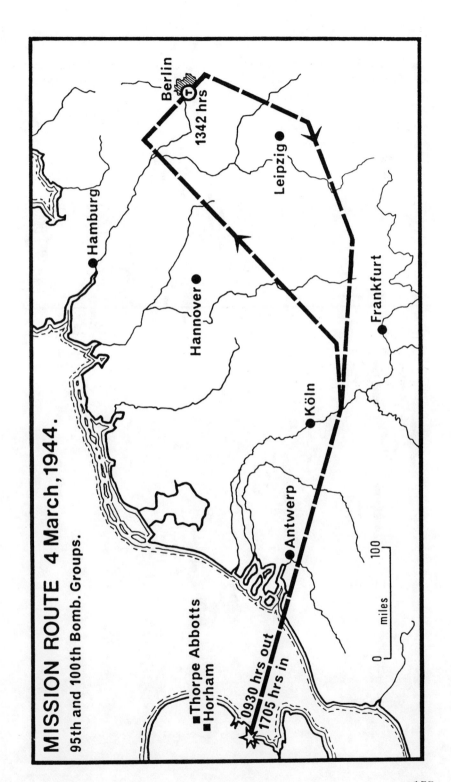

MISSION ROUTE 4 March, 1944.
95th and 100th Bomb. Groups.

Berlin
T
1342 hrs

Leipzig

Hamburg

Frankfurt

Hannover

Köln

Antwerp

Thorpe Abbotts
Horham

0930 hrs out
1705 hrs in

100
miles
0

155

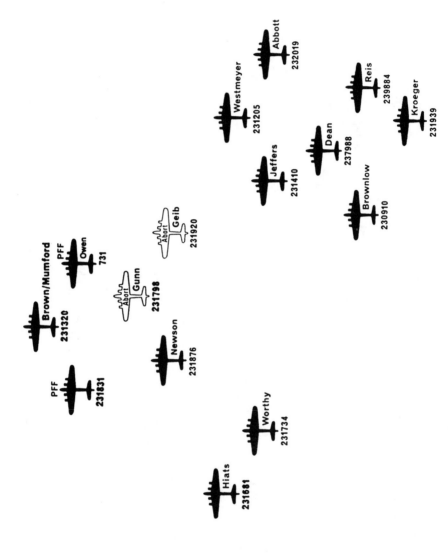

95th Bomb Group (H) Lead Formation Assembly for Berlin, 4 March 1944.

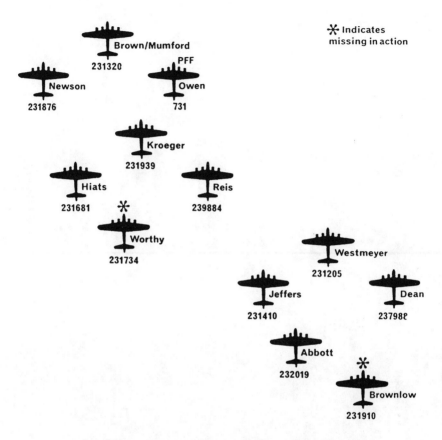

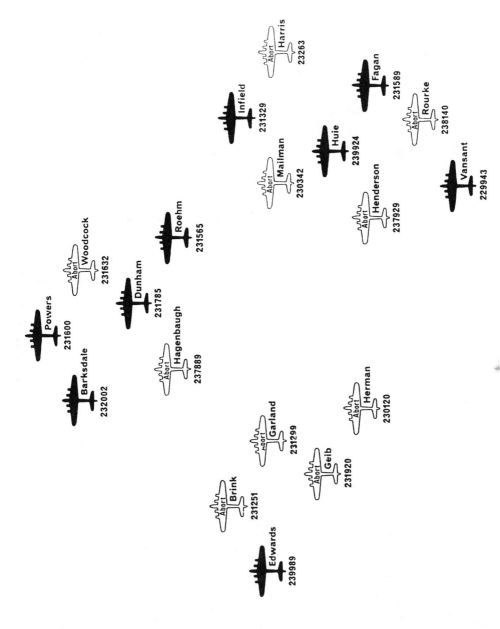

Composite Group Assembly Formation for Berlin, 4 March 1944.

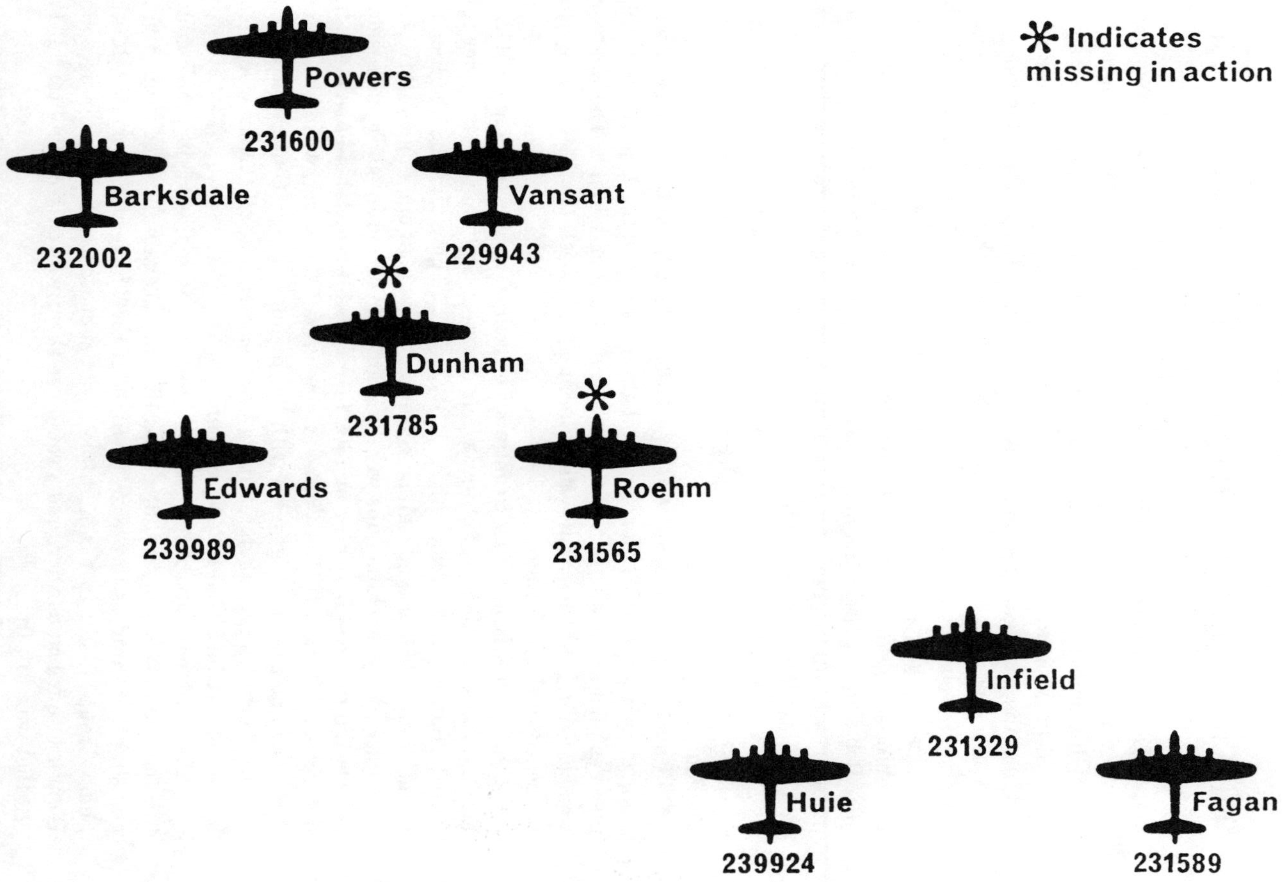

✳ Indicates missing in action

Powers
231600

Barksdale
232002

Vansant
229943

✳ Dunham
231785

Edwards
239989

✳ Roehm
231565

Huie
239924

Infield
231329

Fagan
231589

Composite Formation over Target, Berlin, 4 March 1944.

BERLIN: 6 March 1944

"Ed" Charles, Al Brown, Ralph Bowling, and Lawrence Pifer

Lieutenant Ed Charles, navigator, B-17 231681, 336th Squadron: Two days following the first raid on Berlin, we were briefed to strike the German capital again; this time the weather was favorable for the force of approximately eight hundred heavy bombers. It was to be a maximum effort to return to Berlin and turn the propaganda value of the first raid into irreparable damage.

When our crew took off from Horham at 0830 hours on that Monday morning, I'm sure no one realized that this was going to be the day the Eighth Air Force was going to receive its largest loss in planes and men of the war, sixty-nine heavy four-engine bombers and eleven escort fighters. Nor did my pilot Bob Kroeger and I realize when we'd walked to breakfast earlier that morning with Jim Conley, another 336th Squadron pilot from our barracks, that Jim wouldn't be coming back.

We assembled with the 100th and 390th groups without difficulty and departed the Suffolk coast over Orfordness at about 1030 hours, just behind the Fourth Combat Wing.

Lieutenant Al Brown, pilot, B-17 237882, 412th Squadron: My crew was again to lead the 95th. My former co-pilot, Lieutenant Hank Dippery, flew the plane as pilot and I was in the co-pilot's seat as command pilot. The weather was beautiful, and the route was straight in and back out. A lot of things happened in the meantime.

Lieutenant Ed Charles: We continued on course without incident until just before noon when Charles Schwartz, our engineer and top-turret gunner reported: "Bandits at 12 o'clock high . . . My God . . . There must be a million of them!" You could hear and feel the vibration throughout our ship as all twelve 50-caliber heavy machine guns were brought into action in quick succession.

On the fighters' first pass at 1200 hours (I well remember entering it in my logbook afterward), Jim Conley, flying on our left wing, was shot out of formation and began a big spiral with two engines on fire. Our crew counted only seven chutes getting out, but we later learned that all ten crewmen had bailed out and had been taken prisoner.

After two more attacks in rapid succession the fighters left, presumably to refuel, because twenty minutes later they hit us again. I looked to our right and slightly behind us to where "B" flight of the Thirteenth Wing, the 100th Bomb Group, flying in the high slot, was supposed to be. As far as John Dominick, our bombardier, and I could see there was only one solitary B-17 left that was still flying.

Lieutenant Ralph ("Hoss") Bowling, bombardier, B-17 231251, 334th Squadron: We came under attack for the second time from Me 109s attacking from head on. I was firing my nose gun when our navigator tapped me on the shoulder and pointed to the blazing number 1 engine. As I'd heard nothing on the intercom, I assumed it was time to bail out. I clipped my chest chute on and followed the navigator through the nose escape hatch. I must have passed out for lack of oxygen because the next thing I knew I was falling through space. I immediately pulled the ripcord and my chute snapped open. I saw our ship go down and watched it crash and explode, then the ground appeared to rush up toward me the closer I got to it.

When I tried to get up after landing, I discovered I'd broken my right ankle. Then two young German boys and a man with a rifle, who had watched me all the way down, came toward me. They saw I'd injured my ankle, and they helped me to a nearby farmhouse. The family there was having lunch. They offered me some food, but as I was still in a state of shock, I declined their kind offer. They were friendly but spoke only German so we couldn't converse.

I was given a chair and while I was waiting two more captured crewmen from our plane arrived at the farmhouse. I later discovered that all ten of our crew had mercifully survived, and we became prisoners of war for the next fifteen months.

Lieutenant Ed Charles: The attacks continued at intervals all the way to Berlin, through the IP, and during the bomb run. The flak over Berlin was really dense; at least two B-17s in our formation took direct hits and went down flaming. After we'd dropped our bombs and turned for home, fighters and flak hit us again just north of Magdeburg.

We had our 12-volt heating system to our flying suits shot out, and the only way we could keep warm was to plug in to the 24-volt system for brief periods. While under fighter attack and busy firing my nose gun, I forgot to unplug it and shorted out every connection from my shoes to my shirt. I sustained painful burns to both my heels and back. So much for trying to outsmart the system.

While the flak was exploding all around us, we felt the plane suddenly lurch; our number 1 engine was hit and the prop was feathered. Bob Kroeger asked everyone to check for further damage, but someone kept his mike button pressed down but wasn't speaking. Bob asked me to check, so I put on the "walk-around" oxygen bottle and started toward the rear of the plane.

I passed the top turret and reached the radio room. Our radio operator, George Green, was sitting down at what was left of his table, pushing down on his mike button and staring at a big round hole that a shell had made in the floor of the plane before going on up, between his legs, and out through the roof without exploding. (We've often kidded George many times since then about the only time he was speechless during our missions.)

We returned to Horham at 1610 hours. At the debriefing we learned that our group had lost eight planes and several more had been damaged, some seriously. A little later we discovered the 100th Group had lost sixteen and the 390th two, which ultimately proved to be the Thirteenth Combat Wing's heaviest loss of the war. During the air battle, eighty-seven German fighters were shot down in a vain attempt to stop more than eight hundred bombers from getting through to Berlin successfully.

There were two more missions to Berlin that week, on 8 and 9 March. I don't know if they were easier or just an anticlimax to all that week's activity. At least, for our crew and the 95th Group, they weren't as eventful as the first two raids.

Sergeant Lawrence Pifer, 335th Squadron: During the afternoon of 5 March, Marvin Anderson, our top-turret gunner, and I arrived at the Hermann Goering Hospital in Berlin. Marvin had been injured in his right arm by 20mm cannon shell fragments during the air battle on 4 March. We'd been given no food or drink since starting out on our final mission on 4 March. On arriving at the hospital we were given a cup of black ersatz coffee, cold and bitter, but the pain and exertion of the journey had made me so thirsty that I drank it thankfully. My ankle was put in a plaster cast that night.

The next day, 6 March, the Eighth Air Force bombed Berlin in force, and it was truly awesome. Then on 8 and 9 March they came again and the hospital began filling up with more downed flyers, both theirs and ours.

Lieutenant Al Brown: The city of Berlin was hit hard, and we fought our way home. Our plane had over three hundred holes in it of various sizes on our return, but miraculously no one was injured.

My crew has one special claim. On 27 March we flew our twenty-fifth mission, which completed our tour, to Cazaux, France. We'd finished twenty-five missions with the same crew, at the same time, and not one of us had been so much as scratched. The crew: Al Brown, Hank Dippery, Malcolm Durr, Forrest Flagler, Alan Smith, Frank Atterbury, Elmer Nutter, Bob Raney, Jim Craddock, and Dalton Addison.

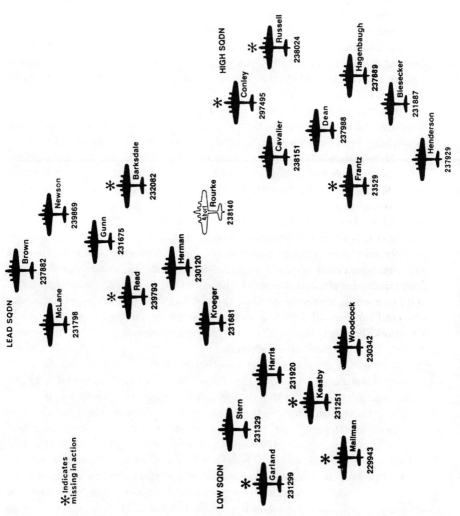

LEAD SQDN

Brown 237882
McLane 231798
Newson 239869
Gunn 231675
* Barksdale 232082
* Read 239793
Herman 230120
Kroeger 231681

Indicates missing in action

Abort Rourke 238140

HIGH SQDN

* Russell 238024
* Conley 297495
Hagenbaugh 237889
Cavalier 238151
Dean 237988
Blesecker 231887
* Frantz 23529
Henderson 237929

LOW SQDN

Stern 231329
Harris 231920
Woodcock 230342
* Keasby 231251
* Garland 231299
* Mallman 229943

95th Bomb Group (H) Formation to Berlin 6 March 1944.

163

BASE COMMUNICATIONS

Taylor Thurman and Cornell ("Corky") Etoll
335th Squadron

As chief of communications assigned to the 335th Squadron at Horham, my duties were many and varied. They grew more complex when I was assigned to group headquarters to join Major Knox's staff to help him locate and assign the best qualified communications personnel to lead the various segments, then assign from each of the four squadrons those best qualified to work under that leader.

Each combat radio operator in the Eighth Air Force had received a thorough and demanding six-month training course in the United States. The electronics curriculum was a solid twelve hours a day for seven days a week. When they graduated they were mentally and physically fit, and knowledgeable in electronics and its applications at that time. Not all made the grade—many washed out—but those that made it were the best that America could produce, and their record proves it. Combat took its toll: many died for their country, many were unsung heroes. We salute them.

The radio operator's duty was to send and receive messages by international Morse code at a minimum rate of sixteen words a minute. He was expected to be able to operate all other electronic communication radios aboard the aircraft. In addition, he was to have the cryptographic codes of the day and be able to decipher them. Direction finding through the use of radio was also used and passed on to the pilot or navigator. The radio operator made sure the IFF (identification, friend or foe) radio was operating or they could be shot down by other Allied aircraft.

The English coast had many direction-finding (D/F) radio stations. All a radio operator need do was call the station on continuous wave and hold the transmitting key down for five seconds. The D/F operator, using a galvanometer, could give him a direction to fly to reach a point on the English coast and then back to base. During the five-second transmission, two sister D/F stations picked up the signal and, using a map and the coordinates obtained in degrees from the galvanometer, drew a line from each station. Where these lines crossed on the map was the location of the plane. The coordinates were given in latitude and longitude. If your aircraft was disabled and going to ditch in the sea, British Air-Sea Rescue boats were there very soon to pick up the crews. A great many crews were saved in this manner, and although this method today is ancient, it proves it doesn't have to be so sophisticated to save lives.

Technical Sergeant Thomas Protheroe was given the responsibility of keeping the 335th Squadron's communications equipment aboard their B-17s in tip-top condition. Each B-17 carried and used the following equipment: a

40-watt command set using an amplitude modulated transmitter and receiver, used primarily for long-distance phone operation; a 25-watt FM transmitter and receiver for interplane communications with a choice of four different wave bands; a radio compass used for homing by the pilot or co-pilot; a 75-watt continuous-wave transmitter and a multiband receiver used by the radio operator; a fixed antenna used for amplitude-modulated command sets, frequency modulated antenna for short-wave very-high-frequency transmission and reception, and a long wire antenna used by the radio operator for full-wave transmission over long distances. This antenna was reeled in and out of the plane using an electric winch and spool. It was a very effective piece of equipment. Finally, there was a ten-position intercom system for use by the crew, a vitally important installation to have, especially during air combat and bomb runs.

Staff Sergeant Arthur Johnson and his assigned men checked and re-checked all radio equipment for satisfactory operation; sometimes they worked throughout the night, until every B-17 met their standards and U.S.A.A.F. standards. Who can ever forget tall and gangling Sergeant Joe McCloskey whose answer to "What's wrong, Joe?" was, "Trouble is what's the matter!" "What's the matter?" sometimes took all night to correct and occasionally longer, but they did it.

Sergeant Medwin White, a steady, quiet man with a purpose to "do it right," and he did. So did his men.

I'm proud of the 335th Squadron's radio maintenance men, because in more than three hundred combat missions, not one had to abort a mission because of radio failures.

Radio maintenance men also installed the control tower equipment, including the VHF command equipment, AM command equipment, and the aerials for them. The power supply for these units was installed in a heavily concreted room at ground level connected to British power lines of 250 volts. A standby gasoline generator was available if regular power failed. As far as I know, an occasion, when power was completely eliminated never happened. But we were ready for it!

Very early on, a need was recognized for the assembly of the group's planes, then in their respective wings, and from there to assemble with other wings over East Anglia.

Sometimes this needed to be accomplished despite a heavy overcast thousands of feet thick. This tightened a few muscles when after take-off each B-17 with twelve 500-pound bombs, 2,700 gallons of 100-octane gasoline, a full complement of guns and 10,000 rounds of 50-caliber ammunition among over 500 heavy bombers climbed for altitude. The risk of mid-air collisions led to the installation of the ground buncher station.

A buncher station consisted of one 75-watt transmitter, an aerial, a power supply, and an automatic keyer to key the transmitter call letters on continuous-wave transmission. The Thirteenth Wing was assigned call letters 8B8, and the buncher station was installed a few miles from Horham airfield in an open area, with only a few houses. One of these empty residential houses was used to house the unit.

Sergeant William Hooley was assigned to maintain the buncher each day a mission was planned. His other duties included obtaining rations for off-base personnel and to drive the communications major on his many rounds. Sergeant Hooley was a personable young man who was liked by all. Sometimes we all felt a twinge of jealousy at his being assigned a jeep when the rest of us either walked or rode a bicycle. (Just kidding—everyone liked Bill Hooley.)

Sergeant Cornell ("Corky") Etoll was in charge of the 95th Bomb Group's transmitter for direction finding. The station itself was of concrete construction, five miles from the base, and housed two 250-watt British transmitters and two 500-watt American BC610 transmitters.

A standby gasoline power unit was mounted on a large two-wheel trailer and was ready for use in case of power failure. A British sergeant was also available to aid in the use of the British transmitters. The building had two bedrooms, a kitchen, a transmitter room, a receiving area for monitoring equipment, and a workbench complete with replacement parts and a tool set.

Corky chose to use our American 500-watt transmitters because of their greater power over the great distances involved in daylight bombing. Daylight hours are simply not as good as night transmission when distance is a major factor. That extra 250 watts was very useful on a number of occasions.

Corky Etoll was a very likeable young man and was an experienced ham operator. Before the war he'd built his own 1000-watt transmitter and antenna complex in his own home and contacted hams all over the world. Although he never mentioned the fact, one of his technicians at the complex said that Corky could send and receive Morse code at more than seventy words per minute. He alone is responsible for the success the 95th Bomb Group combat radio operators had in being able to receive the base station in such distant places as Norway, Leipzig, and Berlin in eastern Germany and Warsaw, Poland.

Incidentally, we also had a friendly DIT DIT transmission with U.S. Naval Ship to Shore (NSS) in San Francisco, California, almost every night. Original contact included the words "U.S. England" with an answering "dit dit" from NSS. "U.S. England" was never repeated, only the dit dits, each operator recognizing each other as a warm friend.

Corky Etoll concludes: The BC610s were really beautiful transmitters. We had two inside the station and one on a mobile transporter. We moved around the countryside and transmitted from various locations to make old Jerry think it was coming from different locations. I'd send fake messages and drive them nuts over there.

Before the invasion in June 1944, we established contact with a bunch of Germans who had a radio station located on the Eiffel Tower in Paris, France. Once we'd located their frequency we got into the biggest and best cussing matches you ever heard. We called them *Schickelgrubbers* and everything else we could think of. Oh boy, the air was blue during those transmissions from Suffolk to Paris, telling those Krauts what we thought of them. They weren't very far away, only across the English Channel.

MORE SHORT BURSTS

William Steele, lead navigator, 335th Squadron: After flying coastal patrols with the R.C.A.F. as an observer from October 1942 until August 1943, I transferred to the Eighth Air Force in London. Subsequently I was ordered to the 94th Bomb Group, Bury St. Edmunds, as navigator on the crew of Lieutenant Michael Tuberose. We flew three missions with the 94th and were then transferred to the 100th Bomb Group at Thorpe Abbots, but on arrival there we were directed to Horham, where we were assigned to the 335th Squadron.

After flying several missions with Lieutenant Tuberose, I was assigned duty as lead navigator for the 95th Group, flying whenever Major Scripture requested.

Of my thirty-nine missions before becoming a POW (after bailing out from the lead plane over Szolnok, Hungary, 19 September 1944), the most dramatic, as I saw it, was my twenty-fifth mission when I was in the lead plane the day the 95th Group led the Third Air Division and the Eighth Air Force to Regensburg and other nearby targets on 25 February 1944.

It was a beautiful clear day with unlimited visibility and bombing results were later described as superb; but what I will never forget was the majestic and quite stunning sight of the First and Second Air divisions forming up close behind us on the way home. Together with our fighter escorts, over 1,600 airplanes participated that day, and it was probably the greatest aerial armada ever visible at the same time, in the history of air warfare.

A few days before my bail-out over Hungary, I was navigator for Major Bill Lindley's B-17 at low level over Arnhem and Nijmegen, Holland, as our VIP passenger, Major General Matthew Ridgway, observed the airborne landings. That was also an unforgettable sight.

****

Rudolph Cooper, transportation section: I had a B.S.T. Chevrolet truck assigned to me, and my main duty was to haul the different types of bombs—ranging from 100-pound incendiaries to the 1,000-pound general-purpose demolition bombs—from the main bomb dump to the flight lines.

On arrival at the hardstands the ordnance section took over, fusing the bombs before winching them up into each B-17's bomb bay. The armament section replenished the twelve heavy machine guns on each ship with long belts of fifty-caliber ammunition where necessary.

I vividly recall one very hectic period, during the invasion of France in June 1944, when we loaded bombs as fast as we could for three successive days. All the group's planes would go out, bomb their assigned targets in France, return, load up, get refueled, and take off immediately. And so it went on. The sky was never empty.

****

John Fisher, lead bombardier, 334th Squadron: On our arrival at Horham in January 1944, we were told the grim news that the 95th Group had already lost over seventy B-17s in combat. Hardly reassuring for an inexperienced and apprehensive replacement crew.

While walking over to the 334th Squadron area, we saw the extraordinary sight of an officer, armed with a wooden club in one hand and a .45 automatic in the other, frantically chasing a scampering rabbit. We immediately thought the worst.

"Who the hell is that?" someone asked incredulously.

"That's your squadron commander. . . ," came the reply.

We exchanged quick and meaningful glances, but nothing was said.

It later transpired the officer concerned was Captain Raymond Abbott, one of the finest and outstanding squadron commanders in the 95th Bomb Group. Very sadly, he passed away in 1970.

****

Leonard Herman, bombardier, 335th Squadron: It is a fact that neither flak nor fighters ask your color, race, or religion when they're shooting at you, and I'm sure we all bleed the same color blood when hit.

When we first arrived in England in May 1943 we thought our crew was the best and that nothing could ever happen to us. After our first mission, which was really a milk run and an indoctrination flight, our confidence rose accordingly. We were cocky, jubilant, gung-ho, and we really thought we were the best.

Other crews were shot down, and then came that terrible Kiel raid when we lost most of our squadron. Only two crews remained from the original nine. That was the beginning.

Shortly thereafter our pilot, Johnny Johnson, was killed. After the numbness and trauma of that mission wore off, the fear set in—the fear of the unknown, the fear of uncertainty. It was not the fear of physical pain—that never bothered me; but it was the gripping, gnawing fear of not knowing what the fates held in store for me.

That dreadful fear stayed with me. Although it slept within me when I was safely on the ground, when we were alerted for a mission it awoke immediately and remained with me throughout every subsequent raid.

When I'd successfully completed my tour of twenty-five missions, it was as though some gigantic iron weight had been lifted from my shoulders. I rushed home in November 1943, but in so doing, I missed a momentous period of history that I'd desperately wanted to be a part of. However, it was not to be. Fear had won out. I wanted to be as far away as possible from that terrible ordeal of combat flying, but I did miss it. Strange how one's mind works.

****

M.J. ("Doc") Steele, bombardier, 336th Squadron: During one of my occasional trips to London between missions in the late summer of 1944, I visited a tailor's shop, just off Oxford Street, and was measured up for a classic "Ike" Eisenhower jacket. I paid £40 in advance and was advised to collect my jacket approximately four weeks later.

On my next visit to London, at the scheduled time, I was shocked to discover the tailor's shop had completely vanished. In its place was a twenty-foot-deep, rubble-filled crater, the results, I was told, of V-1 flying bomb attack.

After expressing my condolences and sympathy to my informant I took the next train back to Suffolk. I subsequently submitted my claim for a £40 refund to the German government, but to date no response has been forthcoming.

****

Wayne Hanson, pilot, 336th Squadron: It was always interesting to watch the mannerisms of new crews as they joined the 95th as replacements. At first they kidded around and played volleyball. After they'd flown a few missions, they wouldn't play around anymore. Only card games, mostly poker, were continued.

At night we could hear the B-17 engines being revved up by the ground-crews up on the flight line, preparing the bombers for tomorrow's mission. When the C.Q. man (charge of quarters, or Wake-up man) left the 336th Squadron headquarters, we could hear the ominous sound of the doorknob being turned.

There is really no way to describe the mixed emotions of fear and getting on with the job, but I always made a point of leaving my wallet with a kind, understanding older sergeant who promised to send it home for me if I didn't come back.

****

Tom Ryan, headquarters staff: For several weeks during January and February 1944, I was assistant to the effects officer. This was a post not included in the table of organization, but this job certainly had to be done. Our task was to collect the personal belongings and effects of those crewmen who were unfortunately listed as missing in action, generally ten names at a time. Our enlisted staff went to the barracks where the missing or dead flyers had been assigned and collected all personal possessions. They were then itemized, listed, and packed for shipment to a main depot in Kansas City until claimed by next-of-kin or by the crewmen themselves, if they had survived, after the war.

There was a certain amount of government property included in the effects, such as flight gear, which we returned to the supply department, but all personal effects were boxed up securely for preservation over an indefinite period of time. (I wonder if any of it is still in storage waiting to be claimed.)

I recall one occasion we were just about to pack a shot-down crewman's belongings for shipment when we were informed that he was *already in Spain* and would be back to claim them personally very shortly. That airman's escape and evasion must have been one of the fastest on record.

****

Glenn Infield, pilot, 412th Squadron: It was the practice for replacement pilots to fly their first combat mission accompanied by an experienced veteran pilot. My crew had arrived at Horham in late September 1943. My first mission was to Bremen, 8 October 1943, as co-pilot with a veteran of twenty-three previous missions flying as pilot.

All went well until we approached the primary target and the two groups ahead of us came under concentrated fighter attack. Three B-17s went down, trailing smoke and shedding parachutes. An enemy fighter, attempting a head-on attack actually collided with another bomber. Both aircraft immediately exploded. The flak grew in its intensity over the outskirts of Bremen and claimed several more planes, one of which was literally blown to bits. It seemed impossible that anyone could have survived that horrific scene.

Shortly after "bombs away," we took a direct flak hit immediately behind the cockpit area, fortunately without any injuries, but it greatly affected the rudder controls. I glanced across at our pilot. He'd "frozen on the stick," evidently as a result of yet one more very close call. And who can blame him?

I managed to get the plane back under control by using differential power on the still functioning engines to counteract a gradual right-hand turn and eventually landed back at Horham with a jammed rudder and numerous flak holes.

A waiting ambulance took the pilot over to the base hospital and from there to a rest home. On Thursday, 14 October our crew flew the Schweinfurt mission, a day on which the Eighth Air Force lost sixty B-17s. It was a traumatic introduction to the air war over Europe, but we survived and completed our tour of missions in the spring of 1944.

****

David G. Cargo, bombardier: The summer of 1944 saw many combat crews flying their missions in a regular and rapid sequence, with very little time off. A bombardier acquaintance flew his tour of thirty-five missions in sixty-six days, because by then the Eighth Air Force had gained considerable air superiority over Europe. Our crew didn't do it that quickly, but there were reasons for our comparatively slow progress.

After we'd flown a few missions we were selected as a lead crew and began our training immediately. Consequently we lost our place in regular scheduling. Then our pilot, Lieutenant James Griffin, came down with the mumps. It was the only case on the base. Some of our crew flew with other crews, but considerable delay resulted.

Just before D-Day, 6 June, all men were required to carry weapons—carbines for enlisted men and the officers carried .45s. This set the stage for another, albeit bizarre, delay. The co-pilot's Colt .45 somehow discharged in its holster while we were in our barracks one evening. The bullet struck the concrete stove base and split into two pieces. One piece passed over several bunks (I was lying on one of them) and went through several garments hanging on the wall. The other fragment ricocheted upward, passing through a finger of the pilot's left hand. Fortunately no bones were broken, but he was grounded again for another week or so.

Both our ball-turret gunner and co-pilot were wounded by the notorious flak over Merseberg on 28 July 1944. The co-pilot's injury was in the left foot, and although the flight surgeons operated on it about three times, they couldn't get the wound to heal. It was several months before they discovered the flak fragment had forced a piece of fur-lined flying boot up into the wound. The leather, of course, didn't show up on an x-ray. Once the boot fragment was removed, he recovered rapidly.

I was quite young at the time (nineteen), but I suppose our tour was about average. Some missions were more trying than others, but apart from the ever present dangers each time we crossed the enemy coast, the flights also had a very interesting geographical aspect. We flew a shuttle mission to Russia and

Italy, and even dropped leaflets along with the bombs on one occasion. But all in all, our crew came out of it with few physical or mental scars.

****

Russell P. Allman, bombardier, 334th Squadron: Our crew flew twenty-two missions together, eleven of which were in February 1944. Of these eleven, seven were flown in ten days, including Regensburg, Brunswick, and a long one to Posen.

We were one of the crews that started on the first daylight raid to Berlin, on 4 March 1944, but were recalled.

Two days later, 6 March we went to Berlin. The closer we came to getting our required twenty-five missions, the tougher they seemed to be. I learned later this mission was a tough one. On our way to the target about 11:00 A.M., under heavy fighter attack and in lots of flak, I was hit in the right wrist while operating the chin turret, and literally spun around on my seat. I do not know what hit me but my arm was 90 percent severed (and later—about 7:00 P.M.— my hand was amputated at the wrist.)

The navigator was one busy fellow from here on. Since he (Elton Skinner) and the flight engineer (Marion Gilman) administered morphine and applied a tourniquet to my arm, I did not lose too much blood or suffer from pain.

In my relaxed state, I didn't realize just how rough a mission it was, and since our plane wasn't damaged, we continued to Berlin. The pilot, G.B. Lloyd, salvoed the bombs.

On our return from Berlin, at about 3:00 P.M., the plane was hit, and we were on fire. G.B. gave the signal to bail out, and within sight of the English Channel, we all hit the silk and landed in Holland. I might add Lieutenant Skinner gave me a little shove out the lower hatch. Since I was wearing a chest chute, I had to reach across and pull the rip cord with my left hand. No, I didn't bother to count to ten—someone else may have as I'm sure I had lots of help that day. Lieutenant Skinner checked me on the ground, then hid out. He was never captured, but after spending six months in POW camp, I beat him back to the United States.

I was taken to a farm house, later picked up by German soldiers and taken to hospital in Leeurwarden, Holland, for surgery about 7:00 P.M. After a few days there, I was taken to Frankfurt for interrogation, and after a time of recuperation near Frankfurt, I went to Stalag Luft III near Sagan, Germany.

In September 1944 I was repatriated and came back to the states as an exchange POW on the S.S. *Gripsholm.*

I went to Battle Creek, Michigan, Percy Jones General Hospital, was fitted with a prosthesis, taught to use it, and retired January 1945. I was the only one of our crew injured. Everyone of the crew except Lieutenant Skinner was captured.

I thank God every day for seeing me through and for bringing me back.
Kriegie #1838   Russell P. Allman
West Camp   0-685753

****

Laur A. Stevens, tail gunner, 412th Squadron: Webster says, "Courage is the quality of being fearless or brave." But if you are startled into sudden terror, then fearless and brave are no longer words to explain one's actions. Panic erases all. We can well remember the full range of emotions in our many missions together. Of any one thing in my past that I can look back upon with pride, it's being together with all the members of my crew. None of you chose me, nor did I choose you, but I consider myself to be a lucky person to have been with each and every one of you. (From a letter written in 1985 to Lieutenant Colonel Albert T. Keeler, Ret., pilot of "Full House").

WE WERE A COMBAT CREW

Vincent Fox, Navigator, 335th Squadron

In 1943, when a four-engine bomber roared serenely overhead, people ran out into the street to stare after it. To those on the ground, the bomber represented a complicated and powerful machine, a symbol of America's military prowess. The human element, the bomber's crew, was scarcely thought of as the great silver bird quickly disappeared from sight. Yet, behind the controls and in the gun turrets of that bomber were yesterday's high school boys—a former clerk in a grocery store, a truck driver, an undergraduate college student, a service station attendant, an insurance office clerk—the unskilled youth of America quickly trained by Army methods to manipulate the machines to spearhead the Allied military offensive.

We were an "all-American" crew, entrusted with a B-17: ten youths hastily trained and haphazardly thrown together by Army methods, but the unfinished product was a potential team of specialists ready to try its luck against the Axis opposition.

"Happy" Hal Powers, the pilot and aircraft commander, was a cocky, blond-headed boy from Orlando, Florida, who thought that anyone born north of Virginia should apologize for being a "damned Yankee." "Mac" McCleod, our co-pilot, was a good-natured, husky boy from the Oklahoma oilfields, with a sweet, blonde wife waiting for him. Herbie Levine, bombardier, was a cocky little Jewish boy from the Bronx who resented anyone associating him with Brooklyn. Knipper, the flight engineer and top-turret gunner, hadn't known a carburetor from a cylinder head before he left Manhattan. Felix could've passed for a junior in any Mid-Western high school, but he'd knocked around plenty before the Army turned him into a radio operator. The ball turret was ably manned by Tom Kennedy, a big-hearted, cigar-smoking little Irishman from Troy, New York, who had more tall stories than Paul Bunyan. Back on the waist guns were O'Keefe and Brashear. O'Keefe was a dark-haired, handsome kid from the Dakota wheat fields, and Brashear got his natural shooting eye from shooting squirrels in the wooded hills of Kentucky. Our tail was defended by tall, easy-going Stan Allard from upstate New York. I was the navigator, the college kid from Ohio, and that made ten of us.

The crew had been formed down at Pyote, Texas. Mac, the co-pilot, and I joined them at Dyersburg, Tennessee, for second-phase training. That was back in June 1943, when Hermann Goering's Luftwaffe still soared virtually unchallenged over the air space of Hitler's fortress Europe and Congress was busily appropriating money and drafting men to fight a global war.

Crew 70, as we were impersonally listed on the operations bulletin board at Dyersburg, Tennessee, was busily occupied dropping practice bombs and flying high-altitude, cross-country practice missions, hoping for a chance to learn formation flying when the ships were available to make up a formation. Powers, fresh out of transition school at Sebring, Florida, demonstrated to us what the B-17 could do when expertly handled, and soon all of us were in love with our Fort. Each crew member practiced his own specialty. Herbie upheld his own reputation and that of the Norden bombsight by demonstrating some good high-level bombing on the practice range near Covington, Tennessee. Our gunners practiced deflection shooting at a tow-target sleeve over the Gulf of Mexico, although we knew that attacking Fw 190s and Me 109s would be a far different proposition when it came to the real thing.

By flying night and day and with an occasional forty-eight-hour pass to Memphis, our two months at Dyersburg passed rapidly. We were supposed to be transformed from ten individuals into a combat-ready team. Each man's judgment regarding his specialty was confidently respected by the rest of the crew, and as our training time wound down we felt a growing confidence in having Powers and McCleod up there at the controls. Although we were still untested rookies we knew we'd earned and deserved a chance to prove we could get the job done, the Army way. We were eager and just cocky enough to think we could survive combat.

On the ground we were a misfit family living and working together; borrowing each other's shoe polish, toothpaste, and money; griping about the food and the stuffy ground-school classrooms; and sharing rooms at the Peabody Hotel in Memphis when out on pass.

At Grand Island, Nebraska, we received our final processing and were given a brand-new B-17G to fly overseas. Wow! Powers popped a couple of buttons when he signed for a ship with only seventeen hours on the clock—the newest plane he'd ever touched. After a session of calibrating the instruments, we were waved off by Mac's wife one early September 1943 morning for our point of embarkation. Our final destination was still a military secret, but we suspected that we were heading for the Eighth Air Force and the European theater of operations.

At Gander Lake, Newfoundland, our suspicions were confirmed. Our route was supposed to be a closely guarded military secret, but two months later LIFE magazine featured an article that gave all the basic information concerning North Atlantic air crossings. We also learned that the Nazi submarine commanders knew all about our route before LIFE told all.

We were finally on our way to do combat, the real thing, and to put to destructive use the accumulated skills we'd acquired through months of hard training, living in tar-paper huts and tent cities. Our average age was twenty-two.

Because of a delayed start and subsequent late takeoff from Gander to Prestwick, Scotland, we were the last B-17 from the Thompson provisional group making the North Atlantic flight that September night, being about two hours behind the main group. Powers and McCleod in the cockpit and Felix in the radio room picked up several "Mayday" calls from our friends ahead of us but we were not close enough to the planes in distress to be able to help. We heard later that five crews from our provisional group failed to make it for a variety of reasons. Because of our late start, I ran out of stars to use for my astro-navigation when the early gray streaks of dawn gradually lighted our lonely world above the clouds and I was unable to calculate a good estimated time of arrival.

Apart from a few glimpses of green, the first real land we saw was Prestwick airfield as we let down through the undercast. They were as glad to see us at Prestwick as we were to get there. One of the ships that had gone down carried our provisional group commander.

The reason we were so welcome in Britain was that due to heavy losses replacement crews and planes were urgently required to fill the gaps. Consequently, our ship was hustled off to a modification center for some armor plating and combat modifications, and we got our first ride on the British railway system to a combat crew replacement center for a week of intensive groundschool on combat tactics in the E.T.O.

For the first time in our Army careers we were "permanent party" when we got to the 95th Bomb Group. We were finally "over there." When we arrived at Horham in the middle of the night, in a drenching rain, the mess-hall was open for us. It seems that replacement crews nearly always arrived late at night, and traditionally it was always raining, so we conformed to the pattern. Down in the 335th Squadron area, our new hut-mates informed us that the beds we were taking over had recently been vacated by some of the boys who'd been shot down during the recent Munster mission. We certainly didn't need a "Lord Haw Haw" broadcast to welcome us to Europe as our new squadron friends were very eager to tell us all about combat in the E.T.O., and what happened to rookie crews flying in the "tail-end Charlie" position.

During the bomb run the bombardier needed to have the aircraft flying straight and level for sufficient time to stabilize the gyroscope in the Norden bombsight and to feed in the groundspeed and drift. This was the basic theory of precision daylight bombing. We were soon to discover that the bomb run was our most vulnerable moments of the mission, because any strategic target worth attacking was always heavily defended by batteries of 88mm and 105mm antiaircraft guns. However, Colonel Curtis LeMay, CO of the 305th Bomb Group and later commander of the Third Air Division, by using an old ROTC artillery manual about the French 75mm cannon, calculated that the probability of a direct hit on a target the size of a B-17 flying at 25,000 feet to be 273 rounds per hit. He thought that gave us pretty good odds. So it became standard operating procedure in the Third Air Division to fly straight and level from the IP to "bombs away." Hermann Goering had promised Hitler that the crazy Americans, flying in broad daylight, would never penetrate past the Rhine River and into the Fatherland in any force.

In October 1943 we had the task of trying to make Goering look bad by getting bombs on targets in Germany, surviving the flak and the fighters, and getting back to England to fly again another day. The Eighth Air Force had been flying missions from England since September 1942, and by the fall of 1943 the loss rate was about 6 percent per mission on average. For the "lucky bastards," a tour of duty was twenty-five missions. It didn't take us long to come to the ominous conclusion that six times twenty-five added up to more than 100 percent.

After a brief indoctrination period, we flew our first combat mission; Powers and McCleod proved they could fly formation. We subsequently graduated from the tail-end Charlie position and worked our way up to squadron lead.

When we got past mission thirteen, we knew we were over the hump and on the downhill side of successfully completing our tour. We didn't dare talk about it but we secretly thought that we had a guardian angel flying with us and watching over every man in our crew.

During an unusual period of clear weather in February 1944, we were a very small part of the huge push—the "big week" operations—that established the Eighth Air Force as a great and powerful force that played a significant role in the ultimate defeat of Hitler's Fortress Europe.

We were there on 4 March 1944 with Lieutenant Colonel Mumford when he led the 95th and 100th Bomb groups over "Big B," when the German capital city felt its first of many thousands of tons of American daylight bombs. We were the first group to accomplish this target goal, and we subsequently appeared on the front cover of *LIFE* magazine as a result of this historic and significant mission.

Did Americans want heroes? Well, we were willing at that point to be satisfied with survival and induction into the 95th Bomb Group's chapter of "the lucky bastards club."

****

Postscript: Nine of the ten original members of the Powers crew successfully completed their tour of twenty-five combat missions.

Major Powers (later colonel) volunteered for a second tour and flew as a command pilot with the 95th Group until he crash-landed in Belgium with two engines out during his thirteenth mission of his second tour.

Captain Fox flew five additional missions as assistant Thirteenth Combat Wing navigator.

All survived to celebrate VE day.

A FATEFUL DAY

Jan Murray (Janofsky) and Max Murray

I was entertaining in England with the U.S.O. during February and March of 1944. My brother, David Janofsky, was a co-pilot with the 412th Squadron, 95th Bomb Group. He and I got together a few times in London when I first arrived in England.

In early April 1944 three members of my show fell ill with pneumonia, which gave me the chance for a week off, after which a replacement dance team and singer would join me. My vacation was due to start on 8 April. My brother and I were jubilant as he'd received permission from his CO for me to spend my vacation at his air base. We made plans to celebrate my son's second birthday, 8 April, together.

Shortly before 8 April I was asked by the U.S.O. to stay in my area for another three days since a new contingent of troops would be arriving from the states and I was the only entertainer in that vicinity. Although I had only one musician left, we performed those three days. I informed my brother in the meantime that I would arrive by train on 11 April. David said if he was flying a mission that day he'd arrange to have me picked up at the train station.

After a long train ride, I finally arrived at the local station. I was approached by a private who informed me that David's CO had asked him to collect me. He took me straight to the CO's office at the 95th Group's base, and there I was told that my brother's aircraft was one of the seven lost by the group that day.

I collapsed . . . stunned. . . . I vaguely recall everyone being so very kind and sympathetic; the rest is a hazy memory. That night I slept on David's bunk.

The next day several Intelligence Section officers gave me their report on that mission. The initial target was Poznan, Poland, but at the last minute was changed to Rostock, Germany. It was there that my brother's plane was hit, as confirmed by some of the boys in other aircraft that were in the immediate vicinity. They couldn't keep up with the formation, two engines were out, and somewhere over the Baltic Sea, they bailed out. I was assured that all ten parachutes opened, although I was told the water is so cold at that time of the year that one could only survive for about fifteen or twenty minutes at the most.

Despite my despondency I clung desperately to the hope that David and his crew had been rescued in time, and they were safely in a POW camp. My first impulse was to return home to be with my father, but knowing my brother had at least got out of the plane made me determined to stay in the E.T.O. as long as possible, hoping and dreaming that someday I'd walk into my brother's prison camp and greet him.

In retrospect it was a childish, romantic notion, but at that time it was the one thing I had to cling to. So I stayed on in England, asking everyone I met at the U.S.O., the Red Cross, and the Air Force if they'd heard any more details concerning my brother. I also wrote to as many families of David's crew that I could locate and assured them all that I was there at the airfield the day their boys hadn't returned, that I had spoken with crewmen in adjacent planes, etc., and gave them assurances there was every reason to have hope that their boys had survived.

After the invasion in June 1944, I was one of the first civilian contingents to go to France, and my show was assigned to the Ninth Air Force. I still had that crazy dream that my brother was a POW and being with the Air Force made me feel close. Every flight crew promised that they'd fly me right to the prison camp when the war was won, and I was also constantly in touch with the Red Cross, hoping for positive news.

Finally, a few days after Paris was liberated, I was officially notified that my brother was dead. I couldn't get any further information; all the Red Cross knew was that the German Red Cross notified the International Red Cross, which informed the American Red Cross, that Lieutenant David Janofsky was dead. I was immediately flown home so that I could be with my father. I contacted the families of the other crew members; apart from me, not one had received any official notification.

After the war I followed every lead, no matter how flimsy, in a determined effort to try to ascertain the facts surrounding my brother's death, but to no avail. Then about 1948 I noticed a small news item in the *New York Times* concerning an American general laying a wreath on the grave of an American soldier who was buried at a church of a small Danish coastal town.

Desperately following every lead, no matter how small and insignificant as this one appeared to be, I called the *Times* and asked for the name of the foreign correspondent who'd written the article. After several frustrating delays (stupidly when I wrote to him I signed the letter Jan Murray instead of my real name, Murray Janofsky), he eventually wrote back saying that he was sorry but the soldier buried in Denmark was not my brother. The name on the headstone was Lieutenant David Janofsky.

The long, agonizing, and frustrating search for David was over. I went slightly crazy. I couldn't call the correspondent because he traveled constantly, so I wrote again explaining everything and that David Janofsky was indeed my brother.

Here is the story. . . .

My brother was buried in a Catholic church graveyard in the small Danish town of Suaneke on the Isle of Bornholm. A Danish priest wrote me a long letter describing what had happened.

A Danish fishermen had recovered David's body from the sea during the late evening of 11 April, the day of the mission. He'd brought the young airman's body to the church at about 5:00 A.M. the following morning, and because the fisherman was a member of the Danish Underground he'd had to wait for an opportune moment to bring the body ashore.

The priest then described my brother: about 6'4", about 200 pounds, and he was wearing a ring that I'd bought him for his high school graduation; as final proof the dog tags gave his name as Lieutenant David Janofsky, Hebrew religion.

The priest, with some local townspeople, then approached the German Army commandant. They told him about my brother, informing him that up until now the Germans on the island had enjoyed a nice easy war, but things would change drastically unless they were allowed to bury my brother in the churchyard with full military honors. They told him if permission was not forthcoming it would mean big trouble in every possible way.

The commandant, not wanting to upset his own easy little war, promptly confirmed they could do what they demanded.

My brother was subsequently buried with full military honors, and because he was Jewish, the priest said the Kaddish, which is the Hebrew prayer for the dead.

The priest then pleaded with me to let my brother remain there as a symbol for the Danish people and a permanent reminder of all the many times the Eighth Air Force had flown over Denmark to give them back their freedom. He added that on Sundays many local people regularly put flowers on David's grave and prayed. He kindly sent me photographs of the grave, and I sent money for the church as we continued our correspondence. Incidentally, my brother wasn't wounded, he'd simply frozen to death during those few short hours in the Baltic Sea. To my knowledge, none of the other crewmen was ever found.

However, my father wanted to bring David's body home to lie beside my mother who had passed away in 1942. I pleaded with him to allow David's body to remain on the Isle of Bornholm. I explained that he was the only American soldier buried there and that the Danish people regarded him as a symbol of all the American servicemen who had given their lives for Danish freedom. But my father was desolate and inconsolable, so we requested that David's remains be sent home.

The final irony was that in the year that it took for my brother's body to arrive, my father died from cancer. On the morning of my father's funeral, I received a call from the port of Brooklyn informing me that my brother's body had arrived from Denmark.

Lieutenant David Janofsky now lies at rest in Washington Cemetery, Brooklyn, New York, beside his father and mother.

****

Max Murray describes what happened to his brother, Ralph Murray, tail gunner on the same aircraft as Lieutenant Janofsky: Ralph flew his first mission (it tragically proved to be his last) on 11 April 1944. His B-17G, named "Miss-Raps-O-Dee" (serial 237876) was hit and went down over the Baltic Sea. All ten crewmen bailed out.

My parents were notified that Ralph was missing in action, and until the end of the war they hoped he was trying to make it back through the Underground or that he was a POW.

Finally, in 1949 my parents received a letter dated 24 August 1949 from Memorial Division, Department of the Army, part of which reads: "On 21 May 1948, the consul general at Hamburg, Germany, transmitted to the American consul general at Hamburg, the identification tags of your son. It was stated that a German fisherman, Hans Conradi, found in his net at 54° 45' 45' N, R 15° east, the bodies of two American airmen, and on the body of one were found the identification tags bearing your son's name and serial number. In view of the fact that the fisherman was not immediately returning to land, the remains of both airmen were sewn in canvas bags and given back to the sea, in true seaman's tradition. We have no conclusive evidence to prove that these were the remains of your son."

No effort was subsequently made by my parents to try to gather more information concerning Ralph's death. It would have been far too painful.

The other eight crewmen who died in the sea that fateful day were Eugene Schiappacasse, Henry Kress, Gerald Taylor, Warren Messmer, Angelo Passere, Harvey Cartrite, Frank Saunders, and Edward Phillips. Although Ralph was a waist gunner, I was told that he flew as tail gunner when he was shot down.

It wasn't until 1985 that I discovered the existence of the 95th Bomb Group (H) Association. I immediately began making relevant inquiries to learn more about the mission and about Ralph. Despite all the help and cooperation from members of the 95th, I've discovered nothing. Unfortunately, Ralph's personal records were destroyed in a fire in 1972, but I will continue in my efforts to complete that part of my family's history.

In the meantime I've met some outstanding 95th Group people, and I hope to keep in touch with them for some time to come.

A CREW CHIEF'S WAR

Martin ("Mitch") Mitchell, Crew Chief, 334th Squadron

I was twenty-one years old when I enlisted in the Army Air Corps on 4 December 1941, at Fort Sheridan, Illinois, just three days before "the day of infamy," when the Japanese devastated our Pacific fleet at Pearl Harbor without even so much as a declaration of war.

From Fort Sheridan I was sent to Jefferson barracks, Missouri, for basic training and aptitude tests. Such was the haste as the United States rapidly mobilized for a global war that I only received a total of nine hours' (one day) basic training before I was sent to Chanute Field, Illinois, where the airplane mechanics school was located.

Following my successful graduation from the five-and-a-half-month-long mechanics course, I went over to the electrical specialists school, also located at Chanute Field. The next phase of very thorough and complex training was in Minneapolis, Minnesota, where our class of thirty studied and absorbed the fascinating intricacies of the automatic flight control electronic (A.F.C.E.) system at Minneapolis Honeywell, a large electronics company. We lived on the campus of the University of Minnesota during this very interesting course.

After graduation, I was then assigned to the 334th Squadron, 95th Bombardment Group (H) at Ephrata, Washington. The 95th then moved to Spokane, Washington, and from there to Rapid City, South Dakota.

At that time I was in the communications section, but while awaiting clearance from the War Department, I went across to the engineering section every day to work with the line crews maintaining the airplanes. (Any airman working near the top-secret Norden bombsight needed special clearance.) Eventually, Lieutenant Dowlin, 334th Squadron engineering officer, arranged with Lieutenant Ford, communications, to transfer me to the line. On 1 February 1943, I was promoted to corporal and a crew chief. Eight weeks later I was promoted to the rank of master sergeant. Having been born and brought up on a farm at Lyndon Station, Wisconsin, (where I still live) and endured all the trials and tribulations of the Great Depression, as had a whole generation of young Americans, I found I never could stay away from grease for long.

When the bitterly cold winter weather hampered our flying training out of Rapid City, we went on detached service to Pueblo, Colorado. It was here that we lost a plane and its entire crew, all of whom I'd known well. They'd asked me to accompany them on that flight, but the fates decided otherwise. I'd worked through most of the previous night, and I explained to them I needed some sack time while they were flying the practice mission.

As an illustration of how easily it can happen, during our flight back to Rapid City from Pueblo our aircraft began to ice up and lose altitude, 1,000 feet per minute, but the de-icer boots on the leading edges of both wings and on our tail-plane saved us from going down.

From Rapid City, the 95th's ground personnel headed for Camp Kilmer, New Jersey. New uniforms were issued and all the attendant paraphernalia of processing was duly completed for our move overseas. On 4 May 1943, we walked up the gangplank of the *Queen Elizabeth*, sailed alone across the pond to Greenock, Scotland, up the Firth of Clyde, arriving 11 May. It was a truly beautiful sight to look out in the morning and see such green-clad countryside. Then on to Framlingham, Suffolk, England.

From there a group of crew chiefs and mechanics went over to Alconbury, where the 95th's planes were stationed with the 92nd Bomb Group. It was at Alconbury while I was working on an engine on one of our B-17s on 27 May that suddenly the whole plane seemed to leap up into the air. A split second later came the sound of a massive explosion. Another of our Fortresses, not too far away, had exploded while the bombs were being loaded, wrecking and severely damaging several other adjacent airplanes. Nineteen 95th ground people were killed and twenty more were injured, some seriously.

The 95th's planes were transferred to Framlingham after flying their first few combat missions from Alconbury. While at Framlingham in mid-June 1943, our group suffered another disaster—the mission to Kiel, which cost ten B-17s and crews—but these early setbacks seemed to strengthen the group's resolve. Later that month we settled in at our permanent base at Horham, Suffolk, for the remainder of the war.

The main duties of the crew chief and his mechanics involved in the servicing of their assigned B-17 included checking and maintaining each of the four 1,200-horsepower engines and their turbo-superchargers; changing complete engines if necessary; filling gasoline tanks, "Tokyo" tanks on long missions; replenishing oil tanks; checking tires for wear and inflation; keeping the plane scrupulously clean both inside and out; checking all controls; maintaining records on all repairs and replacements; preflighting; starting engines before every flight; and being at the flight line when the group returned from a mission.

We would then confer with the pilot to see that everything functioned properly and if not, ensure that the problem part was repaired or replaced as soon as possible. After changing an engine, the plane had to be flight-tested— "slow-timed" was the expression—like "running in" the engine of a new automobile.

During one particular period, the airplanes on which I was crew chief flew seventy-nine consecutive missions without returning because of mechanical failure, and it was for this achievement that I was awarded the Bronze Star.

For our ground crew, it was often exhausting work with long hours on the flight line and being exposed to all types of English weather: sun, rain, sleet, and snow, and of course, the bitterly cold east wind during the winter months, which came blustering across the airfield directly from the North Sea, about twenty miles away. But it was also very interesting and satisfying work despite the continual discomforts. Sometimes crippled, battle-damaged B-17s limped home long after the group returned. The Fortress was certainly a rugged airplane.

Among several interesting missions I flew was the first shuttle mission to Russia in June 1944. On that occasion I went along as crew chief and flew as a tail gunner. I also crewed a Pathfinder B-17 for about six months toward the end of the war.

One of the planes that we maintained was named "Smiling Sandy Sanchez" with a prominent 44 painted on its nose section in recognition of a young and slightly built Mexican-American who flew forty-four missions over Europe before he was ordered back to the United States.

The Nissen hut we occupied at Horham Airfield had fourteen master sergeants, one technical, and one staff sergeant. We got up very early in the mornings to go up to our respective flight lines, and frequently we returned quite late in the evenings. Consequently it left very little time for making up our bunks or sweeping up the floor in our hut. On one of the first inspections of quarters, the officer making the inspection didn't venture further than the door. He took a long critical look and then said, "There's absolutely no point at all in even starting to clean this place up. I respectfully suggest that you just landscape it."

From then on, our hut wasn't inspected.

When the German forces retreated from Holland in the spring of 1945, they blew up many of the dikes that had been constructed to reclaim land from the North Sea. I recall flying over these flooded areas of Holland at tree-top level with the group as we dropped tons of food to the Dutch people, many of whom hadn't had any real food for months.

During the fall of 1985 my wife and I went on a farm tour of several European countries. We visited a Dutch farm that had been part of this reclaimed land, and we saw quite a few interesting sights, at ground level this time. The Dutch people were very friendly, and they were also very grateful for our wartime efforts and achievements.

BERLIN: 29 APRIL 1944

Charles Lajeski, Pilot, 412th Squadron

Naturally, with my usual run of luck, my number one mission had to be a big one, "Big B" to be precise, but I never expected to be thrown to the lions so soon. After all, we had only arrived at station 119, Horham, about a week previously and had precious little time to adjust to life in the European theater of operations. We'd flown practice missions on 24, 27, and 28 April during which we sharpened our skills on formation flying and bombing.

My crew and I were alerted during the evening of 28 April with the "Alert" flag hoisted outside squadron headquarters. I spent some time chatting with combat veterans, pondering the probable target for the next day, and then I tried to get some sleep.

I suppose I was just too nervous and apprehensive because all I did was toss and turn restlessly on my bunk, worrying and pondering the possibilities and probabilities. What was it *really* like? How would I cope with any emergency or desperate situation that might arise? How well had I prepared my crew for a long tour of duty? How well had I prepared myself? The answers to all these questions would come soon, very soon.

The wake up call came about 0300 hours, and after a tasteless breakfast, washed down with brackish coffee, we trooped apprehensively over to the briefing hut at group operations. When the curtain concealing the large-scale map of Europe was drawn back, we saw our target, route in and out, flak areas to avoid, fighter escort points, slide shots of what the target area looked like from various angles, etc.

Quite a roar went up when we saw the colored yarn extended all the way to Berlin, or "Big B" as it was known to the crews. After a very thorough briefing we collected our chutes and escape kits, climbed aboard a truck, and were driven up to the flight line. On arrival at the hardstand, the crew chief and his mechanics were already waiting around our ship, a well-worn B-17G called "A Good Bet," a combat veteran also waiting, poised and ready, to take us to war.

The plane checked out satisfactorily, and in a short while we were lined up, behind other B-17s, on the main runway ready to take off. Assembly, in clear weather, was no problem, and after taking our place in the formation as tail-end Charlie, we were on our way.

Everything was quite serene until we crossed the enemy coast, where we saw our first bursts of flak—ugly, brown-black blobs off in the distance. Eugene LeVan, my navigator reported, "We are now officially feuding."

As we approached the Initial Point, prior to our bombing run, we could clearly see the huge cloud of flak over Berlin that we had to fly through in order to reach and hit the primary target. The actual bomb run was quite frightening as the bursting flak shells appeared to be all around our plane. Directly after bombs away I felt a barrage of hits, and almost immediately number 3 engine ran away and had to be feathered. While heading toward our group's rally point, our ball-turret gunner reported the loss of his oxygen supply as did the other crew stations. Not being able to keep up with the group formation with only three engines, I dropped down to 10,000 feet, where we could breathe normally. I noticed we were quite alone and radioed for our fighter escort, but they were already heavily engaged with the Luftwaffe in a number of air battles taking place high above us.

We could only hope that the German fighters hadn't noticed us as I felt confident we could make it back if no more damage was sustained by our bird.

It is difficult to believe, but we didn't see a single enemy plane after leaving the target area. Navigator LeVan did a magnificent job in guiding us away from the heavy flak areas, and we made it home safely, late, weary, and rather nervous, but also a bit more confident.

The 29 April 1944 mission to Berlin was one of the five heaviest losses suffered by the Eighth Air Force: sixty-three bombers and thirteen fighters were lost that day. The Luftwaffe had also been given a mauling. According to the records, it lost ninety fighters.

That was our first mission. We went back to Berlin on 7, 19, and 24 May. Ball-turret gunner Leonard Prohosky had a confirmed Fw 190 during the 19 May mission.

In conclusion, we felt the Berlin raids were not the roughest for our crew. The very heavily defended oil industry targets at Merseburg, Zeitz, Brux, and one raid on Schweinfurt, when they counted 240 holes in our plane on return, were the worst.

Editor's note: After the war General Adolph Galland, the commander of the Luftwaffe fighter forces, said, "The bombers grounded our fighters by destroying our oil industry."

PATHFINDERS AND NIGHT MISSIONS WITH R.A.F. BOMBER COMMAND

William ("Bill") Owen, Pilot, 412th Squadron

In November 1943 after our first seven missions with the 95th Bomb Group, which included the four raids during the notorious "black week" of mid-October

1943, my crew and I were sent to the 482nd Bomb Group at Alconbury to train on the Pathfinder blind-bombing technique being developed at that time, using the British "Oboe" and "Stinkey" radar equipment.

Within a few short weeks, we were flying to the various Eighth Air Force bases in the middle of the night to join as lead those groups selected to lead the Eighth Air Force, a division, or a combat wing in a daylight mission the following day.

In spite of a shortage of specialized Pathfinder equipment and trained personnel, the 482nd Bomb Group succeeded in furnishing enough trained crews to lead over 80 percent of the Eighth Air Force's missions from early November 1943 to late March 1944. Consequently, the Eighth Air Force actually succeeded in flying more missions during the unfavorable weather conditions of those winter months than it had been possible to fly during the relatively favorable weather conditions that prevailed during the summer of 1943.

By the end of March 1944, each Eighth Air Force bomb group was getting its own B-17s equipped with the American type radar known as "Mickey." This, of course, meant the Alconbury Pathfinders (Stinkey) were no longer required to fly combat. However, a radar school was established at Alconbury to train the Mickey radar operators before leading their own groups. Our navigator, Al Engelhardt, was in charge of this school. It was decided that radar maps, made up from actual scope pictures, would be of great assistance both during actual missions flown by the Eighth Air Force and in instructing the new crews at the school.

This project was assigned to my crew because, I think, we were the closest to completing our tour. One of the Stinkey B-17s was painted black, flame suppressors put on the turbo-superchargers, and a camera—complete with an automatic timing mechanism—was fitted to the radar scope.

The plan was to fly as high as possible (above 25,000 feet) during the eight or nine moonless nights per month that R.A.F. bomber command's heavy bombers flew at that time. We flew pre-determined tracks with the camera taking the scope photographs at regular timed intervals, which enabled a map overlay to be produced.

Flying at that high altitude we would see much of Germany and watched the whole of the R.A.F. mission develop, in stages, through the night. After flying only daylight missions over Germany, it was an incredible sight to behold, and the experience made believers of us all.

With the black landscape below us, any visible light was part of the war: first, the German night-fighter activity, punctuated by occasional bursts of defensive tracer fire, along the seemingly endless stream of British bombers; then the probing fingers of intense light from isolated searchlight batteries; then the marker flares cascading down over the primary target from the British Pathfinder aircraft; then the rapidly increasing movement and activity of searchlights and flak batteries in the target area itself.

As the night wore on, the searchlights, flak batteries, and the raging fires in the target area transformed night into day.

When the German radar-equipped night fighters got among the bomber stream, all we saw was a streak of light, like tracers, then a dull-reddish glow, then falling pieces of burning wreckage as the remains of the bomber plunged to earth. It was entirely different from anything we'd seen during the big daylight air battles that we'd all experienced.

This was a deadly contest of furtive stealth between the hunters and the hunted.

We flew with the R.A.F. during its missions on the nights of 22–23 April to Dusseldorf in the Ruhr Valley to Brunswick, 24–25 April 1944 to Munich and Karlsruhe in southern Germany, and to Bremen, northwestern Germany, 19–20 July 1944. It was during one of these nights that the German fighters were outlining the returning bomber stream against the light band in the northern sky and taking a steady toll. Even on moonless nights, there is more light than one would think.

Being in a single high-flying B-17, needless to say, we were all scared in the beginning. Searchlights would "walk" up to us, hold us briefly, then swing away. During one outbound flight, a high-flying German intruder aircraft followed us back into Germany for some considerable time, but it was apparent that we meant little to the Luftwaffe fighter controllers with all the other activity going on below us at that time.

One extremely interesting night mission was on the night of 27–28 May 1944. We were not aware of the location until the last possible minute, because it was top-secret at that time and had been requested by the senior Allied commanders. Although we'd been briefed earlier to go to Frankfurt, it directed that we were to fly over the south coast of England and take radar-scope photographs of the whole Allied invasion fleet assembled off the south coast. We had all been restricted from flying over that area for some months, but we now had the privilege of seeing a sight, ahead of time, that very few people would see.

On radar, the area of open sea between the south coast and the Isle of Wight was practically packed solid with shipping.

My crew flew again on 6 June, D-Day, and we saw the whole invasion fleet, in daylight, on its way to the beaches of Normandy. It was a sight and an extraordinary feeling that all of us will never forget.

I returned to the 95th in the fall of 1944, flew a few more missions, and after finishing a B-17 tour I was put on detached service with the Third Air Division scouting force with the 55th fighter group at Wormingford, near Colchester, Essex, from where I flew thirty missions in P-51 Mustangs by the time the war ended.

My crew during October 1943 was: Lieutenant W.V. Owen, pilot; Lieutenant F.P. McAllister, co-pilot; Lieutenant A.J. Engelhardt, navigator; Lieutenant M.J. Thixton, bombardier; Technical Sergeant D.E. White, top-turret gunner/engineer; Technical Sergeant L.G. Cain, radio operator; Staff Sergeant G.E. Moffat, ball-turret gunner; Staff Sergeant E.A. Beans, right waist gunner; Staff Sergeant H.V. Stotler, left waist gunner; Staff Sergeant W.A. Galba, tail gunner.

(*Royal Air Force Bomber Command War Diaries* by Martin Middlebrook and Chris Everitt reveal that on these three dates [22–23 April, 24–25 April, 19–20 July 1944] R.A.F. bomber command lost a total of seventy-two bombers, or 3.2 percent of the total force committed to battle.)

D-DAY PLUS ONE

Jack D. Beckelman, Pilot, 336th Squadron

Takeoff and landing were the most difficult and frightening episodes of mission 148, 7 June 1944, as far as I was concerned.

As a young captain and the pilot of a lead crew, one of the unknowns of each mission was the way in which the command pilot would integrate with the crew. Very fortunately for us that day we had Lieutenant Colonel David McKnight assigned as command pilot, and we would be leading the Thirteenth Combat Wing. I'd flown with Dave McKnight previously so I was mentally relieved when I was informed at briefing. I later learned that a command pilot has exactly the same apprehensions when I was given that responsibility on many subsequent lead missions.

Our targets were the railroad marshaling yards and bridge at Nantes, France. Their destruction was imperative to prevent German armored units and troop reinforcements from being brought up to the Normandy beaches where the Allied invasion force was poised for a thrust inland.

As we received a green flare to begin our takeoff, I applied power to all four engines, and our B-17, "Paisano," slowly accelerated with a full bomb load and full fuel tanks. At about eighty miles an hour and halfway down the runway, we heard a loud bang and the aircraft immediately veered to the right. The right landing wheel tire had blown—every pilot's dread, especially with a full load of gas and bombs. It was either a case of fly or ground-loop and burn.

Immediately as he heard the tire explode, Dave McKnight said tersely, "I'm dropping one-third flaps, ease it off." The great airplane left the ground without a moment's hesitation. Gear up, flaps up as airspeed increased, and we were airborne.

Years later, while discussing this incident with Colonel McKnight, he said that he'd discussed this situation with another lead pilot, and they'd agreed on and practiced this emergency procedure. It certainly was fortunate for us to have a quality command pilot aboard on 7 June 1944.

The mission proceeded as briefed with quite accurate flak being encountered. My bombardier, Lieutenant Frank Sohm, "creamed" the target, and the official bombing results were excellent. We were part of a concentrated operation involving nearly nine hundred B-17s and B-24s attacking strategic targets in Northern France and were escorted by nearly fifteen hundred fighters.

The flight back to Horham was uneventful; however, I was apprehensive and concerned that I would be landing at night with a blown tire. To preclude blocking the runway by landing first as was customary for the lead aircraft, Lieutenant Colonel McKnight advised all other 95th Group B-17s that we would land last. By then it was quite dark and we had our navigation lights on.

We were still circling our base at Horham while our other Fortresses were landing when we noticed streams of tracers appearing over the nearby B-24 base at Mendlesham. B-24s in the landing pattern were suddenly catching on fire, exploding in mid-air, and going down. Then the dreaded news came over the radio. German intruder aircraft, Me 410s, had followed the bomber formations back to East Anglia and were having a field day shooting down unsuspecting Allied aircraft as they attempted to land.

Dave McKnight immediately ordered all lights to be switched off to prevent the German pilots picking us up. We had to take our chances on a mid-air collision as opposed to being shot down. My diary indicates three Liberators were shot down and another B-24 crash-landed at another nearby base at Eye, Suffolk.

Our landing was uneventful except we unlocked the tail-wheel lock and allowed the airplane to drift to the right, off the runway. Down safely, mission accomplished, and the time was 2300 hours. The flying time of the mission was eight hours. Lieutenant Colonel Dave McKnight had turned a certain disaster into a routine takeoff and landing.

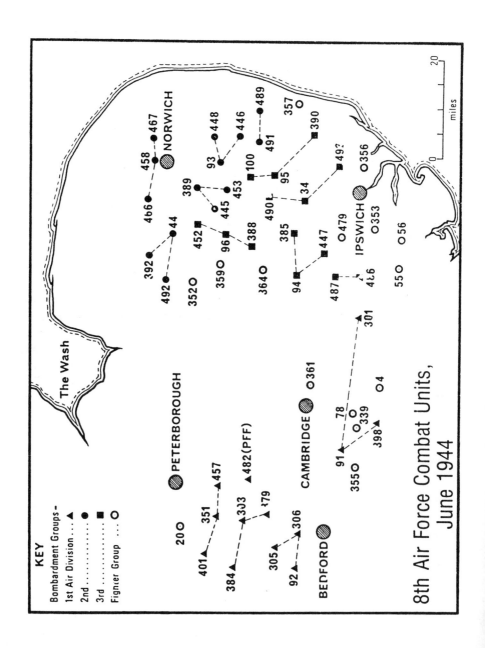

KEY

Bombardment Groups –

1st Air Division .... ▲
2nd .... ●
3rd .... ■
Fighter Group ... ○

20○

PETERBOROUGH

The Wash

401▲
351▲ 457▲
384▲ 303▲ 482(PFF)▲
305▲ ?79▲
92▲ 306▲

BEDFORD

CAMBRIDGE ○361

355○ 91▲
78 ○339
398▲ ○4
301▲

NORWICH
458● 467●
466●
492●
392●
44●
452■ 445○ 453● 100■ 95■ 34■
359○ 96■ 388■ 490L
364○ 385■ 447■
94■
487■ 4?6
55○

389●
93 ○448
446●
491●
489●
357 ○
390■

49?■ ○356
479○ ○353 ○56
IPSWICH

8th Air Force Combat Units,
June 1944

0   20
miles

THE MAN WHO PUT THE 95TH ON WHEELS

Tom Perkins (former Redlingfield schoolboy)

Official transport from Horham to Ipswich, Norwich, and other large East Anglian towns was limited, so when the 95th's off-duty personnel wanted to visit nearby villages the essential piece of equipment was the bicycle. On the many airfields throughout East Anglia occupied by the Eighth Air Force, the lowly bike (as it was known locally) soon became a most valuable and prized possession, jealously guarded by all owners, both civilian and military. The man who had bikes for sale and who would repair them became king due to the insatiable demand for wheeled transport. Such a man was the unforgettable Basil Rodwell.

Basil, a bachelor, had his workshop in the former blacksmith's forge in Horham and, prior to the arrival of the U.S.A.A.F., worked with his father, the village blacksmith. Basil also sold and repaired bicycles for the local communities of Horham, Denham, and Redlingfield. In those days before the war, most English villages had their bicycle specialists, but in my opinion, none had more character than Basil Rodwell. He very quickly established a reputation with the 95th Group as the man to get you mobile again. Inner tubes from 28-inch wheels, no longer repairable in that size, were cut down to make tubes for 26-inch wheels by a clever process of folding the damaged tube back on a broom handle, then applying adhesive. There were many such tricks of the trade known only to the old hands of the cycle repair business.

Needless to say, Basil had many friends among the American airmen, and one of his delights was to be invited to the base for an occasional meal. On one such occasion, when the duty officer was seen approaching the mess hall, the diminutive Basil was unceremoniously deposited out of sight inside the large refrigerator in the kitchen. After the inspection, and the coast was clear, the fridge door was opened; there was Basil, busily demolishing a large bowl of his favorite ice cream!

Sadly, Basil is no longer with us. His bicycle repair shop has also gone, together with the old prewar enameled exterior signs advertising cattle food and car and bicycle accessories.

However, Basil will long be remembered by the many veterans who knew him as the man who put the 95th on wheels; the man who made possible those pleasant summer evening bicycle rides through the beautiful Suffolk countryside to neighboring villages. Memorable and enjoyable journeys to village pubs such as "The Grapes" at Hoxne, Worlingworth, "Swan," Brundish "Crown," Southolt "Plough," while "The Green Dragon" at Horham itself was always a popular haunt with the GIs. Saturday night dances at Dennington Village

Hall and many more similar excursions to other recreational meeting places were also made accessible to the men of the 95th during those momentous days. All of which, of course, brought a much needed and welcome change of environment from the grim realities of the air war, especially for the 95th's combat and ground crewmen.

THE FIRST SHUTTLE MISSION TO RUSSIA FROM ENGLAND

Joseph Moller, Thirteenth Wing Headquarters, Horham, and Lyle Scott, Pilot

Colonel Joseph Moller: About 18 June 1944, we were alerted that we would shortly be flying a shuttle mission to Russia and returning to England via Italy after bombing a strategic target during each flight.

The task force would consist of two wings of three bomb groups each, escorted by a P-51 Mustang fighter group, which would also overfly Germany and land in Russia to be with us on the second and third legs of the shuttle.

We already knew that a cadre of American Air Force personnel, commanded by General Robert J. Walsh, had been sent to Russia to resupply our aircraft with gasoline, oil, bombs, and ammunition. In addition, they had communications capability with England and an intelligence officer. Knowing, however, that our aircraft repair and maintenance would have to be accomplished by our own task force people, we added one ground-crewman per bomber together with his tools, a few spare parts, and some P-51 parts, including spare belly fuel tanks.

The task force was to be led by the 45th Wing (96th, 388th, and 452nd Bomb groups) under the command of Brigadier General Archie Olds, the 45th Wing commander, and the Thirteenth Wing (95th, 100th, and 390th Bomb groups) led by Colonel Edgar Wittan, the Thirteenth Wing commander, who would be flying with the 390th Group. I was to lead the 95th Group and be the Thirteenth Wing deputy lead.

All of us were given numerous injections, special escape kits, language phrase cards, and a long list of instructions. Some of us even got an extra shot or two just before takeoff. After a couple of delays we finally took off on 21 June to fly to Russia. We assembled with the bomber stream, taking our position as the last two wings in the formation of the First and Third Air divisions. We flew over the North Sea and crossed the German border on schedule. As the main force, the First and Third divisions, swung south to attack targets in the Berlin area, we continued east toward our assigned target.

Captain Lyle Scott: We were flying lead crew of the 95th Group with Colonel Moller. My crew that day consisted of Captain John Stack, co-pilot; Lieutenant Frank Butler, bombardier; Lieutenant Claude Anderson, navigator; Technical Sergeant Arthur "Bucky" Harris Jr., radio operator; Technical Sergeant Phil Martin, ball-turret gunner; Technical Sergeant John Seifker, waist gunner; Technical Sergeant Sidney Taylor, waist gunner; and Technical Sergeant Miles Fortner, tail-gunner.

After our task force, led by the 45th Wing, had left the other wings of the main force, we continued eastward and bombed the oil refinery complex at Ruhland, Germany, with excellent and spectacular results.

Me 109 and Fw 190 fighters attacked us near Warsaw, Poland, but the P-51 Mustangs of the Fourth Fighter Group shot down fourteen enemy aircraft in a matter of minutes with no American losses. One of our B-17s had an outboard engine fire and dived out of formation, but it managed to rejoin us when the fire was successfully extinguished.

The 45th Wing landed at Poltava, and we landed at Mirgorod, Russia, after a highly spectacular let-down through and between the anvil tops of the towering cumulonimbus clouds rising majestically over the vast, seemingly endless steppes of Russia. We passed over Kiev, and it really was terribly war damaged.

Colonel Joseph Moller continues: As we passed over the Russian front lines, we were treated to a sample of inaccurate Russian flak. The airfield at Mirgorod was a gently rolling one on which steel landing mats had been laid for a distance of some 1,500 yards, and we were told that Russian women (WACs) had placed the mats.

Some time after we'd landed we saw a German plane overhead and knew it was probably a photo reconnaissance unit aircraft, a PRU. We'd been told in England that, once we were on the ground in Russia, we would be under the control of the Russian military. As we had several of the P-51s on the base that had accompanied us on the mission, Ed Wittan and I agreed that we should request permission to send up two of our fighters and shoot the PRU down, even though the German plane might have already radioed his home base where we were. We would at least prevent him returning with photographs of us on the field at Mirgorod.

Ed went to get the fighters ready for takeoff. I went to the Russian base commander and through an interpreter told him of our plan to send up our fighters. After a lengthy discussion with another Russian, he refused. I asked him why he'd refused; he replied that if we did shoot down the German plane, it would always be said that we'd had to defend ourselves on Russian bases. I then asked him how he proposed to defend us and our parked aircraft against a probable air attack. He had no answer except merely to shrug and turn away.

After circling Mirgorod field two or three times, well above the few meager flak bursts, the PRU aircraft flew off to the west.

Both Ed Wittan and I were extremely concerned, because we knew the

Germans now knew where we were and had seen the dismal performance of the Russian flak. We'd tried repeatedly to contact our people at Poltava by radio and by telephone without any success. After nightfall while Ed was still trying to establish contact with Poltava, I went over to a shack were I was told coffee was available. On the way over I collected my radio operator, who had been trying independently to contact Poltava. We were walking together past some small houses on the edge of the airfield when he suddenly stopped me and brought to my attention the violet blue flashes appearing intermittently from behind the curtains in one of the houses. He told me that he was certain the flashes were caused by a radio transmitting set. We continued on to the shack and got our coffee.

When I returned to the small building, which served as our operations office, Ed Wittan was still trying to contact Poltava by phone, without success. We then talked things over and decided it was imperative that we move our people and planes out of Mirgorod as soon as possible. After much discussion with the Russian base commander, who apparently was very reluctant to make responsible decisions on his own despite the extreme urgency of the situation, he finally agreed that perhaps we were right.

The next problem was where and when we would go. We decided that I'd take the 95th Group to a field near Kharkov that night, the 390th would go to Zaporozke, and Ed would stay in Mirgorod, keeping in radio contact with us and hopefully eventually contacting Poltava to get us our fuel, ammunition, and bombs. Colonel Tom Jeffrey would take his 100th Group to Kirovograd, a Russian airfield south of Mirgorod.

There were no maps and charts of Russia available to us, but the Russian base commander lent me a road map of the Mirgorod and Kharkov areas. We knew the moon would be full, and it would rise in about two hours. The crews were alerted, assembled, and briefed, during which I instructed the pilots to fly in trail, in elements of three airplanes, each element behind the other, always keeping in sight using Aldis signaling lamps in each element leader's tail-gunner's position. It was vital that we keep radio silence during the entire flight, and we timed takeoff to coincide with bright moonlight for our landing at Kharkov.

Just before our departure I remembered to inform the Russian base commander about the radio transmitter in the house near the coffee shack. He asked me to leave my radio operator with him, and he would see that he rejoin us later. I asked my radio operator to select a good operator for me as his temporary replacement.

The night was clear with visibility excellent for pilotage. The terrain was quite flat and level so we were able to cruise in safety at about 1,000 feet. The Russian interpreter, Maja, and her sidekick, a Russian major, whom we called "the gold dust twins," were riding in the nose compartment of my B-17. Incidentally, they'd never flown before but did very well.

About halfway to Kharkov the moon rose, and later on we looked for and sighted a large sandy, desert-like area. Shortly afterward, we located the grass landing strip near Kharkov. It too was a somewhat gently undulating field used by Russian fighter aircraft. The only question was whether or not it would hold the twenty-six tons of B-17 bomber. However, we were relatively light having no bombs and very little gasoline aboard.

At the briefing I'd told our men that my plane would land first and then taxi back, using my landing lights to illuminate the area over which they would land. It worked very well and all landed safely. We slept in or under our planes that night.

The following day we relaxed, ate some K-rations, and a few 95th men walked into town. I was taken into town to meet some of the Russian staff of General Permanoff with whom I had lunch. Kharkov was in a terrible state. Apparently when the German Army had withdrawn a few weeks previously, they'd dropped grenades down the sewer pipelines, and consequently there was no sewage disposal throughout the entire city. The most primitive methods for sewage were in use at that time. It had been the same for the city's main water supply, but several temporary pipelines had been installed to certain central locations where the population could get water and carry it home. In addition, there were large centrally located buildings perhaps one hundred yards square, with many showerheads, using cold water only. Men, women, and children all took showers together.

During the second evening I was invited to a dinner, held outdoors. I was seated at the table with Maja, the interpreter, on my right and on her right was seated a shifty-eyed civilian with a handle-bar moustache. General Permanoff was seated next to him.

I asked Maja who the gimlet-eyed civilian was. She said she didn't know what gimlet-eyed meant so I explained the term, not too well as I recall. Maja then told me he was the commissar of the entire Ukraine, with power of life or death over everyone in it. She also told me he always ranked higher than any officer of the Russian armed forces who happened to be in the Ukraine. To me, he looked like an individual you would be frightened to employ as a day watchman let alone a night watchman.

After a few minutes the commissar pushed Maja back in her seat, leaned toward me, and fired off a question in Russian. From his menacing expression and the tone of his voice, he clearly showed he didn't like me too much. Maja translated his question, which was in effect, "Who did I want elected as president in the coming fall American elections?"

I answered quite simply by saying that I thought President Roosevelt had been president long enough and that it was time someone else became our president. There was complete silence after Maja translated my reply.

After a few more minutes the commissar again leaned toward me, and Maja again translated. He said that perhaps I'd not heard his first question, but now he wanted to know just whom I wanted to see elected as president of the United States in the coming fall elections.

In answer to that I felt I should explain our two-party system and some of our political traditions of free elections, free speech, and so forth, which I proceeded to do. In addition, I pointed out that prior to Mr. Roosevelt, our presidents had limited themselves to a maximum of two terms in office, in accordance with a custom established by General George Washington. I said that Mr. Roosevelt had not followed that custom.

I would say a sentence and wait while Maja translated it, and I thought that I'd made a pretty fair speech. Perhaps I should have been warned by the dead silence. I suppose I somehow felt that I was a political missionary of sorts. In any event, all those present got a pretty good earful about our system of elective government. It certainly ended all further conversations with the commissar.

After dinner we were entertained by a Russian choir with simply beautiful voices. I noted, however, that I was somewhat of an outsider.

The next day I was able to make arrangements to rent one of the central shower buildings to be used only by our people for a two-hour period. The shower building had windows fairly high up, so imagine what we thought when looking up during our showers we saw every window filled with the faces of giggling young Russian women watching the modest Americans taking their showers. This was the only time we were able to get our clothes off until we got to Italy.

During this period I'd been in contact with Ed Wittan at Mirgorod. The 45th Wing had been bombed and decimated at Poltava, losing forty-six B-17s destroyed and twenty-six damaged. Only six planes were salvaged from the entire wing. I had our men gather round in a circle, told them what had happened at Poltava and that we would, with literally half of our original task force left, continue the shuttle mission as planned, attacking the targets as briefed, and eventually return to England.

The next day we flew back to Mirgorod, where I picked up my radio operator. He told me that the Russians had executed the six people found in the house with the radio transmitter.

After landing, our planes were confined to a safe area of the field known to be clear of the butterfly bombs that had been dropped by the Germans during our absence. These were bombs with two metal plates that opened up on impact when dropped, activating the bomb. Thereafter if it was touched or moved the bomb would explode.

We watched a long line of Russian soldiers walking slowly across the airfield searching for those bombs. Every once in a while, they'd stop, one man would raise his rifle and fire. An explosion would mark his target some thirty or forty yards ahead of him. Occasionally, a piece of shrapnel from an exploding bomb would hit one of the soldiers and he'd go down. No one paid much attention to the wounded soldiers except to load them on the truck collecting bomb fragments as the area was cleared.

Our bombs weren't yet available but fuel was, so we refueled and flew back to Kharkov and waited there until our bombs were available at Mirgorod.

Interestingly, when we were briefed in England for the shuttle, we were told that we wouldn't be allowed to take our personal cameras with us because the Russians didn't want us taking photographs of their installations. However, when we arrived in Russia we quietly mentioned that we happened to have a camera or two and when we asked for permission to use them, the Russians laughed and said they didn't mind any photography at all. On the contrary, they said, it had been our General Elliott Roosevelt, head of our photographic section, who didn't want us taking pictures. Quite obviously if his instructions had been implemented, he'd be the only one with a photographic record of the historic Russian shuttle mission.

He didn't allow for the average GI mind.

Early the following morning I received word to bring the 95th back to Mirgorod and load fuel and bombs, which I did.

On 25 June our Thirteenth Wing was intact apart from one B-17. However, we had a problem with some of the crewmen who were apparently suffering from food poisoning, so we checked our crews and found at least one fit pilot for each airplane.

Our informal briefing turned into somewhat of a gab feast. Our morale was high, we knew we'd outwitted the enemy, preserved our wing of the task force, enjoyed a good rest, and we once again had our bomb load and full fuel tanks. Everyone left that briefing in high spirits and a determination to complete the job. It was, for me at least, a very inspiring morning.

We took off, flew to a location within sight of the Black Sea, where, in a phone conversation the previous night with Archie Olds, we'd agreed to rendezvous. He tacked his six airplanes onto the high squadron of our 95th Group.

We flew on to our assigned target—the oil refinery and rail marshaling yards at Drohobycz, Poland—and hit the targets hard with excellent results. As we left the area, we could see black oily smoke towering up to probably 15,000 feet.

Just prior to bombing the target, I was amazed to see several biplane enemy fighters that flew through our formation from head on. They made only one pass, which we thought was rather poorly flown. A little later some Me 109s attacked us, but with no great determination.

We landed at a B-17 base near Foggia, Italy. After going through the delousing building for ourselves and our clothes, we had a fine meal and a wonderful night's sleep in a real bed. The next morning we had a hot breakfast with real coffee. I suppose we in the Air Force had it fairly easy because, if we survived a mission and got back to base, we enjoyed the comparative comfort of good hot meals and slept in real beds—quite different from the infantry men fighting on the ground from muddy foxholes.

All in all things were comfortable in Italy for us. Our planes had been landed on different B-17 bases, by squadron, so as not to overcrowd any one airfield. The bases on which we'd landed contained groups in a wing commanded by Colonel Charlie Lawrence, and while we were there he received his first star. We had quite a star party on the roof of the highest building in Foggia, complete with a U.S.O. show and all the trimmings. I recall asking Charlie how they dared hold a party on top of the building, the lights from which must have been visible for miles, when the German front lines were only a few miles to the north. In England, of course, everything was blacked out because the threat of German intruder aircraft was ever present, any night of the year. Charlie replied there'd been no intruders since he'd been there, and he was not in the least worried. He was right; we saw no intruders, day or night while we were there.

Captain Lyle Scott: We logged nine hours' flying time on the flight from Russia to Foggia. On landing we were assigned to 346th Squadron of the 99th Bomb Group, and by an extraordinary coincidence John Stack's brother, Dick, was there to greet him. Dick was a co-pilot in the 346th Squadron of the 99th Group, which had been flying with the Fifteenth Air Force, first from bases in north Africa since mid-1943, then from the Italian mainland as the war progressed.

From 27 June through 2 July, we spent our time visiting several other bomb groups in the area and got to see a number of former classmates. We visited Foggia and went to Mafardonia to swim in the Adriatic Sea. It was an enjoyable rest and allowed time for repairs of our aircraft and equipment.

Colonel Joseph Moller: All our people went sightseeing in Foggia, Naples, and some went to Rome. On 2 July we attacked the marshaling yards at Arad, Rumania, with excellent results—destroying the yards, a power plant, and some rail-car repair shops.

Incidentally, I was told to take the gold dust twins—Maja, the Russian WAC interpreter and her sidekick, a dour Russian major—to Italy with us. This I did, but where they went after that I've no idea. They simply vanished.

On 5 July we took off for England, picked up our extra high squadron, and proceeded to bomb the marshaling yards at Beziers, near Marseilles, France, again with excellent results. Later, our PRU of the target showed a seventy-five-foot crater in the center of the yards.

We flew on to England and landed back at Horham after a flight lasting ten hours. Although we'd had a great number of interesting experiences, it was good to be home.

As soon as we landed, I phoned Major General Earle ("Pat") Partridge at Elveden Hall over the scrambler phone and gave him my verbal report on the mission and the targets, the bombing of which I might add, was excellent on all four of our assigned strategic targets.

Pat listened for a few minutes and then broke in with the statement that he'd heard I was a Republican. I confirmed that was true, but asked him what that had to do with things. He replied saying that there had been a top-priority message from the Russians stating that one of our task force commanders didn't want to see President Roosevelt reelected in the fall elections. I laughed and again said that was true, but again asked him what did that have to do with things.

Pat said, "Joe, think about it. If a Russian commander of a Russian task force landed in England and had said he didn't want Stalin re-elected, he would have been shot as he stepped out of his airplane upon returning to Russia." I replied that from what I'd heard I thought that was true.

Ever since then I've thought about our freedoms, which we seem to accept so lightly and take for granted. Those many freedoms are worth thinking about and defending.

Shortly thereafter, Pat came down to Thirteenth Wing headquarters at Horham and during our discussions told me that another Russian shuttle mission was planned and asked if I would take command of it. I gladly accepted.

A VIEW FROM THE GROUND UP

(Part II)
Ted Lucey, Radio Technician, 336th Squadron
(Written as personal notes, not originally intended for publication)

17 April 1944: The tannoy announced this morning a number of our men on pass in the nearby villages, while the Jerry air raid was in progress, picked up several incendiary bombs and brought them back to the base as souvenirs! Men ordered to give up their "toys" at once.

A number of times when I've been C.Q., charge of quarters, and so awake all night, a young pilot from Teaneck, New Jersey, would stop by for a chat. He was very nervous and unable to sleep before his missions. His conversation always got around to his belief that a B-17 was safer than B-24, and since he flew a '17 he was safer. But now he and his crew are missing in action.

About ten days ago Crepeau, Dixon, and I visited Elveden Hall, the headquarters of the Third Air Division, for some technical information. Elveden Hall is a beautiful place, an old English country estate complete with a huge mansion, church, pond, ancient trees sedately in a large park surrounding the mansion, and even vividly colored peacocks strutting proudly around the trees. During our stay, we had both noon and evening meals (chow) in the Third Air Division mess hall, which was partly staffed by WACs. The WAC's, we notice, march far better than we do!

21 April: My interphone experiments are coming along quite well. For some reason, there is a distinct loss in clarity in the interphone communication systems at high altitude. About 0700 hours Felmet and Shilton came in from night shift. They'd been working on the line, using a jeep's headlights, when a Jerry plane suddenly came over at very low altitude. It strafed them and the new silver Fortress they were working on. Amazingly, no one was hurt, nor was the Fort damaged. Felmet dived under the jeep, other ground crewmen ran for the cover of darkness, and Shilton had the presence of mind to stop and turn off the jeep's lights as he raced into the night. Then the tannoy blared out its belated red alert (instead of preceding the raid). We later learned the Jerry plane had dropped six bombs near the bomb and ammunition dump. Luckily they were all duds. The fortunes of war. . . .

Later that morning, a practice mission took off from the 100th Group's base at nearby Thorpe Abbotts. While flying low over their base, one ship got caught in the propwash of another and crashed. No survivors.

In the early afternoon, a real mission took off from here, with countless planes in the air. During the afternoon, the ceiling rapidly dropped to less than 1,500 feet. I was working in the radio shack when I heard a lot of yelling. Looking out of the window, I saw a returning B-17, about a mile away, descending rapidly minus its tail section. One parachute blossomed, then three more in quick succession. Two unfortunate crewmen dropped like stones, their chutes failing to open. The Fortress then disappeared behind some trees; there was a huge explosion, and flames and smoked billowed hundreds of feet into the air.

Another Fortress broke up in the air and fell to earth a short distance away. Frank Morley and another telephone engineer were off base and in the immediate vicinity of where all this happened. They watched, horror-stricken, as several aircrew plunged to the ground nearby with closed parachutes, their feet kicking futilely on the way down. One chute, however, did snap open at very low altitude and landed close to them. The airman was conscious, although he was bleeding badly from the cuts on his face and head. He said his ship had been weakened by flak hits and had finally broken up in mid-air. He'd tried three times to escape via the waist exit door of the Fort but, twice, gravity and the centrifugal forces of the spinning plane had tumbled him all the way back to the ball-turret area. On his third attempt, with his face battered by loose ammunition boxes, he jumped, only to have his chute get caught on the ship's tail section. It worked loose in a matter of age-long seconds, and he dropped to safety.

As Frank Morley was rushing the injured flyer to the base hospital in his truck, the second B-17 crashed, and the poor devil, who'd just been through the same terrifying experience, was hysterical as he watched other crewmen drop with closed parachutes.

At dusk the R.A.F. went out again in force.

2 May: Awakened by a series of loud explosions about 0430 hours. From the roar overhead, the sky seemed to be full of planes. Later learned that four Forts had collided in mid-air, crashed, and burned. And a B-24 had jettisoned its bombs in a field near Hoxne, then it had crash-landed in a sheep pasture, killing many animals.

Al Higgins and I were walking to the mess hall about noon when we saw a chute coming down a mile or so away, again toward Hoxne. A Fort circled the chute to keep other ships clear. Apparently A P-38 Lightning had come apart, and the pilot bailed out.

A few days ago Felmet was working in a Fort when a bomb accidentally dropped from the bomb bay, crushing a ground crewman's foot. Shortly after that he was in another plane when another 500-pounder suddenly fell, injuring several mechanics and rolling to the end of the hardstand.

I've twice had similar experiences while lying on my back repairing overhead radio equipment: a sudden warning yell, the sound of running feet, a dull thud as the bomb hits the hardstand, a rumbling noise as it rolls across the concrete . . . and long, helpless seconds of waiting. Of course, the bombs aren't armed while being loaded, but they are extremely temperamental at any time.

On a far more pleasant subject, one evening recently Shilton and I went for a bike ride, going through the villages of Horham and Stadbroke and eventually finding our way to Wingfield Castle. The surrounding countryside is very beautiful, especially at this time of year with all the spring flowers and blossoms coming into bloom.

24 May: We were all sound asleep in our barracks when five loud and very close explosions shocked us into awakening. A Jerry plane, caught in the searchlights and in a panic to get away, had dropped a stick of five 100-pound bombs in a meadow less than a half mile from our base. No one was hurt, but several unfortunate cattle were killed. If the German pilot had held his load for a second or so longer, the bombs would have landed squarely in the 334th Squadron area. And if he'd held on a few seconds more, we'd have got them. Many fellows have collected bomb fragments as souvenirs.

The night before last, about 2300 hours, the R.A.F. were homeward bound from an early night raid. One of their bombers iced up, the crew bailed out, and their plane crashed some distance away. One British airman parachuted down on our base hospital. Extremely good judgment!

Bulletin: Ice-cream making equipment has come to the 95th! And so has every child around, evacuees from London, farm kids from this area, and sometimes the whole family shows up for a treat. We don't even know ourselves in advance that it's an ice cream day, but the kids do! There are often kids on the field. The boys like to watch the mechanics working on the planes and our guys are friendly toward them, although the kids must certainly hear and learn cuss words they shouldn't know!

30 May: Ships returned from a mission at noon. I went out on the line to resume my research for the cause of radio-electrical leakage on ship 8178. Half its bomb load, six 500-pounders were still in the bomb bay. Several armorers and ordnance men arrived to unload the bombs. From their talk I gathered that the bombardier had complained it was impossible to release them. However, nothing was defective. The problem was the bombardier simply didn't know his job—a reflection on hasty training, not on the man.

Early this afternoon one of our new ships circled the field unable to land because only one wheel could be let down. It was ordered out over the North Sea to drop the ball turret, then to head for Honington, a repair depot, for a crash landing.

7 June: Yesterday was D-Day, not too much to our surprise. During the early evening of the 5 June, the ordnance and armament men were called to the flight lines, the engineers went out later. The invasion chatter was very prevalent, then confirmed when the early morning saw two missions, maximum efforts, one at 0330 and the other 0600 hours.

The night was loud with the ceaseless roaring of thousands of planes going over. About 0800 hours, German radio announced Allied paratroop landings in occupied France. No official word from the BBC until later in the morning. When our ships returned, they were immediately serviced for a third mission, which took off about 1730 hours and returned after dark. Returning crews reported thousands of ships of all sizes extended across the English Channel. Colonel Truesdell, our new group CO, led the first mission of the three raids flown 6 June. The weather was beautiful here on D-Day, not a cloud in sight during the morning. Toward noon, however, it suddenly clouded over and except for brief appearances of the sun, we have since had incredibly bad weather, even for England. Predominately low ceiling and a thick blanket of dull, rain-filled clouds. Nevertheless, our B-17s fly even when they shouldn't. They must.

Naturally, accounts of what's happening in France vary widely. The BBC claims Allied successes, while German radio says otherwise. There's a girl with a sexy voice who speaks sweet words to the "misled" Yanks over the German radio. To illustrate the enemy's disdain for our efforts, this girl, Midge, has offered to go to bed with every Yank who walks down the streets of Berlin. She has certainly embarked upon a very considerable undertaking.

23 June: The bad weather continues, there hasn't been one really good day since D-Day. Most days have been cloudy, gloomy, cold, and with lots of rain. Tragic in view of the fact that Allied planes are desperately needed to support the invasion.

Jerry's "secret weapon," the V-1 flying bomb, or "buzz bomb," has done extensive damage in London. The first buzz bomb landed in London on 13 June, but to date, none has fallen near here fortunately.

As radio maintenance work on the line hasn't kept me occupied full time, I've typed out a thirty-two-page radio mechanic's manual for maintenance men newly arrived from the states. It includes a complete servicing program for the liaison set. It's based on the official but dull AAF technical orders and on my practical experience. Third Air Division has asked for another radio booklet, "Cockpit Troubles," a pocket manual for pilots and co-pilots so they'll have an easy-to-understand guide to the nine radios and the ten interphone positions in every plane.

In order to make "Cockpit Troubles" suitable for Liberators as well as Forts, Captain Nastasiak and I visited the nearby 490th Bomb Group B-24 base at Eye. We passed the spot where, a few days previously, a Liberator had exploded just after takeoff. There were no survivors.

8 July: "Cockpit Troubles" was submitted to Third Air Division recently. It came back marked generally OK, but some minor changes were necessary. My first booklet on the liaison radio went from Third Air Division to Eighth Air Force headquarters at High Wycombe then to Bushey Park for printing.

From all accounts the V-1 buzz bombs are doing more and more damage. Several have now fallen near Horham. Very nasty things. It's now forbidden to go to London except on official business.

20 July: Yesterday, one of our Forts, no. 210937 "Ready Freddie," while visiting Duxford, crashed and killed fourteen men who were aboard, in addition to about six ground personnel. Apparently there were several fighter pilots aboard as passengers and the plane attempted to buzz their fighter field. It clipped the top of a hangar, and as it had full Tokyo tanks aboard, the resultant fire must have been ghastly.

29 July: Mishaps and accidents seem to occur in close sequence. Very recently an ordnance man was seriously injured when a 500-pond bomb slipped from its shackles while a Fort was being loaded. Yesterday as our ships returned from a mission, the undercarriage of one plane buckled, causing it to crash on one wing, blocking the main runway. Second ship with tire trouble blocked the second runway and the remainder of the formation began using the third and shortest runway, although the wind direction was unfavorable. A plane landed and taxied to the perimeter, just off the third runway. Another ship came in and slowed down at the end of the same runway. A third B-17 arrived and had to ground-loop to avoid a crash. It went over the perimeter track, spun round in the soft earth and came to a stop, facing in the opposite direction. A little later, as our planes resumed using the main runway, a Fort landed with number 1 and 2 engines feathered and its ball turret missing.

This morning, about 0500, everyone was awakened by a really massive explosion. The beds shook, and stones rattled on the corrugated iron sides and roof of our barracks. Luckily all the windows were open and none shattered. Our first thought was a V-1 flying bomb. We later learned a B-24, with a full load of bombs and fuel, had crashed and exploded shortly after takeoff from Eye airfield. Incredibly, only two crewmen were killed outright, and the others were somehow blown clear with varying injuries.

Again, about 1030, another Liberator blew up while attempting an emergency landing at Eye. And again, amazingly, the crew members were thrown clear. All were injured, some seriously. The blast flattened trees and telephone poles in the immediate vicinity.

When this second explosion occurred, several mechanics were working on a nearby B-24. The crew chief yelled, "Let's get the hell out of here!" and dropped from the hatch forward of the bomb bay. Confused by all the noise and excitement he ran the wrong way, straight into his own plane's spinning propellor blades and was instantly decapitated. All in all, Eye seems to be an unlucky base.

There's a report that buzz bombs fell near our old base at Framlingham early this morning. Flying bombs have also passed over the nearby B-24 base at Debach and fallen near here several times. There's something about buzz bombs that makes them more terrifying than conventional bombs. Probably it's the fact that they have a very distinctive noise, like an idling motor-cycle engine, and you can't help but hear them approaching. When the engine runs out of fuel, gravity takes over and the bomb, containing its load of high explosives, plunges to the ground with quite devastating results.

14 September: Reported to Major Haring at Third Air Division headquarters. He explained that the training section of operations wanted to publish a monthly magazine for combat and ground crews, and I was to produce the first issue. The assignment involved gathering relevant material, traveling to 3AD bases for firsthand accounts of missions, maintenance, etc. Then writing the copy, preparing repro paste-ups, and taking the completed job to London for publication.

25 September: The first copy of the new magazine *Chaff* is ready for reproduction. Doheny, an artist, and I took the copy to London and went directly to Bushey Park to check up on the printing process.

It was a pitiful sight to see the Underground stations even more crowded than before with the additional thousands of people huddled for safety from early evening until morning. Because I was in London on duty, I stayed at the Army's transient quarters located in a tall building at Cadogan Place, Knightsbridge. The first night wasn't too restful with Jerry's V-1s dropping indiscriminately and intermittently in the city. The bombs demolish whatever they hit; inevitably the civilian casualities are very high, and a few days ago a buzz bomb killed twenty-four GIs at Bushey Park.

One early evening as we walked through Knightsbridge during our eight-day stay, we heard the dreaded sound of an approaching flying bomb . . . then its motor stopped. We ran for cover among the mounds of rubble of an adjacent bombed area. In the open street a man also dashed for shelter just as the bomb exploded. The concussion flattened him. He picked himself up, dusted his dark suit, replaced his bowler hat firmly, picked up his briefcase and umbrella, and calmly walked off. The unflappable British!

UNDER ALLIED BOMBS

Larry Pifer, Ball-turret Gunner, B-17G, 231785, "Slightly Dangerous II," 335th Squadron

Following our capture after being shot down and injured during the first Berlin raid on 4 March 1944, Sergeant Marvin Anderson, our flight engineer, and I were taken by train to the Hermann Goering Hospital in Berlin. We arrived during the afternoon of 5 March, racked with pain and bloodstained from our wounds. Sergeant Anderson had 20mm shell wounds in his right arm, I'd sustained a broken ankle and cracked ribs, and on arrival we were given cold, black ersatz coffee. It tasted very bitter but as I'd had no food or drink since before the previous day's mission I drank thirstily. My left foot and leg were put in plaster and my chest heavily bandaged.

The following day, 6 March, the Eighth Air Force bombed Berlin with a force of over six hundred bombers, and it was simply awesome. They hit Berlin again on 8 and 9 March, and the hospital began filling rapidly with more injured flyers. During the night of 12 March, with much of the hospital and surrounding district heavily damaged, the German guards sneaked us out to prevent the panic-stricken and frenzied Berlin civilians from lynching us.

We were taken by railroad to a hospital near Frankfurt, and after about a week I was taken to Dulag Luft in Frankfurt for interrogation and processing. On 22 March a group of us were transported to Frankfurt railroad station and loaded into boxcars. The locked boxcars were then shunted into the middle of the marshaling yards to await transportation after dark. Little did we realize that Frankfurt was to be the primary target for over eight hundred aircraft of R.A.F. bomber command that night for the second night in four, the previous heavy raid having taken place during the night of 18–19 March 1944.

The first indications we heard of the impending raid was the mournful wailing of the air-raid sirens about 9:00 P.M. Then the antiaircraft guns began pounding away into the night sky, and the first of the bombs began whistling down, striking houses, streets, and factories alike with a growing crescendo of ear-splitting explosions. Night was rapidly transformed into day by the vivid flashes of the flak batteries, the almost continuous stunning concussion of exploding British bombs, and the growing intensity of the numerous fires.

Being locked in the boxcars we couldn't get out, and even if we could have, there was nowhere to go.

The raid continued nonstop for one solid hour as the bomber stream unloaded death and destruction on Frankfurt. There seemed little hope of our surviving that indescribable hell on earth.

Finally, after what seemed an eternity, the bombs stopped falling, the guns grew silent, and all we could hear was the hungry crackling of numerous fires, the terrible screaming of injured people, and the hoarse shouts of the firemen and rescuers as they vainly fought the flames. Then, a little while later, the delayed-action bombs began to detonate with earth-shaking explosions as their timing mechanisms expired. It was like another air raid all over again.

Needless to say, there was no possible chance of any sleep that night, and when the pale light of dawn finally came, our guards came and unlocked the boxcars. What an absolutely incredible sight to behold. Mass destruction everywhere, large fires still burning hopelessly out of control, and the grotesquely twisted railroad tracks among the numerous bomb craters in the marshaling yards looked like huge roller-coasters at a fun-fair. Frankfurt's beautiful, glass-domed railroad station had been reduced to a flattened, smoking shambles, but miraculously our seven boxcars, standing all alone, remained virtually intact.

We asked our guards to take us back to Dulag to get something to eat and to be near the air raid shelters, but they told us that the camp at Dulag had been destroyed by a crashed British Lancaster bomber. We were then taken to an air raid shelter at one end of the marshaling yards to wait for the tracks to be repaired.

About noon the following day, 24 March, the nearby flak guns suddenly began firing; apparently the air-raid siren system had been destroyed during the R.A.F. raid. This time it was our own Eighth Air Force that hit Frankfurt again with another heavy bombing raid.

After another three days, during which the uninjured POWs were ordered to assist in the repair of a single-line track out of Frankfurt, we boarded the boxcars again, and we were on our way at last to our permanent POW camps.

We traveled northeast day and night for the next five days, with frequent delays while the railroad tracks were repaired due to damage from the Allied bombing campaign, eventually arriving at Hydekreug, East Prussia, and Stalag Luft 6.

During the following fourteen months of captivity, we were transferred, either by train, forced-march, or ship via Memel, Lithuania, and Sweinemunde, Germany, to POW camps at Stalag Luft 4, Kiefehiede, and Stalag 11-B Fallingbostel (which was very near the infamous and dreadful death camp at Belsen), in order to keep ahead of the Russian forces advancing from the east. Sometimes we could hear the sound of the Russian and German artillery duels in the distance.

With the scarcity of food, we often marched for days without being fed, and with the ever present lice, we became a ragged collection of emaciated and distraught human beings, sleeping in barns, abandoned buildings, open fields, or wherever.

Sometimes we were integrated with retreating German soldiers and were bombed and strafed by our own Allied aircraft. During the march westward from Fallingbostel in April 1945, we'd been issued a few Red Cross parcels on the march to share among ourselves. We'd stopped for rest in a large farmyard when an Allied fighter-bomber, mistaking us for German soldiers, strafed and fired rockets at us as we, like children with Christmas presents, were opening our food parcels. Seven prisoners were tragically killed during this attack.

On 2 May 1945, we finally made contact with the advancing British Army in no man's land, and we were advised to continue until we were behind the main British front line. What a glorious feeling to be free men again! I really believe our prison guards, who'd marched with us, showed more emotion upon reaching British lines than we ourselves did. They threw their rifles away and hugged each other like long-lost brothers, such was their fear and dread of the Russians.

We marched for two more days then boarded trucks, were taken to an airfield, deloused, and flown in C-47s to Brussels, Belgium, and from there to Camp Lucky Strike, where we were processed for the trip home to the United States. From my former weight of 165 pounds in March 1944, I'd gone down to 90 pounds at the time of my liberation in May 1945.

All of us will never ever forget the extremely kind treatment and very gracious hospitality shown to us by the British Army, commanded by Field Marshal Bernard Montgomery, which liberated us and escorted us back to Belgium.

The crew of B-17G 231785 "Slightly Dangerous II" shot down on their 18th mission, Berlin, 4 March 1944 was: Lieutenant Melvin B. Dunham, pilot (POW); Lieutenant Robert T. Renner, Co-pilot (POW); Lieutenant John H. Matthews, Jr., navigator (POW); Technical Sergeant Marvin D. Anderson, flight engineer (POW); Technical Sergeant Lawrence I. Pifer, radio operator/gunner (POW); Staff Sergeant Warren A. Thompson, ball-turret gunner/ass't. radio operator (POW); Staff Sergeant Vince Aiello, right waist gunner (KIA); Staff Sergeant Clarence A. Barstow, left waist gunner (KIA); Staff Sergeant Fred W. Bittner, tail gunner (POW).

THREE FEARFUL EVENTS

Arthur Scroggins, Bombardier, B-17 "Superstitious Aloysius," 335th Squadron

I was a member of one of the first replacement crews assigned to the 95th Group in 1943, but when my crew, commanded by Lieutenant P. V. Milward, completed its twenty-five missions, I didn't return to the United States and continued flying until the end of the war with the group.

On 4 January 1944 our B-17, "Superstitious Aloysius," had two engines shot out over the target—Kiel, Germany—and my original crew was forced to ditch in the North Sea on our way home. We took our ditching positions in the radio room while Lieutenant Milward and Lieutenant Farris, our co-pilot, attempted to put the airplane down safely on a fairly choppy sea.

I was braced under a radio mount to cushion the initial impact of the plane hitting the water and coming to a sudden stop. The airspeed dropped, almost to stalling point, then the aircraft struck a wave, went under, and came back up just like a fisherman's cork float.

The freezing seawater rushed into the plane, almost covering my head. I was very close to panic until I realized all I had to do was duck my head down, clear of the mount, and then stand up. The swirling water was only knee-deep at that time, but it was rising fast as I clambered aboard one of our two life rafts via the waist-door exit hatch.

All ten crew members were rescued shortly afterward by the Royal Navy destroyer, H.M.S. *Verdun,* and we gratefully received excellent treatment and cordial hospitality from her crew. We were back at Horham that same night.

I was rather small in those days, about 135 pounds (somewhat heavier now), and was always ready to try something new and different. Someone higher up thought up a theory of stripping the four 50-caliber machine guns from the nose of a P-38 Lightning twin-engine fighter, installing a bomb-sight and a small, crazy bombardier to accompany the P-47 Thunderbolt and P-51 Mustang fighters, which carried a couple of bombs slung under their wings, on their escort missions.

I was to do the sighting for them and give the pilots a radio order when to release their bombs. The plan didn't work too well because we couldn't get the fighter pilots to fly straight and level through flak.

Colonel Hubert ("Hub") Zemke, the commander of the 56th Fighter Group, the P-47 group trying to prove the validity of the experiment, asked me if I'd like to go to France to bomb a Luftwaffe airfield that he knew about.

The day was very stormy, and the whole Eighth Air Force was grounded. We set off, all alone in our P-38, bombed the airfield successfully, but paid the price. The fighter's braking system was shot out by flak.

On returning to the 56th Fighter Group base at Boxted, Essex, without brakes, we rapidly ran out of runway, hurtled across the perimeter track, demolished a wooden fence, smashed through a hedge, and ended up in the middle of a farmer's field. The aircraft was very severely damaged.

The experiment was canceled, and I returned to the base at Horham. This was probably a lucky break for me because I had to be lifted into the nose section of the P-38 and taken out via a small access panel that involved the use of a screwdriver. In an emergency there was no way of escape.

My third close call happened while I was flying with Hal Powers, a pilot who also flew with the 95th after completing his first tour with the group.

On 17 October 1944, the 95th led the entire Eighth Air Force on a mission to bomb bridges across the Rhine River. Our navigator that day was a major from Eighth Air Force headquarters. During the bomb run, our lead B-17 received a severe flak hit in the nose compartment, which wounded me in both legs, my right hand, and in the head. I looked back and saw the navigator slumped across his table. He'd been killed by a direct hit in his mid-section, almost blown in half.

I managed to scramble back to the bombsight and released the bombs on target. I then realized my oxygen tube had also been hit and grabbed one of the small emergency oxygen bottles before I lost consciousness. Hal Powers managed to get the plane back as far as Brussels, Belgium, and crash-landed on an airfield that only recently had been captured and taken over by the British infantry. After the crash landing, the infantry's medics removed me from the completely wrecked nose compartment and gave me first aid before I was flown back to the hospital in England for specialized treatment.

On my return to Horham from the hospital, friends who'd also flown that mission told me it looked as if every flak shell the Germans fired that day hit our lead plane.

At the end of the war, I was serving as group bombardier and came back to the United States in the same B-17 as Lieutenant Colonel Bob Stewart, the 95th Bomb Group's last commander.

The most gratifying day that I recall during the war was in either January or February 1944, the day the whole Eighth Air Force concentrated its efforts on oil targets for the first time. The 95th was assigned a target deep in Germany, and the previous day it had snowed all over Europe. The day of the maximum effort dawned clear and beautiful but with a blanket of snow. You could see forever. We hit our oil target hard and a huge column of black smoke arose. As we turned back for England, as far as the eye could see, black smoke was towering up from the other oil targets. I remarked at the time to our crew, "Boys, this is the beginning of the end for Germany."

ACHIEVEMENTS, COST, AND THE PRIDE

Adam Hinojos and David Olsson (Ground Personnel)

Adam Hinojos: It was a most rewarding experience to be a member of the 457th sub-depot, which was formed to support the air operations of the 95th Bombardment Group.

By the end of the war in Europe in May 1945, 95th Bomb Group aircraft had flown enough miles to take them around the world twenty-five times, consumed thirty-five million gallons of gasoline, flown 321 combat missions and numerous practice missions, and dropped nearly 20,000 tons of bombs on its assigned strategic targets in Nazi-occupied Europe. The group had 156 B-17 Fortresses shot down, either by enemy flak or fighters, and more than 1,300 aircraft had returned to base with varying degrees of battle damage. Men wounded aboard these returning bombers numbered 192, and 41 of these later died in the hospital.

In addition, the 95th lost thirty-six B-17s due to mid-air collisions, takeoff and landing accidents, and other ground accidents that also resulted in tragic loss of life.

These brief and stark facts summarize the outstanding achievements and the grievous price that was paid by our group's combat crews.

A comprehensive range of highly skilled specialists, tradesmen, and their assistants made up from well over 2,000 ground personnel made the accomplishments of our flight crews possible. From armorers to x-ray technicians, crew chiefs, welders, parachute packers, teletype machine operators, filing clerks, flight surgeons, mechanics, typists, air traffic controllers, radio and radar specialists, hospital porters, meteorologists, truck drivers, bakers, postmen, riveters, machinists, painters, military policemen, Red Cross girls, nurses, sheet-metal cutters, storemen, guards, and cooks—all played an important part in the very complex organization that was the 95th.

The following will illustrate just a small part of the 457th sub-depot's accomplishments. During the ninety-one-day period from 1 April 1944 to 30 June 1944—an extremely busy period of sustained operations that included the three missions flown by the 95th on D-Day, 6 June 1944—the following was achieved, often by working twenty-four hours a day.

The engine maintenance and aero repair section of the engineering department performed during those ninety-one days general maintenance on 570 aircraft (of which 205 were battle damaged), 47 modifications, and changed 153 aircraft engines. The engine-change time—including hanging, pre-oiling, and ground-testing time—averaged one day.

The supply department processed a total of 4,513 vouchers; each voucher contained an average of three items. It handled approximately four million gallons of gasoline and 46,000 gallons of oil.

The parachute department, during those ninety-one days, repacked 2,603 parachutes and fitted 760 sets of parachute harness. Modification of parachutes, dinghies, heated flying suits, oxygen masks, escape kits, and flare kits amounted to 6,595. The flying equipment department completely outfitted 75 new combat crews, ten men to each crew.

In addition, among the items designed and manufactured by the officers and men of the 457th sub-depot at that stage of the war, which had another year to run before it was finally over, were the adjustable vertical stabilizer work stand, the vacuum and hydraulic test stand, adjustable wing rack stand, engine rack mounted on a tractor, wing slot hoist, a parachute tool, which was adopted by the Eighth Air Force, and a circle cutter for sheet metal. On many occasions great ingenuity was shown in modifying and improving existing equipment. The inventions were made by the ground crews and were accomplished without regard to time or effort while working in all kinds of weather. All of these things were a great credit to everyone concerned.

David Olsson concludes: The one word that summarizes the positive attitude of all 95th Bomb Group ground people is *pride*—pride felt by the ground people in the "Square B" and for the airmen who flew with that identification.

There is no doubt that this total dedication by the ground people was sensed by our flight crews, and it must have helped and encouraged them when their own morale dipped following a hard day over occupied Europe. The ground personnel always felt that this pride must have been transmitted to the new replacement crews and helped to assure them that they were not just replacing men who were missing in action, but they had been assigned to one of the very best combat groups, the 95th.

I honestly didn't know or hear of a single 95th support person who didn't express the feeling that we were all working in the best bomb group in the European theater of operations. This has continued to be a great source of pride over the intervening years.

BUNCHERS, BALLOONS, BOMBERS, AND FIGHTERS

Les Lennox, Pilot, 336th Squadron

I arrived at Horham 17 August 1944 and stayed until 20 March 1945. Our B-17G was named "Cadet Nurse" after my co-pilot's girlfriend who was attending nursing school back home in Johnstown, Pennsylvania.

By that stage in the war, East Anglia had many Eighth Air Force bomber and fighter bases and the fact that there were not more mid-air collisions is a tribute to the planners. I recall being shown shortly after our arrival, a large-scale map of all our bases in East Anglia at group operations, showing each bomb group's climb pattern for group assembly. It was an amazing map to look at, very similar to the pieces of a gigantic jigsaw puzzle.

The intelligence officer stressed to my co-pilot, George Marks, and me the absolute necessity of staying within our climb pattern, guided by buncher radio transmissions from the ground, and not straying into someone else's pattern, thus risking a mid-air collision. I'm sure everyone can recall climbing through dense cloud to assembly altitude and then suddenly hitting severe prop-wash, instantly knowing that you had just passed close behind an unseen aircraft and had experienced another near miss. When that happened it meant, of course, that either I was not staying close enough to the buncher radio beacon or that another aircraft had strayed into our climb pattern. At the very least that plan allowed us to have some degree of air traffic control over literally hundreds of bomb-laden aircraft, day after day, with relatively few tragic and frightful mid-air collisions. Lots of close calls, but they didn't count. That was our only air traffic control; there was nothing else but the integrity of each crew flying their own pattern.

The people in air traffic control today would be absolutely appalled if they could see our only method of controlling all those bombers. Taking off at thirty-second intervals and climbing through all types of weather, in daylight or in darkness while maintaining radio silence. When two aircraft have a near miss today it makes national news. We had so many each day that we thought nothing of it. When one thinks back it was certainly frightening, but it was a plan that worked for us and enabled us to launch and assemble a daily air armada, the likes of which will never be seen again.

Before we began flying combat missions, our first flight was to get acquainted with the English countryside, the last leg of which was from Oxford, just north of London, back to Horham.

The weather wasn't too good and although we were flying visual flight rules (VFR) we were in and out of dense clouds. Suddenly I noticed we were over many red-brick buildings, but forward visibility was limited so we couldn't see much ahead of us. I checked with my navigator, Bill Tate, and he said we must have drifted south of our planned course and were now over the northern outskirts of London.

I suddenly remembered the barrage balloons over London that the briefing officer had warned us about and to listen for squeakers. To keep friendly aircraft out of an area that was protected by balloons, with steel mooring cables securing them to the ground, they transmitted a continuous warning signal that could be received on 3105 KC and consisted of a rising and falling tone.

I switched over to 3105 and sure enough, we were well inside the danger area, but the prescribed procedure for getting away from the balloons was both simple and safe. We were told, "At the first indication of squeakers do a 180° turn and fly back until you no longer hear them. Then turn 90° left or right and after a few minutes resume your original heading. If you hear the squeakers again repeat the procedure, and you will eventually get around the area."

The maximum altitude of the balloons was 10,000 feet. We were at 8,000 feet, but eventually we got clear of London and back on course. From then on, needless to say, when we were in close proximity to a balloon area, we listened for squeakers. We concluded that the balloons must have been below us that day or else we would certainly have collected some cable.

Whenever bomber pilots and fighter pilots got together during those hectic and dangerous years, it was inevitable that arguments developed as to who were the better pilots.

In the skies over Germany we had the utmost respect for each other. When they watched us hang in there in our defensive formations through the heavy flak and enemy fighter areas, they knew *we* were good. And they so dominated the skies over occupied Europe when they were defending us that we knew *they* were good. Without the excellent protection they gave us from German fighters, bomber crew losses would have been prohibitive for the American daylight raids. Nevertheless, put a few fighter and bomber pilots together in a bar, and after a few drinks, a highly spectacular and bruising brawl was inevitable.

On 5 October 1944, the target for the Third Air Division was the Luftwaffe fighter field at Handorf, near Munster. The First and Second divisions also had targets in that area, although different from ours.

When we withdrew from the target area that afternoon, the three divisions were flying parallel courses abreast of each other, not in the usual bomber stream, with one division in trail of the other (apart from the B-24s of the Second Division, which always flew separately from the B-17s of the First and Third). It quickly became apparent that we wouldn't be able to squeeze all those bombers through the flak corridor when we crossed the Dutch coast at the Zuider Zee.

We were already starting our let-down as we approached the Dutch coast and we could see the groups ahead of us were attracting some flak so we knew we would too. My navigator, Bill Tate, suddenly called our attention to a lone B-17, probably at about 8,000 or 10,000 feet, slightly ahead and to our left. We couldn't tell whether he had either one or two engines out as he limped homeward below us. With growing apprehension, we approached the coastline and the flak batteries. Sure enough, all flak suddenly ceased at our altitude, and the German gunners zeroed-in on the lone B-17. We just knew he wouldn't make it. Our frustration was mixed with an awful helplessness as we watched the inevitable about to unfold.

But with all those bombers streaming out, so were all our fighters. When they saw what was happening to our buddies, the P-51s hit the deck and began working over those flak batteries. Suddenly all the flak ceased completely, the crippled B-17 maintained its altitude, and the last we saw of him he was safely over the North Sea, heading for home. As we came across the coast, I looked down and watched the P-51s, at tree-top level, spitting tracer bullets all over the area.

Our little friends had given a very graphic demonstration of how they were quite willing to put their lives on the line for bomber crewmen at any time and anywhere. It made me realize that those fighter pilots were the best. I've never forgotten that incident and have told it repeatedly.

BOMBSIGHTS, AUTOPILOTS, AND APHRODITES

Charles Henderson, Bombsight Technician, 334th Squadron

I joined the 95th Bomb Group in November 1943. Captain Malcolm Hanley and Technical Sergeant Clifford Hardessy headed a small number of specialists maintaining the Norden bombsight and automatic flight control equipment (A.F.C.E.) installed in all the group aircraft. All of us had been thoroughly trained in the theory, practical operation, and the maintenance of this highly specialized and top-secret equipment. For example, at the bombardier training school in Texas where I'd received instruction, this equipment was never left in an aircraft without being permanently guarded by an officer or a cadet bombardier.

The autopilot was indeed a marvelous addition to the B-17 or any other aircraft in which it was installed. The pilot could actually control the autopilot from the cockpit by a series of knobs and switches although the aircraft couldn't be banked, climbed, or dived beyond an angle of 30° when the autopilot was engaged. It was the ultimate safety device for the crew, wonderfully smooth in operation, and very dependable. The A.F.C.E., or C-1 autopilot, was a joint product supplied by the Norden and the Honeywell companies. The electronic connection linking the Norden bombsight to the autopilot control was, in fact, on the secret list for much longer than the bombsight.

The Norden bombsight was actually a computer, and it was renowned for unerring accuracy, even when strategic targets were attacked from a height of five miles. But it was only as good and accurate as the bombardier who supplied the relevant information during the bombing run to the target— airspeed, true groundspeed, drift, wind direction and strength, altitude, etc. Some of the 95th Group's bombardiers, people like Dewey Johnson, John Bromberg, and Marshall Thixton, set an extremely high standard of accuracy as proved by the bomb strike photographs time after time.

The bombsight and A.F.C.E. on each aircraft was flight-checked at least once by me, flying with the regular crew of that particular B-17 on practice bombing missions. Although I was with the 334th Squadron I was also assigned to the 335th, which flew Pathfinder B-17s leading the Thirteenth Combat Wing and the Eighth Air Force on several occasions.

I found the work involved to be both stimulating and fascinating, and because I had received excellent training, I was able to solve complicated problems relatively easily.

Mention should also be made of another notable achievement accomplished by the 95th Group bombsight maintenance department. It concerned the electronic control governing the turbo-supercharger mounted on each of the 1,200-horsepower Wright-Cyclone engines of the B-17 Fortress. For some reason the superchargers would unaccountably "run away" at high altitude, causing immediate loss of power to that engine. The aircraft would inevitably become a straggler and be comparatively easy prey for enemy fighters in the vicinity.

Technical Sergeant Arthur Watson, 334th Squadron, designed the necessary component for the turbo-supercharger control, thereby eliminating a very serious problem. It undoubtedly saved the lives of many Eighth Air Force combat crewmen, and he was subsequently awarded a medal for his invention.

Another interesting aspect of the work, not generally known, was the Aphrodite Project. War-weary B-17s and B-24 Liberator bombers were stripped down, then loaded with some 15 to 20,000 pounds of nitro-starch, a very powerful explosive, for attacking special targets such as submarine pens and V-weapon launching sites. The aircraft was manned by a pilot and a specialist A.F.C.E. crewman. The two-man crew would take the flying bomb to the English coast, bail out over land, and a mother ship would then take control by radio signals and guide the pilotless bomber over the sea and onto its assigned target with its ten-ton bomb load. That was the theory, but unfortunately it proved to be a failure in practice.

After several airmen were killed in this hazardous undertaking—including Joseph Kennedy, Jr., President John Kennedy's elder brother, whose B-24 Aphrodite unaccountably exploded over Blythburgh, Suffolk—the project was abandoned.

One of our 335th Squadron B-17s, the war-weary "Brass Rail," was one of the first, if not *the* first, bombers to be used in the Aphrodite Project. Two of our men, Sergeant Phillip Interline and Sergeant John Gelton, actually flew on Aphrodite missions; fortunately they both survived their bail-outs.

RETURN TO POLTAVA, 7 AUGUST 1944

Albert Keeler, Co-pilot, B-17G 297797, 412th Squadron

We were returning from a bombing mission to Trzebinia, Poland, and were well within friendly territory at 10,000 feet and descending on our way to land at our shuttle raid base at Poltava, in the heart of the Ukraine. Our aircraft, "Full House," so named because of its serial number 297797, with the appropriate five-card display on our nose, was leading the high squadron. As we descended through 9,500 feet, I called over the interphone, "co-pilot going off oxygen," meaning that I would remove my oxygen mask and change to a throat microphone for the lower altitude.

Suddenly, a small oxygen explosion occurred under the base of the top-turret gun position occupied by Technical Sergeant Ray Rich, instantly filling our cockpit area with dense smoke. Our pilot, who was still hooked to his oxygen tube and helmet headset, bolted out of his seat, separating his oxygen hose, headset cord, and oxygen mike cord. Because this happened as I was changing to my headset and throat mike, no other crew members had interphone contact with the cockpit. After the pilot had left his seat, I was, of course, flying the aircraft.

The smoke became so dense and choking we could hardly breathe. Fortunately, our B-17 had a small window vent-panel on the front windscreen that could be opened. Frantically I grabbed for it, and immediately the slipstream from the opening cleared the instrument panel so I could check our altitude. We were in a loose formation so I peeled sharply away from the group in a right turn. It was no place for a burning B-17 that could explode and take some of the other aircraft down with it. I leveled the airplane off at a safe distance, at the same altitude and in line with the rest of the group.

The cockpit suddenly became even more drafty. The pilot, who had climbed down into the nose section, ordered our navigator, Lieutenant Frank Morrison, and our bombardier, Lieutenant Foster Sherwood, to bail out through the nose exit hatch, which, of course, they did. Why the pilot didn't bail out himself, I'll never know. Apparently, it suddenly dawned on him that he was the B-17's pilot and that there were other crew members still in the aircraft!

He came back up to the cockpit and said, "We're bailing out!" I had reached for my chest-pack chute to buckle it on while our pilot was down in the nose ... no chute! Evidently my chute had been taken. I yelled, "Hey, Rich! Get me a chute!!" We always carried spares in the lower cockpit area. He threw one up to me, and at about the same time he found a small fire extinguisher. After a couple of squirts from the CO_2 bottle, the fire under the top turret was out.

Just as the smoke was clearing, the door at the front of the bomb bay opened. It was Technical Sergeant Langford, our flight engineer, carrying a large fire extinguisher. He'd been riding as waist gunner and had smelled smoke. Not having interphone contact with the cockpit, he had promptly grabbed the big fire extinguisher and crawled through between the bomb racks, *without a chute*, an extraordinary act of courage in itself, because he couldn't climb through the racks with it on and still carry the extinguisher.

With the fire out and smoke cleared, we rejoined the group's formation, and proceeded to Poltava as briefed. The base of Rich's top turret was red hot, the flames having blasted against the fuel transfer valves and burned the paint from the nameplate. Both Rich's hands were burned, and his chute, which he'd buckled on during the fire, had one end of its packing completely burned away.

Rich climbed into the pilot's seat. Soon, the pilot came back to the cockpit and stood between our seats, silent and ashen.

After landing we were informed that Morrison and Sherwood had been located by the Russian ground forces and would be returning to Poltava. Rich deserved an award, because in fighting and extinguishing the fire, he had saved us all.

This had been our crew's thirty-second combat mission. I was extremely disappointed in the first pilot's lack of leadership at a critical time because, up until then, he'd been a very fine pilot and had led us through several rough missions safety. We discussed the whole incident thoroughly as to why and how so many of us had been deserted in a burning aircraft. Because we were approaching the end of our combat tour, and with three likely milk run missions left (they were), we decided to forget everything. Otherwise a man with a good service record would have probably had a very rough time had the true facts been disclosed.

This unnamed pilot made one statement to me that clinched it all, "Rube . . . you're a hero."

Sadly, the pilot with whom we completed our combat tour died several years ago. It wasn't until the summer of 1984, when we began getting the "Full House" crew members together again, thanks to our navigator Frank Morrison, that any other crew members became aware of the true facts of our return to Poltava. Joe Comeau, our radio operator, said he was totally unaware of what really happened up front that day and thought I'd made the correct decision in keeping the incident quiet. Incidentally, I still have my thirty-five mission "crush" flight cap with a hole burned in the side of it as a souvenir and a poignant reminder of that day. (Editor's note: The name of the pilot in the preceding story has been purposely deleted. The story is worthy of telling without reflecting disrespectfully upon the family of the pilot.)

THE DAY PAUL FIESS BECAME A GENERAL

Eugene Fletcher, Pilot, 412th Squadron

The second shuttle mission from England to Russia was led by General August Kissner (Third Air Division) and the 95th was led by Colonel Truesdell. A few days before the raid, orders came from headquarters that the pilots would be referred to as aircraft commanders, and co-pilots as pilots.

My plane, "Knock Out Baby," was a shiny, bare metal B-17G as were all the 95th aircraft, except that of Paul Fiess, whose regular plane was undergoing maintenance. He flew a war-weary B-17F named "Berlin Bessie," one of the few olive drab aircraft on the base still in use. She was almost covered with mission bombs, with several *B*s printed on the bomb symbols to denote missions to Berlin. In other words, she stood out like a sore thumb.

When we landed on the steel matting at Poltava, we were shown where to park our planes. Fiess pulled in right beside us, and it was then that I noticed several Russian jeeps were following him. As soon as the engines were cut and the propellors jerked to a stop, the Russian surrounded "Berlin Bessie." When the crew emerged from the B-17, there was a lot of handshaking and frivolity going on. A Russian gal in uniform was the interpreter.

The Russian soldiers and airmen pointed repeatedly to the *B* symbols on the bombs and I heard a grinning Paul Fiess say, "Berlin . . . boom! . . . boom!" with the appropriate arm gestures. Of course, the Russians were absolutely delighted, and they all had to hug him and kiss his cheek. Naturally, they assumed he had flown all the missions painted on "Berlin Bessie." The Russians then loaded Fiess and his crew into the jeeps and away they went. I recall thinking it was nice to see him receive such a cordial reception as it couldn't have been much fun flying that old, war-weary airplane. I'd flown her twice previously and she wallowed rather than flew. It really was hard work.

After about twenty minutes a 6 x 6 truck collected our crew along with several others. We went to our temporary accommodations, housing, and mess tents, where we were informed that after chow we should change our flying suits and be in dress uniform because entertainment would be provided in a nearby bombed-out building.

That evening, as we sat in chairs under the night sky in the bombed-out building, I noticed General Kissner and all our high-ranking officers seated in a line on the back of the stage along with the high-ranking Russians. I also noticed a vacant chair between the Russian commander and General Kissner.

Paul Fiess and I were seated about two-thirds of the way back from the stage waiting for the entertainment to start when a young Russian girl in uniform approached us and appeared to be somewhat agitated. In perfect English she said to Paul, "Oh, there you are! We've been waiting for you." Paul, a good-looking young man but quite bashful, instantly turned red as a beet root and whispered urgently to me, "Oh, my God . . . they think I'm the commander." I replied, "That's O.K. I thought I was Napoleon once but I got over it. You'll be all right; just ask her if she has a girlfriend and I'll go with you. Now get yourself up there, you're holding up the show."

In the meantime the girl was gently tugging his arm. Fiess only had time to say, "Shut up! This is no joking matter." I was astonished as I watched the girl lead him to the stairs to the stage. When he reached the stage all the dignitaries stood up, the Russian general greeted Paul heartily and motioned him to take his seat in the vacant chair between him and a bemused General Kissner. Eventually, all were seated and the dancing commenced.

When the party was over and we returned to our tents I asked Paul, "What happened? I saw you whisked away from your airplane in grand style but there must be more to it than that." He explained that when the Russians drove up to his plane they asked one of his gunners, "Where is the commander?" They meant, of course, General Kissner. The gunner, thinking they meant aircraft commander, said, "He will be with you in just a minute."

Fiess, unwittingly, became a commander and was understandably embarassed. He didn't really realize what was going on until that evening's entertainment and the show was being held up.

The next morning, as we stood in the chow line for breakfast a young Russian girl in uniform motioned to Fiess. Apparently she didn't speak English. We were then both escorted into a special mess tent. One of the two tables was already occupied by several dignitaries from our force. We took the empty table.

While we were eating and our coffee cups got low, the young lady appeared with a coffee pot, refilled our cups, and left the coffee pot on our table, ignoring the other table. She then left the tent. One of the group then came over to our table; it could have been General Kissner. Whoever it was had sufficient rank to make mere lieutenants quake.

As I recall, "Regardless of what these people think, we still serve by rank in this man's army, whereupon he took the coffee pot and started back to the other table. As turned away with the coffee pot, I said, "Fiess, won't this make one helluva story when we get back to Horham!" Before he could reply the officer swung round to us and said, "This story stops right here and now. There's been a mistake here that could be very embarrassing to these people if they find out what's happened. Because they're our allies, it goes no further. Now, we've played along with it, but the play-acting is over. Only a few people really know what's happened and you're among them. If word of this ever leaks out we'll know it came from you, and I'll have your hides nailed to the wall as an example for all to see. Is that understood?"

There were several seconds of stunned silence and then a chorus of "Yes, sirs!"

"Good," he said, "Let's go fly."

Paul Fiess had become a general officer and commander for a few brief and unforgettable hours, and true to his word the incident was never mentioned again. We valued our hides and had no desire to risk a court martial or cause trouble, but it surely would have made one helluva story back at Horham.

A SHORT STORY OF A SHORT TOUR

Donald W. Overdorff

No longer rookies, we thought we would get credit for the mission to Trzbenia, Poland, from Poltava, Russia; we were in the air for three hours and ten minutes when we lost an engine and had to abort. If we did, we then could move on to mission thirteen. Apparently, it did not count, so we were flying number twelve on 24 August 1944. We were going through lead crew training, and our crew thought by leading a squadron or group, we would cross over the target before the flak batteries would zero in on our altitude and speed.

Wrong! What one thinks and what really happens are two different things.

Takeoff was terrible up through clouds to rendezvous, then came the flight to Politz, deep into Germany. Our lead crew training had put us into an element lead on one of the first planes over the target. It was really not our day, but it was the beginning of the end of our flying careers. As we approached the target, FLAK—one high, one low—then the third burst was right on our number 3 engine. Soon the cowling and engine were gone and the wing on fire. As the navigator, the escape hatch was only a few feet away from my window.

Bert Powell, our pilot, and Bill Connor, the co-pilot, tried to control the plane while the crew bailed out, but as the right wing broke free, we went into a snap roll. About that time, we were hit again, and the nose section was blown away from the rest of the plane. I found myself on the roof of the astrodome, the glass bubble used by the navigators for celestial navigation. I was trying to beat it out when I should have opened it inward. As Frank Whalen (bombardier) and I were falling, with all the 50-caliber shells, side guns flailing around, maps, and other equipment being thrown about, it became quite a chore to even think of looking for an escape route.

After getting my flak suit off and with help from Frank getting my chest chute snapped on, I started looking for the escape hatch, thinking we would hit the ground at any second. Finally, an opening! But as I started through, my chute got caught and I was stuck fast. The Lord was with me as someone, certainly not a crew member, lifted my chute and pushed me through.

Then I was free, thinking that with all that had happened, I would soon hit the ground. I pulled the ripcord; yes, the chute worked but I found myself surrounded by flak bursting around me. The concussion from the exploding shells caused my chute to oscillate like a pendulum, and at times my chute and I were almost at the same level. Another idea: tilt my chute and get away from it, but again, it didn't work. I grabbed some shroud lines and pulled. I almost died of fright when the chute looked like it was going to collapse. This is where the popular saying, "If it ain't broke, don't fix it" began; at least I was heading toward the ground, still alive. Soon the flak was above and out of range. It was around 1:00 P.M., a beautiful sunny day. I could hear the birds singing, but then I saw a German farmer watching me with a pitch fork in his hands. I saw that there would be no way to avoid a stand of trees. My chute caught in the trees, and I was left hanging about 10 feet above the ground. Knowing that I had been seen, I unhooked my chute and fell to the ground running.

I ran, looking for a place to hide, a stream bank, a ditch, anything. There was no natural hiding place in sight. Finally, I laid down in grass about 18 inches high and took stock of myself. My head was bleeding; my first aid kit was still attached to my chute in the tree. I opened my escape kit. Another surprise! Instead of maps of Germany, my kit had three nylon maps of southern France and northern Spain. There was also a supply of French francs. No great help hundreds of miles from France in northeast Germany.

Well, my problems were just beginning. In the distance, I could hear the Jerries coming toward me. As they came closer, I could see them, approximately thirty feet apart. All I could do was hug the ground. Luckily, they were talking to each other, and I was hiding between them. I can still see the face of the one soldier as I tried to hide my face with grass.

I laid perfectly still for two hours and my first thought was, "Where can I drop a post card to my parents telling them I am alive?" Even without maps, I did know the Russians were about 200 miles northeast of the target.

Since I could not remember being briefed on escape methods in Germany, I had to use my best judgment about traveling. It was a hungry trip for several days. Walking some by day, using back roads and forest trails, avoiding major highways and railroads, I ate little—mostly cold potatoes and turnips with a few wild berries. Sleep at night was fitful as I awakened to every noise. On the fifth day, I was near a railroad and was apparently spotted by people aboard. Soon two men on bicycles came from the rear; one had a rifle and when he took a plug from the barrel, I knew that I was no longer missing in action— I was Hitler's latest POW.

MORE SHORT BURSTS

Lieutenant James Sheller, lead pilot, 336th Squadron: Regarding the return flight from Italy to England, which was the last leg of the September 1944 shuttle mission England–Russia–Italy–England (during which arms, ammunition, and medical supplies were dropped to the Poles in Warsaw), my notes contain the following.

The bomb bay was filled with cases of champagne and brandy supplied by GI bootleggers in Foggia. We were briefed back to England via the Bay of Biscay at low level and no bomb load. I skipped the final briefing where plans were changed to fly a straight course directly back to Horham.

Over the French Alps at 20,000 feet, the champagne bottles exploded and froze the bomb bay doors shut so we couldn't jettison the contraband. The frozen champagne and brandy was starting to melt when we taxied to our hardstand back at the base, much to the joy and delight of our ground crewmen, who held their mess kit cups and coffee mugs under the drain tubes.

Colonel Truesdell's ship had the same problem, but he should have known better because it was he who gave the briefing.

****

Dick Flowerdew, local farmer: Several of the 336th Squadron Nissen huts and headquarters staff huts were built on my land. They were only built to last four or five years but a few of them still stand today (1986), and over the years they've proved very useful for storage and rearing livestock.

During the war, several of the American crews used to come to our farm-house for an evening meal occasionally. They'd bring the food from their stores that my wife then prepared and cooked for them. Home-cooked apple and cherry pies were particularly appreciated.

We got to know them very well as time passed, but when they went out on a mission and didn't return it was most upsetting. This happened to three or four crews who used to come regularly. Finally, it became so upsetting that my wife couldn't face it anymore so, very reluctantly, we had to stop inviting the crews as our guests.

****

Lieutenant Charles Brennan, navigator, 334th Squadron: Our crew was shot down over Augsburg on 16 March 1944 and our pilot, Ed Herman, was the last to leave our plane, which exploded immediately afterward. We were all rounded up eventually and taken to Frankfurt for interrogation, and on the night of 22 March the Royal Air Force virtually destroyed the camp and bombed much of Frankfurt in a truly frightening raid.

We were in an underground shelter, and during the height of the bombing, some R.A.F. flyers who had been shot down on previous raids started singing "The Beer Barrel Polka." We soon joined in to keep up our morale. We emerged from the shelter after the raid to find the whole camp literally flattened as well as Frankfurt's main railroad station. Subsequently we were marched to a small suburban station several miles away. During the march German civilians tried to attack us with clubs and knives, but the Luftwaffe soldiers held them off by using the butts of their rifles.

We were put on a train that night and headed east. We hadn't had any food or water, and I recall our train being shunted into a siding where a German troop train, on its way to the Russian front, was also delayed. Some of the soldiers, when they realized who we were, came over to our train and gave us some of their water and rations.

We arrived at Stalag Luft III, Sagan, the day after the night of the "Great Escape." It resulted in a change of camp commandant, and the new commandant told the senior British officer, Massey, that forty-one of the escapees had been shot while resisting arrest. Massey asked the commandant, "How many of our men were wounded?" He didn't reply.

Later it was discovered that fifty had been murdered by the Gestapo.

****

Albert Finginger, radar navigator, 412th Squadron: We can all recall how difficult it was to keep ourselves warm during the bitterly cold and damp English winters. This was especially true of the airmen's Nissen huts, heated by small pot-bellied coke stoves, located in the middle of the hut, with a small daily ration of coke for fuel.

By way of midnight requisitions and exploring the salvage yard, our hut was able to obtain the necessary equipment (consisting of an old hydraulic tank and tubing, shut-off valves, etc.), to devise a method for augmenting our heating system. By hanging the tank from the ceiling and running the connecting tube down through a hole drilled through the top of the stove, we were able to burn used engine oil, gravity fed, onto a very small amount of coke and so keep our hut comfortably warm.

This arrangement proved to be quite satisfactory until the fire marshal declared it to be a potential fire hazard and ordered us to remove it immediately. This problem was solved by moving the tank outside and acquiring longer tubing. The fire marshal was still not too happy with our new design, but he allowed us to keep it. What he didn't know, however, was that with the tank now outside we had to mix 100-octane aviation gasoline with the oil to keep it from congealing and to allow it to flow into the stove.

Talk about a fire hazard. Well, at least we stayed warm.

****

Joel Bunch, operations officer, 335th Squadron: Before the 95th Group departed from Morrison Field, West Palm Beach, Florida, for England via the South Atlantic route, each aircraft commander was issued $2,500 in cash and treasury checks to pay their crew members and to defray any expense for the aircraft should it be disabled and require landing and repair. The total amount for the thirty-six crews came to $90,000.

Upon arrival at Alconbury there was no finance officer and both the 92nd Group and the 95th Group were paid by the finance officer at Molesworth. Our Group Commander, Colonel A. A. Kessler, thereupon appointed me a Class B finance officer, and instructed all the 95th's aircraft commanders to hand in all remaining funds together with all expense receipts to me. He then ordered me to take the money to the finance officer at Molesworth as we had no safe on the base. I took a staff car to Molesworth and found on arriving that the finance officer was absent, but a technical sergeant invited me to come inside the finance office and wait.

Upon his return, the finance officer, a short fat major, was furious because I was sitting inside the counter, and he ordered me out. I asked him for a receipt for the cash and uncashed treasury checks for security purposes and was told that I had to prepare a separate voucher for each of the thirty-six crews and then to return them together with the funds. On my return to Alconbury I explained what had happened to Colonel Kessler. He was not amused. Neither was I and because we didn't have a typewriter I had to print each voucher, which took about three weeks. At that time, in addition to my duties in group operations, I was also serving as the enlisted men's mess officer and squadron adjutant until the group's ground echelon arrived by troopship from the United States.

After the thirty-six vouchers were completed, another trip to Molesworth proved fruitless because the finance officer refused to accept U.S. currency and he instructed me to change the money into English pounds sterling before he would accept it. Unfortunately, the banks were closed and I again returned to Alconbury to face the wrath of Colonel Kessler. When eventually the U.S. currency had been converted into pounds sterling, a third fruitless trip was made to Molesworth in an effort to hand in the funds, which amounted to approximately 20,000 pounds, a small fortune in those days.

Upon hearing my report Colonel Kessler nearly had a fit and vowed he would have that major's hide as, crimson-faced, he reached for the telephone.

The day I was shot down and taken prisoner, 22 June 1943, I had placed all the money between the mattresses of my bunk and I wondered, and still wonder, what eventually happened to it.

****

Henry Schneider, waist gunner, 334th Squadron: After being shot down during our thirteenth mission (Lieutenant Bert Powell's crew) in August 1944, I was prisoner of war at Stalag Luft I, Barth, and liberated in May 1945. I then took advantage of an opportunity to return to the 95th Bomb Group, Horham, on furlough.

Unfortunately, I had a very severe case of tonsillitis and instead of enjoying myself in the beautiful springtime weather in England, I found myself in the group hospital on the base where I was one of seven patients.

I was admitted to the hospital late at night, and consequently practically no paperwork was completed relevant to my illness. Unknown to me was the fact that all six other patients were recovering from what is known in polite circles as a rather unpleasant social disease. At that time, their treatment consisted of injections of sulfa drugs every two hours.

Shortly after I was put to bed, a new group of doctors and nurses came on duty. At the appointed hour, every patient was awakened for their sulfa shots. Because I'd lost my voice completely as a result of my ailment, I was unable to communicate with the medics. Despite using sign language and frantically attempting to evade the needle thrust, I was forcefully held down by two grim-faced nurses while a third nurse administered an extremely painful injection in a particular tender part of my anatomy. The treatment was repeated two hours later, and it was only after the second injection that I was able to obtain paper and pencil and made the medics aware that I didn't need all that sulfa.

Although I hadn't experienced the joy derived from intimacy, I certainly suffered the agony that often followed. As I look back I find the experience to be humorous and vividly reminiscent of a scene from "M.A.S.H.," but I certainly didn't find it funny at the time.

****

REFLECTIONS ON LIFE AS A "KRIEGIE," 40 YEARS LATER

Lieutenant Leonard Hansen, Co-pilot, 412th Squadron, and Lieutenant Donald W. Overdorff

There is little doubt in my mind that the most memorable period of my life was that from 25 August 1944 to 1 May 1945. It was on the first of those dates that I was shot out of the sky over Politz, Germany, at approximately 1330 hours.

The sequence of events from the moment of the fatal barrage of 88mm flak to my arrival at a Luftwaffe hospital in Griefswald at dusk on 25 August 1944, would be a volume in itself. In the prisoner of war camp we called these tales horror stories. Some were very dramatic and some were less so, but one thing common to all horror stories: it was the day freedom was lost for the duration.

After a brief stay at the hospital, I was shipped out to an interrogation center and from there to Stalag Luft I. Stammlager der Luftwaffe Eins was the full name, which meant permanent camp of the German Air Force number one. Since this was the first permanent POW camp established by Germany for captured Allied airmen, POW no. 1 was in our camp. Germany had the system of handing prisoners of war over to the corresponding branch of their own military machine. Thus, flyers were taken by the Luftwaffe, infantry by the Wehrmacht, political prisoners by the Gestapo.

Stalag Luft I was situated near the village of Barth on the Baltic Sea in the province of Pomerania, approximately fifty kilometers from Peenemunde, where Dr. Werner von Braun was pioneering and developing rocket technology that he would later use in his work for NASA in the United States.

"New kriegies up" was the cry that brought all old kriegies out of their barracks and over to the compound gate to see if any former comrades had suffered a similar termination to their combat careers. Kriegie was the common term we applied to ourselves; it is an abbreviation of *Kriegsgefangen,* the German word for prisoner of war. Seeing some familiar faces and getting some assurance that life in Kriegieland was tolerable made entrance into the permanent camp a little less traumatic. The most oft-asked question, "What are YOU doing here?" usually brought a response of exactly the same question.

Initially we were placed in rooms about 20 feet by 20 feet with ten double bunks. Later, another bunk was added to the top and we then had ten triple-decker bunks per room. What do thirty young men from the far reaches of the United States do? What do they talk about when thrown together in this fashion?

In my room we had the full spectrum of commissioned airmen: pilots of B-17, B-24, B-26, P-38, P-47, and P-51 aircraft, bombardiers, and navigators. We came from California (five), Texas (five), Virginia, Illinois, Alabama, etc. Long hours were spent trying to prove the superiority of one state over another. Among the great questions that were never settled were whether the Texas city of Dallas had the most beautiful women in the world, are earthquakes in California a greater hazard to your health than the winds of Waco, Texas, where it was reported, that they used a length of heavy logging chain for a windsock?

A favorite topic of conversation in Kriegieland was the progress of the war. Everyone was quite certain that the Allies would win the war, but there was always the what if syndrome. What if Hitler really had a secret weapon as he claimed? One of my roommates, a tall Texan named Jim Butler, shook us all up a bit one day when he described what the secret weapon might be.

Jim was a physics major at a Texas university when he joined the Air Corps, and he explained to us how all the great powers had scientific teams at work all attempting to split the atom. This was an idea completely foreign to everyone in the room, except Jim. He then went on to explain how, if they could split the atom and the various particles went crazily searching for each other to reunite, there could be one hell of an explosion. In fact, he said, they couldn't be sure it could be controlled and possibly it could destroy all living matter on earth. None of it made much sense at the time, but it made a lot of sense a year later, in August 1945, when President Harry Truman came on the radio to describe our new weapon, which would be called the atom bomb.

Food was a never-ending source of discussion and controversy. Was southern food really superior, or did the rest of the United States eat just as well? Such arguments were never solved, and just as well, but it was something to talk about. Men copied recipes from each other and pledged to try them out when they got home. I wonder if anyone kept those pledges any more than I kept my pledge never to drive my car without a box of Hershey bars in the glove compartment. How quickly we forget!

Kriegie craftmanship was a real testimony to the ingenuity of fertile young minds. Tin cans that brought us Klim (powdered milk) and other foods in Red Cross parcels were fashioned into everything from baking pans to slide rules and even a complete pendulum clock that worked and kept very good time! Wool sweaters that didn't fit were unraveled and crocheted into socks and caps using a crochet hook formed from a toothbrush handle.

My reflections wouldn't be complete without mentioning the spiritual side of life in a POW camp. There is an old saying, "There are no atheists in foxholes or on the lower end of a parachute," and I believe that to be true. It was interesting to observe how the interest in church attendance progressed during my Air Corps career. Being brought up to go to church every Sunday, I naturally kept to this routine in the Air Corps when possible. At the training bases in the West Coast Flying Training Command, I would estimate that Sunday worship was attended by less than 10 percent of the cadets. As we got commissioned and began taking combat readiness training, chapel attendance increased to about 50 percent. After the first rough combat mission when several 95th Group crews were lost, just about everybody found the time to get to the base chapel, and in POW camp where we were ministered to by a British chaplain, who voluntarily stayed behind at the time of the Dunkirk evacuation in June 1940, *everyone* came to the chapel services at some time.

I wonder how many promises to God made at that time assuring Him of lifetime obedience to His Will in exchange for safe return home have been and are being honored. I am very grateful for His granting me a safe return and my prayer is that I will never fail to keep that commitment I made there at Stalag Luft I in 1944 to serve Him wherever and however He leads me.

The guards in our camp were not the typical militaristic German soldiers of the German armed forces. Some were placed there because of their knowing the English language, some because of partial disability, and others because they were too old to fight. By the time I arrived at Stalag Luft I (Paris was liberated the day I was shot down), the Germans realized that their cause was lost and their prisoners would soon be the victors. I'm sure this affected their attitudes very considerably.

However, they were still very much in charge, and we were kept very much aware of that fact by daily roll calls, guards in every watchtower with machine guns, and double barbed wire fences. Strict rules regarding our behavior when Allied planes came over, en route to a target, were rigidly enforced. Daylight raids by the Eighth Air Force came directly over our camp when heading for the famous Peenemunde rocket testing center. A rule was posted forbidding us to leave the barracks during an air raid alert. One POW forgot and jumped out of a barracks window; he was shot and died instantly.

"Mail call!" to any serviceman was a highlight of any day during his military career. In a POW camp you can imagine the excitement and anticipation of every Kreigie that *this* time he will get a letter or letters. We were allowed to send one letter and three postcards per month and hoped at least that many would come from home. I was fortunate in that regard as my fiancée (now my wife) kept me informed regularly of all the latest news from home in California.

Some prisoners received letters with tragic messages, and some were downright ridiculous and humorous like the POW who wrote to a Red Cross knitter who had put her home address inside the sweater of his gift parcel. Her response to his letter of thanks was, "I am sorry to hear that a prisoner is wearing the sweater I knitted for a fighting man." One well-meaning aunt wrote, "I am enclosing a calendar. I thought that it would be appropriate and come in handy as it has several years ahead on it." A sister wrote, "I'm really worried about our cat. I took her to the vet and he said her diet was insufficient." Fortunately, most letters from home brought good news, hope, great encouragement, and assurances that our families and friends were praying daily for our safe return.

Words are totally inadequate to describe the physical, mental, and moral support provided to Allied prisoners of war in Europe by the International Red Cross and the International YMCA. The Red Cross provided physical support through food and clothing, while the YMCA ministered to our morale by providing reading materials, musical instruments, and athletic equipment. Upon assignment to our permanent POW camp, we were given a capture parcel from the Red Cross. It contained towels, socks, handkerchiefs, soap, toothbrush and powder, shirt, tie, sewing kit, pipe, tobacco, underwear, toilet paper, wool sweater, razor, and a first aid kit. This indeed was a very welcome sight because these were the vital items that the Germans did not provide. Weekly food parcels, one to each prisoner, was the goal of the Red Cross. These came quite regularly to Stalag Luft I until January 1945 when the Germans' shortage of petrol and manpower became so acute that they couldn't deliver them. When the German camp commandant, a colonel, had to abandon his staff car and ride around the camp in a horse-drawn surrey, we were assured the claims of a petrol shortage were genuine!

The times were not bad while the food parcels lasted, and a thriving POW economy came into being; miniature trading posts were established. Non-smokers came to trade their cigarettes for food, spam haters could trade for cheese or corned beef, etc. Understandably, there was always a surplus of cigarettes, and these made excellent black market trading stock with wayward German guards who would risk being transferred to the dreaded Eastern front (to fight against the advancing and vengeful Russians) to get American cigarettes in exchange for fresh vegetables and spices.

But the inevitable happened in January 1945; there were no Red Cross parcels during the next four months until our camp was liberated by the advancing Russian Army in early April 1945. During this time to add to our misery, German rations to the camp were severely curtailed until we were existing on about 800 calories a day. It was extremely cold during those winter months and fuel was in very short supply. During that time we learned you can be quite thin and still lose weight!

The provision by the YMCA of athletic equipment and reading materials was a godsend to our morale and our sanity. I read twenty-eight books, one per week, while a POW. Some were not so good, and others like *The Robe, This Above All,* and *Goodbye Mr. Chips* were classics. The YMCA also sent us playing cards, musical instruments, bibles, and testaments. It is not hard to see why words are inadequate to describe what these two great organizations did for us all.

****

Donald W. Overdorff: I finally ended up in Barth, Germany, Stalag I, Kriegie #5353. Being a POW meant many things: very little food, a one-minute bath (usually every two weeks), cold nights on a mattress filled with straw, and long hours wishing the war would end.

With time on our hands, in our room number 6, block number 3, North Compound II, we were always thinking of ways to keep up our morale.

The days were much the same. Twice a day we were assembled by barracks in rows of five in an open area and counted to check whether anyone had escaped, an almost impossible task.

As Christmas was near, our room, headed by Charles ("Mole") Wilson decided on a plan. With material furnished by the YMCA, we cut letters from paper and on Christmas morning, we took the first row of the barracks waiting to be counted, and at a signal the letters were flashed in front of each Kriegie. As the Jerries and the other eight barracks looked on, the front row spelled "MERRY CHRISTMAS, ROOM 6" much to the delight of all.

WILLIE GREEN'S FLYING MACHINE

This is the fable of Willie Green
Who invented a kriegie flying machine,
'Tis as weird a tale as ever you heard
Yet I'll swear by the truth of every word.
The man who first heard it, suspicious as I,
Swore by his chocolate 'twas all a great lie,
But imagine his surprise, the gleam in his eyes,
When Willie's machine was seen to fly.
The parts were gathered—'tis no secret now—
But Willie alone knows the secret how.
They were hidden away in corners and places
While he carved away on the spars and braces.
The tin can piles were low indeed
When W.G. performed his deed
There is still talk of that famous day
As the last Klim-can was hidden away.
The engine was the first of the plane to be made
With crankshaft of steel from the missing spade
While in Klim-can cylinders with mighty sound
The butter can pistons went up and down.
The flashy propellor so aerodynamic
Was carved from a board in the barracks attic
While this peculiar strand that made the ignition
Was a length of barbed wire from the compound partition.
Fuel was no problem for a man with a head
And Willie got gas from cabbage and bread.
In case of emergency, Willie held
The thing could easily be rocket propelled.
The side of the bed the fuselage made
The stick, the handle of the fore-mentioned spade
The instruments, it could be seen at a glance,
Was none other than the seat of Willie's pants.
Two locker doors the wings did make
With dihedral taper and negative rake
And a Red Cross box from a racket source
Serve as a tail for his flying horse.
The question of wheels was mighty hot
Till Willie remembered the communal pot
While Kriegies were wondering how it disappeared

Willie's machine became tricycle geared.
There were no guns on Willie's steed
Its only defense was its excessive speed
To weight down the tail our hero used
A size "12" pair of British shoes.
And when it was done our Willie cried,
"Enough, enough, I'm satisfied."
And one dark night when conditions were best
Willie's machine was put to the test.
The prop turned over, the engine caught,
"Ah," said Willie, " 'twas not for naught."
The plane jumped forward, started to fly
And was over the fence in the wink of an eye.
The guard yelled "Verboten" and started to shoot
But all his efforts were as good as "Kapoot."
Willie flew on and into the dark
Toward Ellis Island and Battery Park.
The plane flew on until Willie spied
The lights that mark the other side.
He felt so good, and oh so free
His Red Cross box fell into the sea.
A crowd was there when he landed his crate.
"Where am I?" he asked. "It sure looks great."
"Why where," they cried, "were you headed for?"
"This my boy . . . is Stalag Luft Four."

(Submitted by John Welles)

Emmett Dedman

THE FINAL FLIGHT OF "FIREBALL"

Stewart Evans, Friends of the Eighth (FOTE), England

On Saturday, 9 September 1944, twenty-eight B-17 Fortresses of the 95th Bomb Group took off from Horham Airfield as a part of a 1,000-bomber raid by 8th Air Force B-17s and B-24s to attack strategic targets in the industrial Ruhr Valley and other towns in southwestern Germany. The 95th Group's assigned target was Dusseldorf situated in the Ruhr Valley.

Aircraft 231876 QW-Q "Fireball," piloted by Second Lieutenant Billie B. Lahl, aborted the mission over the North Sea and turned back with number 4 engine feathered.

The B-17 arrived over Horham at an altitude of 16,000 feet, descended, broke out of low cloud at 1,500 feet, and turned into a final approach without making a full pattern landing. Lowering the landing gear and flaps was delayed until well into the final approach. As Lieutenant Lahl leveled off for the landing, the flight engineer reported that the tail-wheel wasn't fully extended. The control caravan at the far (downwind) end of the runway urgently flashed a red light at the aircraft as it approached the runway with its two main landing wheels still retracted.

The pilot added power to maintain altitude until the landing gear was lowered and in doing so, the B-17 drifted off the line of the runway and over the bordering grassed area. As there were still five 1,000-pound general-purpose bombs aboard, the remaining three engines were unable to supply sufficient power to prevent continual descent, and the aircraft landed on wet grass about four hundred yards from the approach (upwind) end of the runway, slid along the grass parallel to the runway, across the eighteen-yard-wide perimeter track, and into a pile of concrete rubble.

There were no injuries to the crew, but "Fireball" was damaged beyond repair.

ARNHEM—OVERFLIGHT TO BATTLE

Robert Hastie and Bill Lindley, 334th Squadron

The 95th Group was on standdown on Sunday, 17 September 1944, when my crew and I received instructions to meet Lieutenant Colonel Bill Lindley at 334th headquarters for a special assignment. Our regular airplane, "Excelsior," was already loaded with parachute supplies, supply canisters, ammunition, small arms, food, etc., for a mission to besieged Warsaw, Poland, which had been delayed for several days. We were assigned another B-17, "Screaming Eagle," for this unexpected operation.

We loaded the required supplies, my crew installed the machine guns, and we took off for an airfield near London with Bill Lindley and veteran squadron navigator Bill Steele aboard. The crew that day was completed with Charles Cupskey, engineer and top turret; Art Niemzyk, radio operator; Lindsey, ball-turret; Bob Morgan as waist gunner, and Floyd Alford, tail gunner.

Bill Lindley recalls: Colonel Truesdell, 95th Group commander, had called me the previous day and told me to report to Third Air Division headquarters for a special assignment. He knew none of the details. Everything crossed my mind from being transferred to headquarters to being shot at sunrise.

A short jeep ride put me in the office of the deputy for operations, where I was briefed on a large scale paratrooper drop scheduled for the next day on Arnhem, Holland. General Matthew Ridgway (U.S. Army) was one of the Allied commanders of the operation and wanted to be in the dropping zone (DZ) when the operations got under way. That was my assignment. Take him in and bring him back, both at 20,000 feet. He was to be picked up at an airfield in southern England and from then on I was to follow his instructions implicitly.

Back to Horham I go, all fired up at the prospect of being a part of the largest airborne operation of the war.

The next morning, right on schedule, we landed at the designated base and met General Ridgway and his aide. The general reaffirmed that he wanted to be in the DZ when the first paratroopers arrived and that he would tell us when to return to base. He then asked what we could expect to see from an altitude of 20,000 feet. I replied, "Not a hell of a lot." This got his attention and he asked, "What height do you recommend?" The only thing that made any sense was to go in with the C-47 Dakotas and the gliders and stay in their immediate area, at their altitude. The heavy flak we could dodge, and with all the planes in the air for the Germans to shoot at one more wouldn't make that much difference. He bought the whole package.

Robert Hastie continues: We fitted General Ridgway and his aide with the two spare parachutes and harnesses that we had brought along. Of course, both these two gentlemen were highly experienced paratroopers whereas none of us had ever bailed out. Nevertheless, we felt very confident in briefing them on the appropriate use of the parachute.

We all piled into the plane and took off for the English Channel toward Holland. It was a warm, sunny September morning and we flew at an altitude of about 5,000 feet to a flight plan that avoided the known heavy flak concentrations in Holland. A let-down was made over the unpopulated area of Holland, where we intercepted the first waves of C-47s, C-46s, and then many other types of transport aircraft towing gliders. What an absolutely incredible sight!

They were cruising at 2,000 to 3,000 feet. It was a clear day, and the vast formation of aircraft extended to as far as the eye could see, flying in long straight lines. Our airspeed was greater than that of the "gooney birds," and we had to drop 15 degrees of flap in order to slow down and do wide S turns in order to stay with the front rank of C-47s and the following formations.

It was really quite an amazing and startling sight to see so many aircraft fanned out from horizon to horizon. We could also clearly see the people standing around the streets of small towns and villages in their shirt-sleeves looking up and watching this great aerial armada heading toward the Rhine River area. As we approached Eindhoven, we could see the orange smoke billowing upward that marked the front line of the Allied ground forces. Ahead of us P-47 Thunderbolts were beating up all the hedgerows, roadside farmhouses, and haystacks, which were all blazing and smoking.

It was just beyond Eindhoven that the first of the paratroopers began bailing out. The sky suddenly filled with thousands of variously colored supply parachutes. At first we couldn't comprehend the magnitude of the drop until we looked between all those colored chutes and could see a multitude of olive-drab personnel chutes. They nearly blanketed out the ground below as we flew directly over them. The paratroopers appeared at the doorways of the C-47s, looked up very briefly, then in rapid succession, launched themselves into space. In less than two minutes, they were on the ground, scrambling around, picking up their supply canisters and equipment, and then sprinting to take up their positions in the hedgerows that bordered the flat fields of the DZ.

This was the first time that we had been exposed to low-level ground fire. There was tracer fire, both 20mm and 40mm, also some small flak bursts but much smaller than 88mm bursting around the transport aircraft. We could see the paratroopers on the ground moving into position and a great deal of fighting ensued as they clashed with the German defenders. We circled this area for awhile and then moved forward to Nijmegen where the same thing was occurring.

Bill Lindley recalls: I was flying the B-17; General Ridgway and his aide were down in the nose compartment when the aide called me on the interphone and asked if he and the general could fire the nose guns and the chin turret. From then on they kept the guns busy and used all the ammunition in the nose. A fresh supply was then taken to them from the upper turret. The ball-and tail-turret gunners got into the act, and everyone shot at anything on the ground that moved as we approached the Nijmegen DZ. In the middle of all this, the second jump started, and the crew witnessed again a sight that few people have ever seen. It was possible to see the paratroopers jump, assemble, and then move off to their assigned objectives. Although several C-47s in our immediate area were shot down, we were lucky, not a hit.

Robert Hastie continues: After a survey of the Nijmegen area, we went on to Arnhem, where the ground fighting was far more intense. This has been well recorded in the movie *A Bridge Too Far.* During the operation I don't recall seeing any C-47s dropping out of formation prior to dropping the para-troopers but very shortly afterward I saw quite a number of them fall lazily off on one wing and plunge to the ground in flames. There were also a large number of CG-4 gliders that still had invasion stripes painted on them being towed by British transport aircraft. We left the Arnhem area at the Rhine River and flew back over the drop zones at Nijmegen and Eindhoven, circled around very briefly, observing the ground fighting in those areas, and then climbed to about 5,000 feet to head back to England as instructed by General Ridgway.

We experienced the usual feeling of relief and exhilaration on returning to England from occupied Europe, but this time it was rather subdued and dampened with the knowledge of the great numbers of our people that were left behind involved in intensive ground combat.

Bill Lindley: The flight back was without incident. General Ridgway thanked the entire crew individually for what he said was the best command post ever.

Robert Hastie: The overall plan of the operation was for the ground forces, under the command of General Bernard Montgomery, to spearhead through and relieve the three drop zones, which included vital bridges spanning the Rhine River, in a time span of forty-eight hours. The paratroopers gallantly held out for, I believe, seven days before being forced to withdraw after sus-taining very heavy casualties. The ground forces had encountered fierce and unexpected opposition and couldn't force their way through.

On the return flight that memorable day, I asked Bill Lindley, considering the length of time he'd been flying, why he was still messing about in B-17s. His reply was that the Fort was as good as any fighter or any other type of aircraft. I said, "Well, Bill, when I complete my tour, I'm not staying with these babies in this kind of business."

As we approached the base in England he stood the airplane on a wing, dropped through a hole of the overcast, and kicked it around in line with the runway. I considered that we were too high and far too close for any sort of landing, and with General Ridgway up there in the nose, Bill proceeded to chop back power and poked the nose into the air until we were just staggering along. Then, he walked it down to a stall—something I've never seen a B-17 do—and just before we got to touch-down level, he clammed the power to all four engines, dropped the nose, and wheeled her in to one of the smoothest landings I've ever seen.

He then looked across at me and said, "You can do any damn thing with a B-17 that you can do with any fighter."

Bill Lindley concludes: A month or so after this mission and with several more missions of my second tour under my belt, I awoke one morning, looked around, and suddenly realized that most of the old and familiar faces were gone. The fun wasn't there any more. It was time to pack it in, head back to the states, get married, and raise kids.

Every good thing comes to an end sooner or later, and so it was with the crew of "The Zootsuiters." While I flew with several different navigators and bombardiers, the enlisted men of my crew stayed the same. A finer group of individuals never existed. They flew when I flew, never doubting our ability to get safely through the war. They never questioned any of my decisions and were always there when I needed them. Every mission we flew, of course, was made possible by the untiring efforts of our ground crew, the backbone of any outfit. Parting was tough.

The 95th Group was good to me in both promotions and responsibility. I hope my efforts were in keeping with its high standards of combat operations.

WELCOME TO COMBAT!
ONE CREW'S FIRST MISSION

Glenn Purdy, Pilot, 335th Squadron

Editor's Note: The waiting prior to the first exposure to combat generates untold uncertainties that cannot be adequately described. Each individual faces the prospect of war and deals with it accordingly. Emotions run the full spectrum from anxiety to desire, fear, self-doubt to full self-confidence.

Even though by December 1944 the Luftwaffe no longer resembled an effective fighting organization, combat crews on occasion faced aroused fighter opposition, but more ominous for combat crews was the antiaircraft fire—the flak. Upon the request of the 335th Bombardment squadron commanding officer, Lieutenant Glenn T. Purdy, a 21-year-old engineering student, drafted a report of his crew's first mission. Below is Lieutenant Purdy's report of his crew's first mission in B-17G 338760, named "Lucky Lady," which had previously logged fifteen missions. It was Christmas Eve 1944, the target: Biblis, an airfield near Frankfurt.

The Crew: P Glenn T. Purdy, *CP* Theodore R. Harris, *N* William A. McEwan, *NT* Carl B. Strauch, *TT* Henry J. Miller, *RO* Edward W. Schneider, *BT* Horace ("Gene") E. Hampton, *WG* James P. Ganster, *WG* Robert J. Spitznagel, *TG* Richard "Red" A. McCain. Robert Spitznagel, though assigned to the crew, did not participate on this mission. Additional information appears within brackets throughout the text.

TO: Commanding Officer, 335th Bombardment Squadron

SUBJECT: Lieutenant Purdy's Crash Landing in Alsace-Lorraine, France.

1. We were participating in the mission of 24 December and were flying ship 338760, number 3 in the low element of the low squadron (95D), when hit by flak. Our position was directly over the target at 25,000 feet, time approximately 1445 hours, a few seconds after the scheduled time of "bombs away," but the group did not drop so we still had our bombs. Tail gunner "Red" McCain had been calling out flak at six o'clock level when all of a sudden there was a crash and the ship lurched upward. Lieutenant T.R. Harris, my co-pilot, was flying at the time, and the next thing I knew he was turning up the turbo charger to see if number 4 engine power could be increased. We noticed that number 4 engine fuel pressure was almost zero, so I switched number 4 booster pump on, but pressure did not rise. So Harris hit number 4 feathering button, I switched the fuel valve closed, and we (after several attempts) completed the feathering procedure. I tried to contact Fire Ball E, EASY (call sign for 95D) and give the abortion message (the phrase used was "Mexican hay ride") but could not contact him. We were now slightly behind the formation and I had planned to cut them off on the next turn, but number 2 was leaking oil—it was heating up—and number 1 manifold pressure was falling off. We salvoed the bombs and ordered the crew to stand by to abandon ship, but they were instructed to keep on the interphone and at their positions. About three to five minutes later number 2 went out—we couldn't keep it cool. Oil pressure went to 30 pounds per square inch, cylinder head shot up to 230° and then over; the oil temperature was over 100°. Number 2 began putting out black smoke, and black oil was coming out from under the top cowl flaps. It quit and we feathered it. Number 1 would only pull about 20 inches of manifold pressure, so the crew was ordered to throw everything out such as bail-out packets, emergency equipment, flak suits, helmets, dinghy radio, and all ammunition except that which was already loaded. Extra radio tuning sets and the rear door were also discarded. Ball-turret gunner Gene Hampton stayed in the ball turret, and the gunners kept some ammunition in case of fighters. I *did not* drop the ball turret because I wanted it in case of fighters. The 100th Bomb Group had passed over us and to the left. Previously, Lieutenant W.A. McEwan, our navigator, had given me a heading of 190° and we were high tailing it for home on the briefed course. His Gee box was inoperative. We were losing

approximately 500 feet per minute; air speed was between 100 and 110 mph and number 3 was wide open pulling 57 inches and 2500 rpms. It ran this way for fifty minutes and never gave any trouble. I was hoping that as we got lower in altitude, number 1 manifold pressure would build up but it never did. Its maximum was 20 inches. We couldn't roll any aileron trim as the knob was stuck.

2. Lieutenant McEwan gave us slight course corrections, and I kept asking him if we were still over Germany. All he'd say was, "I'm afraid so!" I was planning on everyone bailing out but was waiting for our front line. At 9,000 feet Sergeant Hampton got out of the ball since the navigator said we were almost to our lines. We were just about to the line, altitude approximately 9,000 feet, when we encountered heavy flak. We tried evasive action, but it went where we did. It came from the vicinity of Bitche (Alsace-Lorraine). At 5,000 feet the navigator said we were just over the lines, and I was just going to have the crew bail out when T.R. (Harris) spotted a good field ahead and at about two o'clock. I nodded so he called the crew and asked, "How'd you like to ride her down?" Everyone said, "OK, Roger," so I called for ditching positions. We were on a heading of 270° and upstairs the wind was from 68° but down there it was due 90° according to the smoke from the small town we passed over. At 3,000 feet Harris pointed to a large field on his right at about three o'clock. It looked better than the rest as it had no fences. They were all set in the radio room so we made a 180° approach turning right into the final. I had number 3 on until I was sure we wouldn't undershoot, then I cut power, Harris lowered the flaps; the indicator didn't work. We both got on the controls, sideslipped to the right, and came in at 110 mph. Made a regular (wheels up) landing on the upslope of a small hill, slid up to the top, and stopped on the other side. Nothing unusual occurred. She slid on the tires exposed from the nacelles and the ball (turret) and belly. The plexiglass nose broke open. Props were bent, numbers 2 and 3 engine mounts broken, and the ball turret busted in two. The ball did not come loose at the top support. The time was 1550 hours.

3. We cut all switches just before the plane stopped, exited immediately via cockpit windows, crew by the waist exit and we started to run but we spotted two American MPs in a jeep. One MP stayed with the crew and the ship while Harris and I went in the jeep to Sarrable. Reported to the provost marshal and another guard was sent out with a truck for the rest of the crew. Reported to Captain Iye, Seventh Army, 15th Corps Command Flight Control. Ship was pinpointed at three miles out highway number 56, 300 yards northwest of the road, seven miles behind the front lines. Sarrable was almost nine miles from the front.

4. Thirty minutes after landing a *complete* SOP (standard operating procedure) message was sent to Eighth Air Force in England, relayed by radio, and Twelfth TAC advance was also notified.

5. Spent Christmas eve with the Seventh Army, Fifteenth Corps Com-

Walter   Fred   Howard
Ray   Voltz   Eaton
   Louis   Edward   Jim
   DeLuca   Pachnik   Drexler

                              Chuck
                              Moody
Russian Yak Fighter at Air Field

Part of the 95th crew of Fred Voltz who made a forced landing on an
airfield very recently liberated by the Russians. They continued to
Moscow to start a long trip back to Horham.

John Bromberg is congratulated
by a friend for another award.

German bombers destroyed 45 American B-17s at Poltava during the
first shuttle mission to Russia, 21 June 1944.

War map shows 7,000-mile route of the first shuttle mission to Russia, 21 June to 5 July 1944.

Control tower at Mirgorod, Russia, where 95th planes were based during the first shuttle mission to Russia. Other facilities were equally rustic.

Mirgorod Hilton, June 1944. Crew accommodations.

All targets were destroyed on the first Russian shuttle from England. Shown are (*top*) oil refinery—Drohobyer, Poland. Center, oil refinery—Schwarzheide, Ruhland, Germany. Bottom, marshaling yards, Beziers, France.

American officers shown with Russian officers and soldiers. The girl in the center is Maja, Russian interpreter.

American airmen from the 95th with kitchen helpers at Mirgorod.

95th crewman with Russian soldiers, male and female.

Main dining room at Mirgorod Hilton.

Typical friendly
greeting when the
95th planes landed at
Mirgorod, June 1944.

Russian commander greets
Paul Feiss on the second
shuttle mission to Russia.
The 95th planes landed at
Poltava in August 1944.

Malcolm Durr, 95th
navigator with a Russian
sentry. Second shuttle
mission to Russia, August
1944.

P-51 Mustang fighters with long-range drop tanks escorted the B-17s on all missions during the 7,000-mile shuttles to Russia, Italy, France.

Colonel Truesdell is greeted
upon the return of the third
shuttle mission to Russia and
Italy, September 1944.

Dignitaries arrive for awards
ceremony to honor the 95th
Group, which dropped needed
supplies to Polish Freedom
Fighters in Warsaw during
the third shuttle mission,
September 1944. *L to R:*
Colonel Moller, General
Partridge, General Harbold,
General Sosnokorosky (others
unknown).

olonel Carl Truesdell
ceives Poland's highest
ard as leader of the supply
ssion to Warsaw.

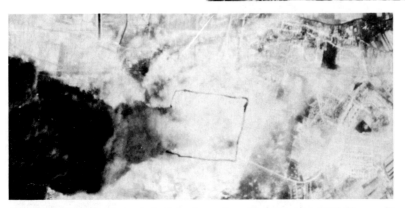

A few of the many targets left destroyed and burning by 95th Group B-17s. *Top*, Zeitz. *Center*, Ludwigshaven. *Bottom*, Politz.

Familiar sights at Horham,
1943, '44, '45. Flyers
lounge, Red Cross building,
a mess hall, briefing room.

336th Squadron plane came to rest across a ditch after crash landing at Horham.

95th crewmen saw many B-24 Liberators in flight. This one is from the
93rd Bomb Group, Second Division.

Proud award recipients. The broken arm was the result of a fall from a bicycle!

A R.A.F. Lancaster visited Horham in 1945. A most interesting name—
and with many missions to its credit. (This plane is now on display at the
Royal Air Force Bomber Command Museum, London, England.)

General LeMay with General Carl Spaatz, SHEAF and General "Jimmy" Doolittle, Eighth Air Force at Elveden Hall, 1945.

A planning session at Elveden Hall, early 1945. Major Ellis Scripture reviews mission flight plan for General Doolittle and General Spaatz while Lieutenant Colonel H. Griffin "Grif" Mumford watches. General Partridge, Colonel Hunter Harris, Colonel Carl Norcross at the right.

Major General Curtis E. LeMay, original commander of the Fourth Bomb Wing, which became the Third Air Division as more groups arrived for duty with the Eighth Air Force. Later he commanded SAC and was chief-of-staff.

Major General Earle Partridge succeeded General LeMay as commander, Third Air Division at Elveden Hall. Later he became Chief of Operations for the U.S. Air Force and the First C.G. of NORAD.

Elveden Hall, headquarters for the Third Air Division, Eighth Air Force.
This beautiful country mansion was adapted for wartime operations, thus
the stark, drab appearance.

B-17G No: 48640 from the 95th was the last plane lost in action by the
Allies in WWII on 7 May 1945. This crew picture was taken earlier in
happier days. Eleven men were killed, including four ground crewmen
and photographers along for the final mission.

Rhenania oil plant, south of Hamburg, Germany, goes up in oil smoke to 19,000 feet, clouds at 18,000 feet; planes at 26,000 feet. Bombing done by radar technique.

Me 410 narrowly misses a mid-air crash in a concentrated attack. (Photo from 388th Bomb Group).

German Luftwaffe Messerschmitt (Me 109) with rocket launchers under the wing.

German Focke Wulf (FW 190) fighter plane.

Vital rail and road systems lay in total ruin at war's end. Concentrated, accurate high-altitude bombing was effective.

Entrance to the American cemetery, Cambridge. The British people
deeded this property to the U.S. government so that American men killed
in action could be buried on American soil.

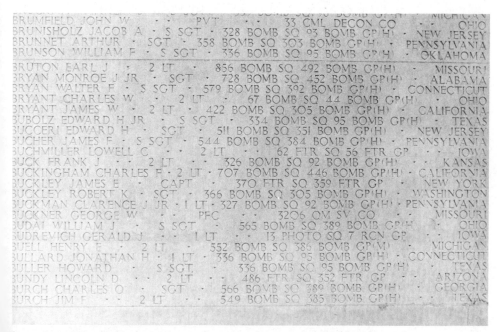

BRUMFIELD JOHN W	· ·	PVT	· ·	33 CML DECON CO	· ·	MICHIGAN
BRUNISHOLZ JACOB A	·	S SGT	· 328 BOMB SQ	93 BOMB GP(H)	·	NEW JERSEY
BRUNNET ARTHUR	·	SGT	· 358 BOMB SQ	303 BOMB GP(H)	·	PENNSYLVANIA
BRUNSON WILLIAM F	·	S SGT	· 336 BOMB SQ	95 BOMB GP(H)	·	OKLAHOMA
BRUTON EARL J	·	2 LT	· 856 BOMB SQ	492 BOMB GP(H)	·	MISSOURI
BRYAN MONROE J JR	·	SGT	· 728 BOMB SQ	452 BOMB GP(H)	·	ALABAMA
BRYAN WALTER F	·	S SGT	· 579 BOMB SQ	392 BOMB GP(H)	·	CONNECTICUT
BRYANT CHARLES W	·	2 LT	· 67 BOMB SQ	44 BOMB GP(H)	·	OHIO
BRYANT JAMES W	·	2 LT	· 422 BOMB SQ	305 BOMB GP(H)	·	CALIFORNIA
BUBOLZ EDWARD H JR	·	S SGT	· 334 BOMB SQ	95 BOMB GP(H)	·	TEXAS
BUCCERI EDWARD H	·	SGT	· 511 BOMB SQ	351 BOMB GP(H)	·	NEW JERSEY
BUCHER JAMES F	·	S SGT	· 544 BOMB SQ	384 BOMB GP(H)	·	PENNSYLVANIA
BUCHMILLER LOWELL C	· ·	2 LT	· ·	62 FTR SQ 56 FTR GP	· ·	IOWA
BUCK FRANK J	·	2 LT	· 326 BOMB SQ	92 BOMB GP(H)	· ·	KANSAS
BUCKINGHAM CHARLES F	· 2 LT	· 707 BOMB SQ	446 BOMB GP(H)	·	CALIFORNIA
BUCKLEY JAMES E	·	CAPT	· 370 FTR SQ	359 FTR GP	·	NEW YORK
BUCKLEY ROBERT K	·	SGT	· 366 BOMB SQ	305 BOMB GP(H)	·	WASHINGTON
BUCKMAN CLARENCE J JR	· 1 LT	· 327 BOMB SQ	92 BOMB GP(H)	·	PENNSYLVANIA
BUCKNER GEORGE W	·	PFC	· 3206 QM SV CO	· ·	MISSOURI
BUDAI WILLIAM J	·	S SGT	· 565 BOMB SQ	389 BOMB GP(H)	·	OHIO
BUDREVICH GERALD J	· ·	1 LT	· ·	13 PHOTO SQ 7 RCN GP	· ·	IOWA
BUELL HENRY E	·	2 LT	· 552 BOMB SQ	386 BOMB GP(M)	·	MICHIGAN
BULLARD JONATHAN H	· 1 LT	· 336 BOMB SQ	95 BOMB GP(H)	·	CONNECTICUT
BULLER HOWARD	·	S SGT	· 336 BOMB SQ	95 BOMB GP(H)	·	TEXAS
BUNDY LINCOLN D	· ·	2 LT	· ·	486 FTR SQ 352 FTR GP	· ·	ARIZONA
BURCH CHARLES O	·	SGT	· 566 BOMB SQ	389 BOMB GP(H)	·	GEORGIA
BURCH JIM F	· ·	2 LT	· ·	549 BOMB SQ 385 BOMB GP(H)	· ·	TEXAS

A portion of the Wall of Honor at the American Cemetery, Madingly,
Cambridge, England. The names of 114 men from the 95th whose
remains were never found are among the 5,123 names on the wall.

The 300th mission of the 95th Group was flown successfully on 20 March 1945 and was celebrated with this remarkable montage of people, planes and events.

Slave laborers and ex-POWs await 95th B-17s for trip back to Belgium and France. May 1945.

Slave laborers and ex-POWs walking to 95th Group B-17s for trip to freedom. These planes ferried thousands of men to France and Belgium, May 1945.

Photos reveal complete destruction of German ports and industrial installations by Allied bombing.

Crew of "Knock Out Baby" at Horham, 1944. *Front row (left to right):*
Eugene Fletcher, Myron Doxon, Robert Work, Frank Dimit. *Back row
(left to right):* Kenneth McQuitty, Robert Lynch, Martin Smith, Joseph
Firszt, Edward Brown, George Hinman.

Seattle, 1985. Nine members of the crew of "Knock Out Baby" survived
to fly "The Last Mission" in a B-17 of the Confederate Air Force.

A very small part of the thousands of planes that participated in Operation Varsity, the final airlift over the Rhine River, 24 March 1945.

Exploding C-47, west of the Rhine River after dropping paratroopers, 24 March 1945.

Three burning straw stacks mark an isolated target for planes dropping supplies to French Resistance fighters (*Maquis*).

Cannisters float on parachutes to drop area.

Arms and ammunition safely on target for Operation Cadillac, 14 July 1944, in the remote Jura Mountains of southern France.

Lead plane from 390th Group, led by Colonel Joe Moller, releases the
first food packages over Holland in Operation Manna/Chowhound, 1 May
1945.

Food parcels drop to feed
the starving Dutch
population, May 1945.
Operation Manna/
Chowhound.

Thousands of tons of food
were dropped at specific
target areas by Third Air
Division planes.

Returning 95th Veterans joined the people of Horham to dedicate the community's memorial to the group.

IN MEMORY OF THE MEN OF THE
95TH BOMBARDMENT GROUP WHO
SERVED AT HORHAM AIRFIELD
AND TO THOSE WHO GAVE THEIR
LIVES IN THE CAUSE OF FREEDOM,
1943 — 1945

★   ★   ★

334TH, 335TH, 336TH AND 412TH BOMB.
SQUADRONS AND SUPPORTING UNITS.
HEADQUARTERS 13TH COMBAT BOMB.
WING, UNITED STATES 8TH AIR FORCE

★   ★   ★

DEDICATED 19TH SEPT. 1981

The Memorial Plaque dedicated by the citizens of the Horham area, 19 September 1981.

Contrails from thousands of planes above the skies of Europe are a sight to be remembered—and never to be seen again.

"Old Glory" flies proudly her people live in Freedo ... The reason for it all!

mand in an old German headquarters. Departed in the morning for Twelfth TAC advanced at Saverne. Arrived that afternoon, reported to Major Reichert, A-3, and he started to plan our trip home. Again SOP messages were sent to the Eighth Air Force and to the Ninth Service Command. No answers were received. Finally the Ninth SC answered and said to wait for transportation from the Eighth. We waited and sent SOP messages every evening until January 1st when Twelfth TAC received a telegram from A-95, Major Swindon Flight Control, that a B-17 was there and requested a pilot to get it out of the way as they had to keep it on a runway. Twelfth furnished transportation to A-95, and we arrived there that evening. The B-17G was 338814 a 95th aircraft (named "Cadet Nurse the 2nd," this aircraft landed on 5 November and would not return to combat duty until late March 1945). It needed an oil filter, so we stayed with the P-47 boys that night. Departed 2 January with a sergeant, who was working on the B-17, from A-95 to A-70 where he said we would get help. At A-70 we were informed that their facilities had moved to B-53, Merville. Stayed at A-70 the night of 2 January, arriving at B-53 the next evening at 2000 hours. Our driver had to drive with lights out, so he didn't see a turn; we hit a telephone pole and the truck ended up in a ditch. No one was hurt. So we walked the rest of the way to B-53, stayed that night, and sent SOP messages to the Eighth Air Force again. Departed by C-47 4 January and landed at Horham that afternoon. Glad to be back!

6. All crew members were especially outstanding in the fact that they chose to ride her down. Lieutenant Harris did an excellent job of flying and checking the engines properly and feathering correctly. His calmness and judgment were truly praiseworthy; he kept me from getting rattled. Lieutenant McEwan did an excellent job of navigation. His Gee box was out. He brought us out through the flak corridors by pilotage and dead reckoning. Before take-off, he had drawn in the flak areas on his Gee map and the front lines. I'm glad he did. He steered us clear of one town, which shot up flak, so it went to our right. His anticipation of the front lines was perfect. He was calm and collected at all times. He did an excellent job. Sergeant Strauch, immediately after the flak struck, called for an oxygen check. This kept the crew from getting excited and kept them from calling me on the interphone. All the way down he got oxygen checks, and I noticed that he did this every time the crew seemed nervous. It gave them something else to think about. I know they were wondering when they were going to jump. Sergeant Hampton had his chute in the ball and stayed there until the front lines in case of fighters. His vivid description of a P-51 strafing a train gave the crew something else to think about. He was most calm and collected. (Ed Schneider, radio operator, later let the crew know that a piece of flak passed between his legs, tearing his clothing and flying suit just below his crotch without inflicting any injury.) All members did an excellent job of ditching positions and showed excellent teamwork and obedience. They had a first aid kit ready and open just in case. I'm proud to say I'm *their* pilot. Their confidence was wonderful.

7. Our trouble rested with the fact that the return facilities were changed 24 December, and stations on the continent were not as yet notified. This is why we were directed to A-70 by mistake.

8. The foreign phrase sheet was especially helpful, and the escape kit razors and soap well used.

9. We returned all parachute harnesses and flying equipment per S/O (standing order). Some personal equipment was thrown overboard.

10. I might add that dog tags are essential. We were picked up in Saverne because they thought we were paratroopers. AGO cards were always requested of officers. We had none. The FFI (friend or foe identification) is not to be taken lightly, and passwords are always requested. Also the personal interest of General Walker and the Seventh Army and Fifteenth Corps command was praiseworthy. The Twelfth TAC provided for us for a week, and we were truly grateful. The treatment of our enlisted crewmen was excellent.

11. Battle damage and engine information: Engine number 1 drew 18 to 20 inches (of manifold pressure when a full emergency turbo supercharger setting was used) until landing, and we did not feather. Oil temperature was 65° and the cylinder head temperature was 180°. (It was later discovered that the intake manifold ring, which feeds the air/fuel mixture to the cylinders, was punctured by flak, causing the fuel mixture to leak. This accounted for the very low power output). The engine nacelle had four flak holes.

Engine number 2 was hit and when it failed we had been pulling 38 inches of manifold pressure and it feathered OK. (This engine caught fire, probably from an oil leak, before feathering took place and was extinguished by putting the aircraft in a steep dive.)

Engine number 3 had holes in the wing next to the fuel line. (This engine proved to be the workhorse as it drew 57 inches of manifold pressure at 2500 rpms through the critical period for nearly fifty minutes of emergency turbo supercharger setting until the aircraft crash-landed.)

Engine number 4 had a large hole near the check plate and had lost oil. (Almost no fuel pressure; it seems as though the fuel booster pump was damaged. The engine feathered properly after several attempts. This was the first engine to be feathered as a result of the flak hit over the target area.)

Flak hole about four inches long, below the flight deck under the pilot's seat, that cut the hydraulic lines, cut the heating duct in two and the oxygen feed line, but fortunately missed the control cables.

LETTERS TO MOTHER

(Continued) 1944
Harry Conley, 95th Bomb Group, 93rd Combat Wing

18 January: Things have been very quiet for the past month. We have been operating as often as possible but have been restricted by rather severe fog. We have been quite fortunate, and all of our trips have been quiet. It has just been our luck to be in the middle of the procession into the targets and, except for flak, have not had any difficulty. It has been our luck not to have seen any fighters for some time. They seem to attack the front and rear groups and leave the others alone, simply because they do not have enough aircraft to attack us all. It is some change from the old days of last year when we fought for our lives every minute we were over enemy territory.

14 February: We have been going pretty hot and heavy, and even if we don't go on the missions, the staff do get up for the briefings and were up most of the previous night on the planning.

23 February: The weather has been quite cold and we have had considerable snow, but it doesn't stay on the ground very long—just about like San Francisco snow. However, it is mean for flying because it impairs visibility and makes it nasty. It hasn't stopped us, however; as you probably see by the papers, we are really putting forth a maximum effort. As I see it, it looks like the prelude to the big show. We are attempting to knock out the Luftwaffe before the main event starts. If we can succeed, it will mean saving thousands of lives.

Churchill finally came out and told the British yesterday that the war over here may not be over in 1944. This is going to be a hell of a rough go when they start across the Channel. People at home have no conception of just how tough it is going to be.

6 March: We have bombed Berlin twice this week. The big news in that being that the first time the weather was extremely bad and the only group that got over the city was the 95th (of course!). The boys were led that day by Grif Mumford of San Jose. He is the #1 hero of these parts at present. General LeMay came over and awarded him the Silver Star for the occasion.

The weather was so bad that day that everyone turned around and came home except Grif and he went the whole way with twenty-nine airplanes. They went again today, and the whole Air Force made the trip. It was pretty rough, and we suffered our share of the losses.

The 95th started for Berlin on my twenty-fifth mission and got within eighty miles of the city, but we had to turn around because of weather. The weather was not as anticipated. We climbed through solid clouds the whole way and finally broke out at 28,000 feet southeast of Hamburg only to be confronted by another wall of clouds that reached to about 35,000 feet. As we had planned to fly at a considerably lower altitude, we had neither sufficient gas nor oxygen to climb the necessary amount to get to the target and return. Needless to say we were all greatly disappointed. The next day Grif found a hole in the weather and sneaked through. It really has put the 95th on top of the heap. We have been swamped with newspaper men and photographers from all the papers and magazines. Some excitement.

We have had quite a bit of snow the last few days. The other day, when we took off for my last mission, it was in a blinding snowstorm. The ceiling was about 100 feet and visibility about 100 yards. I've never seen worse conditions. How we manage to get up and down through the stuff is a mystery to me.

28 March: You wrote that you thought that as operations officer, Grif Mumford didn't fly combat. That is the secret of our success and high morale in the 95th. All staff officers fly in their turn. The four squadron commanders, group CO, operations officers, air executive—all take their turn in rotation. I was out in my turn the other day. Number 27. It was an uneventful trip.

In the Berlin deal on 6 March, we bore the brunt of the fighter attacks. I wasn't along, but our squadron lost half the boys that were on the mission.

Today we received good news; one of our crews that was knocked down in southern Germany a couple of weeks ago made it to Switzerland. We got a wire today reporting the above.

From what I have seen of the news reports of the London air raids in the American papers, it is greatly overplayed. The Jerries have not been over in force. The bombing has been by individual aircraft and consequently scattered and not very effective. The London flak is terrific and quite a show. Proportionately, they seem to score many more hits than the Jerry flak.

9 April: Colonel Gerhart (John K.) was given command of a new wing (the 93rd) to be formed here in the Eighth Air Force, and he asked for me as his chief of staff.

As our station is not completed, I am now living with Colonel Gerhart in his quarters at Air Force headquarters. We expect to be here about a week or ten days before we can move into our own station.

Curiously enough, the group that will be on the field with us and one of the groups in our wing will be the old 34th Bomb Group to which I was attached in Spokane.

Our headquarters will be only ten miles from the 95th, so I'll be able to visit them frequently. After all, that is still home to me.

16 May: As for the debut of our new outfit, the first group will be ready in about a week. Colonel Gerhart and I will fly with them the first couple of times out, then I'll only fly combat a couple of times a month.

We have put them through a really intense training and now time will tell. I chase them around the sky each day in my fighter, herding them into formation, and observing their technique. Incidentally, we gave up our P-51 and now have a P-38. We just got it today, so I'll try it out tomorrow.

This is certainly a marvelous experience in administration. In the past six weeks, we have set up three complete air bases. As the new outfits come over here, all of their ground personnel have to be reassigned to meet the requirements of local conditions. It is a most interesting assignment, and all of us have learned much.

27 July: Events of the past week on the German political scene look most encouraging. However, we are watching the progress of our ground forces. They are fighting in most difficult terrain for mechanized offensive, and everyone here is looking for some signs of progress. Despite this lack of progress, I surely feel that the end over here is close at hand. It will come suddenly when it terminates. Then we will be able to move eastward and give our undivided attention to the "sons of the Rising Sun." That will be a pleasure. After fighting in this theater with its terrifically developed flak defenses and hordes of fighters, it should be considerably easier in the Land of the Rising Sun.

8 August: Actually, the buzz bombs aren't too bad. One can see them coming, and they are all blast effect. No shrapnel.

As for the current combat situation, we were out last week to Brussels. Encountered a little flak and that was all. The boys were flying a new formation we worked out here in the wing. We flew alongside to take pictures and see how it worked. While they bombed, I circled off to the side and watched the show.

You asked about the ribbon on the right side of our uniforms. It is a presidential citation given to the 95th for Munster last 10 Oct. We also wear a cluster on it for an additional citation for the Regensburg raid.

17 August: Happy Regensburg Day! It is the first anniversary of our shuttle raid today. It certainly doesn't seem a year since that memorable day. How clearly one can remember every detail.

26 August: We are very busy supporting the ground troops as well as carrying out our own strategic bombing.

12 September: We've had three big parties this week! To start, a week ago Sunday night Colonel Gerhart, "Jiggs" Donohue, our intelligence officer, and I were invited to a party at the 95th to say goodbye to Dave McKnight, one of our original boys who has been deputy group commander for the past year. He is going home after making forty-two missions. A well-deserved rest. He is a hell of a popular guy, and it was a real get-together. A lot of the old fighter boys were there as well as all the old 95th boys, who are left over here. It was a wet old time!

The next Saturday and Sunday the 95th had a two-day celebration of our 200th mission. It was a little late as they are well past that figure now, but they waited until they could get what they wanted in the way of entertainment. It was well worth waiting for as you will admit. We had Glenn Miller and his band, Bing Crosby, and Dinah Shore. What a party it was! The Air Force gave the group a two-day layoff, and the carnival spirit reigned. Dancing all day and all night, two big turkey dinners, and plenty of liquor. All work stopped on the entire base, and every man participated in the celebration.

Then two nights ago we held a private goodbye for Dave McKnight. He delayed going home because he got a chance to go to Paris for three days, which he did. So he didn't leave for home until yesterday. This little party was just the colonel, Dave, Jiggs Donohue, and me. We sat around the fire after dinner and sipped a few and reminisced about the old boys. We stayed there until the wee hours.

We got in a couple of good raids last week. As you have probably seen in the papers, we have been beating at Germany's heart again in force. On both these days our wing had the honor of leading the whole Air Force (over 1,600 aircraft) into Germany. We got in a pretty fair scrap for a few minutes with about forty fighters. We only claimed four fighters out of the lot and lost pretty heavily. Our formations and defenses are not as tight as they used to be. More intensive training is on the agenda!

8 October: It looks as though the war will continue indefinitely over here. By all rights the Germans are beaten and should give up, but under the surrender terms offered them, they will probably fight on from house-to-house. If so, it will take years to finish the job.

11 November: Had a wonderful day Thursday! The colonel and I took a B-17 and flew over to Reims, France, for the day. We left here at daybreak and didn't return until after dinner. We flew the whole trip below 1,000 feet and circled all of the former targets on the continent and had a wonderful time! At Reims we loaded the airplane with champagne. Boy, we bought it by the gallon! All the good French champagne comes from there. None of the towns in northern France have been damaged to speak of, but every airfield, railroad yard, and bridge is smashed to bits. Actually, we never realized how good our bombing really was. We did a great deal more damage than the photos indicated, especially to airfields where installations were hidden in woods and didn't show in the pictures. Also the fighters really took their toll on German transport. The roads are all lined with strafed vehicles of every description.

The story of the French Underground and Resistance movement is one of the great stories of the war. I'm sure there will be many books about it, so I won't attempt to tell stories here. It would take too long. But it must be said that they have been positively amazing in their deeds.

19 November: There isn't anything new from here. Rumors are plentiful. We are about to undergo a reorganization and nobody in the Air Force knows what job they will have next week. We are hoping to get some definite word in the next day or so. As you can readily understand, no one can possibly leave until we know just what the future holds.

Editor's Note: Harry Conley continued to serve as chief of staff to Brigadier General John Gerhart in the 93rd Combat Wing after he completed his official tour of duty.

THE JOHN BROMBERG STORY

Reprinted from *Contrails* (1947)

His name is John S. Bromberg, ace bombardier. The story starts with his thirty-fourth mission, on a shuttle from Russia to Italy on 19 September 1944. He was lead bombardier and the primary target was a railroad complex at Szolnok, Hungary. Just before reaching the target, his aircraft was hit twice by flak. The second flak burst knocked him off his seat out on the catwalk at the escape hatch. He crawled back to the bombsight, however, and managed to drop his bombs on the target before he was forced to bail out of the burning Fortress.

As he floated to earth a convoy of enemy troops fired at him, wounding him in the foot. Soon after he landed in a cornfield, vehicles drove up and sprayed the area with machine-gun fire. German S.S. troops and Hungarian soldiers discovered him, chained his wrists, and after beating him, dragged him to a nearby truck. He was taken to a farmhouse and put under guard, but not before several women and children struck him with fists and sticks. Later he was locked up in a village cell without windows, lights, bed, or chair. Still without receiving any medical attention for his wounds or the beatings he had received after landing, he was taken by trolley and train to Szeged near the Rumanian border on a trip that lasted several hours. He was locked in another cell, again without light, bed, or chair. All his personal belongings were taken away. He was kept in the cell for twenty days.

During that incarceration, he was interrogated by a Luftwaffe major, but he refused to divulge any information other than his name, rank, and serial number. The major then threatened to turn him over to the Gestapo and demanded information on captured equipment shown to him—bombsights, radar sets, and aerial cameras. Bromberg wouldn't talk.

He was taken into another room where two nice-looking young men beat him up with rubber hoses and the liberal use of fists and feet. Bromberg lost consciousness and suffered a broken rib and left collar bone. He was given no medical attention and had no water or food for several days. He was then given some thin, black ersatz coffee and put on a railroad prison car with other prisoners. For several weeks they traveled on a jagged route, changing trains frequently because of bombed-out tracks. His only food on the journey was black coffee and occasional thin soup.

At Dulag Luft in Oberursel, he was put in a cell with no ventilation. A large heater was turned on to make the cell unbearably hot, then turned off to make the room intensely cold. Bromberg was interrogated again and divulged no information.

The next day he was taken to Wetzlar prisoner of war camp where he was offered some solid food but was unable to eat it. Subsequently he was sent to an infirmary and fed liquids. From there he was put on a train again and at

Fulda an air raid was in progress. Bromberg and his two guards went to a shelter, but a bomb exploded nearby nearly killed the two guards and knocked Bromberg unconscious, with steel fragments buried in his legs.

Eventually he was put on a stretcher and loaded on another train but near Eisenbach it was strafed by P-47s and wrecked. One of his guards was killed but other guards took over and took him to an Allied hospital at Obermisfeld, which was run by the British under the jurisdiction of German guards, where he received his first medical attention since bailing out.

When the hospital was liberated by the Eleventh Armored Division six months later, Bromberg went into action with tank and infantry units. During patrols, he killed a German general who tried to shoot him as he entered a house.

****

Editor's note: John Bromberg and Bill Steele were flying as bombardier and navigator on the last plane in which Colonel Carl Truesdell flew as mission commander. By an ironic cruel twist of fate Bromberg's B-17 was not shot down during the mission on 19 September 1944.

Lieutenant Eugene Fletcher, pilot, B-17G "Knock Out Baby," 412th Squadron: When we left Poltava, Russia, on the next leg of our flight to Foggia, Italy, I flew in the 95th's lead squadron and was in a position to monitor Colonel Carl Truesdell's lead aircraft. We saw his aircraft hit and catch fire; most of the flames appeared to be under the left wing and number 1 engine. It appeared to us that the B-17 could blow up at any moment. We relayed to him what we could see, and he made the decision to leave the formation. Colonel Truesdell then wiggled his wings to signal to his left wingman to take over the lead position as he was leaving, but both his wingmen didn't understand the signal and left with him in a gradual descent.

We immediately called them to come back to the formation because if the lead ship exploded, we would lose all three aircraft instead of one. They then returned to the formation. Since I was flying in the diamond with two wingmen, we formed on the high element and they became the lead.

We soon lost track of Colonel Truesdell's airplane and it wasn't until we reached Foggia that we discovered the fire in his left wing had gone out, but not before four members of the crew had bailed out. Colonel Truesdell and the remaining crew members continued the flight to Italy.

MEMORIES OF HORHAM AIRFIELD

Graham Shipley

I was five years old at the beginning of the war in September 1939 when my three brothers, one of my two sisters, and I were among the first of thousands of children to be evacuated from London to relatively safer parts of England to avoid the blitz bombing of the city that followed in 1940–41. My youngest sister stayed in London with my parents, but the rest of our family found ourselves in completely new surroundings at the small Suffolk village of Worlingworth, quite close to Horham.

We took a few personal belongings with us, including a gas mask and a ration card. In those days if a householder had sufficient room it was compulsory to provide accommodation for an evacuee. The government paid a small weekly allowance for the evacuee's room and board. This money and ration card were very welcome, but in many cases the evacuee was an inconvenience and an extra mouth to feed.

I recall always being hungry, often eating frost-covered brussels sprouts from the fields on my way to school during the winter months. Meat, butter, sugar, and tea were all rationed and even fresh eggs were a rare luxury. Practically every family in Britain had to endure these hardships. The average income was generally speaking very low in East Anglia, where the main industry is farming.

It was while out walking alongside the railway track from Worlingworth to Horham during the summer of 1943 that I first discovered the airfield at Horham. I saw a four-engined aircraft circling the area, then it disappeared behind some distant trees, but didn't emerge from the other side. Being a very curious youngster I ran across the fields toward it, thinking that the plane had made a forced landing. I came to a high hedge, clambered through it onto a narrow country road. There, in front of me, was the amazing sight of Horham Airfield: three long, intersecting concrete runways, an encircling perimeter track, with American Fortress bombers parked all round, and several large buildings.

The temptation to explore further proved too great and I walked across to the nearest plane. I recall poking my fingers into the barrels of the two tail machine guns and looking at the curved perspex of the tail gunner's position. I then walked to the front of the bomber under one huge wing, seeing the massive landing gear, wheel, and engines at close range.

Suddenly a door on the side of the fuselage opened and an American airman emerged with his tool box. This was to be the first of many meetings with Hank, a friendly aircraft mechanic with the 335th Squadron, 95th Bomb Group.

After explaining that I was an evacuee from London now living at Worlingworth, Hank asked me over to a workshop near the two hangars. The workshop was where the magnetos from the B-17s' engines were repaired and maintained. Hank gave me a box of candy and some chewing gum, then introduced me to some of the other mechanics who also gave me gifts of sweets and gum. From then on I was a regular visitor to the airfield every opportunity on nonschool days during the next two years.

Hank showed me all around the interior of the B-17s he worked on: the gun turrets, bomb bays, the cockpit, etc., and he explained how everything functioned. The first B-17 that I went in was named "Roarin' Bull," which had a picture expertly painted on each side of the plane's nose section of a bull snorting steam from its nostrils and pawing the ground with its front hooves. This bomber was parked near one of the two hangars and the remainder of the 95th's B-17s were parked at regular intervals around the 3½-mile-long perimeter track. Each aircraft had a different painting and distinctive name.

Although much of the maintenance work was done on the aircraft while they were out on the concrete hardstands in all types of weather, the two hangars were constant hives of activity. B-17s that had suffered major damage during a mission were repaired by the specialized engineering trades. The graveyard where all the wrecked and salvaged planes, and wings, fuselage, and tail sections were dumped was at Whitehouse Farm, quite close to the two hangars. This provided the mechanics with a ready source of spare and replacement parts.

The American airmen were very generous, especially to the local children. I recall a mechanic asking me if I had a penknife. When I said I hadn't, he replied, "Every young boy should have a penknife and a piece of string." He then gave me a pearl-handled penknife, which had three blades, a corkscrew, a bottle-opener, and one or two other useful attachments. To this day I always carry a penknife. I was given generous meals with the airmen at the messhall, including ice cream and coffee. When my mother and father came to visit us from London, Hank always ensured that they went back with large parcels containing coffee, food, including tins of fruit, fresh oranges, and cigarettes.

Hank was a great influence on my life. One day one of the Americans lit a cigarette and gave it to me saying it was good for me. I hadn't taken many puffs, when Hank arrived and said, "Who the hell gave you that?" He immediately took the cigarette and stamped on it, saying I was not to smoke. When it was raining my boots used to get covered in mud while I was at the 335th Squadron flight line. Hank gave me a shoebrush and a tin of shoe polish, telling me to wipe the mud off and polish my boots before going home. He always encouraged me to be neat and tidy before I went home, and he always ensured that transport was available, either a truck or jeep, to take me home at the end of the day.

I also vividly recall the aircrews being driven out to their waiting planes, the tremendous noise generated by the 95th's four squadrons as they took off for a mission, and the very stirring sight as they formed up into formation. In the late afternoons, on their return, I recall seeing the red flares emerge from damaged planes signaling wounded men aboard. I used to sit in a B-17 under repair listening to the radio messages from the returning aircraft to the control tower as the damaged planes were given priority in getting down first, while the remainder would continue circling the base at low altitude.

A little later, when all the group's planes had landed and parked, I went into one or two B-17s. The floor was usually littered with empty cartridge cases, jagged holes in varying sizes graphically illustrated the effectiveness of the flak and fighters on the daylight bombers. It also proved the rugged qualities of the Flying Fortress and its ability to absorb severe damage and still bring its crew home to fly another day.

I clearly remember a returning B-17 with two engines out landing safely when one of its two main landing wheels suddenly collapsed. It continued along the runway then, as if in slow motion, one wing dipped and touched the ground. The bomber's forward momentum spun it off the runway onto the grass, then the other landing gear collapsed under the strain. The plane then plowed straight on, showering earth and grass high into the air, finally coming to a stop near the edge of the base. On that occasion the entire crew was uninjured.

We could always tell when a raid had been successful or not. The crews were either boisterous and shouting cheerfully to each other, or strangely subdued and quiet if they'd suffered heavy losses. I recall, most vividly, the jubilation following the first daylight mission to Berlin in early March 1944, the unforgettable concert given by Glenn Miller and his Army Air Force band in one of the hangars during the late summer of 1944 (which I saw after Hank had made all the necessary transport arrangements for me), and the film shows in the base theater.

I also have fond memories of the visits to the local village pubs—"The Swan" at Worlingworth, "The Grapes" at Hoxne, and "The Green Dragon" at Horham, standing outside drinking lemonade and eating a packet of Smith's crisps that Hank bought for me while he was inside enjoying a pint of beer and a sing-along with the other airmen.

Very regrettably, I never did discover Hank's surname, and despite making numerous inquiries over the years I've been unsuccessful. I didn't even have the chance to say goodbye and thank him for all his kindness and generosity at the end of the war. My parents arrived at Worlingworth, but there was insufficient time to visit the base before we had to catch the train back to London.

It's all a long time ago and a part of history now, of course, but Margaret, my wife, and I occasionally travel from our home in Essex to visit friends at Horham. I always take the opportunity to go to what now remains of the old airfield at Horham, and it all comes flooding back: the distinctive noise of a B-17's engines starting up, the tinkle of a dropped spanner on concrete, the smell of aviation fuel, the squeal of heavy bomber's brakes, the laughter, the sorrow, and the painful grief.

It was a precious part of my life and one which I will never forget.

THREE FINE MEN

Joel Bunch, Operations Officer, 335th Squadron

There are those who disapprove of my candid, loose-lipped, and down-to-earth verbal designations and expressions but I classify everyone as son of a bitch. To my friends it is an expression of endearment; to those unfriendly souls, tough, but that's life. Everyone who worked with or who passed through the 95th Bombardment Group knew, appreciated, and greatly admired the sterling leadership of Dave McKnight, Harry G. "Grif" Mumford, A.A. "Aaron" Kessler, and others. But the three most unforgettable characters in my memory were Dr. Elvin D. Imes (flight surgeon), Leonard Herman (a bombardier and nose gunner), and Bill Lindley (a seemingly carefree, irresponsible, and "devil-may-care" pilot).

"Doc" Imes found no injury too small to merit his close attention, nor was he ever too busy to tend the lowest in rank as quickly as the brass. He risked his life to participate in several tough bombing missions to learn, and experience personally, the effects of high altitude, freezing temperatures, combat fatigue, strain, and other factors that the combat crews experienced. Doc Imes asked for nothing more than a chance to serve his God, his country, and his fellow man. A *great* S.O.B.

Leonard W. Herman was the most visibly fearful of any crew member within the limits of my memory. I think being Jewish added to his fears, because I believe that fear of Nazi torture was much worse than death itself should he have to bail out over Germany and be captured. But Leonard never missed a briefing, and he never missed a tough assignment. In spite of his apparent and visible fear, Leonard truly had the courage that makes men great. In my opinion he was a *heroic* S.O.B., one that overcame fear to serve his country well.

William C. Lindley, like most young Army Air Corps pilots, had been told that he was the finest pilot that ever strapped an airplane to his rear end and flew away. And, like most young pilots, Bill Lindley believed it. He subsequently made all the mistakes and violated all of the rules and regulations that young pilots make and violate; but Bill was one of those rare people who would volunteer for any assignment, regardless of the hazards and the dangers involved. His "let the hide go with the horns" attitude was only his expression of his faith and his confidence in his abilities. Many doubted that "Wild Bill" Lindley would advance to the rank of captain, but he became a major general as he continued to follow a productive military career and to do the jobs well that make American fighting men respected throughout the world. A *brilliant* S.O.B.

A VISIT TO BERLIN

Willard W. ("Bill") Brown, Group Navigator

After I was shot down during the Kiel mission in mid-June 1943, I was imprisoned at Stalag Luft III, Sagan, Silesia, and remained there until late February 1945. Then the camp was abandoned, and we were transferred to another POW camp, further to the west, as the Russian ground forces advanced from the east. We were liberated by the Allies in May 1945.

During the long months of captivity at Sagan, I made three escape attempts, all of which proved unsuccessful, but the temporary freedom they gave was a most welcome tonic. After my second escape attempt, the escape committee in the British compound became interested in my activities and invited me to become the "Mr. X" in the American officers' (center) compound. Mr. X was the person who was responsible for all escape plans and intelligence communications. A very good friend of mine, Roger Bushel, was the Mr. X in the British (north) compound.

Much has been recorded, both in print and on film, concerning the activities of the escape organizations during the Second World War, and in my opinion, the movie made of "the Great Escape" from Stalag Luft III, which took place in the spring of 1944, was among the best. It was about 75 percent accurate in its portrayal of actual events.

However, what is probably not so well known are the following events concerning the attempts at shortening the war that took place during mid-February 1945.

At that time a few of us were sent up to Berlin. General Bannerman, Colonel Spivey, and Colonel Kefty were all senior American officers at Sagan. I was taken along as a so-called escape expert in case things didn't work out.

As it happened, the day we were scheduled to meet Hitler at his chancellery headquarters in Berlin, 14 February, the Eighth Air Force bombed Dresden. Hitler ordered us to be shot in retaliation, and he gave the direct order to carry out our executions to the commander of the Waffen S.S., Lieutenant General

Jon Berger. General Berger was, among other things, responsible for all prisoners of war plus the army of Ukrainians that had been hastily formed to fight the advancing Russians. These were Russians willing and able to fight Russians.

Fortunately, General Berger didn't carry out Hitler's order. What he did was talk with General Bannerman, Colonel Spivey, and Colonel Kefty. He said to them, "I'm going to send you back to the United States with this message to be conveyed directly to President Roosevelt and General Marshall in Washington:

"1. The German armed forces will make a stand and hold the line against the Russians at the Oder River (the old Polish/German border). We will then wait for the arrival of American and British Forces, our common enemy being Stalinist Russia.

"2. I will assume personal responsibility for eliminating both Hitler and Heinrich Himmler (chief of the Gestapo).

"3. The Americans or British are requested to appoint anybody you like to administer the postwar affairs of Germany.

"4. Abandon the terms of unconditional surrender.

"5. Abandon the policy of the Morganthau Plan, which would reduce the postwar German economy substantially."

These proposals made a lot of sense.

Berger then took the dangerous risk, as far as his own life was concerned, of transporting Bannerman and Spivey to Switzerland in his personal staff car. These men were then flown to Washington, where they reported to President Roosevelt and General Marshall.

The proposals were heard with interest, but no action could subsequently be taken because commitments had already been made at Yalta among Roosevelt, Churchill, and Stalin, a few weeks previously.

However, what Bannerman and Spivey did achieve was most important to all POWs! They obtained promises from Berger concerning the future safety of all the POWs in Germany, which, at that stage, was very precarious. Apparently, there was a plan in the pipeline for transporting all Allied prisoners down to the last redoubt in the Bavarian Alps with every man perishing in one final collapse.

When the Nuremberg war trials took place after the war, both Bannerman and Spivey went to Germany and gave evidence on Berger's behalf. Consequently, his sentence was reduced to five years. He died soon after being released during the early 1950s.

MORE SHORT BURSTS

Irv Rothman, top-turret gunner, 336th Squadron: Paul Keith, our co-pilot, had an English bike, which he absolutely adored. He went everywhere on it until one very wet day in December 1943. He zoomed down a hill just outside the base, lost control, hit the roadside bank at high speed, catapulted over the handlebars, crashed straight through a thorn hedge like a train, went arse over elbow, and landed in thick, stodgy English mud.

His bike was a write-off, and he looked as though he'd gone three very tough and bloody rounds with a tractor when he staggered into our barracks.

****

James Johnson, S-2 (Intelligence Section): We were constantly warned that "careless talk costs lives" by large posters and signs virtually everywhere we went, and security was, generally speaking, rigidly observed.

However, we had been at Horham for quite some time when two of our Intelligence Section people went to London for some much needed rest and relaxation. On the train from Diss to London, one of them got talking to an R.A.F. officer, the way fellow airmen do. During their conversation, our man casually mentioned some aspects of our method of decoding the field orders when they arrived via teletype machine from Third Air Division headquarters prior to a bombing mission.

On the train's arrival at Liverpool Street Station, the R.A.F. officer immediately summoned two military policemen and ordered them to arrest our man. He was subsequently court-martialed and served a lengthy prison sentence at Leavenworth Prison, Kansas.

****

Raymond Murray, co-pilot, 336th Squadron: Our replacement crew, commanded by Lieutenant Dave Taylor (a really top-notch pilot) left Grenier Field, New Hampshire, for Goose Bay, Labrador, in late September 1944. When we landed at Goose Bay, a howling blizzard greeted us. It continued snowing for the next two days and after three days there we eventually took off for the next leg of our flight to England, which was Keflavík, Iceland.

After about an hour's flying out over the North Atlantic from Goose Bay, I saw what looked to be a submarine on the surface. We were at about 500 feet so I called the crew on the interphone telling them, "Look at that submarine down there . . ." as it certainly was an extraordinary sight. Just as I'd finished speaking, the submarine blew a long column of water skyward. It was the biggest whale I'd ever seen! In fact, it was the *only* whale I'd ever seen except in the movies.

****

C.H. Upchurch, top-turret gunner, 336th Squadron: Our crew was among the first to be assigned to the 336th Squadron at Greiger Field, Washington, in October 1942. We arrived at Alconbury, England, on 12 May 1943, operating with the 92nd Bomb Group, which had been in England since August 1942.

During the mission to Rennes, France, on 29 May, two weeks after our arrival, our B-17 was hit hard by enemy fighters while leading the combat wing. Our pilot, Lieutenant L.D. Clark, was killed in one of the first attacks, and there was an oxygen fire in the nose section of our airplane. Despite the flames, our co-pilot managed to hold the burning aircraft in level flight long enough to enable us to bail out. Major Edgar Cole, 336th Squadron commander, was flying with us as mission commander. He was picked up by the French Resistance and was back in England after an interesting stay on the continent. Lieutenant Fisher, bombardier, also evaded, but he took eleven months to get back. The remaining survivors all landed near St. Malo, on the French coast, and we were all quickly captured as the area was thick with German troops. I spent the next two years at Stalag XVIIB, Krems, Austria.

Tragically, our B-17 exploded before our co-pilot, F/O Y.S. Berntzen, and waist gunner, Staff Sergeant C.J. Mayo, could bail out.

****

John Bright, ground crewman, 335th Squadron: One of the numerous notices that appeared on the bulletin board at the base stated that there was to be no more pheasant or partridge shooting as they were deemed to be "the King's birds." However, I was on a bike ride in the countryside around Horham during the summer of 1944 and I got talking with a friendly farmer, Mr. A.E. Garner at Fairstead Farm, when I mentioned the lack of fresh meat at the base. He kindly invited me and a few of my buddies to hunt and shoot rabbits and hares while his fields were being harvested. During the fall and winter of 1944, Mr. Garner also gave us permission to hunt pheasant, partridge, and pigeon on his two farms, which totaled 500 acres.

The moral of this story is, Don't believe everything you read.

****

Raymond Murray, co-pilot, 336th Squadron: Our crew arrived at Horham on 1 October 1944. While we were in training we were filled with horror stories by the men who had experienced combat. By that time, very few of the original crewmen were around. It came as a very nasty shock to be told that almost all the 95th's original crewmen were either dead or prisoners of war.

I vividly recall being up at the flight line the day the medics had to drag a crewman out of a badly shot-up B-17 in a straitjacket. Apparently it was only his fifth mission, but on each previous raid one of his fellow crewmen had been killed. During this particular mission his co-pilot had been decapitated and two other crewmen had also been killed.

****

Theophil Ross, transportation section: I enlisted in 1942 and completed basic training at Victoria, Texas, and from there I went to Lake Charles, Louisiana, where I was a crew chief on an AT-6 single-engine training aircraft. It became increasingly and painfully obvious that my first sergeant didn't approve of the name Ross and put me on KP duty every other day. Eventually and inevitably I grew so disenchanted with him that I put my name on the transfer list.

After being in the service eight months, we were allowed a furlough. When the eight months were up, I immediately applied for that furlough, had my papers signed on the Friday night, and was ready to leave for home at three o'clock the following Saturday morning. In the meantime my first sergeant came around and said, "Ross, you're shipping out."

When we shipped out, our troop train passed within thirty miles of my home. I was ready and willing to go AWOL right there and then. We boarded the *Queen Elizabeth* in New York, came across to Scotland, and were greeted by a pipe band. We headed south by train and eventually arrived at Horham at about two o'clock in the morning.

It seems that I was the sad sack of the 95th Group. The following day my first duty was the honey pot detail. Apparently, Captain Herron didn't know what to do with me so the powers that be decided I had volunteered for the honey pot detail. Fortunately, it only lasted three or four days when they discovered that I was an aircraft mechanic. I eventually ended up as a dispatcher in the transportation section.

****

Irv Rothman, top-turret gunner, 336th Squadron: After a unique bombing mission of the V-1 flying bomb sites in northwestern France in December 1943, we returned to a snow-covered East Anglia.

The aircraft that landed ahead of us couldn't stop due to the exceptional amount of frozen mud, ice, and snow on one of the two shorter runways. The plane slid off the runway's end, across the perimeter track, plowed through a hedge and a ditch, then ground looped, and came to rest just beyond the ditch.

We couldn't stop in time either and ended up with our landing gear in the bottom of that ditch, our nose crashed against his left wing, and our number 3 engine sustained all kinds of damage amidst showers of sparks and clouds of steam. Wonderful.

Captain Campbell, group armaments officer, magically appeared from nowhere, jumping up and down about five yards away screaming, "Get out! Get out! Before she blows up!" Every one got out. I was the only one hurt; coming through the radio room I forgot to duck and the swinging flex gun gave me a superb egg-head.

The damn plane wasn't even ours. It belonged to a crew on leave in London, and we'd been assigned to it while ours was being repaired. When they came back, you would have thought we'd done the whole mess on purpose. All that was left of their B-17, of course, was the empty shell of the plane. Every crew chief at Horham had scrounged and cannibalized whatever spare parts he needed.

****

Raymond Murray, co-pilot, 336th Squadron: About mid-way through our thirty missions, we became a lead crew. Taylor was an excellent pilot, Fred Carter was a crack bombardier, and Jesse Attebern was A-plus when it came to navigating. We went to Berlin at least five times, and on my last mission, to Oranienburg in April 1945, there wasn't a single burst of flak. It wasn't always like this, but we were very fortunate; not a single member of our crew got a scratch.

There was no ducking anything for us in the box barrages of flak we flew through up at Merseburg, the Luna oil plant. There was nothing you could do but sit there and say Hail Marys as fast as you could. Planes were going down all around us, but I'll always remember the first one. I was looking right at this plane because I was flying on him when it took a direct hit between number 3 and number 4 engines. I saw the wing rise up in the air, the pilot turned his head very slowly and looked out at me with no expression. Then we saw parachutes spilling out, a couple of them bursting into flames as they opened. Then the plane started cartwheeling and spinning. Not too many chutes got out, possibly four or five. Then the aircraft exploded, and that is when I became a very religious man.

I was 19 years old at that time, and I suppose that my mind was so young that with the passing years time has erased most of the bad things I'd seen. The only memories that I now have of a combat mission are hours and hours of boredom interrupted by moments of sheer terror when nearby aircraft would suddenly take a hit and go down; but I felt detached, I didn't have anything to do with it, I was never going to get hit.

I talked to our 336th Squadron flight surgeon about this one day. Captain McKittrick was a very nice guy. He said, "That's why we give you whiskey, and that's why you're all so young. If you thought about it, you wouldn't fly combat."

The older I get and the more I think about it, I realize he was telling the truth. I didn't believe that I was going to get killed, I knew I was going to come through it, and I suppose people who were shot down felt exactly the same way.

I have fond memories of most things that happened with the 95th Group, but the death of one of my really close friends, Paul Facteau, a navigator, really knocked me for a loop. He was killed because someone was careless. I saw him that morning and they were packing his things together that night. Other than Paul, I didn't know any of the other people I saw get shot down.

A VISIT TO MOSCOW

Edward Pachnik, Co-pilot, B-17G 338199, 335th Squadron

On 15 February 1945, the primary target for about 450 B-17s of the Third Air Division was the railroad marshaling yards at Cottbus, deep in eastern Germany, about seventy-five miles southeast of Berlin and only twenty-five miles from the Polish border.

This was our second mission. Our crew consisted of the following: Fred Volz, pilot; James Drexler, navigator; Charles Moody, bombardier; Stanley Wooden, top-turret gunner/flight engineer; Howard Eaton, radio operator; Louis DeLuca, ball-turret gunner; Walter Ray, waist gunner; and Joseph Smith, tail gunner.

At the early morning briefing, the intelligence officer warned us not to land in Russian territory if we got into trouble. As subsequent events transpired, we had no alternative. Due to battle damage sustained by our airplane shortly after bombing the primary target, we lost altitude, and there was no possible way that we could make it back behind Allied lines in liberated France.

Numbers 1 and 3 engines were hit, and although number 3 was feathered successfully, the propellor gear housing to number 1 had broken free, tilting the propellor forward about 15°. It was windmilling at flat pitch and at very high rpms. Consequently, it pulled us into an uncontrolled turn to the left but eventually we were able to fly straight by using differential power on the remaining two engines and the rudder.

James Drexler, our navigator, advised that we could make it to the Vistula River in central Poland with the help of strong westerly winds. We knew that the Russian Army had crossed the Vistula a few weeks before during their bitterly fought advance from the east.

During the mission I saw another 95th Bomb Group B-17 in similar trouble. It was an olive-drab (camouflaged) Fortress and one of its engines was on fire. We flew on across German-occupied Poland with scattered snow squalls occasionally restricting visibility. We missed the airfield at Deblin; then, mercifully, a gap in the clouds revealed a large clear area. This had to be our landing site, because the sun was setting. It turned out to be a frozen swamp, and we discovered later that the German Air Force had used this field as a fighter base during the winter months. It was ten miles north of Deblin Airfield.

We spent most of the first night trying to establish contact with the Russian Army by radio. Eventually a Russian colonel arrived, and he arranged transport and accomodation for us in a bomb-damaged hotel in the city of Deblin.

We were assigned a mess sergeant, two orderlies and a Russian captain who was in charge of a twenty-four-hour guard for us. This was necessary, so we were told, because there were several German Army stragglers in the vicinity who were trying to get back to their own lines. We were also visited and interviewed by a young Russian officer and his equally young female assistant. These two, we later discovered, were members of the NKVD, the dreaded Russian secret police.

Basically, we were treated well and fed adequately. We could go almost anywhere as long as we were accompanied by the captain of the guard during the next eight days. On 25 February 1945, a Russian general from Poltava sent his IL-2 (a Russian version of the Douglas DC-2) to collect us. We left that same day and, accompanied by the two young secret police, we flew to Lublin in southeastern Poland and then on to Moscow.

We landed in Moscow in freezing temperatures during the evening. The Russians then took us to a large banquet hall, where they treated us to a farewell dinner of roast goose. Very enjoyable.

About 11:00 P.M., the Russians escorted us to the American embassy in Moscow. Averell Harriman, United States ambassador to Russia, was there to greet us at the embassy door. The next day we met Robert "Rosie" Rosenthal of the "Bloody Hundredth" Bomb Group. His right arm was in a sling due to being fractured during his bail-out over Russian lines while flying his last mission. Rosie had flown over fifty missions with the 100th Bomb Group since arriving at Thorpe Abbotts in October 1943.

The following day our crew, with Rosie Rosenthal, traveled by train to Poltava where we were delayed for about a week. From Poltava we flew in a C-46 transport plane to Iran, where we stopped overnight. Next morning we flew to Payne Field near Cairo, Egypt. After three days in Cairo, we flew to El Adane, a British base, then to Athens, Greece; Naples, Italy; and Rome, where we transferred into Winston Churchill's converted B-24 Liberator for the flight back to St. Mawgan's, near Land's End in southwest England. A U.S. Navy DC-3 then flew us to Bovingdon Airfield. Here we were stranded until we found an abandoned B-17G parked out of sight back in the woods. Its serial number was 43-38346; we flew this airplane back to the 95th Bomb Group at Horham two days later.

On our arrival we found all our personal belongings had been shipped out. After spending two days searching in Liverpool, we found our belongings at Stanley warehouse.

After Fred Volz was transferred to group operations, I took over as pilot in our new ship and Lieutenant Claybourn joined our crew as co-pilot. It wasn't until after the war and we'd returned to the United States that we discovered that we'd been given missing-in-action status. This entitled us to an additional one month's leave and orders to Atlantic City for rest and recuperation.

Postscript: The 95th Bomb Group lost two aircraft during the mission to Cottbus, our crew and the other was probably "Big Casino's" crew. About four or five years after the war the War Department in Washington contacted me again. They wanted to know if there was any other information I could give them in addition to the information I'd given during de-briefing on our return from Russia. It seems that I was the last person to see the olive-drab B-17 from the 95th Bomb Group with an engine on fire over enemy territory.

Fortunately, Air Force records show that "Big Casino's" crew was all taken prisoner and survived the war. The men involved were: pilot, C.D. Schaad; co-pilot, T.E. Flora; navigator, J.C. Keeney; nose gunner, H.W. Vaughn; top turret, E.C. Hemmingway; radio operator, L.G. Bassett; ball turret, B. Glanzer; waist gunner, L.T. Harman; tail gunner, W.S. Mazurek.

FLIGHT SURGEON

Dr. Jack McKittrick

I joined the 95th Bombardment Group at Rapid City Air Force Base, South Dakota, on Christmas Eve 1942. The group was composed of the 334th, 335th, 336th, and 412th squadrons, and I was assigned to the 336th with whom I stayed at various airfields in the United States and in England until the end of the war.

Eventually, after many trials and tribulations, the 95th Group arrived at our permanent base in Horham, Suffolk, in June 1943. We tried to make the base as much like home as we could for the duration of the war. Sports teams were formed for basketball, football, volleyball, and tennis. Our baseball team was called the Bombers.

During the first few months of flying combat missions, there were two major problems. One was frostbite. We had the old model B-17F that had no windows in the sides where the two waist gunners were. At 30,000 feet it didn't take long to freeze both hands. Of course, the gunners were supposed to wear silk gloves and then the electrically heated gloves on top. But their guns would jam, they'd get excited and tear their gloves off to clear the jammed guns. Then their hands would literally stick to the bare metal of the 50-caliber heavy machine guns.

The other big problem was battle fatigue. The men would start arguing about who was going to pass the butter, or they would deliberately pick a fight, or have battle dreams and wake up screaming in the middle of the night. Before we established "flak shacks" for their rehabilitation, it was a very real problem.

Some crewmen would approach me and say, "Captain, you can do anything you want, but I just can't fly this next mission. I'm too scared." Sometimes I would try and get them by on a medical, but it was difficult because Article of War 6-4 could land me in deep trouble. I recall one particular time in 1943, when the Eighth Air Force was going through a very rough period of heavy losses, one of our good pilots got hysterical on the truck taking us down to the mess hall. He went absolutely berserk.

Sometimes it would get so bad we'd have to transfer them out. But what we'd usually do was to send them over to the nearby 64th general field hospital. Frequently the doctors there would use sodium pentathal injections to get them to recount their experiences because a lot of these boys couldn't express themselves when they were conscious. Getting it out of them was an important form of therapy.

I vividly recall the several cases of battle fatigue that came during the big week in late February 1944 when the 95th flew deep penetration raids every day. The boys were getting exhausted, and they were coming home so terrified they couldn't eat or sleep. And they'd have to get up at 0300 hours and start all over again.

The flight surgeons sent a letter, over the heads of our group and squadron commanders, to General Curtis LeMay, commander of the Third Air Division at Elveden Hall, Suffolk. When he received the letter he got on the horn, called every damn flight surgeon in the Third Air Division over to division head-quarters, and reamed us out but good. I can still see him sitting there with a big cigar in his mouth, and he said, "Gentlemen, I know you are professionals but we are too. I don't want you to interfere with the way we're running the war . . . and we will not appreciate any more letters."

But we were getting so much pilot fatigue that we were getting silly accidents. The crews got liquor rations after a mission during debriefing. It was done very methodically; it did a great deal to settle them down and it gave them a little more appetite. It helped to relax them slightly from the horrors of a particularly terrifying mission that, all too often, surpassed fiction. And I'll be damned if the Women's Christian Temperance Union didn't try their best to put a stop to that.

I went to the first 150 briefings and noted that when the briefing officers discussed the weather and the flak areas en route to the target they were usually only about half right. I became a hero worshipper, because I saw so many boys that went on missions when they were absolutely scared to death to go. It wasn't a question of if they were going to be shot down, but rather when they were going to be killed, injured, or if they were lucky, taken prisoner, or even luckier still, to complete their tour of combat missions. But they still kept on going.

The first mission I flew was in April 1944 to the V-1 flying bomb launching sites at the Pas de Calais, France. I was scared, and I wondered what I was doing there. Just before I made this mission, I'd been delegated to lecture the 100th and 390th Bomb groups about first aid, frostbite, and the insidiousness of anoxia. So the first mission I made, what happened?

Somebody gave me an old A-10 oxygen mask, which I found out later, had a 25 percent leak in the nose. I went up and when we were over the target I had this very pleasant feeling of euphoria, like a cheap drunk. I recall thinking, "Lord, this is the best time I've ever had in my life."

The next thing I knew I was sitting in the nose section on an ammunition box. Our navigator looked back and had seen that I was purple. He switched the emergency oxygen supply on and I quickly recovered, but I had a king-sized headache for a week and the whole 336th Squadron kidded me for weeks afterward about it.

My second combat mission was in July 1944 for the carpet bombings of St. Lo, France. We bombed from about 12,000 feet, and I had a very vivid demonstration of the mighty Eighth Air Force during that run. There were 2,700 heavy bombers, medium bombers, and their fighter escorts in the air. We picked up the rally point at Caen, and when we were returning over the English Channel, bombers and fighters were still heading in the opposite direction. The narrowest escape I had was over Warsaw, Poland, on my third mission when we were dropping supplies to General Bor during the 1944 Warsaw uprising. We were hit by a burst of flak and lost two engines. We were forced to leave formation, and there were two Me 109s ahead of us. How they missed seeing us I'll never know. They hit two B-17s behind us and shot them both down. But they missed us.

We finally landed at Poltava, Russia, arriving an hour behind our group. I was scared, sick to my stomach, spitting cotton, and couldn't see straight when I lowered myself from the nose hatch and stepped on to the concrete hardstand.

With the huge numbers of aircraft, I don't know why we didn't have more mid-air collisions than we actually experienced over east Anglia. Most of the time the weather and cloud conditions were such that a pilot was flying blind and on instruments from the time his bomber left the runway until he broke through the undercast of cloud above his base prior to assembling into group formation.

Even so, from around mid-1944 onward, almost every morning there would be a mid-air collision. I could hear the eerie wailing of a bomber out of control and spinning down. Then I'd hear the crash and the bombs exploding just a few miles away. If I was the officer of the day I'd have to go and pick up whatever was left. Occasionally I found that I'd known some of the crewmen that were involved.

A mid-air crash is the worst crash in the world, and you compound that with 500-pound, high-explosive bombs. I can remember going along and picking out a perfectly dissected human heart from a bush. The twisted remains of a crewman would resemble a gnarled tree trunk. It was horrible. . . . The first time I did it, I couldn't eat for a week.

Then there were those seemingly endless periods of boredom and the occasional attacks of homesickness. I remember when we had been overseas for about a month or so and one of the fellows came up to me and asked, "Doc, what do you have for nostalgia?"

One diversion from homesickness and boredom was a forty-eight-hour pass to London. I was in the city when the first V-1 buzz bombs fell shortly after the invasion in June 1944. The flying bombs sounded like a motorcycle coming down the road. When the engine suddenly stopped, you knew you'd better duck because 1,000 pounds of high explosive was on its way down. When the V-2s came along, you didn't hear anything, just an eerie whistle after the massive explosion. I was within a block of one of them when it landed and killed a number of civilians and GIs in a tavern. There wasn't much left of the tavern or the people when I got to the scene . . . utter devastation.

I found myself in the middle of history in London on V-E night. One of General Patton's chief surgeons was lecturing at a meeting at the Royal College of Surgeons. It was my birthday, 7 May, and after the meeting finished I went to a little theater on Leicester Square. I heard all this commotion and went outside. The streets were so packed with people it took me two hours to get to Piccadilly Circus. British Tommys and GIs were packed together in and on taxis, buses, and firetrucks. That night I couldn't buy a drink in London. Everything was free. I was at the Dorchester Hotel and we all listened to Winston Churchill's speech; it was the most exciting night I've ever seen. They lighted all the lights for the first time in six years; big department stores, Piccadilly Circus, Oxford Street, the Houses of Parliament were all shining brightly.

One thing I will always remember was the quietly spoken Englishman who said to me on that joyous night, "Thanks, Yank, we couldn't have done it without you. . . ."

GALLANT TO THE END

George Hintz, Ball-turret Gunner, 336th Squadron

On 25 February 1945 the briefed target for the 95th Bomb Group was the sprawling railroad marshaling yards at Munich in southern Germany. It was a maximum effort with all three air divisions of the Eighth Air Force attacking different strategic targets throughout southern Germany.

After an early morning takeoff and assembly, the outward flight was relatively uneventful until approximately eight minutes from our target. We were at 24,000 feet when number 4 engine was put out of action by a flak hit. Losing altitude we turned back toward the French border while under attack from enemy fighters and surrounded by exploding flak. Part of the nose was shot away, both wings took numerous hits, and the tail gunner had his guns literally shot out of his hands.

During the battle we dropped our bombs on an unidentified town. Someone said it was Augsburg, Germany. Then our number 3 engine took a hit and the propellor was successfully feathered in time. The loud hissing of punctured oxygen tanks below the flight deck and the leading hydraulic tank just above those oxygen tanks increased the possibility of an explosion.

Holes suddenly appeared through the radio room fuselage, the radio table was hit, number 2 engine caught fire, and flames threatened to explode the leaking fuel tanks. The order came to bail out instead of our intended crash landing and, although we were now at a dangerously low altitude, we all made it, landing near the Swiss-German border but, very luckily for us, on the Swiss side.

Incredibly, our severely damaged and now pilotless B-17 flew on and made a respectable crash landing in a forest clearing at the southern end of the Baldegger Lake, Switzerland.

We were interned at Addobolten, Switzerland, and released after a few weeks. Our gallant Fort was dismantled at its final resting place, the parts were taken to Dubendorf airfield for storage and eventual scrapping after the war.

Crew of B-17 231989: Pilot, Lieutenant Karel Havelik; co-pilot, Lieutenant Donald Johnson; navigator, Lieutenant Lloyd Brandborg; bombardier, Sergeant Robert Welsh; engineer, Sergeant John Maruk; radio op., Sergeant Thomas Conry; ball turret, Sergeant George Hintz; waist gunner, Sergeant Wilbur Schrander; tail gunner, Sergeant John Charles.

REFLECTIONS

R.E. ("Lefty") Nairn, Toggelier/Armorer, 336th Squadron

As a young 22-year-old replacement crew member of a B-17, commanded by Lieutenant Tom Gibson, the startling sight of all those wrecked B-17s and B-24s lying scattered haphazardly and grotesquely across the snow-covered countryside of southern and eastern England that I saw during the train journey from Valley, Wales, to Diss, Norfolk, in early January 1945 shocked me into an awareness and stark realization that here was the real war. By that time, of course, the war was almost over and the wrecks awaiting salvage were a somber reminder of all that had gone before.

How many more wrecked Allied bombers, I wondered, were now lying scattered and smashed across continental Europe and in watery graves at the bottom of the North Sea and the English Channel? Would I be yet another statistic? Victory in Europe was a mere six weeks away when on 21 March 1945, during a mission to Munster-Handorf Airfield in western Germany, my apprehensions, fears, and anxieties, call it what you will, were answered. It was the 95th's 300th combat mission. A chunk of jagged steel shrapnel from an exploding flak shell struck me in the left shoulder, fracturing both arm and shoulder. The truly agonizing pain, however, didn't come until I was lifted from the B-17's nose-hatch back at Horham and transferred to the 65th general field hospital at Botesdale, near Diss.

The ambulance driver, from Brooklyn, New York, must have been in serious training for the Indianapolis 500 race. Bouncing around in the rear of that speeding GI ambulance along those winding country roads was probably the most painful period of my being injured and that includes the actual impact of flak into my shoulder.

After lengthy periods of hospitalization in England and the United States, my wounds healed satisfactorily and I am truly very grateful for my good fortune. Many, many others were far less fortunate.

Quite apart from those many thousands who gave the greatest sacrifice— their young lives for our freedom, whose names have been quite properly recorded for all time—are those who survived and whose injuries resulted in severe physical disablement with the attendant emotional trauma, whom everyone, apart from their relatives and close friends, appear to have forgotten.

I sometimes wonder, especially at our annual reunions, how many Eighth Air Force veterans and, more specifically, 95th Group veterans who were severely disabled during missions from England and are now confined to Veterans' Administration hospitals, are unable to cope successfully with life, or even to provide for themselves adequately.

Truly, these are the forgotten heroes.

A TRIBUTE

Leonard Herman, Bombardier, 335th Squadron

This article is dedicated to all the aerial gunners of the 95th Bomb Group, but more particularly it is dedicated to Staff Sergeant Donald Crossley.

There is not the slightest doubt in my mind that had our bomber's crew been less proficient and had our gunners been less skilled and accurate, I would not be alive today to write this memorial tribute.

Donald Crossley was a handsome young devil and had a charming yet wicked smile. He had the spirit and verve of a young stallion. The girls all loved him!

Better still, our crew all loved him. And why not? After all, he was a really excellent shot, and he kept us alive on a number of occasions. He certainly knew how to handle his guns in our tail turret position.

Donald Crossley's picture graced the front cover of the 10 October 1943 issue of the *New York Times Magazine.* The article was headlined "Sharp Shooter of the Air." Other news clippings said, "Gunner Honored as Best in Europe," (dated 17 September 1943, London, U.P.) "He has been credited with having shot down 22 German fighters in 20 missions." (A later article stated that Donald Crossley now had 12 German planes to his credit.)

Don completed his combat tour at about the same time as I did, and I left Horham very soon afterward for the United States but I later learned that Don did not come home at that time. Evidently, he'd been transferred to the 100th Bomb Group at Thorpe Abbotts as a gunnery instructor, crashed into a brick wall while driving a jeep, and died in the base hospital as a result of his injuries.

I will always remember him.

A voice from the past—a happy ending: Sometime during May 1984, several months after we started our quest for wartime experiences and other relevant information in order to compile this group history, I contributed the small dedication to our tail gunner, Donald Crossley. It was sent to Ian Hawkins in England.

Shortly before our group's annual reunion at Las Vegas in September 1984, I received a telephone call from the west coast. The caller stated that he was Don Crossley and he wished to speak to Leonard Herman to ask if he was the same person who flew with the crew of a B-17 named "The Brass Rail," 95th Bomb Group, Eighth Air Force, during World War II.

I took the call and told the gentleman that I thought it was a very sick joke to use a dead airman's name in order to have a phone conversation. "Leonard," the voice exclaimed, "I *am* Don Crossley and I'm damned if I'm dead!"

Apparently, Don had read the small article I'd written in the *Disabled*

American Veterans Magazine, requesting information from 95th Group veterans for our anthology.

Knowing Don Crossley, I should have asked him where he was calling from. Most certainly science has advanced tremendously and of course communications are now being received from all parts of outer space.

It transpired that after crashing into the wall and being rushed to the hospital the medics had given Don up, and he was not expected to live more than twenty-four hours. Thus the story was circulated that Don had passed away. In fact, I checked with many people and they'd all heard the same sad story. Well, it *was* Don Crossley on the phone, he *was* alive, and he was going to attend our 95th Group reunion. As a result of my conversation with him, I was able to contact a few other crew members of "The Brass Rail" whom I hadn't heard from since 1943.

The reunion took place in Las Vegas, and it was a great emotional experience. Randall Cowan, our top-turret gunner and his wife appeared, and I was finally reunited with Don Crossley at about midnight at the hotel bar. We reminisced into the early morning hours, drinking toasts to each other and to all the members of our crew.

So now my dedication is to a real living person. Nothing changes that dedication except, by the grace of God, he is alive. Donald Crossley has beaten the odds again, and he can still talk about it. Here's to you, Don!

OPERATION CADILLAC AND OPERATION VARSITY

Ellis B. Scripture, Group and Third Air Division Navigator

After the Allied invasion of continental Europe in early June 1944, two or three large-scale missions were flown by the Third Air Division during which we dropped arms and supplies to the French *Maquis*, members of which were some of the most honored fighters in the Underground and Resistance movement in Europe. Numerous resupply missions had, of course, been flown throughout the war to France and to other occupied countries by the Royal Air Force and select American units although on a much smaller scale and mostly at night.

The 95th Group participated in two of these post-invasion daylight supply drops, one of which was code-named Operation Cadillac and took place on 14

July 1944. I was assigned to one of the missions as lead navigator. On this day we flew over the German front lines at a rather high altitude of 20,000 feet and then dropped down to 1,000 feet after flying some distance into the occupied French interior. Our target was three burning straw stacks in a field in an isolated area of France, to the east of Lyons, and in the foothills of the Swiss Alps. Some of the other Third Air Division groups were assigned to resupply other locations.

We located the target on time and dropped our canisters by parachute from an altitude of 500 feet.

One interesting aspect of this mission is that as the canisters were being packed, the American airmen wanted to show their admiration for the French resistance fighters. We scattered packages of cigarettes into the canisters, and later that night, when the coded acknowledgment came over the radio to notify us the arms and supplies had been received safely, the message read: "DAYLIGHT DROP SUCCESSFUL. CIGARETTES ALSO RECEIVED. MANY THANKS."

Needless to say that made us feel really close to the Resistance fighters in the French Underground movement.

Another extremely interesting mission in which I participated was Operation Varsity, the airborne crossing of the Rhine River in March 1945.

On 21 March 1945, the 95th Bomb Group was scheduled to fly its 300th mission, a unique and historic occasion for the group. I'd flown the first mission with the 95th on 13 May 1943, the 100th mission on 22 March 1944, and the 200th mission on 27 August 1944. Needless to say I was very much looking forward to the opportunity of probably being the only original crewman who would also fly the 300th mission.

However, it was not to be because at that time I was serving on the staff at Third Air Division headquarters at Elveden Hall as division navigator. On the day before the 95th Group's 300th mission, Third Air Division was requested by the Allied command to furnish two radar-equipped B-17s to lead the paratroopers and the glider troops across the Rhine River for the final assault on Germany. This mission promised to be one of the highlights of the Second World War. The 95th was assigned a rather minor role for its 300th mission: to fly a diversionary mission to Handorf, Germany, on 21 March, which didn't promise much action.

I asked General Earle Partridge, Third Division commander, for permission to fly as navigator in the B-17 that would lead the paratroopers across the Rhine River to their dropping zones. Permission was granted. On 24 March 1945, we met our stream of C-47 Dakota troop-carrying aircraft north of Paris and headed for the assigned drop zone. We were scheduled to lead them across the Rhine River at 1000 hours, at 500-feet altitude with air speed at 120 knots. We arrived at the assigned target, on time, at 500 feet.

It was a beautiful spring morning and it was a tremendous thrill for us as we led the C-47s to the middle of the Rhine and then flew back across the Rhine River, two or three miles away from the action to watch the stream of planes as they came through. Hundreds and hundreds of aircraft came flying over, first with paratroops, then came the gliders towed by Stirling bombers and C-47s. The thrill was the climax of the entire war as we realized that we were quite literally pouring tens of thousands of troops across the final barrier to the Fatherland. At last this was the beginning of the end of Hitler's Germany.

The records reveal that the stream of Allied aircraft on that memorable day consisted of 1,696 transport planes, 1,348 gliders, and 889 fighters for escort purposes. An additional 2,153 combat airplanes participated in this operation, silencing and suppressing the German defenses in the drop zones. In addition to these, another 2,596 heavy bombers and 821 medium bombers were attacking strategic targets in Germany. A total of 9,503 aircraft graphically demonstrated the truly overwhelming superiority of Allied air power at that stage in the war.

Our B-17 remained at a very low altitude, circling for about two hours, while we took photographs and watched the action. It was an absolutely stunning and amazing sight for us to witness this great number of airplanes assigned to this one operation.

There is one thing that stands out vividly in my memory of this momentous day. I took several photographs of C-47s crashing very soon after they'd recrossed the Rhine and headed back to friendly territory. We counted as many as eighteen C-47s that turned after dropping their paratroopers, crossed the river, and a few seconds later would literally explode in mid-air. At that low altitude, of course, the pilots had no chance of bailing out.

These extraordinary incidents were photographed and discussed when we got back to our base in England, but we never did file a formal mission report.

About two weeks later I was on leave in London and ran into a highly decorated paratrooper captain in a bar. We were talking, as combat people always do, and I related what I'd seen during the Rhine crossing.

His story was something like this: "Major, I can tell you precisely what happened. The pilots and co-pilots of those airplanes are trained to drop paratroops at 500 feet, flying straight and level, going at no more than 120 knots. If they do that we keep our paratroopers grouped together so that when we reach the ground we are a compact fighting unit, entirely dependent on our collective firepower if and when there's a reception committee.

"However, many times some of these pilots get real cute as they approach the dropping zone. They very quietly raise their altitude up to about 1,000 feet, then cunningly increase their airspeed as they drop to 500 feet—the purpose being, of course, to save their own skins. If they're going a little faster or a little higher it gives the enemy gunners on the ground less opportunity. The pilots drop their troops and then scoot out of the way at full throttle, getting clear as quickly as possible.

"We don't like that because when they do that it scatters us all over the place and it results in death and injury for many of our men as we're not a fighting unit when we hit the ground.

"Sometimes when this happens the last angry man out pulls the pin from a hand grenade and tosses it into the airplane just as he jumps. That's what you saw, Major. They kill us, we kill them."

Needless to say, I was disappointed that I was unable to fly the 95th Bomb Group's 300th mission, but the crossing of the Rhine River was one of the most interesting experiences that I had during my entire combat career. To top it all off, when we landed back at our home base, I found my chest-pack parachute on the table exactly where I had left it when we got onto the plane that morning! There is no question—someone up there was watching over me that day—and every day for nearly two years.

MORE SHORT BURSTS

William Binnebose, waist gunner, 334th Squadron: We were shot down over Belgium during the Schweinfurt-Regensburg raid, 17 August 1943. It was our fourteenth mission, and while firing at the attacking German fighters, I was hit in the legs. Shortly after I'd been injured, we received the signal from our pilot, Lieutenant Walter Baker, to bailout. All our crew managed to evacuate our burning B-17, named "Our Bay-Bee," successfully.

I was picked up and taken to a hospital at Beverloo, Belgium, with the other two wounded members of our crew. We were joined by a Luftwaffe Me 109 pilot who had also been wounded that day and had been forced to bail out.

His name was Werner Kraft, and it was his attack that had finally finished us off. From the way he described the action, it had been my gun position that shot him down. It was really quite extraordinary, something that very rarely happened, for any of the boys from both sides to meet the way Werner and I did.

****

Ellis B. Scripture, group navigator: The 95th Bomb Group flew its first mission to Nazi-occupied Europe on 13 May 1943. It flew its final mission on 7 May 1945, having completed a total of 321 missions with the loss of 192 B-17 Fortresses and 1,774 casualties. (Planes lost include those that crash-landed on the continent and were damaged beyond repair.)

The heaviest aircraft and crew losses in the group were: *Kiel, 13 June 1943*, 10 planes from 26 (38.5 percent); *Brunswick, 10 February 1944*, 7 from 21 (33.3 percent); *Berlin, 6 March 1944*, 8 from 23 (34.8 percent); *Munster, 10 October 1943*, 5 from 22 (22.7 percent); and *Rostock, 11 April 1944*, 7 from 37

(18.9 percent). These numbers do not necessarily reflect the intensity of those great air battles and the total jeopardy of the crews; nor do these bare statistics indicate the countless acts of heroism and courage displayed by the crewmen who participated in these five traumatic missions.

The statistics do, however, indicate the 95th Group's dogged determination and esprit de corps in rebounding from adversity to an even greater combined and individual effort that undoubtedly minimized later losses through self-discipline.

****

Tom J. Tower, pilot, 334th Squadron: Merseburg, 28 September 1944, was our baptism by fire. The oil refineries there were ringed by some 400 heavy antiaircraft guns, which turned a cubic mile of sky into a solid steel wall of flak. This resulted in our most unbelievable sight of witnessing the tragic loss of Lieutenant Wright and his crew.

Our two B-17s were flying almost next to each other when what must have been a 105mm shell went through his number 2 gas tank and set his airplane on fire. We could clearly see the crew's faces in the cockpit and waist position. Lieutenant Wright immediately swung his ship away from the formation, and as he banked, we saw that the shell had made a hole in his wing as large as a fifty-gallon drum. The molten aluminum was flowing back along the fuselage and over the tail section. Suddenly, the ship nosed over and went straight down. Sergeant Parsons, our tail gunner, watched them as far as he could, but no one got out.

This happened again in very similar circumstances during our second raid to Merseburg, 30 November 1944, when we witnessed Lieutenant Don Miller's airplane take a direct hit while over the target.

Again, our two ships were close together, almost eyeball to eyeball. An 88mm shell hit his tail section just behind the tail gunner. It sliced a hole through the control area of the vertical and horizontal tail section and blew out the tail gun position. My waist, ball, and tail gunners saw the trapped gunner fall, his back blown open.

Lieutenant Miller and his co-pilot skillfully nursed the damaged ship back as far as the Belgian coast where he decided that they better bail out while still over land, which they did. The humorous story came from the bombardier who landed in a tree and was jerked upside down by the branches and knocked unconscious.

He came to, still upside down and unable to do anything about it except yell and shout for help between dizzy spells. Eventually, to his intense relief, he saw two black-clad figures rushing toward him. They turned out to be two little old ladies who incredibly, climbed the tree with remarkable agility, went right past him without saying a word, and reached the billowing folds of his tangled parachute. They then each produced scissors from within their long black dresses, promptly cut the silk parachute free, and dropped the fabric to the ground. They scrambled down past him, again not saying a word, grabbed the precious parachute, and took off at high speed.

Finally, a couple of men working in a nearby field heard his shouts, came over, and rescued the incredulous bombardier from the tree.

I'll bet some Belgian girl still has some fancy silk petticoats made from that parachute!

****

Zach Stanborough, co-pilot, 336th Squadron: At the time of the mission to Oschersleben, 28 July 1943, I was temporarily grounded with blocked sinuses. Lieutenant Willis Parker took my place in the cockpit beside Lieutenant Francis Regan, our pilot.

Shortly before reaching the enemy coast, their B-17 was lagging behind due to engine malfunctions. Two Fw 190s were seen heading in their direction and very soon after that a B-17 was seen going down, out of control, in flames, and crashing in the North Sea.

That was the end of Lieutenant Regan and my original crew. It would have been my fifth mission.

****

Technical Sergeant James Johnson, S2 (Intelligence Section): We were transferred from Alconbury to Framlingham on 12 May 1943. That same evening, "Lord Haw Haw," broadcasting from Berlin announced on our radio: "Welcome to your new airfield at Framlingham, you American airmen of the 95th Bomb Group."

****

Willard Brown, group navigator: I was married very soon after the war. My wife, of course, wanted to see Europe and some of the places I was familiar with over there. About 1947 we decided to take our vacation in Europe.

While we were driving through Germany, I showed her some of the places where I'd hidden during my unsuccessful escape attempts. One of these places was a barn located at an isolated farm. The German farmer had found me hiding there but did not turn me over to the German authorities.

We drove up to the farmhouse in a prewar Pontiac and I immediately recognized the adjacent barn. That same German farmer was working nearby and he recognized me, but before I could say hello and ask him how he was getting on, he strode rapidly into the house. Almost immediately afterward we heard a lot of yelling and shouting coming from within. Wondering what all the commotion was about I went to the front of the house and quite soon the farmer emerged accompanied by his daughter, a pretty girl about twenty years old.

Cradled in her arms was a little guy, about two years old.

She looked at me, then looked at the father and shook her head no. That's how you spell R-E-L-I-E-F!

FATE IS THE HUNTER

Tony Braidic, Bombardier, 334th Squadron

In the fall of 1944 I completed my training at Drew Field, Florida, with a B-17 crew commanded by Lieutenant Lionel ("Spider") Sceurman. In January 1945 we arrived in England and were assigned to the 95th Bombardment Group. We had flown six combat missions when I was removed from active duty and chosen to begin B-29 Superfortress training for the Pacific theater. Staff Sergeant Dave Condon replaced me.

I was still at Horham during April and May, however, and participated in the Eighth Air Force Chowhound project, dropping urgently needed food supplies from low level to the starving Dutch people. I flew four of these mercy missions with various other crews, and on 7 May 1945, I was to fly with Lieutenant Paul Crider's crew. At the briefing as were told that this was the final day of the war, Victory in Europe (VE) Day, but it wasn't yet officially announced to the world.

At the flight line my original pilot, Spider Sceurman, approached me saying he wanted to celebrate the end of the war with the same crew he'd trained with and would I change places with Dave Condon so that this could be accomplished. No one would know the difference. I declined—why, I don't really know.

Paul Crider took off and we flew, with other Third Air Division bomb groups, to Holland. We dropped our load of food containers from low altitude near Hilversum. We then proceeded across other areas of Holland, the tulip fields, the dykes, canals, the windmills, the rusting hulls of half-sunken ships in Rotterdam harbor. We also saw crowds of people looking up and waving to us from the town square in Amsterdam. We even flew over Antwerp, Belgium, before we turned for home.

As we walked up the slope from the flight line to the 334th Squadron area, we were told by some of the other crews that Lieutenant Sceurman's B-17 had gone down on the return flight. Halfway across the North Sea his number 2 engine had caught fire and it was doubtful if there were any survivors.

That night at the base hospital we were overjoyed to discover that two crewmen had survived, Jim Schwarz, co-pilot, and Dave Condon. But in another area of the hospital were the four bodies that had been recovered from the sea: Spider Sceurman; Russ Cook, navigator; Norbert Kuper, armorer-gunner; and one of the five passengers from the photographic section who had gone along for the ride. Another body was recovered later, but the other five were never found.

A medical technician, somewhat inebriated, allowed us to view their remains at the hospital. It was a terrible mistake, because afterward the other crews in the 334th area endured several fitful and sleepless nights as we consequently experienced nightmares and woke up screaming.

I attended the funeral service and burial of my former crew members at the American Military Cemetery, near Cambridge, as did other members of the 95th Group, including several representatives from the photo section.

In early May 1985, twenty Eighth Air Force veterans and about 120 Royal Air Force Bomber Command veterans who had participated in the food drop missions were invited back to Holland for the fortieth anniversary celebrations of Operation Manna/Chowhound. I viewed the celebration as a tourist at the resort city of Scheveningen and was deeply impressed by the emotional welcome shown by the appreciative Dutch people.

Incidentally, B-17G 48640, 334th Squadron, 95th Bomb Group, was the last Eighth Air Force B-17 to do down during the war in Europe. It is indeed fitting and appropriate that Mr. Hans Onderwater, a member of the Dutch Organizing Committee for that memorable occasion dedicated his excellent book, *Operation Manna/Chowhound*, to my former crew and the other 95th Bomb Group personnel who died tragically on 7 May 1945.

Was it an unconscious premonition that warned me to decline Lionel Sceurman's suggestion on that fateful day? I shall never know.

Note: Page 139 of *Operation Manna/Chowhound* (appendices) states: "Over Ijmuiden two B-17s (95th B.G. and 385th B.G.) were fired upon by German machine guns. The 95th B.G. B-17G crashed into the North Sea. Of the crew of twelve, only two survived."

PRISONER OF WAR AT STALAG 17B

Warren Thomas, Radio Operator, B-17F "Fritz Blitz" 335th Squadron

Our crew was shot down over Munster, 10 October 1943, during my 25th mission. All of our crew, commanded by Lieutenant Eldon Broman, with the exception of top-turret gunner Sergeant Rightmire, survived and became prisoners of war.

After two weeks' treatment at a prison hospital in West Germany for my burns sustained during my bailout, I was taken by train, under guard, to Frankfurt's interrogation center. From there, a week later, I went to the infamous Stalag 17B POW camp at Krems, Austria. I was given a number, 99131, had my hair completely shaved, and began my first day as an ex Luft-gangster. My first meal, Jerry soup, had a number of fat, white grubworms floating on top. I carefully removed the worms and then drank the soup, but during the next eighteen months of imprisonment I began to find the grubs a quite delicious addition to our near-starvation diet.

Incoming prisoners were not completely accepted at first, only after being positively identified did we become true Kriegies. Each tarpaper-covered hut contained triple-decked bunks, forming each interior side of the hut with a small, narrow aisle down the center. The wooden slatted shelf bunks were furnished with a straw-filled sack mattress. Five huts formed a fenced-in compound; the fences consisted of a double barbed-wire main fence with guard towers, complete with searchlights and heavy machine guns placed at strategic points along the fence, fully manned around the clock. Tin cans, in the thousands, were piled along the length of the main outer fences, which rattled if men tried to cut their way to freedom. About five yards inside each compound and running parallel to the main fence was a knee-high warning fence. This was a single-strand warning wire and had signs in English that read: "Do not touch this wire or pass into the warning area or you will be fired upon immediately without warning." The watchtower guards certainly weren't fooling.

We had two to three roll calls every day. The guards came around with their loud and piercing whistles and ordered everyone outside to be counted. Each roll call took one to three hours and they were really rough; mud, rain, snow, and sleet made no difference. Following an escape, we'd be kept outside all day, even in freezing weather, with countless number and photograph checks.

Red Cross food parcels were issued on Fridays if any were available. Stalag 17B seemed to be the end of the line for the parcels to be delivered. Each American prisoner averaged 1½ parcels per month, and a hungry man could devour the contents in one day. When the parcels arrived, the Jerries punctured all the canned goods with bayonets. This prevented food being kept for escape attempts.

The huts were gradually stripped of all spare wood for our stoves and shoring material for escape tunnels. Before we left the camp, the huts were only bare shells of their former materials.

The prison camp was necessarily very well organized. Leaders were elected to head each hut, compound, and camp. The escape organizing committee was excellent, and other court activities were very efficient. Most of the escape attempts arranged without the knowledge of the escape committee ended in death and disaster.

Flea bites, lice, and chilblains were constant companions. Fortunately, our health remained comparatively good, and only one American prisoner died of natural causes. The Germans gave him a full military funeral when he was buried. Those who were killed during escapes were not accorded this honor.

Due to a typhus epidemic many, many Russian prisoners died at Stalag 17B. The bodies were wrapped in heavy paper and buried in mass graves. We Americans were very thankful for our typhus shots that we'd had before capture. A small dispensary, manned by medics, was located in our area and captured French doctors had a dispensary in the German area of the camp. We were only able to use the facility if and when we were extremely ill.

I shall never forget the endless hours of boredom during captivity. Seconds became minutes, minutes became hours, hours crept by like days. The sports equipment was given to us by the YMCA through the International Red Cross. Many softball games were thoroughly enjoyed after the equipment arrived, but card games, compound walks, work on court activities, reading, and picking fleas from clothing seams were the usual activities.

One memorable night the R.A.F. came over, and their Pathfinders dropped orange flares to mark the boundaries of our camp. To our great relief the bombers hit targets in the nearby town of Krems and not our camp in error.

We had many different types of radios. Most were small crystal sets but adequate to receive news bulletins broadcast by the BBC in London. We kept up to date with the progress being made on the various war fronts. We occasionally allowed our guards to discover some escape materials and radio equipment during their hut searches. This always seemed to satisfy them and then we resumed our usual activities.

The German guards were as a rule quite fair in their treatment of prisoners. They were just German GIs doing a job. Many of them had been to the various fronts, been wounded, and invalided to the POW camps for guard duty. Other guards were less friendly, just plain mean, or sadistic. Some guards had been tricked into helping our cause under the threat of exposure, but very few were completely in sympathy with us. They all had to be extremely careful not to show their true feelings about the war to their superior officers; otherwise they'd have probably been shot or sent to the Russian front, which virtually meant the same fate.

We had an Englishman in our hut posing as an American who had departed the stalag, and to our great surprise, an enlisted medic at our camp turned out to be a French general. His English was perfect, but why he was posing as an American was never divulged. We also had three Australians with us. They'd arrived late at night to impersonate three Americans who joined a group of commandos in an escape. Three Russian prisoners were also in our compound—Nicholi, Alex, and Sergi—posing as Americans. The Australians reached liberation with us but the three Russians were taken away. I wish I knew how they fared on their return to Russia.

On 8 April 1945 we began our march westward during a blizzard. The guards said it was to protect us from the Russian Army, whose big guns could be heard rumbling quite close to Stalag 17B during the previous two days. We marched in eight large groups of 500 men each through mud and snow for about eighteen days, covering about twenty kilometers per day, through all types of weather and on every type of road and track. At Linz, Austria, we hurried through as it had recently been bombed, and the civilians were in a very angry and ugly mood toward us. We went through the forested area of Braunau, Hitler's birthplace, toward the end of the march. During the nights, we sheltered in farmer's barns and any large buildings we came across. Earlier in the march, we'd seen the absolutely sickening sight of a few thousand very emaciated Jewish people being marched to their deaths at Mauthausen concentration camp. They were guarded by S.S. troops and many were falling by the roadside because of their exhausted condition. It was horrifying to see their S.S. guards club their heads with rifle butts and be absolutely powerless to intervene.

When we finally reached our destination on 25 April, some of us were very weak due to the complete absence of food during the last few days of the march. Eventually a convoy of white trucks, bearing the Red Cross insignia, arrived from Switzerland with British drivers. They carried food parcels; each prisoner received about half a parcel, which was indeed very welcome, but those who made the mistake of trying to eat their entire ration at one sitting became very ill.

The Thirteenth Armored Division arrived at our temporary camp on 2 May and an officer told us we were free men at last. Our guards were disarmed and marched away. Within a few hours our camp became a madhouse with ex-POWs scouring the surrounding countryside for additional food.

We were soon flown in B-17s and C-47s to Camp Lucky Strike in France. I was taken to a hospital at Nancy, France, where I spent four weeks recovering from a few medical problems. I then went to England and sought transportation home, eventually finding a place on an L.S.T. in convoy with other L.S.T.s. We limped across the Atlantic at a snail's pace via the Azores and Bermuda, then to the U.S. Navy base at Norfolk, Virginia. While on hospital leave at my home, I heard the Japanese had surrendered. The war was finally over.

My postwar career included flight school, aircrew duties in B-29s, B-50s, B-36s, and finally a fleet of GMDs (gray, metal desks).

THE MANNA/CHOWHOUND MISSIONS

Ellis B. Scripture, Third Air Division Navigator

During the latter days of April and the early days of May 1945, the B-17 Fortresses of the Third Air Division and several squadrons of Lancaster bombers combined forces in a series of missions of mercy to drop thousands of desperately needed food parcels to the starving Dutch people. Holland at that time was still occupied by the German armed forces, which had denied the entire populace food and fuel during the harsh winter of 1944–45. By the end of April 1945, over 18,000 Dutch people had starved to death and more than 3,000,000 were desperate for food; but their resistance to the Nazis continued— as a nation and as individuals who loved freedom.

The food drops in specified dropping zones were carried out from low altitude. Food dropped eventually totaled more than 24 million pounds of urgently needed rations. The R.A.F. bomber command aircraft flew 3,358 sorties for Operation Manna, a term derived from biblical times when the Israelites in the wilderness miraculously received food from Heaven. The ten participating bomb groups of the Third Air Division flew 2,268 sorties during Operation Chow Hound. The entire operation was planned initially by the Royal Air Force, and the bombers were used because all the transport aircraft were busily occupied in other operations.

Practice drops were made at Horham to determine the feasibility of low-level flights, and the 95th was one of the groups selected to drop food to the beleaguered Dutch people. The three groups of the Thirteenth Combat Wing were fully involved in every mission. The first Chowhound drop was led by the 390th Group, with "Colonel Joe" Moller as mission commander. Joe is very familiar to many as the man who joined the 95th in mid-1943, wrangled himself into a combat assignment, and flew fifteen missions with the 95th Group before becoming the 390th Group commander. Joe continued to fly actively and most honorably in combat until the war's end. All of this at an age when he could have been called "daddy" by most of the kids who were crew members. There were about 23,000 Third Air Division men involved in these missions. It should be noted that the only airplane lost in all of the 5,626 plane missions flown was from the 95th. This was the last combat casualty in the Eighth Air Force: Eleven men from the 95th were lost as their plane went down at sea.

Much will be written and remembered over the years by the men who flew those missions and by the Dutch people. Much will also be remembered by the men who were invited to spend a very moving and memorable week, from 28 April to 4 May 1985, in Holland to celebrate the fortieth anniversary of those missions. The Dutch people remembered so vividly after forty years!

Many honors were graciously bestowed upon the representatives of the six nations representing the R.A.F. and the Eighth Air Force that flew the food-drop missions (British, Canadians, New Zealanders, Poles, Australians, and Americans). That visit to Holland will be a highlight in the lives of all the veterans and their wives for all time. None of us privileged to be present had ever seen such a display of genuine emotion and great national pride as we witnessed during that memorable week.

The Chowhound operation of 5 May 1945, was the last mission flown by Grif Mumford and me; we represented the original cadre of men that formed the 95th Bomb Group in 1942. For both of us, it was a most rewarding and satisfying way in which to end a WWII flying career that spanned almost two years in combat. This was not a combat mission in any sense of the word, but we had no firm assurance that the Germans would not fire at our airplanes as we dropped the food parcels. As stated earlier, the one plane that was lost could, in all probability, have been the target of small arms ground fire from frustrated Nazi troops.

It was certainly a wonderful feeling to be able to do something constructive, instead of destructive, as we ended our flying service in the European theater of operations. It was doubly rewarding, forty years later, to discover the full details of what actually had been accomplished by these missions and to personally witness the emotional thanksgiving of an entire nation.

29 APRIL 1945

Swarms of swallows bringing food
Visions of victory,
Thoughts of freedom
For the starving,
For the powerless,
For the discouraged ones.
They all laugh and cry. . . .

They waved from bridges
From canals
From squares and viaducts
They climbed on roof tops
Once bent down they straightened
Their backs again
And shook hands

And cheered at every place
For this was a miracle
Salvation from above
Manna-rain
Bringing relief, true blessing
Mighty moment
We waited for months to see it

By Elisabeth van Maasdijk
(From *To The Ones Who Fell*, The Hague, Holland, 1945)

A VIEW FROM THE GROUND UP

(Part III)
Ted Lucey, Radio Technician, 336th Squadron
(Written as personal notes, not originally intended for
publication)

8 May 1945: Victory in Europe, or V-E Day, found me at Elveden Hall, Third Air Division headquarters, celebrating with the party to end all parties. It was held in the stable yard and garden at Elveden Hall which, in all its centuries, had never witnessed its equal. I enjoyed several postwar baseball games between teams of officers and enlisted men. I recall one game in particular in which a brigadier general, who was long on nerve and short on hair, was on second base. He tried to reach home base on a single as a thousand GI fans howled, "Slide, Baldy! Slide!" Our local R.A.F. staff stood stunned and agape at such lèse-majesté.

During June 1945 I was detached from 3AD and sent to Knettishall, Suffolk, the home of the legendary 388th Bombardment Group. Perhaps no other group in the Eighth Air Force quite matched its flair for relaxation and hospitality. But it is equally famous for being up there where the shooting was heaviest and the flak was thickest. For example, during the Stuttgart raid of 6 September 1943, the Eighth Air Force sent out 338 bombers, of which forty were shot down. The 388th lost eleven of those Forts, including all the planes from one of its three squadrons. It was one mission among many, many other rough, tough missions that the Eighth Air Force flew in Europe.

I turned homeward with the 388th Group in August as with so many other units. We rode a much happier train as it headed toward Greenock, Scotland. One evening before sailing I saw a beautiful double rainbow with one leg in the Firth of Forth and the other in Loch Lomond. I marveled at the poker and crap games that ran nonstop during the five days it took the mighty *Queen Elizabeth* to reach New York harbor. As the huge ship glided serenely past the Statue of Liberty, all the other ships in the harbor sounded off their sirens in a crescendo of "welcome home." Milling crowds of relatives and friends lined the jetty. The wheel had turned full circle.

There were so many who did not come back . . . thousands and thousands: the amiable GI lieutenant who hitched a ride in a mission-bound Fortress that didn't return from that raid; the Teaneck pilot who made himself fly, despite his great consuming dread; and "the man who came for breakfast." Were they killed? Prisoners of war? Perhaps no one knows what happened. Perhaps their names live only in memory among 5,123 others that are inscribed on the Wall of the Missing at Madingley, the American military cemetery near Cambridge.

I know that in the ebb and flow of the fortunes of war, I was lucky. I wasn't in combat, not as the flyers were. They were the ones who took all the risks and who did the dying. The flyers of the Eighth Air Force were the bravest men I have ever known, together with the men of the Royal Air Force and those of the Luftwaffe.

If I had been assigned to a B-17 or a B-24, I would have flown. If the selection process had put crossed rifles on my lapel, instead of a propellor and wings, I'd have slogged along with the infantry. If my uniform had been blue, I would have taken my chances against a U-boat or a Kamikaze.

Time has gone by and places far away exist only in my memory. Neither I nor anyone else will ever again see a thousand planes in the same sky. I will never again know the same excitement and boredom, the comical and the sad, the brilliance and the stupidity, the selfishness and the selflessness.

I will never again see Framlingham, Horham, Elveden, and Knettishall as they once were, for time has worked its wondrous changes and nothing is quite the same.

In May 1985, my wife Rosemary and I drove to the beautiful Black Hills area of South Dakota near Rapid City, the 95th Bomb Group's training base in 1942–43. This was my first sight of the place in forty-two years. Today the old training area is called Ellsworth Air Force Base, and it's huge by comparison with its size in WWII. Because it is a Strategic Air Command base now, admittance is restricted. However, I had my 95th Bomb Group Association membership card and this together with my sad tale of returning after an absence of forty-two years had the desired effect.

We were permitted to drive to the museum, a wooden frame building, and I immediately recognized it as the base headquarters building in 1943. It's the only building still standing from the old days as far as I could determine.

The museum was surrounded by a number of Second World War planes but a B-17 Fortress was nowhere to be seen. On inquiry I was informed the

Fortresses are so scarce today that even a non-flyable B-17 would cost the museum (which is not government-supported) some $500,000. After the war several thousand Forts were flown home from Europe for storage and eventual salvage at Kingman Air Force Base in the Arizona desert. It was said that a flyable B-17 Fortress could be purchased for the price of the gasoline in its fuel tanks.

At the museum I was told reunions of the 44th and 490th Bomb Group associations would be held in Rapid City in late May and that in all, eleven bomb groups were trained at the old base during the Second World War. Nothing is quite the same.

A VIEW FROM THE OTHER SIDE

Hubert Kosters

By the end of the war in May 1945, virtually every major city and town in Germany had been devastated by the Allied bombing offensive. I had last seen my home city of Munster on a beautiful spring morning in April 1942, and at that time Munster had been virtually untouched by bombs.

In December 1941, I'd been conscripted into the Luftwaffe at the age of eighteen as a radio operator and had served for the rest of the war in Italy (Sicily, Naples, northern Italy) and Villach, Austria, where I was taken prisoner by the British Army in May 1945.

I was then transferred to an American-run POW camp near Stuttgart and subsequently released in June 1945 to make my own way home. It was a hard journey. Hardly any trains were able to move on the railway system in Germany since it had been almost completely destroyed by bombs. During the day I hitched rides on trucks, and at night I slept in abandoned railway carriages. I finally arrived in Munster in early August 1945.

The city was one huge heap of rubble with many bombed-out, roofless buildings. A few people still lived in half-demolished houses; the bulk of the population had found temporary accommodation in the surrounding small towns and villages. It was very painful and heart-breaking for me as I saw my home town so completely and utterly destroyed. Wrecked cars and trams had been pushed aside by bulldozers to make temporary roadways through the mass of rubble. My parents' home was somewhere under one of those mounds of broken bricks. I turned away with a heavy heart and started off in the direction of Wolbeck, about twelve kilometers from Munster, to where my family had been evacuated.

I was the first son in my family to return home from the war. My parents were overjoyed and deeply relieved to see me. My two brothers had served on the Russian front. My elder brother had died of wounds there on 5 October 1942, and my younger brother had been taken prisoner. It wasn't until September 1949 that he was released and returned home from Russia, a broken man.

Life in Germany, as in many other European countries during the immediate postwar years, was very harsh. There was a severe shortage of food and clothing and the barest necessities were obtainable only by barter, but the will and determination to rebuild was stirring.

Helped greatly by the Marshall Plan, it now seems hardly possible that a new city had been completely rebuilt from the ruins of Munster that I saw in 1945.

We who have lived through and experienced all the horrors and heartbreak of war can only fervently hope that people everywhere will learn to live in peace and friendship and so ensure the future of mankind.

A VIEW FROM AN EAST ANGLIAN

Roger Freeman

Editor's Note: In October 1977, Roger Freeman, the renowned English author and foremost authority regarding the history of the United States Eighth Air Force in England during the Second World War, was invited to St. Louis, Missouri, by the Eighth Air Force Historical Society as its guest and principal speaker at its annual reunion.

Over 1,000 Eighth Air Force veterans, many of them from the Third Air Division and the Thirteenth Wing, were present to hear the author of such definitive volumes as *The Mighty Eighth, 8th Air Force War Diary*, and *Fortress At War*, deliver a memorable speech.

After he'd recalled numerous lighthearted and humorous anecdotes relevant to their varied and occasional outrageous activities both on and off their wartime bases in England, most of which, Mr. Freeman assured the veterans, were a mixture of truth and rumor, he then spoke of their achievements; and the cost of those achievements:

I have my own memories of you good people. I remember you on your bicycles, the laughter, the singing, and the shouting, how you would go to the local pubs, complain bitterly about the wet, warm English beer and then drink the pubs dry. I recall your generosity with the local children, how you would give them sweets, make a fuss of them, and arrange parties for them. I think most of us in England remember those cheerful young men that you were.

I have other memories and I make no excuses for changing the mood here. These are some of my memories that I have and they're true.

I remember being terrified as a B-24 Liberator spiraled down with one wing aflame and I was down there on the ground and some equally terrified, or far more frightened young men, were parachuting down from that blazing bomber. I recall watching the pilot of a P-38 Lightning being literally lifted out of his cockpit because he was so cold and numb after a long fighter escort mission to Berlin. I remember seeing a B-17 Flying Fortress in a cloudless summer sky limping home from a raid with a shattered tail and with holes so large blown through both wings you could see daylight through them. When this bomber finally came in to land at the local airfield, I recall seeing the humps on the stretchers being carried to the waiting ambulances.

I also remember those bitter winter days in England, watching the ground-crews working on the engines. Their hands must have been as numb as they could possibly be because you couldn't wear gloves for some of the intricate jobs they had to perform.

And I remember a burning mass in an English field that, a few seconds previously, had been a P-51 Mustang fighter, and I knew that somewhere in that mass was a charring body that had once been a human being.

I also recall the noise as I lay in my bed early in the morning. The constant noise that you couldn't escape from anywhere in East Anglia in those days as the bombers and fighters were warming up, taking off, and going to war.

I recall the contrails in the skies as hundreds upon hundreds of your bombers flew out, all heading eastward. And on days when you couldn't see the sky because of an overcast, I can recall seeing the colored assembly flares slowly dropping through.

I also remember the fighters sweeping back in the late afternoons, the colors of their heraldry flashing in the sunlight, and the bombers coming home, some limping, but usually in good formation.

These are my memories. I know there are memories that you have that I cannot share, although I know what they are.

Such things as the flak clouds over Berlin, over Merseburg, over Hamm. Such things as the smell of smoke and human sweat in the oxygen systems. Such things as the tired grip of an oxygen mask on your face for ten hours, the vibration and the noise of riding those bombers. Such terrible things as seeing your comrades, whom you probably had breakfast with that morning, go down in the plane next to you and being helpless to do anything about it, and perhaps worst of all, those empty beds that had been full the night before.

These are your memories and they are just a small part of the story of the Eighth Air Force. The Eighth Air Force . . . I'll remind you again, the largest air striking force in history ever committed to battle, the supreme realization of the American dream of daylight strategic bombardment. Yes, a great force indeed.

I know that the men of the Ninth Air Force bled as freely, those of the Fifteenth Air Force died as cruelly, and all the other air forces of that war have their pride, and rightly so. But no one can take away from you a record that is unsurpassed in courage and endeavor. And the evidence is there: 47,000 men killed or missing by the end of the Second World War, half the top awards for bravery earned by the American air forces were for the Eighth Air Force, so that speaks for itself.

Sadly, today there are people, some of them young, who would scoff at all this. They would say that you have come here to wallow in old glories, to gloat over a victory over another nation, that you achieved nothing, that your comrades who are not here with you died in vain, and in any case they are forgotten. Well, it goes without saying that there are men here tonight, with mental and physical scars obtained during those dark days, who could tell any peacenik far better than I could, that there is no glory in war.

Of course you're not here to gloat over a victory over an old enemy. I have German friends and I'm sure some of you do. No, you're here because you take an honest pride, and I think, if you won't admit this, it is probably the basic element of your all being here. You have an honest pride of being part of the Eighth Air Force, indeed you do.

And as for having achieved nothing, that is nonsense. You were part of the decisive victory over the worst tyranny that man has ever known, and you should be proud of it. Your courage and endeavors are not forgotten; neither are the people who died. Any young life is a wasted life, but nobody died in vain. All those boys whom you lost died in a damn good cause.

I mentioned honest pride; if you want to keep faith with the sacrifice of your buddies of years gone by there is no better way than to promote that pride. Pride in the Eighth Air Force—the greatest air force your country has ever produced and one of the most famous fighting units in history. Cherish that pride.

Most of you wear the Eighth Air Force symbol in some form or another, either in the badge of this society or sister societies. I say to you, gentlemen, you have every right to wear that with pride; wear it with pride and so keep the courage and endeavor of the Eighth Air Force shining brightly for future generations.

Thank you.

As one, the veterans rose and gave their guest speaker from England a two-minute standing ovation.

REMEMBRANCES: October 1942 to June 1945

H. Griffin ("Grif") Mumford, Group Air Executive; Director of Operations, Third Air Division

4 March 1944. 28,000 feet over Berlin. The first of many. God, it's cold. Look at that outside air temperature gauge—minus 65 degrees, and it isn't designed to indicate anything lower. Wonder what the temperature really is. Forget the temperature. Look at that flak. The bastards must have all 2,500 guns operational today. This has to be the longest bomb run yet. Krumph . . . boy, that was close and listen to the spent shrapnel hitting the airplane. Look at the gaping hole in the left wing of number three low element . . . an 88 must have gone right through without detonating. Damn, won't we ever drop those bombs? Bombs away . . . the sweetest words on any mission. OK, let's go home.

Wow, look at our little friends. Love those long range droptanks! That old "escort you across the Channel" crap just wouldn't get the job done. Not to worry in the target area today about the Me 109s and the Fw 190s. Only wish our little friends could stay with us all the way home. What with the weather it would be nice to not have to contend with both the flak and the fighters on the way back.

What a great crew I have the good fortune to fly with today. Certainly makes a commander's job easier. Al Brown has fine tuned his crew as well as any I have flown with: well-disciplined, possessing great spirit and courage, with each prepared to go to the limit and then a little something extra thrown in. Today certainly proves that point.

I wonder if they realize the significance of this mission, that it could be the turning point of the war. Stinking weather, fighter attacks, and flak over Berlin so heavy it could be walked upon is enough to make one anxious to get out of this wieners-and-krautland and back to Jolly Old . . .

We made it. Wonder what old "Iron Ass" LeMay will think of the show his boys put on today.

Where did it start?

When will it end?

Geiger Field, Washington, late 1942. Colonel Alfred A. Kessler, the first 95th Bomb Group commander. "Uncle Ugly" his peers used to call him; I think it was his West Point classmate General Peck who hung that name on him. Cruel perhaps, but it fit. Heaven knows that no one in the 95th ever called him that, at least not to his face. Mixed reviews on "Aaron" (Colonel A.A. Kessler). There were some of us who felt that what success he enjoyed was due to his good fortune of having as his air executive a head-screwed-on-right Air Corps reservist, John H. ("Jack") Gibson. Jack went on to gain fame as a

B-24 group commander in England, but we never held that against him. Those of us in the original group always felt that Jack belonged to us anyhow.

Activation, organization, manning, and getting it all sorted out filled those early days at Geiger and Ephrata. And what a Godforsaken spot Ephrata was in those early winter days. Dismal weather. Cold huts. The chaplain caught stealing coal from Colonel Kessler's coal bin one night. Dave McKnight and Bill Brown trying to solicit members for their five o'clock morning exercise and jogging club. Sandy Baldwin, a most able and dedicated member of our support group whom I shall fondly remember because of the extras he did to make life more bearable for the 412th squadron.

Finally on to dear old Rapid City for crew and unit training. This west Texan's first encounter with really cold weather. Aircraft not hangared overnight couldn't be started the next morning. Some of us took our wives to Rapid City much to the consternation of Colonel Kessler who then edicted that all 95th personnel would live in barracks on the base, but we could leave base during weekends to see our wives. What brave and wonderful ladies! Quietly and courageously smiling for us, praying for us, while accepting hours and days of loneliness as a way of life.

We experienced a thorough indoctrination in cold-weather operation and flying in inclement weather. However, in retrospect, we probably would have benefited from another two or three months of training in those miserable conditions. But there was a war to be fought and the 95th Group was soon to play its part.

Kearney, Nebraska, for further outfitting with combat gear. Heady stuff for my squadron bombardier who got slightly juiced the night he was issued his .45 and on returning to the barracks proceeded to start shooting at the ceiling. Needless to say, at that point the 412th lost its squadron bombardier to the provost marshal while the remainder of the flight crews processed through Gulfport, Mississippi, and West Palm Beach, Florida, for the flight across the South Atlantic to Africa and then to England.

All aircraft were flown separately so that any problem with one wouldn't delay the entire group. And there were problems. The first 95th aircraft had landed in England while I was still in Trinidad having a wing tank replaced on my B-17. Apart from that delay and having to feather an engine at about two o'clock in the morning mid-way across the Atlantic and a three-day weather delay in North Africa, my flight to England was uneventful. Finally, the 95th was together again in late April 1943 at our first home in England—Alconbury.

Formation flying, bombing practice over the wash, dead-reckoning navigation over the English countryside (that took a bit of doing), and we were ready to get on with winning this war. But first a lesson in humility.

It was at Alconbury that one of the most tragic events of the war would strike the 95th—an explosion in one of the aircraft being serviced and loaded with bombs for a mission. Men and aircraft were blown to bits with parts of both scattered over much of the field.

Nineteen men killed and twenty injured, four aircraft completely destroyed. We were to suffer the loss of many men and aircraft while flying combat missions in the months to come, but 27 May 1943 will remain the 95th's most disastrous ground accident of the war.

May 1943. Last to arrive, squadron commander's duties, familiarization/ training flights, and low man on the totem pole among squadron commanders delayed my first combat mission some six weeks after arriving in England. Emden, then Flensburg . . . both uneventful. Kiel, and the roof fell in. I think that the Krauts were saving that one for us. On a percentage basis, the worst drubbing that the Eighth Air Force was to take on any combat mission during the war.

Deadly accurate flak and an aggressiveness on the part of the German fighter pilots that equaled any that I encountered thereafter. Al Wilder lost . . . first of our squadron commanders. Willard Brown parachuted into the North Sea, survived the frigid waters, and spent the remainder of the war in a German POW camp. General Nate Forrest lost . . . he promoted me to captain. Chalk up 13 June 1943 for the other side but we would be back to settle that score and more.

"Jiggs" Donohue. To all who knew and worked with Jiggs, he was one of the unsung heroes of WWII. Can a group intelligence officer play a major part in winning the war? You bet he can if he is a knowledgeable and dedicated professional, a compassionate and understanding human being, old enough to be the father to his boys—the combat crews—and a handsome Irishman. As I remember, it was only when Jiggs would take a rare day off to go to London that he wouldn't personally brief the intelligence for every combat mission. We miss you, Jiggs, but hundreds of fine young men will always remember you fondly.

Long missions. All of us had a few. Mine were La Pallice, Marienburg, and Rostock, all eleven hours. Most of those eleven-hour missions were spent with your ass chewing on cushions, except for those rare occasions when you could relax and look for something different to do. Like the day I was flying with John Storie and his crew, and John decided to relieve himself in his flak helmet because the relief tube was frozen solid. Opening his side window he managed to throw the contents of his helmet in that direction, but the incoming blast of wind won that one.

Al Wilder, squadron commander, 334th; Dave McKnight, squadron commander, 335th; Ed Cole, squadron commander, 336th, and the second to be shot down; "Grif" Mumford, squadron commander, 412th . . . the originals. Many were to follow as time went by: Harry Conley, Bob Cozens, Bill Lindley, John Storie, to name a few from the original Geiger Field contingent.

Gale House, Bill Lindley, and John Storie, the original 412th flight commanders. Gale, quiet and serious, wounded in the Alconbury bomb loading accident and again while flying a combat mission, was sent home early. John Storie and Bill Lindley were the fun-loving, recalcitrant, non-conformist types who added that all-important and much-needed levity to the serious business of flying combat missions. All three outstanding crew and flight commanders.

Thoughts of John Storie and Bill Lindley (it used to be Wild Bill but it's Sweet William now; he retired as a major general), brings to mind our original group bombardier, Wayne Fitzgerald ("Meet me at the round-house, Nelly, they can't corner us there"), and a replacement pilot, the equally fun-loving Rodney Snow. Great guys who did much to lighten the emotional and psychological load that all were carrying in those trying and testing times.

I remember flying a mission with Bill Lindley, and since ours was the lead aircraft upon which the remainder of the 95th aircraft were forming, Bill decided to fire the assembly flares out through the open cockpit window instead of the flare pistol opening in the ceiling of the aircraft. After firing several flares out of the window, he took aim at the instrument panel and, forgetting that the pistol was loaded, he pulled the trigger. Needless to say the two of us spent the next few hectic minutes chasing those two damn flares as they bounded and danced around the cockpit.

So much of what happens in one's life can be attributed to luck, or fate if you will. And it was my good fortune to have assigned to the 412th squadron more than my share of outstanding personnel: John Miller and Dick Ogden, "Pappy" Smock and Clyde Bingham, Steve Stone, George Billie and Frank Belk, Chester Peek (engineering officer), Vincent Cicero, Jerome Hines and John Gira, and so many more whose names slip my mind.

And last, but not least, a special word of admiration and praise for my dear friend of these many years, Jay Schatz, my squadron navigator, whose combat tour ended all too abruptly when he was seriously wounded during his fourth mission, spent the next six months in the hospital at Oxford, and then another year back home in the hospital at Battle Creek. The assistance and encouragement that Jay has given to so many people, both in and out of the military, is legendary, but then that could be the subject of an entire book. Great guy.

Sadness mixed with pride when I moved up to the position of group operations officer, and subsequently to the position of group air executive when my good friend, Dave McKnight, was transferred back to the United States.

In group headquarters I had the opportunity and pleasure of working more directly with perhaps the most able and by far the most admired of the 95th Bomb Group commanders, John Gerhart, who subsequently retired as a four-star general from the duties of commander in chief of N.O.R.A.D. Sadly, he passed away in 1983.

John was our second group commander and he probably flew more combat missions than any of the other four. He was respected and admired by all and obviously by higher authority because he was first transferred up to the Third Air Division headquarters and shortly thereafter he was given command of the 93rd Combat Wing. Not only did we lose John, but he also arranged the transfer to his wing headquarters of the very able and dedicated Harry Conley, Jiggs Donohue, and Bill Pratt.

Fortunately, the 93rd Wing was close by so we were able to maintain our close relationship with these ex-95ers. John's mess at the 93rd was legendary, and as I remember, I availed myself of every opportunity to plan a visit there at mealtime.

Kessler, Gerhart, and then, in less than twelve months, came our third group commander, Chester P. Gilger—"Cheerful Chester". And he was. I never saw him angry or utter a cross word. Chester was not the most forceful or dynamic of our commanders; rather he was content to delegate to the talent and experience within the group that by then abounded. The 95th established itself as one of the premier heavy bomb groups in England, and Chester was happy to be a part of that glory.

Carl Truesdell. Dave McKnight loves to tell the story about Gilger, Truesdell, and him at the skeet shooting range a few days after Truesdell arrived to replace Gilger. Apparently Carl was at number 1 station, waiting for the signal that the skeet was ready for launching. Cheerful Chester was standing behind him with Carl's cap in his hand. Dave yelled, "Pull!" Chester immediately threw Carl's hat high in the air and Carl peppered his own hat with both barrels of buckshot. Chester departed the next day and peace returned to the commander's quarters.

Carl lacked the finesse of John Gerhart and wasn't as easygoing as Chester Gilger, which meant that he rubbed some the wrong way. To say the least Carl was controversial, but then aren't we all to some extent? I managed to get along well with him and am indebted to him and his father, a highly respected old-line Army major general, for helping me to obtain a regular commission in 1946.

Jack Shuck. Our fifth group commander and fresh from the United States with the air material command. Jack came aboard just as I was preparing to depart for a new assignment, and consequently I didn't know him as well as his predecessors. I must say, however, that at that late date in the war I didn't envy him coming in to command an outfit of baptism-by-fire, tough-and-ready combat individuals.

Another group commander was to follow, but by then I had been transferred to my new duties as director of operations at Third Air Division headquarters and never really had any close association with the last 95th Group commander in England, Robert H. Stuart.

My disappointment in leaving the 95th was compensated for by my good fortune of working for two highly respected and outstanding people—Hunter Harris, my immediate boss as deputy chief of staff, operations, and Pat Partridge as commander, Third Air Division. I would have the great pleasure of again working for both these individuals later in my career. Two very able gentlemen who helped make my thirty years in the Air Force so pleasurable.

Working at Third Air Division headquarters afforded me the opportunity to once again work on the staff with my dear friend Ellis B. Scripture, who had been the 95th Group navigator. Scrip and I were to make three more flights together before the war ended. In addition I was to have the great pleasure of flying the British Mosquito aircraft on a combat mission into Germany.

The first flight was one for pleasure into Paris for a few days after it had been liberated. I was advised to take a small aircraft because of the crowded conditions at the Paris airports so I selected an AT-6. En route to Paris and while over the channel the fuel pump malfunctioned. Scrip paid for his pleasure by having to work the wobble pump the rest of the way into Paris and again on the journey back to England when we returned because the fuel pump couldn't be repaired in Paris.

The second flight of our own victory tour was also a joy. We flew as a lead crew on the Manna/Chowhound relief food supply mission to Utrecht's drop zone on 5 May 1945, one day before the Canadians marched into Holland as liberators. This flight was a double thrill. We dropped our food supplies from low level as part of the air armada, then left the stream of B-17s to make a special delivery letter drop for Captain Cornelia Visman, aide to Third Air Division commander, Major General Earle Partridge. Captain Visman's sister had married a citizen of the Netherlands and lived in a small village in eastern Holland. After three low-level passes over the town square filled with hundreds of people celebrating the war's end, we dropped Cornelia's letter in a quiet park nearby, with a heavy Hershey bar attached to the small parachute and letter. A note also attached said: "Please deliver the letter and keep the chocolate bar." After the war Cornelia wrote: "Yes, the letter was delivered."

We had the good fortune and rare privilege of visiting London on VE Day and the same night watching the street lights being switched on again after six long years of blackout. It was then that I finally realized that the war in Europe was over, and with it an overwhelming sense of pride and satisfaction that I, in some small way, had contributed to lifting the yoke of deprivation and suffering from our dear friends and allies, the brave British people.

Scrip and I made our third post-combat flight together as pilot and navigator when we headed a small contingent of Eighth Air Force personnel on a "show-the-flag-goodwill-mission" into Copenhagen two days after VE Day. We had the rare pleasure of flying low-level all the way from England, across the flat lowlands of the Netherlands, and parts of Germany into Denmark. It certainly looked different than it did at 25 to 30,000 feet, with no flak or fighters. We saw many German soldiers walking along the roads of Denmark on their way back to Germany, and didn't feel a bit sorry for them.

In Copenhagen we were directed to our landing by a German air controller and given a celebratory "thank you, Yanks" welcome. Three days of sightseeing, signing autographs, wining and dining, and then back to Elveden Hall to await transport back to the United States of America. Wow, what a way to end a war!

I couldn't possibly end these recollections without comment and tribute to others who contributed so much to the honor and the outstanding history of the 95th. People like "Curly" Burt, our ground executive; Ed Russel, our adjutant; "Doc" Bill Harding, our group flight surgeon; Clarence Fields, our group maintenance officer; and all our devoted ground crews to whom all who flew in a 95th aircraft owe an eternal debt of gratitude; John Bromberg, perhaps the most proficient bombardier in the Eighth Air Force (my dear friend and protector who always wanted to accompany me to London and act as my bodyguard; he could, he was a professional wrestler before the war).

Last but not least, one of the most loyal, dedicated, and competent individuals to come to the 95th—Joe Moller. Joe was on temporary assignment as a pilot to get combat experience before being assigned to command a combat group. I can't remember how many missions Joe flew with us (Joe and I flew together on one of his first), but there were many, despite the fact that he was old enough to be the father of many of our combat crew pilots.

Joe was assigned to the 390th Bomb Group at Framlingham, which, under his command, became one of the most distinguished in the Eighth Air Force. Of course, we in the 95th knew it was because of the outstanding indoctrination that he received with us. A great guy who contributed much to the 95th, and to the total war effort.

Where did it start? There isn't any one answer to that because each of us have our own time and place.

When will it end? The war in Europe was over on 8 May 1945. What has not and will not end are the memories of our comrades who rest in peace having made the supreme sacrifice; and the esprit de corps, the honor, and the satisfaction of having faithfully served as a member of the 95th Bomb Group.

Earlier I pondered what General Curtis E. LeMay might say about the 95th's effort against Berlin on 4 March 1944. Those who knew him, and I had the pleasure of working with him later in the Pentagon, would describe him as being a dedicated, hard-working, exceedingly competent, and tough Air Force officer who demanded perfection of himself and those working under his command. When deserved, he gave credit and praise, and a commendation from him was to be cherished.

Recognizing the outstanding contribution that the 95th Bomb Group made to the war effort, General LeMay on 31 March 1944 presented to the 95th one of the most laudatory commendations made to any bomb group in the Eighth Air Force.

Awarded on the occasion of our having completed our first 100 heavy bombardment missions, this commendation, perhaps better than any of the others awarded to us, attests to the honor and glory of all who served in the 95th during those hectic and dramatically eventful days of 1942–45. It is indeed entirely fitting and appropriate that we record this much-valued commendation in this, our first-person record for history.

COMMENDATIONS AND CITATIONS

RESTRICTED: HEADQUARTERS 3RD BOMBARDMENT DIVISION APO 559

SUBJECT: Commendation   31 March 1944
TO: Commanding Officer, 95th Bombardment Group (H), AAF Station 119, APO 559

It is my pleasure and privilege officially to commend the officers and men of the 95th Bombardment Group (H) for its outstanding achievement in successfully completing, from 13 May 1943 to 23 March 1944, *one hundred (100)* heavy bombardment missions against the enemy. Engaged in daylight aerial combat against a mighty foe armed with the world's most concentrated anti-aircraft and fighter defenses, our bombers and crews each day are carrying the war home to Germany with increasing destruction to her war plants and installations.

In this gigantic undertaking, no bombardment group has earned more enthusiastic praise than the 95th. Some of the engagements in which it has participated will be recorded as the greatest air battles of this war. At Huls on 22 June 1943, great devastation was rained down upon the plant producing twenty percent of the enemy's synthetic rubber. On 17 August 1943, the 95th added its fury to the assault that wrought destruction to the all important Me-109 plant at Regensburg, then producing one-third of Germany's fighter planes. Results on the new and most vital fighter assembly plant at Marienburg on 9 October 1943 were so satisfactory that General Arnold proclaimed the attack as "the best precision bombing of the war." Accuracy again characterized the Schweinfurt raid on 14 October 1943, when the largest ballbearing works in Europe was blasted. Requiring expert navigation to strike a small distant target, on 16 November 1943 this group combined with others in crippling seriously the plant at Rjukan, Norway, manufacturing nitrogen and other chemicals used for explosives. On 4 March 1944, this intrepid group led the first daylight bombardment of Berlin by American heavy bombers, a feat for which it has already won world renown. Other deadly blows in which the 95th has contributed magnificently to the success of our aerial invasion of enemy territory are the raids on La Pallice 4 July; on Paris, 3, 9, and 15 September 1943; on Bremen, 16 and 20 September 1943; and on Berlin, 6, 8, 9, and 22 March 1944.

The success of the group's bombing operations testifies indisputably to the meticulous care with which its missions have been planned and executed and to the discipline, skill, and gallantry of its combat and ground personnel, not only in the group, but in the related attached units of the station.

Commended alike are the officers and men now present for duty and those whose absence is keenly regretted. To you and to them are due eternal praise and gratitude for heroic accomplishment in battles well fought, worthy of the highest tradition of the Army of the United States.

I am confident that you will bring added honor to yourselves and your country in the future great air battles which must be fought to bring our common endeavor to a victorious conclusion.

CURTIS E. LE MAY
Major General, U.S.A.,
Commanding

HEADQUARTERS EIGHTH AIR FORCE
Office of the Commanding General
APO 634

9 February 1944

GENERAL ORDERS
NUMBER 35

CITATION

The 3rd Bombardment Division (H) (then the 4th Bombardment Wing [H]) is cited for outstanding performance of duty in action against the enemy, 17 August 1943. This unprecedented attack against one of Germany's most important aircraft factories was the first shuttle mission performed in this theater of operations and entailed the longest flight over strongly defended enemy territory yet accomplished at that date. For four and one half hours, the formation was subjected to persistent, savage assaults by large forces of enemy fighters. During this bitterly contested aerial battle, 140 German fighter aircraft were definitely destroyed and many more damaged. In spite of desperate attempts by the enemy to scatter the bombers, the groups of the Third Bombardment Division maintained a tight defensive formation and coordinating as a perfectly balanced team, fought their way to the assigned target at Regensburg. Though weary from hours of grueling combat, the bombardiers released their bombs accurately on the target and wrought vast destruction on an aircraft factory of vital importance to the enemy's war effort. The high degree of success achieved is directly attributable to the extraordinary heroism, skill, and devotion to duty displayed by members of this unit. Their actions on this occasion uphold the highest traditions of the Armed Forces of the United States.

By command of Major General DOOLITTLE:
JOHN A. SAMFORD,
Brigadier General, USA
Chief of Staff

OFFICIAL:
/s/ Edward E. Toro
/t/ EDWARD E. TORO,
   Colonel, AGD,
   Adjutant General

RESTRICTED
GENERAL ORDER) Headquarters 3rd Bombardment Division
APO 559
NO. 138) 23 May 1944
CITATION OF UNIT

Pursuant to the provisions of Executive Order No. 9396 (Sec 1, Bull 22, WD, 1943) and Section IV, War Department Circular 333, 22 December 1943, the 95th Bombardment Group (H), this command is cited for outstanding performance of duty in action against the enemy in connection with the bombing of an important target at Munster, Germany, 10 October 1943.

The 95th Bombardment Group (H) led the Third Bombardment Division and the Thirteenth Combat Wing (H), in the air, on this highly successful five (5) hour operation which involved a flight of five hundred twenty (520) miles at an altitude of 24,000 feet. During the period of no friendly fighter support, the group was subjected to the violent and concentrated attacks of approximately two hundred fifty (250) enemy fighters, chiefly Fw 190s, Ju 88s, and Me 110s and 210s. Choosing the 13th Combat Wing (H) as the focal point, the waves of attackers, after shooting down all but one (1) of the aircraft in the low group and eight (8) of the aircraft in the high group, concentrated on the 95th Group. Twin-engined enemy fighters, firing 20mm and 37mm cannon and rocket projectiles, attacked in staffels of twelve (12) to fifteen (15) each. Losing five (5) aircraft to this concerted opposition, the unit maintained a cohesive combat formation throughout the attacks. The 95th Group is officially credited with the destruction of forty-one (41) enemy fighters, five (5) others probably destroyed, and nineteen (19) damaged. Beginning at Dorsten and continuing through the target area, the group also encountered extremely intense and damaging antiaircraft fire. Ten (10) of the remaining aircraft in the unit were damaged. Rallying the remaining aircraft of the lead combat wing, the 95th Group led a six (6) minute bombing run in a highly effective formation, dropping its bombs directly on the main point of impact. Flying directly through the antiaircraft barrage, which grew increasingly heavy as the bomb release point was reached, the unit took more than the usual amount of time on the turns, so that the following groups, which were also undergoing vicious fighter attacks, could rejoin the formation and receive the benefit of defensive fire power. The bombing results were superior to those of any other bombardment group participating in the operation. Of the 102,000 pounds of bombs released by this unit, 36 percent hit within 1,000 feet and 69 percent fell within 2,000 feet of the assigned aiming point. The bombing pattern was excellent. Testimony to the highly successful bombing of the target was the award of the British Distinguished Flying Cross to the lead bombardier for his work on this mission. After the bombing, the group led the division's forces to the rally point where friendly fighter support was met. As a result of the savage enemy opposition, fifty-one (51) of the unit's personnel are missing in action, and four (4) were wounded.

Distinguishing itself by courageous resolution in overcoming vicious enemy fighter attacks, and heavy antiaircraft artillery fire, the 95th Group displayed extraordinary valor, audacity and courage under fire. By heroic strength of purpose, it led the way over the target to successfully carry out its mission. This unit's personnel performed its task with coolness, skill, and self-sacrifice in the face of unusually determined and damaging enemy fire. The extraordinary devotion to duty and disregard of personal safety displayed, above and beyond that of all other units participating in the same operation, resulted in a vital blow at the German war effort. The outstanding valor and bold vigorous heroism displayed on this occasion presented an inspiring example for other units of the Army Air Forces.

By command of Major General LE MAY:

A.W. KISSNER

Brigadier General, U.S.A.

Chief of Staff

OFFICIAL:

O.T. DRAEWELL

Major, Air Corps

Adjutant General

CONFIDENTIAL

HEADQUARTERS 3D BOMBARDMENT DIVISION

Office of the Commanding General

APO 559

GENERAL ORDERS

No. 923   3 November 1944

UNIT CITATION

Under the provisions of Executive Order No. 9396 (Sec I, Bull 22, D, 1943) and Sec. IV, Cir 333, D, 1943, the 95th Bombardment Group (H) is cited for outstanding performance of duty in action in connection with the first aerial daylight attack by United States heavy bombers on Berlin, Germany, 4 March 1944.

The energies of the entire Eighth Air Force were devoted to this vital operation but only the 95th Bombardment Group and twelve aircraft from one other group got through to the primary target and bombed it.

At takeoff time, the weather conditions were so bad that one entire division was forced to cancel the mission. The 95th Group assembled in proper formation and departed the English coast as scheduled, despite local snowstorms and generally adverse weather. Soon after the continental coast was crossed, all participating units of the Eighth Air Force except one wing either abandoned the operation or attacked other targets because of treacherous, towering cloud formations and dense, persistent contrails, which made formation flying difficult. The one wing, led by the 95th Group, resolutely continued on to the objective. In the target area twenty to thirty single-engine enemy aircraft pressed home vicious attacks, mostly in elements of two or three aircraft at a time. Friendly fighter support was inadequate and enemy ground positions fired heavy concentrations of antiaircraft fire at the attackers. Nevertheless, the 95th Group maintained a tight defensive formation and released forty-two-and-a-half tons of high explosives on the cloud-covered German capital. Even after the target was bombed, enemy fighters continued to attack the formation until the rally point. The courageous crews of the 95th Group destroyed three of the hostile fighters, probably destroyed one, and damaged one more. A safe withdrawal was completed, although it was necessary to fly directly through solid clouds since the exhausted oxygen supply made it impossible to rise above them. Nine bombers were damaged by enemy action, four were lost. Forty-one officers and enlisted men were missing in action, and four were wounded.

By heroically electing the more hazardous of two equally acceptable and honorable courses of action, the 95th Bombardment Group clearly distinguished itself above and beyond all other units participating in this momentous operation. The extraordinary heroism, determination, and esprit de corps displayed by the officers and enlisted men of this organization in overcoming unusually difficult and hazardous conditions brought to a successful conclusion our country's first combat operation over the capital of Germany. The fortitude, bravery, and fighting spirit of the 95th Group on this historic occasion constitute a noteworthy contribution to the war effort and add notably to the cherished traditions of the Army Air Forces.

By command of Major General PARTRIDGE:

OFFICIAL:

                                    N.B. HARBOLD
                                  Brigadier General, U.S.A.
                                  Chief of Staff

JOHN P. THOMAS
Major, Air Corps
Acting Adjutant General

HEADQUARTERS 3D BOMBARDMENT DIVISION
Office of the Commanding General
APO 559

200.6   1 September 1944
SUBJECT: Commendation
TO: Commanding Officer, 95th Bombardment Group (H), APO 559
    1. I wish to extend my most hearty congratulations to all personnel of
your station on completion of the *200th mission* performed by the group.
    During the last 100 missions, your organization has participated in op-
erations which have materially contributed to the successful outcome of the
war. Prior to 6 June 1944, you were primarily engaged in defeating the German
Air Force and in preparing for the assault on the continent. Subsequent to 6
June 1944, you have supported the ground operations and have intensified the
operations against strategic targets in the German homeland.
    These last 100 missions have been carried out in 160 days, and the delivery
of that number of effective attacks in such a short period is a tribute to the
teamwork and coordination of your personnel.
    2. Please extend to all officers and men on your station my appreciation
for the outstanding work which they have done. Their achievements reflect
the highest credit upon themselves and the Army Air Forces as a whole.
                         E.E. Partridge
                     Major General, U.S. Army
                           Commanding

FAREWELL TO ENGLAND, HOME AGAIN!

Stephen G. Stone, Jr., Adjutant, 335th Squadron

Friday, 3 August 1945, will be a banner day in the memories of all members
of the ground echelon of the 95th Bombardment Group. On that day we prepared to leave Horham, Suffolk, our home for the past two years, and headed
for the port of embarkation at Glasgow. For most of us it had been twenty-
seven months to the day since we boarded the *Queen Elizabeth* at New York.
    This momentous day was spent mostly in making the base ship-shape so
that the holding party of about 100 men under the command of Major R.H.
Hepner, squadron finance officer, would not have too great a task on their
hands. All day long jeeps and trucks from the 100th made shuttle runs to
Horham, transferring stores and expendable supplies to be used at Thorpe
Abbotts during their tour of occupation. All bunks and other barracks fixtures

were turned in to quartermaster. By late afternoon the men were sleeping on the floor or sitting Indian fashion playing cards.

By the time evening rolled around, the local gentry had begun to arrive to bid us fond adieu. The early part of the evening was spent issuing K-rations to the men for sustenance during the rail trip. About 2100, the Red Cross provided us with coffee and doughnuts, which were ravenously consumed. About 2200 we had roll call and lined the men up in embarkation roster order. By 2230 the trucks began to arrive and the men started to embark. By 2315 we were all embarked, and at 2330 we started off for the railhead at Diss seven miles away. As we passed through the great metropolis of Eye the local burghers were on deck to give us a rousing send-off, many of them were around later in the evening than they had ever been in their lives.

At Diss we lined up on the platform some 700 strong and awaited the arrival of the train, which pulled in at about 0015. By 0030 we were all aboard and the train departed on schedule. A bright and fair dawn found us in Peterborough, and by noon we had crossed the River Tweed at Berwick and were on our way toward Edinburgh. We were really getting a good tour of Britain, because on the way south two years ago we had gone through the Midlands and on our way north now we were skirting the east coast. As we passed through Glasgow later in the afternoon, the populace was again on hand to wish us Godspeed as they had been two years previously. By 1700 we had arrived at Greenock where we boarded the ferry that was to take us to the *Queen Elizabeth*, majestically at anchor in midstream.

All day Sunday we were aboard getting settled and finally on Monday at 1630 we weighed anchor and glided slowly down the Clyde followed by a small steamer on the deck of which was assembled a band of pipers in Scottish regalia skirling out with stirring Scottish marches. They concluded with "Auld Lang Syne," which proved to be very moving as played on the pipes, and they returned to Greenock, leaving us to slip quietly past the headlands and out into the broad Atlantic taking with us memories, both pleasant and unpleasant, of our starred and checkered careers in merrie England. The five-day trip was uneventful, the sea being calm as a mill pond. The men had much better accomodations than they did on the trip over, when they had to sleep one night on deck and the next inside.

11 August 1945 was another red-letter day in the lives of the ground echelon of the 95th Bombardment Group. Just before dawn the pilot came aboard, and by the time it began to grow light we could discern the coastline of Long Island. As we entered the outer reach of New York port, we were met by dozens of flag-bedecked boats, both large and small, all with whistles tooting and some with horns blowing. It is impossible to describe the feeling of each individual as we saw again the Statue of Liberty; suffice to say the primary feeling was one of boundless joy.

We docked at 0830 and then began the lengthy process of debarking close to 15,000 men and women. It fell to our lot to be designated as police detail, which meant we were the last men off the ship. However we were off by 1730 and on our way to Camp Kilmer, which we reached by 1930. There we were introduced to the transportation corps board of efficiency, which was nothing short of remarkable! Each and every one of us was completely processed and ready to head for home within twenty-four hours.

By 2400, 12 August 1945, the 95th Bombardment Group (H) had entered a period of suspended animation, which lasted until 27 August when Order #116 Sec. II Par #1 Hq 2AF terminated the existence of one of the Eighth Air Force's finest bomb groups.

THE 95TH RETURN

Ian L. Hawkins

Following a memorial service at St. Mary's Church in Horham on Saturday, 19 September 1981, the impressive memorial to the airmen of the 95th Bombardment Group was unveiled by the U.S. vice-consul from the American Embassy in London, Mr. Frederick Vogel. The unveiling followed a speech delivered by Colonel Sam Morgan, the base commander at U.S.A.F. Bentwaters, Suffolk, during which the colonel said:

"Today we, the Americans and the British, share almost everything we have. The very roots of our nation, the United States, come from Britain. Our values are the same, our language is the same, and I think it's marvelous that the Friends of the 95th were able to arrange this ceremony and memorial for the airmen who were over here with you during the war.

"It is a chance to think and talk about what used to be, and it's a chance for me to give thanks for what we have today. This outstanding air force, of which I am a part, started long before I came along. Veterans of the 95th who are present today, like Lefty Nairn, Al Brown, Arthur Frankel, and Dave McKnight, helped put it all together. You have given a great deal to me personally, and I don't need to speak from a prepared text at a ceremony like this. There is so much to it that the challenge is to sort out what should and should not be said.

"Years ago you heard the song by Simon and Garfunkel 'Where have you gone Joe DiMaggio? We turn our shining eyes to you . . .' It was a plea for the existence of heroes such as we used to have, the men and women who rose to the challenge of the Second World War and fought that great battle. I know very well, I believe, the experiences and thoughts that you had then. When we arrived at Horham today my wife, children, and I drove out to your former airfield and drove down the runway. We could see then the ghost of a B-17 going off into the distance, joining the orbit where you got the great formations together.

"I have been in combat, I have turned with the MiG 21s and seen the missiles as they streaked through the air, and the description of flak being thick enough to walk on is not a misnomer. It really does look just like that. I've also known the trauma of seeing a comrade engulfed in a ball of fire and go down, to be with us no longer. Notwithstanding all of that, war is a great experience . . . for those who don't get shot down . . . and those are whom we have with us today. But we are also taking a moment to reflect on both those whom are here and those whom are not, and think about the heroism of the people of the 95th and the heroism of the people of Britain who shared that war.

"The most important thing to a person is his reputation, followed by a sense of values. In other words, when he is presented with a challenge, how does he rise to that challenge? How does he react? Does he have the courage and stamina to look out ahead of him and see the flak and the fighters and still hold the course, even though all around him may be coming apart? Even in the face of odds that look like he will never be able to make it through? It goes back to the ground crews who shared the trauma when their planes failed to return and their crews were no longer among them.

"In the years afterward you can look back and think upon those experiences and those challenges that confronted you at that time. All of you here, all the men and women of the 95th, the people of Horham, the Friends of the 95th, you can look straight into any man's eye and know that your values were straight and true, and when presented with the problems of the past, you met them head on and surmounted them admirably.

"Today, you have given me a tremendous opportunity just by being here for the unveiling of this monument. I can tell the next generation that I was somewhat a small part of the tremendous organization of the 95th Bombardment Group.

"Thank you very much, and the least that I can say to you of the 95th is that I, and the current Air Force, salute you and all that you stood for."

Several 95th veterans returned Colonel Morgan's salute amidst applause from the circle of many listeners.

Mr. Vogel then made a short speech during which he summarized the achievements of the 95th and the cost:

"It is equally an honor for me to have this opportunity to meet with you all and to participate in this ceremony. It is also most appropriate that an embassy representative be here. I understand that one of the pilots and comrades was the son of the then United States ambassador to the Court of St. James, and while flying with your wing, was shot down over Germany and captured. We dedicate a memorial here today so that those events of yesterday will not be forgotten and that tomorrow will not demand the same of you and yours again.

"The 95th Bombardment Group flew 321 missions and lost 192 aircraft in battle: 192 aircraft, 1,774 men . . . comrades, fathers, husbands, brothers, and sons of our people. You have returned here today to commemorate heroism, but more so to honor the sacrifices of those times when you gave up your boyhood, your youth, your very lives to achieve a great and lasting victory. The 95th Bombardment Group won three Presidential Distinguished Unit citations for your courage and daring, the only combat group to have that great honor. It is a tribute to you, and to our Allies and friends as well, that such valor remains strong in memory still.

"Let those who would challenge us today note well, and take heed, that the sons of Britannia and Columbia still regard such valor as a highest virtue. We dedicate this memorial to you veterans of the 95th Bombardment Group who have returned. Let us also honor those who could not: comrades fallen . . . friends lost; they bore the banner, they paid the price of victory. . . ."

Mr. Vogel then unveiled the marble memorial, carved in the shape of a B-17's tail surmounting a marble plinth on which was laid out the pattern of Horham's wartime runways. On one side of the B-17's tail was a bronze plaque of remembrance, and on the other was the distinctive Square B, the Group marking of the 95th.

Colonel Arthur Frankel, secretary of the 95th Bomb Group (H) Association in the United States, then responded with a short address:

"Without the seeds that were sown several years ago by our English friends, this truly beautiful memorial to our men would not be here today, because it was the Friends of the 95th, the English, who really gave it the impetus for which we are so deeply grateful.

"Both our countries are pacifists; we don't believe in war. In 1938, Prime Minister Chamberlain stepped from an airplane on his return from Germany, waved a piece of paper in the air and declared, 'We shall have peace in our time. . . .' Well, we all know history.

"Yes, we are pacifists, but not the type of pacifist that we find in our world today who actively encourage the dissolution of our strength and so invite our destruction. We are standing here today, the lucky ones, because of that strength.

"Again, our very grateful thanks to you all."

The memorial was then blessed by Colonel Caspers, the base chaplain from the nearby American airfield at Bentwaters.

That Saturday evening, the veterans of the 95th and their wives again joined local people in a convivial dinner/dance at nearby Stradbroke High School. Before the sixteen-piece band began playing the haunting and nostalgic music of the legendary Glenn Miller, the after-dinner speech was made by Roger Freeman. He said:

"I have many personal recollections of Horham. In 1942 I was a thirteen-year-old schoolboy, and I occasionally stayed with my cousin at Dennington, which is a village about five miles south of here. We young boys were both 'aeroplane mad.' On this occasion my cousin said, 'Let's cycle up to a place called Horham. They're building an aerodrome there.' So we cycled from Dennington, through Worlingworth to Horham. I remember how impressed I was by the wide, open landscape on our arrival. This was long before prairie farmers, and the huge gaps in the countryside caused by the construction of this airfield was really something to behold. It seemed to stretch to the far horizon.

"Well, that was not the last association with Horham, because as luck would have it for us both, my uncle, who had been in the First World War and was a squadron leader in the Royal Air Force during the Second War, was given command of Horham Airfield before the construction had been completed. He was, in fact, the first commanding officer of Horham Airfield and he moved here in late 1942. His son and his nephew (me) made the most of that. In fact, it was at Horham in December 1942 that I had my first look inside an American bomber.

"My uncle eventually turned the airfield over to the American authorities and moved on to other jobs. After the war I asked him what he remembered most of his stay at Horham when the Americans were there. He answered immediately, saying that his most difficult task was trying to get the Americans to pronounce Horham correctly, instead of their consistently saying, 'Whoreham'!

"Anyway, my cousin and I continued to cycle over to Horham, peering over the hedge and watching the big bombers . . . and they were Flying Fortresses. Now, in those days we didn't know that the unit occupying the airfield was called the 95th Bomb Group, because there was such a thing as security. We therefore labeled the bombers that flew from Horham as the 'B in the Square' because the B in the Square was what they all carried on their tails. In fact, the Big B turned out to be a very appropriate marking because Big B was the nickname for the enemy capital, Berlin, and it was the 95th that on 4 March 1944, became the first of forty-odd American bombardment groups to strike the capital city of Germany.

"In fact the 95th, probably unbeknownst to the English people around the base, had a very tough time of it during the early days. There was a time when it was suffering a 35 percent survival rate for its crewmen. Though I say suffering a survival rate, because if you saw your buddies go down you were suffering too. And the fact was that there was only one in three of the original crews who survived. It was very tough indeed and a very bloody war that they fought.

"The 95th, as you have already heard today, was awarded three Presidential Unit citations—they didn't give these away—they were really hard won. As you also heard, the 95th was the only group in the American air forces in Europe to come away from that war with three such citations. That gives a fair indication of the sort of battles that it fought. Another indication is that the gunner with the most claims of enemy aircraft shot down while flying in bombers was also based here at Horham. Yes, the 95th had a very hard war, very hard indeed.

"It's all a long time ago now, of course, but when the 95th first arrived at

Horham in June 1943, there's no doubt that the local people at least or at best viewed them with a certain amount of suspicion . . . these strange, brash young men from across the sea from a place called America which the locals only associated with the film stars of Hollywood.

"There is the story, probably not true at all but it was told in those days, about the farmer who lived near Horham. The base was built around his farm. After a few months following the Americans' arrival, he went to the local cattle market and there he met another farmer. The other farmer greeted him with, 'Well, hello Bill. How are you getting along with them there Yankees?'

"Thereupon Bill exploded, 'Gettin' along with 'em? Gettin' along with the blighters? I'll tell you how I'm gettin' along!! Why, since they've been here my cows have gone off the milk, my chickens have gone off the lay, my gatepost has been knocked down, my dog has been run over, my apples have been stolen, my daughter's pregnant, my wife's run off with one of 'em, and I can't drown my sorrow because the blighters have drunk all the pubs dry!'

"Well, it wasn't long before the people of Horham, Denham, Stradbroke, and the surrounding district began to realize what was going on. They would watch the bombers go out and they saw them come back, sometimes full of holes, and they also saw some of the terrible crashes that occurred. They got to know the GIs in their smart uniforms who seemed to be everywhere in the ubiquitous jeeps, and soon they developed quite a liking for these strange young men from across the water. They soon began to refer to them as 'Our boys.' It was our boys that went out today. It was our boys who had got badly shot up.

"By the time they went home in 1945, perhaps the Americans did not realize this but there was a certain fondness toward them. And as for the Americans? Well, they went home, those that were lucky enough to go home, and what did they do? They married, they had children, and they got on with life. They didn't want to remember the war in which they had escaped with their lives. But now, if I may say it, they're sliding past middle age, they are retiring, and it's time to think. They think about what must have been the most traumatic moments and days of their lives. They think about the Second World War. And what, specifically, do they think about?

"You can't go back to a battlefield in the sky. The 95th struck at targets as far afield as Norway, occupied Poland, down to Africa, and you can't go back to those battlefields way up in the clouds.

"So you come back to the only place you can return to—the old airfield at Horham, in Suffolk County, England. That's the focal point of your interest. To all those men, however short a time they spent here, this little spot in England will always mean something to them. And for the locals? They have realized now that when this airfield was built in their village, it was the most momentous thing that ever happened to this ancient village and probably will ever happen to it. They realize that it is a part of their history just as it is part of the history of the men who flew from Horham Airfield years and years ago.

"It is a long time since the inhabitants of Horham have been woken up in the early morning by the dull roar of Flying Fortresses grinding off the end of the runway with their loads of bombs to distant targets, a long time since their contrails crisscrossed the sky, a long time since Adolf Hitler was a household name. But, as you have seen, veterans of the 95th and your ladies who have returned with you, the sort of welcome extended to you, and you suddenly realize, don't you, that those funny old English have a big soft spot for 'our boys.'

"I've said it before, and I'll say it again. We see lots of Americans over here at American NATO air bases. Americans? They are quite nice, friendly people. But anyone who served with the Eighth Air Force is something really special. Welcome back!"

****

Among the returning 95th Bomb Group veterans was William Charles, a 336th squadron navigator, who had flown over fifty missions with the group. The following day he went for an early morning walk in the chill September mists. He recollects:

I walked alone along the same paths, now overgrown, from my former barracks' site in the 336th squadron area to the combat mess hall. The thirty-eight intervening years suddenly evaporated in the mists of time, and it was as if I was doing it all over again as I trudged toward a breakfast that existed only in my memory.

From there I walked to the group operations building, dilapidated but still standing, where we had received our specialized briefings before each mission, wondering if I'd return and how many of the boys I would ever see again.

Eventually, I reached our squadron's flight line. I am not a sentimental man, but it was so uncanny how the years seemingly rolled back, just as the opening scenes of *Twelve O'Clock High* when the ground executive officer cycled back to his abandoned bomber base after the war and he stood alone at the end of the deserted runway seeing and hearing the roaring engines of a ghostly B-17.

I went to the site of the officers' club, now demolished, and the first thing that crossed my mind was how we used to stand around a tinkling piano being expertly played by Dr. Jack McKittrick, our squadron flight surgeon. I recalled the beautiful tenor voice of Lieutenant Stevens, a bombardier on Lieutenant Bullard's crew, from our barracks.

I also recalled, most vividly, the morning Lieutenant Bullard's navigator received a Dear John letter from his wife. He also had a young daughter whom he had never seen. Naturally, we'd joined him in trying to drown his sorrows at the club that night, and we had ended up singing a storm. The very next day John Bullard's crew was shot down, all killed in action.

Later that morning, I went to the Red Feather Club with my good friends

Dave McKnight, Al Brown, and John Miller, all of whom I had known well and with whom I'd flown many, many missions. We were joined by English Friends of the 95th. While there, we drank a toast to our fallen comrades and absent friends, probably the first drinks to be consumed there for almost forty years. The club, with its colorful wall murals, breathes a special atmosphere.

Dave McKnight is, of course, a special friend because he set such an inspiring example for all replacement crews to emulate during those dangerous and eventful years. I have always felt that I was living on borrowed time when I look back, and I wonder how I ever survived all that I did. I am convinced that my mother's prayers had a lot to do with God sparing my life, although I sometimes think that I haven't done much with the life that He gave me, I'm still very thankful.

That Sunday afternoon we went out to the American military cemetery at Madingley, near Cambridge, surely the most beautiful and impressive of all American cemeteries, and surely our comrades of days gone by could not have been laid to rest in greener pastures than these.

It was not until I saw all the names of John Bullard's crew among the 5,000 or so names which are carved on the Wall of the Missing that I finally learned their fate. I had never heard whether or not they had survived but the hope had always existed. It was a highly emotional moment for me personally, and it was as if I had secretly known all these years but couldn't accept the fact.

****

In late November 1981, Ellis Scripture, the 95th Bomb Group lead navigator during 1943 and early 1944, wrote:

We are getting ready to celebrate Thanksgiving in the United States. This is our traditional family reunion each year when we pause to thank God for all our many blessings. Too often we forget!

I shall always be very grateful that I was allowed to continue my life and to enjoy the laughter of children and grandchildren. We hope that they will be spared the heartbreak of war and its terrible destruction.

The great tragedy was that the peoples of the whole world were forced to barbaric acts against each other because of the political ambitions of a few hated men. The world's history has always been thus, and unfortunately, the trend continues today in so many areas. All of us grieve for those who continue to be exploited in the name of political gain.

Our weapons are now so deadly and uncontrollable that the world would indeed be devastated if man allowed his senses to get out of control. We must do all possible to prevent another outbreak of man's hatred.

Man was made to create, not destroy.

THE LAST MISSION

Eugene Fletcher, Pilot, B-17G, "Knock-Out Baby," 412th Squadron

We never thought we'd ever see each other again after we came home and went our different ways at the end of the war in Europe. But in late July 1985, all members of our crew, apart from one who sadly passed on a few years previously, got together again at Seattle, Washington, to attend the fiftieth anniversary celebrations of the B-17 Flying Fortress. An estimated 12,000 Air Force veterans from WW II, including some 400 veterans from the 95th Bomb Group Association, were also present for that very special occasion.

When we departed Horham and came home in 1945, my crew and I thought that our paths would never cross again. Then, all of a sudden, we were back together. We were just kids again, and for some reason we felt like crying.

At Seattle we were honored and privileged to meet Ed Wells, the designer of the B-17, which first flew in July 1935. Apparently, he worked on the principle of Murphy's Law, which states: 'If anything can possibly go wrong . . . it will,' so design accordingly.

The result was the legendary B-17, which was quite capable of absorbing tremendous structural damage during combat and still bring its crew safely home. The B-17 brought my crew home safely from thirty-five missions between June and December 1944 and none of us even suffered a scratch. Those thirty-five missions were dangerous; they involved flying through both fighters and flak to reach the primary target. We would see the black clouds of exploding flak shells through which we had to fly, and we'd turn white. It was a most terrifying sight. Our bombardier, Frank Dimit, summarized our thirty-five missions when he said: "As far as the target and up to the release of the bombs we were working for the government. From that point on and all the way home we were working for ourselves."

A special bond of friendship developed within our crew, as with all crews. We were very much dependent upon each other; we trusted and respected each other's specialized ability. Right from the beginning I felt we were the best, and we were indeed very fortunate to participate together in one last mission during the Seattle reunion. Our flight in the B-17G "Sentimental Journey" (owned by the Confederate Air Force based in Texas) was arranged and filmed by a local TV company for a documentary program about the Eighth Air Force.

During that memorable flight, all the once familiar sounds, the long forgotten details, the emotion, and the memories returned to each individual member of the crew. It goes without saying that we considered ourselves extremely fortunate and we are very grateful, but we couldn't help thinking of all those many thousands of crewmen who didn't return from their last mission.

Let us never forget those fine young men who loved their country and freedom enough to lay down their lives to preserve all that is good in America and the free world.

FROM AN ORATION BY PERICLES

Athenian Statesman and Military Commander
circa 495–425 B.C.

Each one, man for man, has won imperishable praise, each has gained a glorious grave—not that sepulchre of earth wherein they lie, but the living tomb of everlasting remembrance wherein their glory is enshrined. For the whole earth is the sepulchre of heroes; monuments may rise and tablets be set up to them in their own land, but on the far-off shores there is an abiding memorial that no pen or chisel has traced; it is graven, not on stone or brass, but on the living heart of humanity. Take these men as your example. Like them, remember that prosperity can only be for the free; that freedom is the sure possession of those alone who have the courage to defend it.

BIBLIOGRAPHY

R.A.F. Bomber Command War Diaries, Martin Middlebrook & Chris Everitt; Viking, London, U.K.

Mighty Eighth War Diaries, Roger Freeman; Jane's, London, U.K.

Contrails: The 95th Bombardment Group (H), U.S.A.A.F., David Henderson; Ashland, Kentucky, U.S.A.

Munster: Bloody Skies Over Germany, Ian Hawkins; TAB Books, Blue Ridge Summit, Pennsylvania.

Operation Manna/Chowhound, Hans Onderwater; Luchtvaart, Weesp, Holland.

Verse from the Turret, Squadron Leader William Rainford, MBE, R.A.F., (Retd.); Geni Printing, Gloucester, U.K.

Life Magazine, New York, U.S.A.

Eighth Air Force News, Hollywood, Florida, U.S.A.

Eighth Air Force Historical Society, Hollywood, Florida, U.S.A.